5-14-96

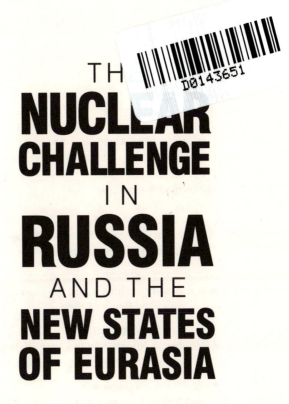

THE
NUCLEAR
CHALLENGE
IN
RUSSIA
AND THE
NEW STATES
OF EURASIA

THE INTERNATIONAL POLITICS OF EURASIA

Editors:
Karen Dawisha and Bruce Parrott

This ambitious ten-volume series develops a comprehensive analysis of the evolving world role of the post-Soviet successor states. Each volume considers a different factor influencing the relationship between internal politics and international relations in Russia and in the western and southern tiers of newly independent states. The contributors were chosen not only for their recognized expertise but also to ensure a stimulating diversity of perspectives and a dynamic mix of approaches.

Volume 1
The Legacy of History in Russia and the New States of Eurasia
Edited by S. Frederick Starr

Volume 2
National Identity and Ethnicity in Russia and the New States of Eurasia
Edited by Roman Szporluk

Volume 3
The Politics of Religion in Russia and the New States of Eurasia
Edited by Michael Bourdeaux

Volume 4
The Making of Foreign Policy in Russia and the New States of Eurasia
Edited by Adeed Dawisha and Karen Dawisha

Volume 5
State Building and Military Power in Russia and the New States of Eurasia
Edited by Bruce Parrott

Volume 6
The Nuclear Challenge in Russia and the New States of Eurasia
Edited by George Quester

Volume 7
Political Culture and Civil Society in Russia and the New States of Eurasia
Edited by Vladimir Tismaneanu

THE INTERNATIONAL POLITICS OF EURASIA

Volume 6

THE
NUCLEAR
CHALLENGE
IN
RUSSIA
AND THE
NEW STATES
OF EURASIA

Editor:
George Quester

M.E. Sharpe

Armonk, New York
London, England

Library of Congress Cataloging-in-Publication Data

The nuclear challenge in Russia and the new states of Eurasia /
edited by George Quester.
p.   cm.   —   (The international politics of Eurasia ; v. 6)
Includes bibliographical references and index.
ISBN 1-56324-362-8.   —   ISBN 1-56324-363-6 (pbk.)
1. Nuclear weapons—Government policy—Former Soviet republics.
2. Nuclear arms control—Former Soviet republics.
I. Quester, George H.   II. Series.
UA770.N83 1995
327.1'74'0947—dc20   95-7709
                                            CIP

Printed in the United States of America

The paper used in this publication meets the minimum requirements of
American National Standard for Information Sciences—
Permanence of Paper for Printed Library Materials,
ANSI Z 39.48-1984.

BM (c)   10   9   8   7   6   5   4   3   2   1
BM (p)   10   9   8   7   6   5   4   3   2   1

Contents

List of Maps   vii

About the Editors and Contributors   viii

Preface
Karen Dawisha and Bruce Parrott   xi

1. Introduction: Nuclear Weapons and the Russian Littoral
   George Quester   3

2. The Post-Soviet States and the Nuclear Nonproliferation Regime
   William C. Potter   10

3. Technical Aspects of Proliferation and Nonproliferation
   Oleg Bukharin   35

4. Russian Control of Nuclear Weapons
   Bruce G. Blair   59

5. Russia and Nuclear Weapons
   Steven E. Miller   89

6. Is START Stalling?
   John W.R. Lepingwell   100

7. The Sources and Conduct of Ukrainian Nuclear Policy:
   November 1992 to January 1994
   Sherman W. Garnett   125

8. Belarusian Denuclearization Policy and the Control of
   Nuclear Weapons
   Vyachaslau Paznyak   153

9. Kazakhstan's Nuclear Policy and the Control of Nuclear Weapons
   Murat Laumulin   181

10. The Nuclear Problem in the Post-Soviet Transition
    Craig Nation   212

11. U.S. Nuclear Arms Control Policies Toward Russia and
    the Former Soviet Union
    Michael Nacht   239

12. Conclusion: The Importance of Nuclear Weapons
    George Quester   252

Appendix: Project Participants   263

Index   265

List of Maps

Russia's Nuclear Weapon Infrastructure   88

Nuclear Weapons and Other Sites of
Proliferation Concern
    Ukraine   124
    Belarus   152
    Kazakhstan   180

About the Editors and Contributors

George Quester is professor of government at the University of Maryland. He has taught at Harvard University, Cornell University, the National War College, and the U.S. Naval Academy. He is the author of numerous books and articles on military doctrine and nuclear weapons in the United States, the former Soviet Union, and China.

Karen Dawisha is professor of government at the University of Maryland, College Park. She graduated with degrees in Russian and politics from the University of Lancaster in England and received her Ph.D. from the London School of Economics. She has served as an advisor to the British House of Commons Foreign Affairs Committee and was a member of the policy planning staff of the U.S. State Department. She has received fellowships from the Rockefeller Foundation, the Council on Foreign Relations, and the MacArthur Foundation. She is a member of the Royal Institute of International Affairs and the Council on Foreign Relations. Her publications include *Russia and the New States of Eurasia: The Politics of Upheaval* (coauthored with Bruce Parrott, 1994), *Eastern Europe, Gorbachev, and Reform: The Great Challenge* (1989, 2d ed. 1990), *The Kremlin and the Prague Spring* (1984), *The Soviet Union in the Middle East: Politics and Perspectives* (1982), *Soviet-East European Dilemmas: Coercion, Competition, and Consent* (1981), and *Soviet Foreign Policy Toward Egypt* (1979).

Bruce Parrott is professor and director of Russian Area and East European Studies at the Johns Hopkins University School of Advanced International Studies, where he has taught for twenty years. He received his B.A. in religious studies from Pomona College in 1966, and his Ph.D. in political science in 1976 from Columbia University, where he was assistant director of the Russian Institute. His publications include *Russia and the*

New States of Eurasia: The Politics of Upheaval (coauthored with Karen Dawisha, 1994), *The Dynamics of Soviet Defense Policy* (1990), *The Soviet Union and Ballistic Missile Defense* (1987), *Trade Technology and Soviet-American Relations* (1985), and *Politics and Technology in the Soviet Union* (1983).

Bruce G. Blair is senior fellow at the Brookings Institution. He holds a Ph.D. in operations research from Yale University and has been an adjunct professor at Yale and Princeton. Dr. Blair's latest publication is *Global Zero Alert for Nuclear Forces* (1995).

Oleg Bukharin was trained in physics at the Moscow Institute of Physics and Technology and in international security at the Woodrow Wilson School of Public and International Affairs at Princeton University. Dr. Bukharin recently had a long-term fellowship as an SSRC-MacArthur Foundation Fellow on Peace and Security in a Changing World.

Sherman W. Garnett is senior associate for Russia, National Security at the Carnegie Endowment for International Peace in Washington, DC. He received an M.A. from Yale University in 1979 and a Ph.D. from the University of Michigan in 1982. Dr. Garnett has held several positions at the USD/P which include: Principal Director for Russia, Ukraine, and Eurasia and Director for Russia, Ukraine, and Eurasia. He was also Deputy Assistant Secretary of Defense (Acting) and Director for European Security Negotiations.

Murat Laumulin works at the Ministry of Foreign Affairs of Kazakhstan, in the Department of International Security and Arms Control. He received his Ph.D. from the Institute of History in Moscow in 1990. Dr. Laumulin was previously senior research fellow at the Institute of History and Ethnology in Almaty, senior research fellow at the Center for Oriental Studies, Almaty, and lecturer at Kazakh State University.

John W.R. Lepingwell is assistant professor of political science at the University of Illinois at Urbana-Champaign. His research interests include Soviet and Russian civil–military relations and the development of post-Soviet security affairs. Dr. Lepingwell has published articles on these topics in *World Politics*, *Orbis*, *International Security*, and the *RFE/RL Research Report*.

Steven E. Miller is director of the International Security Program at the Center for Science and International Affairs of the Kennedy School of

Government at Harvard University. He is also editor in chief of the journal *International Security*. Previously Dr. Miller was senior research fellow at the Stockholm International Peace Research Institute (SIPRI) and taught defense and arms control studies at the Massachusetts Institute of Technology. He is coauthor of the recently published monograph *Soviet Nuclear Fission: Control of the Nuclear Arsenal in a Disintegrating Soviet Union.*

Michael Nacht is assistant director for Strategic and Eurasian Affairs at the U.S. Arms Control and Disarmament Agency, where he has primary responsibility for the agency's work on nuclear arms reduction and missile defenses with Russia and the other states of the former Soviet Union. Formerly dean of the University of Maryland School of Public Affairs and a faculty member at Harvard University's Kennedy School of Government, Dr. Nacht is the author or coauthor of five books, including *The Age of Vulnerability: Threats to the Nuclear Stalemate* and *Beyond Government: Extending the Public Policy Debate in Emerging Democracies.*

Craig Nation is resident associate professor and coordinator of Russian area and East European studies at the Johns Hopkins University's School of Advanced International Studies, Bologna Center. He received his Ph.D. in Soviet studies and contemporary history from Duke University. Dr. Nation previously taught at Duke University, Cornell University, and the University of Southern California.

Vyachaslau Paznyak is director of International Programs, Minsk Center for Nonproliferation and Export Control. He received his Ph.D. from Belarusian State University. Dr. Paznyak was previously project director and chief expert of International Security Affairs at the National Center for Strategic Initiatives in Minsk, as well as assistant professor in the Department of Political Science and Sociology at the National Institute for the Humanities, also in Minsk.

William C. Potter is professor and director of the Center for Nonproliferation Studies at the Monterey Institute of International Studies (MIIS). He also directs the MIIS Center for Russian and Eurasian Studies. Dr. Potter is author or editor of numerous works, including *Nuclear Profiles of the Soviet Successor States* (1993) and *International Missile Bazaar: The New Suppliers' Network* (ed., 1994), as well as a contributor to many other books and journals. His current research focuses on nuclear exports, nuclear safety, and nonproliferation problems involving the post-Soviet states.

Preface

This book is the sixth in a projected series of ten volumes produced by the Russian Littoral Project, sponsored jointly by the University of Maryland at College Park and the Paul H. Nitze School of Advanced International studies of the Johns Hopkins University. As directors of the project, we share the conviction that the transformation of the former Soviet republics into independent states demands systematic analysis of the determinants of the domestic and foreign policies of the new countries. This series of volumes is intended to provide a basis for comprehensive scholarly study of these issues.

The collapse of the Soviet Union has demolished the international political order of the past half-century and created a host of new states whose security policies must be devised even as their political and national structures are being built. This book analyzes the problems posed for Russia's relations with its neighbors by the existence of nuclear weapons. Just as in the years of the Cold War, such nuclear weapons are double-edged in their impact, seen by some states or factions as a reinsurance against political threats or conventional military attack, but seen more widely as posing unbearable risks of mass destruction. This book must thus be read in conjuction with the volume edited by Bruce Parrot on the role of conventional forces along the Russian Littoral. The variety of interpretations of the nuclear role here intersects with varying national interests, now that the Soviet Union has been broken up.

This book is an outgrowth of a conference jointly conducted by the Russian Littoral Project, the Department of War Studies at King's College, London, and the International Institute for Strategic Studies. We owe a special debt of gratitude to Lawrence Freedman of King's College and to

Gerald Segal of IISS for their intellectual contributions to the conference and their willingness to provide institutional co-sponsorship of the enterprise.

We wish to thank the contributors to the volume for their help in making this phase of the Russian Littoral Project a success and for revising their papers in a timely fashion. We are especially grateful to George Quester for supporting the project since its inception, for contributing insights that were pivotal in structuring the projects treatment of military and nuclear issues, and for editing this book. We are also are grateful to the numerous conference discussants—particularly Roy Allison—whose comments and suggestions substantially improved the quality of the final papers. Special thanks are due to Janine Ludlam and Florence Rotz for their skillful handling of the pre-conference logistics and for their unstinting labor on the book manuscript. We also wish to express our appreciation to Fiona Paton and Kjetil Ribe for their able support in administering the conference.

The Russian Littoral Project

The objective of the Russian Littoral Project is to foster an exchange of research and information in fields of study pertaining to the international politics of Eurasia. The internal development and external relations of the new states are being studied in a series of workshops taking place in Washington, D.C., London, Odessa, and other locations between 1993 and 1996. Scholars from the new states, North America, and Europe are invited to present papers at the workshops.

Focusing on the interaction between the internal affairs and the foreign relations of the new states, the project workshops examine the impact of the following factors: history, national identity and ethnicity, religion, political culture and civil society, economics, foreign policy priorities and decisionmaking, military issues, and the nuclear question. Each of these topics is examined in a set of three workshops focusing in turn on Russia, the western belt of new states extending from Estonia to Ukraine, and the southern tier of new states extending from Georgia to Kyrgyzstan.

The Russian Littoral Project could not have been launched without the generous and timely contributions of the project's Coordinating Committee. We wish to thank the committee members for providing invaluable advice and expertise concerning the organization and intellectual substance of the project. The members of the Coordinating Committee are: Dr. Adeed Dawisha (George Mason University); Dr. Bartek Kaminski (University of Maryland and the World Bank); Dr. Catherine Kelleher (The Brookings Institution); Ms. Judith Kipper (The Brookings Institution); Dr. Nancy Lubin (Carnegie Mellon University); Dr. Michael Mandelbaum (The

School of Advanced International Studies); Dr. James Millar (The George Washington University); Dr. Peter Murrell (University of Maryland); Dr. Martha Brill Olcott (Colgate University); Dr. Ilya Prizel (The School of Advanced International Studies); Dr. George Quester (University of Maryland); Dr. Alvin Z. Rubinstein (University of Pennsylvania); Dr. Blair Ruble (The Kennan Institute); Dr. S. Frederick Starr (the Aspen Institute); Dr. Roman Szporluk (Harvard University); and Dr. Vladimir Tismaneanu (University of Maryland).

We are grateful to the John D. and Catherine T. MacArthur Foundation and the Ford Foundation for funding the conference from which this book is derived; we are especially grateful to Kennette Benedict of the MacArthur Foundation for her firm support of the whole project from the beginning, and to Geoffrey Wiseman of the Ford foundation.

We wish also to thank President William Kirwan of the University of Maryland at College Park and President William C. Richardson of the Johns Hopkins University, who have given indispensable support to the project. Thanks are also due to Dean Irwin Goldstein, Associate Dean Stewart Edelstein, Director of the Office of International Affairs Marcus Franda, and Department of Government and Politics Chair Jonathan Wilkenfeld at the University of Maryland at College Park; to Provost Joseph Cooper and Vice-Provost for Academic Planning and Budget Stephen M. McClain at the Johns Hopkins University; to Professor George Packard, who helped launch the project during his final year as dean of the School of Advanced International Studies, to SAIS Dean Paul D. Wolfowitz, and to SAIS Associate Dean of Academic Affairs Stephen Szabo.

Finally, we are grateful for the guidance and encouragement given by Patricia Kolb at M.E. Sharpe, Inc. Her faith in the idea of the project and in the publication series has been crucial to the success of the whole endeavor.

Karen Dawisha
University of Maryland at College Park

Bruce Parrott
The Johns Hopkins University
School of Advanced International Studies

THE
NUCLEAR
CHALLENGE
IN
RUSSIA
AND THE
NEW STATES
OF EURASIA

1

INTRODUCTION
Nuclear Weapons and the Russian Littoral

George Quester

The Cold War is over, and the West won. In fact, the West won quite totally, as communism was renounced even within the Soviet Union, and as the USSR broke into the separate republics whose interrelationships are the subject of this entire series of volumes on the International Politics of Eurasia.

The special question for this volume is how nuclear weapons affect these interrelationships. And the general answer, developed very well in each of the separate chapters, is that such weapons are enormously complicating and troublesome.

For all the reasons cited in this book, the West indeed won the Cold War much more than it should have dared to. By the basic logic of mutual nuclear deterrence, as taught in courses on Cold War military strategy all across the United States, no one in Washington or any of the other democratic capitals could have expected to depose the communist rulers so totally, without in the process risking the most dire consequence, an all-out nuclear war.

If Nuclear Weapons Did Not Exist

If nuclear weapons did not exist, if Albert Einstein's theories had been wrong, there would not be this volume in the series. And if nuclear weapons did not exist, a total victory over the communist rulers in the Soviet Union would have been much more straightforwardly welcome; the division of the Soviet Union into "Russia" and its littoral states would have been more clearly the goal.

The old approach was "divide and conquer," or more precisely, "divide and avoid being conquered." This was nothing more than the basic principle of a "balance of power" system, whereby Britain and every other major power had for centuries worked to prevent any conglomeration of power sufficient for hegemony or world empire. The essence of an empire was that it would put kingdoms out of business. Any one of the kingdoms, in the old balance of power system, would have liked to become an empire itself. But each one of them would work to keep any other from becoming an empire, joining coalitions again and again against the strongest single power.

But such a balance was then inherently threatened by geography, in what Mackinder and others were to label the "drives of geopolitics," whereby any such state that controlled the center of Eurasia would have an inherent military advantage against the peninsulas sticking out from the world's largest continent.[1] Russia, already in the days of the tsars, thus wielded a threat to achieve and impose a hegemony, and to become a world-dominating empire; the British task, captured in the analysis of Mackinder, but already for a century or so understood by British planners to be "the great game," was to keep Russia from exploiting this power.

The United States after World War II basically inherited what the British had thus regarded as their great burden, to counter the inherent advantage of the position governed from Moscow. Mackinder had alerted the British to expect particular difficulties once the Russian internal lines of communication were enhanced to allow rapid movement of forces. His great 1904 attention-capturing lecture to the Royal Geographic Society was tied to the imminent completion of the Trans-Siberian Railroad, and Mackinder included a prediction that was monumentally wrong, that Asia soon would be "crisscrossed" by similar railroads.

These railroads never were built, but the Soviet successors to the tsars were to be important developers of another means of internal mobility for military forces, the tank. Possessing some eighty thousand tanks at the end of the Cold War, Moscow had thus reified Mackinder's worst fears for Britain, the fears inherited by the United States and all its NATO partners.

Soviet-built tanks invaded South Korea in 1950, and they were the crucial tool in the final communist takeover of South Vietnam in 1975. For all the years of the Cold War, they sat continually poised to threaten Finland and Scandinavia, Turkey and Greece, and above all Western Europe.

If nuclear weapons did not exist, the Western choice would thus have been limited to two basic options, either to trust the intentions of Stalin and his successors, or to expend enormous resources in trying to guard against such a tank attack. Few Westerners were ready to adopt the first choice, in light of Stalin's policies in Eastern Europe, and in light of the invasion of

South Korea. But the second approach would have very much slowed down the economic growth that characterized West Germany, Western Europe, and the entire free world after the introduction of the deutsche mark in West Germany in 1948.

Since Nuclear Weapons Do Exist: Extended Deterrence

The basic American and Western approach to this political-military problem was thus neither to trust Moscow nor to match the Soviets in numbers of troops and tanks, but rather to rely on the threat of nuclear retaliation to deter Soviet aggressions, to deter around the rim of Eurasia any repetitions of the attack on South Korea. The "containment" of communism, the prevention of Soviet hegemony, depended on nuclear weapons.

These were the decades when Moscow obviously wished such weapons did not exist and strove to delegitimate them, strove to get the West to accept the policies proposed in the "Rapacki Plan" of "nuclear free zones" and "no first use." These were the decades of the mature Cold War, when the United States, West Germany, and the other powers facing the Soviet bloc had to maintain policies of "flexible response." This was hardly ever a clear policy; it amounted basically to saying that the West would attempt to hold back a Soviet-launched conventional attack for a few days by conventional means; if this did not succeed, the United States would then escalate to nuclear warfare, allegedly aimed at reversing the battlefield outcome, but actually very plausibly leading to further escalation—to all-out thermonuclear war. The mere prospect of all this, hopefully, would keep Moscow from ever launching such a tank attack in the first place.[2]

While the United States possessed a monopoly on nuclear weapons, its threat to use such weapons if Soviet tanks rolled forward was quite plausible. Once the Soviets demonstrated nuclear weapons of their own after 1949, however, it was much more difficult to make any such American threats of nuclear escalation credible because the price of an attack on a Soviet city would be the corresponding destruction of American cities.

The Soviet-backed North Korean armored invasion of South Korea in 1950 thus saw no American use of nuclear weapons, and there were analysts who expected the same if Soviet forces were to invade West Germany and the rest of Western Europe. The decades of the Cold War were thus largely shaped by the effort of succeeding American administrations to maintain and restore the threat of American nuclear weapon use in the event of a purely conventional armed attack on Western Europe, or once again on South Korea, or on any other such exposed position.

Since Nuclear Weapons Do Exist: Basic Deterrence

The impact of nuclear weapons, until the Warsaw Pact and the Soviet Union collapsed so suddenly and dramatically, was thus basically twofold. First, such weapons were widely and plausibly seen as compensating for Moscow's advantage in conventional military strength and the advantage of its central geopolitical position, now so greatly enhanced by the enormous Soviet investment in mobile armored warfare. But doubts remained, never to be erased completely even as the Cold War was ending, about whether American nuclear retaliation could be made credible, if the United States itself were not invaded or if American cities were not subjected to any nuclear attack themselves.[3] This aspect of nuclear weapons thus amounted to what would be labeled and debated as "extended nuclear deterrence."

A second impact of nuclear weapons was more basic, and indeed is often labeled "basic nuclear deterrence," for such weapons were also seen as an inherent brake on how far either side could ever go in advancing with victorious conventional military forces; a losing side would lash out and retaliate if it were about to lose everything, if it were about to be subjected to total defeat and unconditional surrender.

By the logic of basic nuclear deterrence, of mutual assured destruction, there would never be a hostile army, Soviet or otherwise, allowed to occupy Washington, DC, and the rest of America, because the United States would have nothing left to lose, and would have no reason to hold back its nuclear force. And similarly there would never be a hostile anticommunist force allowed into Moscow and all of the Soviet Union, because the Soviets would then have no reason to hold back their nuclear force.

The inference here was that the Allies would have had to stop short of going all the way to Berlin in 1945 to depose Hitler, if Hitler had somehow possessed intercontinental missiles with nuclear warheads. The core of deterrence was that one should never dare to put an opposing side into a position of "use them or lose them" with regard to its nuclear missiles, for it was only the prospect of still having something left to lose that kept such missiles from being fired.

Washington was occupied by the British in 1814, when the White House and the Capitol were burned, and President Madison and his government were forced to flee. Moscow had been occupied by Napoleon in 1812, resulting also in the destruction of what had been, and was to become again, Russia's capital city. By the basic logic of weapons of mass destruction—that horrendous retaliation would follow if one ever imposed so total a defeat and humiliation on an enemy—no one would get to occupy or burn these capitals again. All war would now have to be limited in ends, as well as in the kinds of weapons used, and victors would have to settle for containment rather than rollback.[4]

Yet in 1991 we did see "anticommunist forces" in the streets of Moscow, and this leaves much to be explained, and much to be worried about. If someone had gone to sleep, Rip van Winkle–style, in 1984 and awakened in 1994, he would have been amazed about what he had slept through.

By any normal humane standards, he would almost surely have been pleased, as free markets and free expression—despite all the shortcomings and disappointments recounted in these volumes—are surely preferable to what they replaced.

By the traditional standards of international power politics, this modern van Winkle would also have been pleased, as the conglomeration of power controlled from Moscow is much less extensive than what Stalin or the tsars commanded. All of Western Europe and all of the rest of the world have less to fear in terms of conventional Russian military power, and in the extended and central position from which it works.

But if this van Winkle had gone to sleep aware of the theme of this volume, the impact and role of nuclear weapons, he would also have awakened with some disquiet, with a host of worrisome unanswered questions about how such a total victory could have been possible in a situation of mutual assured destruction and how all the nuclear issues are to be handled from here on.

A Reversal of Roles

One very elementary consequence of the way the Cold War ended must thus be noted here at the very beginning. Until 1989, Americans and their allies were probably glad that nuclear weapons existed, while the regime in Moscow was not. After 1989, this might all be reversed.

This is not to argue that, if the West had engaged in unilateral nuclear disarmament during the Cold War, the Soviets would have followed suit. Stalin and his successors were surely capable of understanding the advantages of a monopoly of nuclear weapons and could have used such a monopoly well as a way of advancing "socialism." Yet, since the Americans had such weapons first, and then even when both sides had them, such weapons tended to negate the conventional military power and geopolitical position commanded from Moscow. If Moscow and its allies were expected to have the advantage without nuclear weapons, they would seek to eliminate them from the scene.

Since 1989, however, it is plausible instead that the United States and its allies wish that nuclear weapons had never existed; and conversely, it might be the Russian military planners who would now welcome the scientific facts of nuclear physics with some relief and would extoll the advantages of "flexible response" rather than "no first use."

Some Americans might now wish that nuclear weapons could disappear from the scene for more narrow and nationalistic reasons. The totality of the political victory over communism has been followed by the shift of all of Eastern Europe from alliance with Moscow into a de facto alliance against. Such political shifts were accompanied by the dramatic and easy victory of American conventional weapons in Operation Desert Storm against Iraqi forces equipped with Soviet weapons. All this suggests that the West may never have been as disadvantaged as it had feared in the conventional realm,[5] and that the West as a whole now has the advantage against mere Russia. Rather than worrying about the "Asian hordes" commanded from Moscow, we could speculate about "American hordes" (after all, the United States now exceeds "Russia" in total population).

Yet, since the West has now indeed so totally won the Cold War, there is less reason remaining for most Americans to be savoring another forward march against Moscow. For most of the Cold War, Americans and other Westerners had shared a feeling that they were somehow losing the struggle, that containment was working only imperfectly, that the Soviet Union and its allies were militarily spreading "socialism" around the world. If anyone then had predicted that there would, by the middle of the 1990s, be only Cuba, Vietnam, China, and North Korea styling themselves as "Marxist" (with China indeed pursuing "socialism with Chinese characteristics"—which amounts to something very capitalist—and with Vietnam matching the Chinese "reforms"), that person would have been dismissed as wildly unrealistic and out of touch with the world. But all this has happened.

Much less competitively, and with more of a general world interest at heart, the majority of Americans may thus wish to be free of the nuclear shadow because of all the problems analyzed in this volume, and because of the aftermath costs of their victory, rather than because of the prospects of new power struggles and new victories.[6]

Among the problems to be dissected here, we will be analyzing the issues of command and control over Russian nuclear weapons, as well as the more basic issues of custody over fissionable materials and the secrets of weapon design. We will similarly have to wrestle with the issue of the nuclear weapons that were in the custody of Belarus, Ukraine, and Kazakhstan, which have generated a type of nuclear proliferation that none of the proliferation literature had very much anticipated. Of possibly comparable concern will be whether Russia can be fully and effectively enlisted in slowing and preventing nuclear proliferation in North Korea and in Iran and Iraq.

We have already noted the strategic problem of whether the Russians will now have to reverse their attitudes on no first use of nuclear weapons and nuclear-free zones, in light of the change in apparent strengths of the conventional forces facing each other.

The basic moral issue of nuclear deterrence—whether it is appropriate, or instead morally "mad" (mutual assured destruction), to aim retaliatory nuclear forces at opposing urban centers—has been much debated during the Cold War. It acquires a new spin when Russian President Yeltsin grandly announces that Soviet nuclear weapons will no longer be aimed at American cities, or indeed at any American targets, and when the United States makes a reciprocal announcement. What such announcements mean in practical reality may be outweighed by the political impact of what they could *seem* to mean. The moral issue also acquires a different spin when the Russians who would have been aimed at are voters who actually have some voice and responsibility for Russian military and diplomatic policy, rather than, as in the Soviet days, people denied any such voice or responsibility.

Finally, hanging over this entire volume is the more basic question of how important nuclear weapons are, whether they make much of a difference in how much respect or deference anyone gets. The thrust of most of the chapters, and indeed of this volume as a whole, is that such issues remain very important.

Notes

1. Halford J. Mackinder, "The Geographical Pivot of History," *Geographic Journal*, 1904, vol. 23, pp. 21–44.

2. For a basic analysis of the problems here, see Glenn Snyder, *Deterrence and Defense* (Princeton: Princeton University Press, 1961).

3. For a good example of an expression of such doubts, see Henry A. Kissinger, *The Necessity for Choice* (New York: Harper and Row, 1961).

4. Morton Halperin, *Limited War in the Nuclear Age* (New York: John Wiley, 1963), provides a valuable overview of the theory that developed here.

5. An example of such an earlier argument that NATO might have the conventional advantage can be found in Paul Bracken, "Urban Sprawl and NATO Defense," *Survival*, vol. 18, no. 6 (November–December 1976), pp. 254–60.

6. For an example of such arguments, see Jonathan Dean et al., "The Paris Summit: Beginning of a New European Security System," *Arms Control Today*, vol. 20, no. 10 (December 1990), pp. 3–7.

2

The Post-Soviet States and the Nuclear Nonproliferation Regime

William C. Potter

It has not escaped the notice of the critics of the Nuclear Nonproliferation Treaty (NPT) that the most ardent proponents of nonproliferation
generally have included those states with the largest nuclear arsenals.
Such was the case with the Soviet Union. At the time of its collapse in
December 1991, it simultaneously supported a massive nuclear weapons
complex, which consumed a large portion of the Soviet national budget,
and championed the major pillars of the nonproliferation regime—the
NPT, the International Atomic Energy Agency (IAEA), and the Nuclear
Suppliers Group (NSG). Notwithstanding its own active nuclear testing
program, it also promoted the early conclusion of a Comprehensive Test
Ban (CTB).

Since the disintegration of the Soviet Union, Russia has retained a
smaller, but still sprawling, nuclear weapons complex. It also has continued
to pursue nonproliferation aims that in many ways resemble those of the
Soviet Union. Less continuity, however, is apparent in the nonproliferation
perspectives of the non-Russian successor states. This chapter seeks to discern the major elements of continuity and change in the nonproliferation
policies of the post-Soviet states. Particular attention is given to the analysis
of post-Soviet state attitudes toward and behavior regarding nuclear exports
and export controls, international and national safeguards, the 1995 NPT
Extension Conference, and proliferation "problem countries." An effort also
is made to identify measures that might promote greater cooperation for
nonproliferation among the post-Soviet states.

The Historical Context

The basic premise that underlay Soviet nonproliferation policy was that Soviet military and political interests were best served by prevention of the spread of nuclear weapons to other states. This perspective, shaped first and foremost by the fear that nuclear weapons might be acquired by states hostile to the Soviet Union, remained remarkably constant for well over a quarter century.[1] Soviet support for nonproliferation also was motivated by concern that an increase in the number of states with nuclear weapons would increase the risk of local conflict escalating to a superpower confrontation.[2]

Although much of Moscow's nonproliferation rhetoric and elements of its nonproliferation behavior can be explained in terms of narrow self-interest, the range and consistency of its nonproliferation efforts, as well as certain specific actions, indicate that the Soviet leadership appreciated the global risks posed by the diffusion of nuclear weapons. One therefore finds Soviet support for nonproliferation not only in declarative policy but also in concrete behavior, including endorsement of the Partial Test Ban Treaty of 1963, the Treaty for the Prohibition of Nuclear Weapons in Latin America of 1967, and the Nuclear Nonproliferation Treaty of 1968, and, for much of the period since 1958, stringent Soviet nuclear export policy.

Although prevention of access to nuclear weapons by traditional adversaries was a major concern of Soviet foreign policy, nonproliferation was not in itself a primary policy objective. The topic was rarely the subject of Politburo deliberations, and, especially after West Germany signed the NPT, there was a noticeable decline in the perceived urgency and magnitude of the proliferation threat expressed in Soviet nonproliferation pronouncements.

A decline in the priority of nonproliferation as a Soviet foreign policy objective, however, by no means meant neglect of the issue. Indeed, if one focuses on behavior rather than rhetoric, one can observe a subtle shift in Soviet policy in the mid-1970s in the direction of more pragmatism and cooperation in the area of nonproliferation. This change entailed movement away from the post-1958 approach—driven by the Soviet experience with China—which had been characterized by the notion that "there would be no proliferation problem if all countries would follow the policy of the USSR and 'each take care of its own.' "[3] Soviet involvement in the Nuclear Exporters Committee (or the Zangger Committee, as it is usually known), the London Suppliers Group, the NPT Review Conferences of 1975, 1980, and 1985, and the International Nuclear Fuel Cycle Evaluation, for example, reveals increasing Soviet recognition of the complexity of proliferation problems and the utility of coordinated, multinational action.[4]

Soviet nonproliferation policy during this period also was noteworthy for the unusual degree to which it was in concert with that of the United States.[5] This cooperation persisted even during the most troubled periods of the superpowers' relations in the 1970s and 1980s and was reflected in regular bilateral consultations and a variety of multilateral forums, including the IAEA, the London Suppliers Group, the Nuclear Exporters Committee, and the NPT Review Conferences.

Probably the most unusual example of Soviet cooperation with the United States on nonproliferation measures occurred in the summer of 1977, when the USSR shared intelligence information with the United States that indicated the possibility that South Africa had constructed a nuclear test site in the Kalahari Desert.[6] The Soviet Union also subsequently respected American requests not to interfere with a U.S. initiative to gain South African adherence to the NPT and international safeguards.[7] This behavior is particularly significant as an indicator of the Soviet Union's genuine interest in nonproliferation, because it occurred behind the scenes and did not afford the Kremlin the opportunity to exploit its nonproliferation vigilance or anti–South African stance for propaganda purposes— something it had certainly done during the Kalahari Desert episode.

Ironically, given the Cold War history and Western stereotypes about Soviet misbehavior, the long-standing experience of U.S.-Soviet cooperation on nonproliferation actually appears to have made U.S. policy makers less attentive to, and less concerned about, the signs of the change in Soviet nuclear nonproliferation policy that began to emerge in the late 1980s. Indications of change were most apparent in the area of nuclear export behavior.

Under former General Secretary and President Mikhail Gorbachev, the Soviet Union in the late 1980s and early 1990s undertook a number of nuclear export initiatives that signaled a less prudent approach to nonproliferation. These initiatives, although for the most part unsuccessful, included efforts to market nuclear goods and services to non-NPT parties (e.g., Argentina, India, Israel, and Pakistan) without requiring the application of international safeguards on all the recipient state's nuclear facilities (i.e., so-called full-scope or comprehensive safeguards). During the same period, the Soviet Union adopted a more lax nuclear export policy toward NPT states and expressed a readiness, for example, to sell South Korea sensitive nuclear technology, including uranium enrichment and fast breed reactor processes.[8] Although none of these export initiatives were prohibited by the NPT, they implied that even longtime supporters of nonproliferation were, for the right price, prepared to sell nuclear equipment, technology, and services to potential proliferators.

These nuclear initiatives coincided with the decline of the Soviet Ministry of Foreign Affairs' influence on nuclear export decisions, and the corresponding rise in power of the Ministry of Atomic Power and Industry (MAPI). MAPI's export policy appeared to be driven primarily by hard currency considerations, with little regard for the foreign or defense policy implications of the export of sensitive technology. MAPI's ability to pursue an export policy that emphasized profit considerations was facilitated by the absence in the Soviet Union of any domestic legislation governing nuclear exports. It also benefited from the absence of public scrutiny, due to the lack of Soviet journalists or independent experts knowledgeable about nonproliferation issues.

The Post-Soviet Period

The end of the Cold War, the collapse of the Soviet Union, and the nuclear inheritance by the Soviet successor states have created both new proliferation risks and nonproliferation opportunities. Although the dangers generally have overshadowed positive developments, one should not overlook recent nonproliferation advances involving the post-Soviet states. A summary of the status of major nonproliferation activities of the new independent states as of August 1994 is provided in Table 2.1.

On the positive side of the nonproliferation ledger, one can point to the redeployment on Russian territory of thousands of tactical nuclear weapons that previously were dispersed in at least fourteen of the republics. Considerable progress also has been made in gaining post-Soviet state adherents to the NPT. As Table 2.1 indicates, by the end of July 1994, ten of the fourteen non-Russian successor states had joined the NPT as non-nuclear weapon states, and an eleventh, Moldova, appeared poised to do so.[9] Adherence by two of these states—Belarus and Kazakhstan—is crucial since they, along with Ukraine, were the non-Russian states upon whose territory the Soviet strategic nuclear arsenal was based.

Many of the post-Soviet states also are parties to other significant, if less well known, nonproliferation organizations, treaties, and regimes. Belarus and Ukraine, for example, were members of the IAEA (and the United Nations) long before they achieved meaningful independence. They also were long-standing parties to the Partial Test Ban Treaty, the Seabed Treaty, the Outer Space Treaty, and the Antarctic Treaty. Although it is not widely known, officials in Ukraine twenty-six years ago sought approval from Moscow to join the NPT. At that time, however, the Russian-dominated Politburo was not prepared to see Ukraine join the NPT either as a nuclear weapon state or as a non-nuclear weapon state.[10] More recently, Belarus and Ukraine have become parties to the Convention on the Physical

Table 2.1

NIS Nonproliferation Status Report, August 1994

Country	NPT Treaty	IAEA Member	IAEA Safeguards	NSG Member	Zangger Committee	Partial Test Ban Treaty	Antarctic Treaty	Outer Space Treaty	Physical Protection	Seabed Treaty	1992 Minsk Accord
Armenia	X	X							X		X
Azerbaijan	X										
Belarus	X	X				X		X	X	X	X
Estonia	X	X									
Georgia	X	X									
Kazakhstan	X	X									X
Kyrgyzstan	X										X
Latvia	X	X	X							X	
Lithuania	X	X	X						X		
Moldova	X[a]										
Russia	X	X	b	X	X	X	X	X	X	X	X
Tajikistan											X
Turkmenistan											X
Ukraine		X				X	X	X	X	X	
Uzbekistan	X	X	X								X

Sources: Inventory of International Nonproliferation Organizations and Regimes (Monterey, CA: Monterey Institute of International Studies, 1994); and William Potter, *Nuclear Profiles of the Soviet Successor States* (Monterey, CA: Monterey Institute of International Studies, 1993).

[a]At the time this chapter was revised in August 1994, Moldova's parliament had approved accession to the NPT, but instruments of accession had yet to be deposited.
[b]Voluntary safeguards.

Protection of Nuclear Material, as have Armenia, Estonia, and Lithuania; Latvia has joined the Seabed Treaty; and Armenia, Estonia, Kazakhstan, Latvia, Lithuania, and Uzbekistan have become members of the IAEA. Most of the post-Soviet states, including those that have not yet acceded to the NPT (e.g., Ukraine), also have initiated negotiations with the IAEA to place their nuclear facilities under international safeguards.

Having identified these positive developments from the standpoint of nonproliferation, one must note a number of areas in which the nonproliferation practices of the post-Soviet states remain, at best, underdeveloped. Three areas of particular proliferation significance are export controls, international safeguards, and national safeguards.

Export Controls

The basic economic and domestic political conditions that encouraged a reorientation in Soviet nuclear export policy under Gorbachev remain today in Russia and the other Soviet successor states, but in a more acute form.[1] Nuclear goods and services, along with other defense-related products, are among the few commodities from the former Soviet Union that are in demand abroad and are able to generate hard currency. Particularly worrisome is the danger that private firms and/or organized crime may acquire and sell some types of sensitive nuclear material, equipment, and technology.

The West, until May 1994, was extremely lucky regarding nuclear smuggling from the former Soviet Union. Despite frequent sensationalist headlines to the contrary, for three years the West avoided an influx of militarily significant nuclear goods from the ex-USSR. This luck has now run out, as evidenced by a series of seizures in Germany in the summer of 1994 of weapons-grade material of NIS origin.

Although the threat of illicit international trade in nuclear weapons material is no longer theoretical, it remains important to distinguish between confirmed cases of diversions of weapons-grade material from nuclear facilities in the former Soviet Union and the transport of such material to other states. To date, there are surprisingly few cases of confirmed—as opposed to reported—diversions involving weapons-grade material. The most serious involve the disappearance of an undisclosed quantity of highly enriched uranium (HEU) from the "Luch" nuclear research facility at Podolsk near Moscow, the theft (and subsequent recovery) of three fuel elements containing HEU from a naval base in Murmansk, and the case mentioned by FBI Director Louis Freeh involving the investigation in St. Petersburg of the possible theft of two or more kilograms of HEU. Most other alleged thefts of weapons-grade fissile material, including the sixty kilograms of HEU cited by Seymour Hersh in his widely publicized *Atlantic Monthly* exposé, in fact involved low-enriched uranium of no direct use in a nuclear weapons program.[12]

There also are only a few confirmed cases in which NIS-origin weapons-grade material—as opposed to dual-use nuclear commodities (e.g., zirconium, beryllium, and hafnium) and proliferation-sensitive radioactive elements—have been seized abroad. As of this writing, all involve material seized in Germany during a four-month period in the spring and summer of 1994.

An extended analysis of the recent cases of nuclear smuggling is beyond the scope of this chapter. Several points, however, should be emphasized.

The news media generally have lumped together what they refer to as four confirmed cases of weapons-grade material smuggled from Russia to Germany: (1) 6 grams of extraordinarily pure plutonium 239 inadvertently discovered in Tengen on 10 May 1994; (2) 800 milligrams of uranium enriched to 87.8 percent U–235 confiscated in Landshut on 13 June 1994; (3) between 300 and 350 grams of 87 percent pure plutonium 239 (part of a larger quantity of mixed oxide, or MOX, fuel) seized by German police from a passenger leaving a Lufthansa plane that arrived in Munich from Moscow on 10 August 1994; and (4) .05 milligrams of plutonium 239 confiscated by German police in Bremen on 12 August 1994.[13] Although there is substantial evidence that at least the first three cases involved Russian-origin material, the four seizures differ significantly in terms of their nonproliferation implications. Most serious from a nonproliferation standpoint are the Tengen and Munich cases. The significance of the former derives from the fact that it is the only seizure that was not a "sting" operation and may have been part of a serious effort by representatives of an aspiring nuclear weapon state to procure nuclear weapons-grade material. The unusual quality of the plutonium—99.75 percent pure—also points more clearly to the production source, most likely the Arzamas–16 nuclear weapon laboratory. This super grade of plutonium must have been extremely costly to produce, however, and probably was not available in large quantity. In contrast, the seizure in Munich is important primarily because of the relatively large quantity of material and indications that its sellers were in a position to deliver considerably more—perhaps enough to construct a crude nuclear weapon. Neither the Tengen and Munich contraband nor that taken at Landshut appear to have been the product of dedicated nuclear weapons production. Collectively, however, they demonstrate that a variety of weapons-grade material is available from multiple sources in the former Soviet Union.

Until recently there was little possibility of illegal (as opposed to unwise but state-sanctioned) nuclear exports from the Soviet Union, due to the absence of private trading companies and the operation of stringent national controls over the production and sale of all commodities. The export monopoly in the nuclear sector belonged to Tekhsnabeksport, a state-controlled company most lately associated with MAPI and previously with the Ministry of Foreign Trade. Since all nuclear export activities were carried out by a single governmental subsidiary under contracts and conditions approved by MAPI and the Ministry of Foreign Affairs, it was relatively easy to enforce stringent export controls. These regulations took the form of decrees issued by the USSR Council of Ministers. The enactment of comprehensive national legislation governing nuclear exports was deemed unnecessary.

Today, the nuclear export control machinery in Russia and the other successor states is in a state of flux. Governmental oversight responsibilities and jurisdiction are diffused, and the virtual bankruptcy of the entire defense sector has created an environment in which it is possible for private entrepreneurs to sign contracts with nuclear scientists and export nuclear goods and services. The activities of the International CHETEK Corporation, which included efforts to market peaceful nuclear explosives (PNE) services at home and abroad, are only the best-known example of a more general phenomenon.[14]

What was particularly dangerous about CHETEK's nuclear activities was the incestuous relationship it enjoyed (and it and other firms may still enjoy) with MAPI and its successor agency, the Ministry of Atomic Energy (MINATOM). This relationship involved substantial CHETEK financial subsidies to MAPI in return for exclusive marketing rights to Soviet PNE services and access to MAPI's nuclear test site(s). According to Viktor Mikhailov, a major promoter of CHETEK and now the head of MINATOM, the arrangement was the only way to preserve the research programs of Russia's nuclear labs and avoid the layoff of large numbers of scientists.[15] What Mikhailov did not note was the potential for conflict of interest and export control abuse when a cash-starved national ministry with export control responsibilities is dependent on an export-oriented private firm dealing in nuclear goods and services. The fact that nonproliferation advocates in the Russian government also tended not to recognize the impropriety of the MAPI/CHETEK deal suggests the more fundamental problem the successor states to the Soviet Union will have in balancing the principles of export control, private enterprise, and profits in an economically depressed environment.

A major potential for conflict of interest also exists in the staffing of senior positions in the export control structures of a number of the post-Soviet states. In Russia, for example, a tradition has developed for the head of the Export Control Commission—the body with responsibility for coordinating Russian export control policy—to serve simultaneously as head of the Commission for Military and Technological Cooperation (Kommitet po voenno-tekhnicheskomu sotrudnichestvu, or KVTS). The conflict of interest arises from the fact that the main purpose of the latter body is to promote the export of Russian defense products. The situation nearly became much worse in the early summer of 1992, when the head of both commissions, Georgii Khizha, sought to merge the two bodies. A decision to block the merger was made by President Boris Yeltsin only after forceful intervention by the Ministry of Foreign Affairs. Although Khizha subsequently was removed from his posts, the tendency for a conflict of interest remains, as Deputy Prime Minister Oleg Soskovets has succeeded him in both positions.

The danger of new efforts to weaken the Export Control Commission is heightened by the fact that the entire Russian export control structure, as well as that in the other newly independent states, continues to derive its legal basis from executive branch decrees rather than parliamentary legislation. In addition, poor pay, alternative employment opportunities in the private sector, and the perception of a reduced impact on policy outcomes are leading to a brain drain from the Ministry of Economics and the Ministry of Foreign Affairs. Such an exodus will clearly impede the development and implementation of a sound nuclear export and nonproliferation policy. New and vocal champions of exports without regard to nonproliferation implications also have emerged among Russian parliamentarians.

The economic and political constraints under which the Russian export control system functions are evident in the decisions, apparently sanctioned by the new Export Control Commission, to sell Iran two nuclear power reactors and provide China with nuclear assistance, including reactors[16] and a uranium enrichment plant. Russia previously had concluded an agreement for the sale of nuclear reactors to India (which collapsed when Russia was unable to provide the credit promised by the Soviet government) and is reported to have pursued reactor sales with Pakistan and Algeria. Although these sales do not violate Russia's NPT status, nuclear exports to states lacking comprehensive safeguards (e.g., Pakistan and Algeria) would be contrary to Russia's obligation to support the 1992 Nuclear Suppliers Group consensus. Such export initiatives are at odds with prudent nuclear export policy and also have the effect of encouraging other Soviet successor states to subordinate nonproliferation objectives to considerations of economic gain.

Notwithstanding certain shortcomings, Russia generally has taken positive steps to regulate nuclear exports. However, these actions are undermined by the absence of well-developed or parallel export control bodies and procedures in the other post-Soviet states. A very important measure designed to correct this situation was the agreement on export control coordination signed in Minsk on 26 June 1992 by eight of the Soviet successor states.[17] The agreement specifies, among other things, that parties "will create national export control systems at their earliest convenience," and "will coordinate their export control policies." It remains problematic, however, whether the measures called for by the Minsk accord will actually be implemented.

The obstacles to implementation of the Minsk accord are numerous. A problem common to most of the non-Russian states is the absence of virtually any export control structure or a cadre of personnel trained in matters of export controls, material accounting, physical protection, and international safeguards. Although some progress has been made in developing new export control procedures in Belarus and Ukraine,[18] budget deficits, a tremendous demand on very limited resources, strong pressures to export anything that can be sold abroad for hard currency, and a preoccupation with other domestic crises combine to relegate the issue of export controls to the bottom of the decision-making agenda in all states of the former Soviet Union (if it is on the agenda at all). There are also powerful domestic political reasons for the leadership of some of the successor states to avoid the appearance of cooperating too closely with Russia. All these factors suggest that for many of the post-Soviet states, the failure to develop export controls is not the result of conscious national efforts to obstruct nonproliferation. The consequences, however, may be the same.

It is tempting to dismiss the often naive marketing and public relations activities of the new private nuclear entrepreneurs ("PNEs for environmental purposes") as inconsequential or even as a bad joke. More often than not, the directors of these firms are unsophisticated in the ways of Western business practices. These nuclear entrepreneurs partially fill a need, however, by absorbing some of the Russian nuclear scientists and engineers who otherwise would be unemployed as a consequence of the end of the Cold War and the slow pace of defense conversion. As much as 20 to 30 percent of the workforce at the Russian nuclear weapons laboratories, for example, are reported to have left their state jobs during 1991 and 1992, many presumably for work in the private sector.[19] The percentage of this workforce that will ultimately find its way onto the international black market is uncertain. What is clear is that unless domestic economic opportunities for employees at the formerly closed nuclear sites improve, their rate of migration abroad will increase.

This statement is not intended to sensationalize the threat of nuclear mercenaries or impugn the loyalty of nuclear scientists in the former Soviet Union. An exodus of nuclear know-how still appears to be more a potential risk than a fait accompli. The dedication of even the most loyal scientists, however, will be severely tested in an environment of job insecurity, food and housing shortages, plummeting prestige, political turmoil, and lucrative offers from abroad. The problem is compounded further by the perception on the part of many of the midlevel scientists in the formerly closed nuclear cities that their bosses are corrupt and interested only in lining their own pockets. Western promises of assistance by means of international science and technology centers, joint ventures, and direct financial aid, unfortunately, remain unimplemented for the most part and contribute to growing cynicism among both nuclear scientists and the population at large.

A tendency to emphasize profits over proliferation may be reinforced by the new trend in Russian foreign policy that seeks to assert a more influential and independent role for Russia in world affairs. Although this development may not interfere with Russia's long-standing cooperation with the United States on nonproliferation and export control issues, the potential for strained relations already is apparent in recent U.S.-Russian skirmishes over Moscow's missile-related sales to India, the appropriate means to curb North Korea's nuclear ambitions, and the continuation of UN sanctions toward Iraq. The proliferation danger represented by Russia's new foreign policy assertiveness is that traditional proponents of export control restraint in the Foreign Ministry will find it more difficult politically to control the export of proliferation-sensitive goods. Russia also may be more reluctant to endorse nonproliferation initiatives that bear a clear U.S. imprimatur.

International Safeguards

The most immediate, visible consequence of the collapse of the Soviet Union was the nuclear inheritance by its successor states. Although the issue of nuclear inheritance is commonly thought of in terms of nuclear weapons, it also encompasses a variety of nuclear assets not confined to Russia. They include uranium mining and milling centers in Estonia, Kazakhstan, Kyrgyzstan, Tajikistan, Ukraine, and Uzbekistan; nuclear research and training centers in Armenia, Belarus, Georgia, Kazakhstan, Ukraine, and Uzbekistan; and research reactors at many of these centers, some of which are fueled with highly enriched uranium (HEU).[20] There is evidence, for example, that thirty-three to thirty-five kilograms of weapons-grade uranium is stored at the Institute of Power Engineering Problems at Sosny, near Minsk. At least twenty-two kilograms of uranium enriched to

90 percent also are present at the Baikal–1 and IGR reactor complexes at the Semipalatinsk test site in Kazakhstan. Over three times that amount appears to be stored in bulk form at the Kharkiv Technical Institute in Ukraine, although Ukraine has reported only a small portion of that amount to the IAEA. There are also fourteen nuclear power reactors in commercial operation in Ukraine, two in Lithuania, and one in Kazakhstan. Those of the RBMK (Chernobyl) variety in Lithuania and Ukraine are high-power versions of the plutonium production reactor used for military purposes. The reactor in Kazakhstan at Aktau (formerly Shevchenko) is a liquid metal fast breeder used for both desalination and electricity-generation purposes. It is capable of producing over one hundred kilograms of plutonium a year. Kazakhstan also is the site of the Ulba Metallurgy Plant, the major facility in the former Soviet Union for fabricating nuclear fuel assemblies. This plant at Ust'-Kamenogorsk in eastern Kazakhstan produces nearly all the fuel pellets used in Soviet-manufactured reactors. In addition, the plant is the largest producer in the former Soviet Union of beryllium, a metal used in civilian nuclear power reactors and also in the manufacture of nuclear weapons. Other major production sites for dual-use nuclear-related items, such as hafnium and zirconium, are found in Ukraine.

Although the nuclear assets of the non-Russian republics (with the possible exceptions of Kazakhstan and Ukraine) are unlikely to support an indigenous nuclear weapons program, they do pose significant risks in terms of diversion and unregulated nuclear exports. Those dangers are heightened by the primitive state of export controls in the former Soviet Union outside Russia, the underdeveloped state of material accounting and physical protection in most of the successor states, and the failure to enlist any of the non-Russian successor states as members of the Nuclear Suppliers Group.[21] The risk of division also is aggravated by the absence of international safeguards at most nuclear facilities in the newly independent states.

According to the NPT, each non-nuclear weapon state party to the treaty is required to conclude a safeguards agreement with the IAEA within eighteen months of accession. Technically, therefore, Azerbaijian, Estonia, Latvia, Lithuania, and Uzbekistan already should have safeguards agreements in place. To date, Latvia, Lithuania, and Uzbekistan have concluded the required agreements, and one with Estonia is nearly complete.[22] Kazakhstan also signed a safeguards agreement with the IAEA in July 1994 that will come into effect upon ratification by the Kazakhstan parliament. The principal delay in implementing the accord will be the lack of trained personnel.

The safeguards situation is more complex in Ukraine. Despite Kiev's ambiguous NPT stance, serious deliberations have been under way for nearly a year between Ukraine and the IAEA over conclusion of a safe-guards accord. In September 1993 Ukraine proposed that it conclude a so-called INFCIRC–66 type safeguards agreement. This kind of agreement would have placed safeguards at specific nuclear facilities but would not have been comprehensive or "full scope" in nature (i.e., it would not have placed all of Ukraine's civilian nuclear facilities under safeguards, as is required of all non-nuclear weapon states that are parties to the NPT).[23] Although the United States initially appeared to endorse the Ukrainian initiative, it was unacceptable to other IAEA members. Subsequently, in June 1994, Ukraine and the IAEA agreed *ad referendum* to a draft comprehensive safeguards agreement under which all nuclear material in all peaceful nuclear activities of Ukraine would be covered by safeguards. It is expected that the agreement will be submitted for consideration by the IAEA Board of Governors at its September 1994 meeting.[24]

The absence of safeguards at Ukraine's nuclear facilities has jeopardized nuclear fuel shipments to Ukraine and has placed Russia in violation of its NPT Article 3.2 obligations. This article prohibits NPT parties from providing "source or special fissionable material" (including low enriched nuclear fuel for civilian power reactors) to non-nuclear weapon states that do not have "full-scope" safeguards in place. Although the 14 January 1994 Trilateral Statement explicitly sanctions Russian supply of fuel assemblies to Ukraine in return for the transfer to Russia of two hundred nuclear warheads, Russia and the United States regard this exchange as a temporary arrangement that cannot continue if Ukraine does not conclude a safeguards agreement with the IAEA. Russia also is obliged under the Nuclear Supplier Group guidelines to confine its nuclear exports to states with comprehensive safeguards in place.[25]

National Safeguards

International safeguards are designed to detect and deter national governments from diverting nuclear material from peaceful to military purposes. National safeguards, in contrast, refer to measures undertaken by national governments "to detect, deter, prevent, or respond to the unauthorized possession or use of significant quantities of nuclear materials through theft or diversion and sabotage of nuclear facilities."[26] They tend to emphasize the provision of physical security and material control and accounting and are directed at nonstate actors. All the post-Soviet states with nuclear assets suffer from major deficiencies in national safeguards.

According to conventional wisdom, the Soviet nuclear fuel cycle was very secure from penetration by outsiders because of the country's authoritarian political system, its pervasive network of internal security, and the close integration of its civilian and military components.[27] The vulnerability of the most sensitive nuclear facilities—uranium enrichment and conversion plants and reprocessing and plutonium storage facilities—also was reduced by their location in relatively remote and stable regions of Russia.[28] Although physical protection probably remains quite high at Russian uranium enrichment and plutonium production sites,[29] security is more suspect at nuclear fuel storage facilities for propulsion reactors, plutonium storage facilities for dismantled nuclear weapons, and sites for research reactors, critical assemblies, and fast breeder reactors.

The most dangerous and immediate problem involving inadequate physical security concerns the large stockpile of highly enriched uranium in the form of fuel for Russia's nuclear propulsion reactors. This fresh fuel, some of it enriched to 70 to 90 percent, is concentrated at shipbuilding plants that in 1993 supported 228 nuclear-powered ships in the Russian navy's northern and Pacific fleets, as well as 7 civilian nuclear icebreakers. These ships contained a total of 394 nuclear reactors.[30] An associated but subordinate physical security problem relates to the spent fuel from the reactors of 113 nuclear-powered submarines that have been decommissioned as of early 1994 (56 from the northern fleet, 47 from the Pacific fleet).[31]

Very little information is available in the public domain regarding physical security at fuel storage sites for naval reactors or at the sites for decommissioned submarines. Interviews with knowledgeable Russian nuclear engineers, naval experts, export control officials, and environmentalists, however, suggest that significant problems exist. They pertain to lax security at storage sites, confused lines of authority regarding material control at these facilities, and suspect reliability on the part of those charged with responsibility for securing access to the nuclear material.

Security is especially suspect at some of the makeshift interim storage sites for fuel rods from decommissioned submarines. Photographs of such sites in the Kola Peninsula indicate huge open-air piles of fuel rods protected only by barbed wire.[32] Russian Foreign Ministry officials involved in nuclear export controls also recently have expressed alarm regarding minimal security at these sites.[33]

According to experts at Moscow's Kurchatov Institute, fresh nuclear fuel stockpiles for naval reactors are under the control of two different bodies, although the stocks are colocated. New fuel for naval reactors is under the custody of the Ministry of Shipbuilding, while strategic stocks of fuel (much of it HEU) are under the control of the State Committee for the Defense Industry.[34] This duality of control, the existence of dual material accounting systems, and the reluctance of either body to date to cooperate with the Russian nuclear regulatory body, Gosatomnadzor, create conditions that could be exploited by individuals or organized groups seeking access to the HEU. Although separate material accounting systems exist on paper at the nuclear fuel stockpiles, no physical inspections or checks of the nuclear material inventories have been conducted in the past decade—if ever. Material accounting, to the extent that it was employed, tended not to be facility-specific and was used mainly for central planning and financial purposes.[35] Material control relied on a system of personal responsibility in which a designated person was entrusted with the nuclear material until it was passed on to another designated individual.[36]

A team of safeguards experts at the Kurchatov Institute is now attempting to persuade Russian authorities to introduce a modern system of material control and accounting at the propulsion reactor fuel storage facilities. At the present time, however, Gosatomnadzor, which technically has authority for assuring physical protection and material accounting, at best can provide an item count of sealed fuel containers. Access reportedly is limited because of bureaucratic resistance to what is perceived as undue intrusion by another organization and because of concern by the Ministry of Shipbuilding and the State Committee for the Defense Industry that Gosatomnadzor will discover that something is amiss, if not missing.

The problems of inadequate physical protection and underdeveloped material control and accounting are not confined to large fuel stockpiles for propulsion reactors. Indeed, lax physical security and shoddy material control and accounting can be found in most, if not all, civilian nuclear facilities in the former Soviet Union. One recent indication of this danger was a decision taken by Gosatomnadzor in 1994 to shut down for six months the All-Union Research Institute for Nonorganic Substances in Moscow because of lax security involving plutonium at its facility.[37] At another major nuclear research center at Sosny in Belarus, senior authorities at the Institute of Power Engineering Problems acknowledge privately that due to sloppy past accounting practices they cannot now determine the quantity of HEU even at their own facility.[38] Given the small amount of material in question at Sosny (between thirty-three and thirty-five kilograms of HEU enriched to 90 percent), one can imagine the uncertainty at nuclear facilities in Russia that possess HEU and plutonium stocks thousands of times larger. Under such conditions, it is probably impossible at the present time to distinguish between "material unaccounted for" and material that has been stolen. Assertions by MINATOM officials immediately after the seizures of nuclear contraband in Germany that all weapons-grade material is accounted for, therefore, are disingenuous.

Until recently, it generally was assumed in the West that, notwithstanding possible shortcomings in the civilian nuclear sector, physical security was high in the military domain. Although security at military facilities probably remains much higher than at civilian nuclear sites, the situation appears to be more dangerous than previously recognized.

The most chilling and compelling account of a near theft of a nuclear weapon is provided in a new book by William Burrows and Robert Windrem.[39] It involves an operation, conceived by William Arkin at Greenpeace in late 1990, to purchase a fifteen hundred–pound Scud warhead from a Soviet lieutenant, purportedly in charge of a shift of guards at a missile installation in East Germany. The transaction, which was prepared over a period of six months, was supposed to be consummated on 7 September 1991. It reportedly collapsed, however, with the disappearance of the lieutenant at the end of July 1991, a change in security at the base in question, and the withdrawal of the last warheads from Germany to Russia in mid-August 1991.[40] Although it is impossible to corroborate some of the key elements of Arkin's story (as recounted by Burrows and Windrem), unlike other unsubstantiated reports of Soviet warhead thefts,[41] this case appears plausible. The danger of theft and/or unauthorized use of nuclear weapons from the former Soviet stockpile would appear to have diminished with the redeployment of all tactical nuclear weapons on Russian territory. The security of these weapons, however, may be compromised by the absence in Russia of adequate storage facilities for the influx of nuclear warheads. According to one recent report, "many nuclear warheads are now being stored in facilities constructed for the storage of conventional munitions under less than adequate physical security."[42] These warheads may be particularly vulnerable to theft by disgruntled past or present Russian Special Operations (*Spetsnaz*) soldiers, who are trained to use atomic demolition weapons and may have special knowledge of and even access to nuclear weapon storage depots.[43]

MINATOM officials recently have acknowledged that interim storage facilities for plutonium from dismantled weapons are "not very safe" and are not adequately guarded.[44] This expression of concern may be designed to increase pressure on the United States to expedite Nunn–Lugar funding for a plutonium storage facility long sought by MINATOM. Nevertheless, the explicit acknowledgment that plutonium storage facilities are vulnerable to theft must be taken seriously, especially in light of a number of complicating factors: the enormous quantities of weapons-grade material in question, the growing disaffection of large segments of the Russian population, plummeting morale in the Russian military and the nuclear industry, the widespread disregard in Russia for law, pervasive corruption throughout the government, the increasing reach of organized crime, and an economic malaise that encourages the plunder and sale of government property. Perhaps the most significant indicator that MINATOM's warning was not primarily designed for external consumption is the fact that in 1993 it strongly endorsed internal measures to strengthen safeguards, especially security of HEU and plutonium, although financial difficulties and interagency bureaucratic battles have delayed their implementation.[45] Among the specific safeguards deficiencies noted by MINATOM are the shortage of trained personnel and modern equipment, inadequate transport control procedures, and the lack of storage and processing facilities.[46]

Perspectives on the 1995 NPT Extension Conference

The disintegration of the Soviet Union into fifteen independent states already has yielded ten new adherents to the NPT. Their support for the treaty may prove significant at the 1995 NPT Extension Conference, at which parties to the treaty will decide "whether the Treaty shall continue in force indefinitely, or shall be extended for an additional fixed period or periods" (NPT Treaty, Art. 10.2).

At prior NPT review conferences, held at five-year intervals since 1975, the Soviet Union often was an ally of the United States and other countries that sought to fend off challenges to the treaty and strengthen the international nonproliferation regime. Although the two superpowers did not concur on all the substantive and procedural issues at prior review conferences, they shared similar perspectives on most of the major issues. The Soviet Union, for its part, also was able to deliver support for these positions from the caucus of communist NPT parties.

This bloc of votes is no longer certain in the post-Soviet environment. Many if not all of the East European states probably will stake out independent positions at the 1995 conference, without particular reference to the preferences of Russia or the other successor states. Most of the post-Soviet states party to the NPT also are not inclined to mimic the stance adopted by Russia. Their ability to formulate independent but constructive positions on the often esoteric provisions of the NPT, however, is severely constrained by a paucity of nonproliferation specialists, almost all Soviet experts having been absorbed by the Russian Foreign Ministry. This shortage of experienced personnel, combined with the relatively low priority attached to the issue by most of the successor states and the short time available for preparation before the conference opens in April 1995, makes it difficult to predict how the non-Russian participants will align themselves. Although many of the states sent representatives to the first two conference preparatory meetings in May 1993 and January 1994, they generally did not play an active role at the meetings and gave few clues about their positions on key issues likely to be contested at the April 1995 conference.[47] Indeed, discussions with senior foreign ministry officials from four of the states in question indicate that little advance work has been undertaken and that national positions on the major issues have not yet been formulated.[48] These discussions do reveal, however, a desire to understand better the reservations about the NPT held by India, Pakistan, and, until recently, China.

Despite the uncertainty regarding the NPT perspectives of the non-Russian successor states, the key elements of Russian policy toward the NPT are likely to continue to resemble those of the Soviet Union. This includes a strong endorsement for the indefinite extension of the NPT, support for enhancing the effectiveness of the IAEA safeguards system, and readiness to consult and cooperate routinely with the United States in order to secure a mutually beneficial conference result. If anything, U.S. and Russian perspectives on an issue that is likely to be very contentious at the extension conference—the Article 6 debate over a Comprehensive Test Ban (CTB)—are apt to be more congruent at the 1995 meeting than at prior review conferences. This development is due mainly to a shift in U.S. policy, which is now more supportive of a CTB.[49]

To the extent that U.S. and Russian positions at the 1995 conference diverge, these divergences may involve debates over access by the developing world to nuclear energy, the merits of a ban on plutonium reprocessing and use, and the readiness of the nuclear weapon states to extend meaningful security assurances to non-nuclear weapon states. A number of the post-Soviet states (especially the Baltic states, Kazakhstan, and Ukraine, should it accede to the NPT) are likely to focus on the latter issue with respect to Russia; they are also likely to press Russia to commit itself to a timetable for disarmament. The United States and Russia also may find themselves at odds over the appropriate role of the UN Security Council in enforcing the 31 January 1992 declaration that "the proliferation of all weapons of mass destruction constitutes a threat to international peace and security." The salience of this issue and its potential divisiveness are likely to hinge on progress made toward defusing the nuclear crisis in North Korea.

Problem Countries

Soviet declaratory policy during most of the Cold War period identified the Federal Republic of Germany, Israel, and South Africa as the most worrisome would-be nuclear proliferants.[50] Although it was prepared to discuss other proliferation problem countries in private during bilateral U.S.-Soviet consultations in the 1970s and 1980s, the Soviet Union generally seemed confident that NPT membership, IAEA safeguards, and/or its own political influence in a country were sufficient to prevent diversion from civilian to military nuclear programs. This stance was apparent in Soviet nuclear trade with Argentina and India and nuclear assistance programs to Cuba, Iraq, Libya, and North Korea.[51] It also was reflected in Soviet linkage of nuclear assistance to Libyan and North Korean accession to the NPT.

The deposition of West Germany's instruments of accession to the NPT in 1975 greatly reduced Soviet concerns about the Federal Republic's nuclear weapons ambitions. South African accession to the NPT in 1991 similarly appears to have removed any serious worries in Moscow about Pretoria's nuclear program.[52] Public commentary about the dangers of Israel's nuclear arsenal also largely have disappeared from mainstream public commentary, although outspoken critics of Israel's nuclear policy remain entrenched in Russia's foreign and defense establishments.

Not surprisingly, Ukraine has replaced Germany as Russia's principal "problem country" from the standpoint of nuclear proliferation. It is beyond the scope of this chapter to analyze the nature of Ukrainian-Russian nuclear relations or assess the prospects for Ukrainian assertion of control over the nuclear assets on its territory. Here it is sufficient to note that despite successful implementation to date of the 14 January 1994 Trilateral Statement by the presidents of the United States, Russia, and Ukraine, over fifteen hundred nuclear warheads remain in Ukraine, with little prospect for their prompt removal. The size of this arsenal, Ukraine's hesitance to accede to the NPT, and serious economic, political, and military grievances between Ukraine and Russia combine to make Ukraine's nuclear future a problem not only for Russia but also for the entire international community.

Aside from Ukraine, the only other state Russia regards as a serious nuclear proliferation threat is North Korea. Soviet/Russian policy makers were very slow to recognize this danger, having long been engaged in assisting North Korea with its civilian nuclear program. Although pressure from the Soviet Union largely was responsible for the decision by Pyongyang to accede to the NPT in 1985, Russia was reluctant to abandon its nuclear assistance despite repeated North Korean delays in concluding a safeguards agreement with the IAEA.[53]

Senior Russian officials continue, at least publicly, to discredit reports that North Korea has developed nuclear weapons, and they continue to oppose harsh measures (including sanctions) directed against North Korea.[54] Russian officials have criticized the United States in particular for failing to consult adequately with them on its sanctions approach and have advocated a more cautious policy that features an international conference on the subject of the North Korean nuclear program. Russia, however, has supported IAEA efforts to gain North Korean compliance with its safe-guards obligations, and Foreign Minister Andrei Kozyrev has indicated that Russia would agree to sanctions as a last resort if North Korea actually quit the IAEA.[55]

Policy Recommendations

The breakup of the Soviet Union and the nuclear inheritance of its successor states belatedly focused Western attention on the proliferation risks in the region. Although considerable progress has been made recently toward de-nuclearization in Belarus, Kazakhstan, and, to a lesser degree, Ukraine, serious proliferation dangers remain. Most of them are deeply rooted in the difficult economic, political, and social conditions of contemporary Russia and the other post-Soviet states. As such, they are unlikely to be resolved until progress is made in stabilizing the economy and restoring public trust in governmental institutions, law, and social justice. These changes will not occur soon, and the United States can make a difference only at the margins, at best. We can and should, however, try to make that difference.

There is no shortage of good recommendations, some of which actually have been adopted as U.S. policy. They include efforts at encouraging post-Soviet state accession to the NPT, putting in place international nuclear safeguards, fostering more routine and extensive sharing of U.S.-Russian intelligence regarding nuclear exports in general and organized crime activities in particular, and expediting the delivery of financial and technical assistance in the areas of export controls, physical security, and material control and accounting.

What too often has been lacking in U.S. policy is prompt implementation. The bureaucratic reasons for delay by the U.S. government and by the recipient side are well known. Also inhibiting the pace and impact of U.S. denuclearization assistance efforts, however, have been a poor understanding of the nuclear infrastructure and domestic sources of nuclear policy making in the former Soviet Union (especially in the non-Russian states) and the hesitance of U.S. governmental agencies to work more closely with nongovernmental organizations in pursuit of mutual nonproliferation objectives.

Illustrative of these difficulties is the problem the United States has had in providing timely assistance to key organizations in Belarus, Kazakhstan, Russia, and Ukraine with expertise in and responsibility for export controls, physical protection, and material control and accounting. If the U.S. government is unable to reach interagency agreement on who those parties are and/or is incapable of persuading the lead actors on the recipient country side (e.g., MINATOM in Russia) to utilize the funds as intended, it should engage U.S. foundations or nongovernmental organizations with good ties in the former Soviet Union to dispense at least a portion of the funds while they may still do some good. A nongovernmental Center for Nonproliferation and Export Controls in Belarus is available today to begin training export control officials, but it has no funds; a modern system for material control and accounting has been developed by a team at the Kurchatov Institute in Moscow, but it cannot get money to test the system; the Export-Technical Committee in Kiev would like to train personnel on dual-use export controls, but it lacks resources; the nuclear regulatory agencies in all the successor states desperately seek access to nuclear trade publications, but they have no hard currency for subscriptions. Delivery of funds for these small but important activities should not have to wait until another sensationalist report about nuclear smuggling turns out to be true.

The United States and its Western allies also have erred by not expanding the Nuclear Suppliers Group (NSG) to include successor states other than Russia. This policy failure stems from the West's fixation on Russian nuclear assets to the neglect of those in other post-Soviet states. It also displays ignorance of the export role played by countries such as Belarus and the Baltic states, which lack substantial indigenous nuclear and dual-use production capabilities but serve as major points of transit for such commodities. These countries should be encouraged to join the NSG, while other successor states, at a minimum, should be invited to participate at NSG meetings as observers.[56] The engagement of these states is important not only as a means to share technical information and secure policy commitments but also as a vehicle to create and/or strengthen internal institutional mechanisms within the governments with responsibility for nuclear export controls.

Western efforts to encourage nuclear export and nonproliferation restraint in the post-Soviet states also are undermined by the perception that Washington, Bonn, Paris, and London often do not practice what they preach. As a consequence, their ability to gain allies in the former Soviet Union for the 1995 NPT Extension Conference may well turn on the perceptions in Almaty, Minsk, and Tallinn of the consistency with which the West applies its nonproliferation standards and the extent to which the Western nuclear weapon states (as well as Russia) are prepared to forgo nuclear testing and reduce their own nuclear arsenals.

Policy makers in the post-Soviet states generally assign a lower importance to nuclear nonproliferation than do their counterparts in the West. This lower ranking is not because they disagree about the dangers of the spread of nuclear weapons, but because they have only a faint understanding of the issue's relevance to their immediate situation, in which they are struggling to survive from one crisis to the next. In such an environment, it is especially important to increase public awareness of the security risks posed by nuclear proliferation. This task, however, is a difficult one, since the issue generates little serious analysis in the mass media and only a handful of journalists and scholars write knowledgeably on the subject (with the important exception of Ukraine).

Some steps are being taken today in the nongovernmental sphere to build communities of independent nonproliferation specialists in the former Soviet Union. A much more substantial commitment to this effort, however, must be made by the U.S. government—in partnership with nongovernmental organizations—if we are to avoid future unpleasant proliferation surprises in the post-Soviet states.

Notes

1. Denial of nuclear weapons to the Federal Republic of Germany was the overriding objective of Soviet nonproliferation policy.
2. For a discussion of Soviet nonproliferation incentives, see Benjamin Lambeth, "Nuclear Proliferation and Soviet Arms Control Policy," in *The Soviet Union and Arms Control*, ed. Roman Kolkowicz et al. (Baltimore: Johns Hopkins University Press, 1970), pp. 70–115; Toby Trister Gati, "Soviet Perspectives on Nuclear Nonproliferation," *California Seminar on Arms Control and Foreign Policy Discussion Paper*, no. 66 (November 1975); Joseph C. Nogee, "Soviet Nuclear Proliferation Policy: Dilemmas and Contradictions," *Orbis* (winter 1982), pp. 751–69; William C. Potter, "The Soviet Union and Nuclear Proliferation," *Slavic Review* (fall 1985), pp. 468–88; and Peter R. Lavoy, "Learning and the Evolution of Cooperation in U.S. and Soviet Nuclear Nonproliferation Activities," in *Learning in U.S. and Soviet Foreign Policy*, ed. George W. Breslauer and Philip E. Tetlock (Boulder, CO: Westview Press, 1991), pp. 735–83.
3. V.S. Emel'ianov, cited by Gloria Duffy, *Soviet Nuclear Energy: Domestic and International Policies*, R–2362-DOE (Santa Monica, CA: RAND Corporation, 1979), p. 12.
4. See, for example, A. Mikhailov, "Effective Control Over Nuclear Exports," *International Affairs* (June 1982), pp. 19–25; V. Emel'ianov, *Problems of the Nonproliferation of Nuclear Weapons* (Moscow: Nauka Press, 1982); I. Dmitriev, "Postavit' nadezhnyi bar'er," *Pravda*, 8 July 1977; and V.F. Davidov, *Nerasprostranenie iadernogo oruzhiia i politika* (Moscow: Nauka Press, 1980).
5. See William C. Potter, "Nuclear Proliferation: U.S.-Soviet Cooperation," *Washington Quarterly* (winter 1985), pp. 141–54; and Lavoy, "Learning and the Evolution of Cooperation."
6. See Murrey Marder and Dan Oberdorfer, "How West, Soviets Acted to Defuse South African A-Test." *Washington Post*, 28 August 1977. For a Soviet account of the episode, see Valerii Davidov, "Iadernaia ugroza u mysa Dobroi Nadezhdy," *SShA* (December 1977), pp. 48–49.
7. On this point, see Joseph Nye, "The U.S. and Soviet Stakes in Nuclear Non-proliferation," *P.S.* (winter 1982), p. 36.
8. The sale of enrichment technology, had it been concluded, would have been contrary to the recommendations of the 1977 Nuclear Suppliers' Guidelines, which the Soviet Union helped to draft and to which it subscribed. I am grateful to David Fischer for reminding me of this point.

9. Moldova's parliament approved accession to the NPT in early 1994, but at the time of this writing, Moldova had yet to deposit its instruments of accession.

10. The Politburo rejected the latter option due to the international safeguards requirement it would have entailed. Interview with senior Soviet official who drafted the policy recommendation for the Politburo in response to the Ukrainian request, Washington, DC, November 1991.

11. This section draws on William C. Potter, "Exports and Experts: Proliferation Risks from the New Commonwealth," *Arms Control Today*, vol. 22, no. 1 (January/February 1992), pp. 32–37; and idem, "Nuclear Exports from the Former Soviet Union: What's New, What's True," *Arms Control Today*, vol. 23, no. 1 (January/February 1993), pp. 3–10.

12. Seymour Hersh, "The Wild East," *Atlantic Monthly* (June 1994), p. 75.

13. For more detail on these cases, see "Illicit Transactions Involving Nuclear Materials from the Former Soviet Union: A Chronology of News Reports" (CIS Non-Proliferation Project, Monterey Institute of International Studies, Monterey, CA, 26 August 1994). The fourth case, involving the seizure of a minuscule amount of plutonium, now appears to be a "nonissue." The material in question reportedly was from a smoke detector.

14. See William Potter, "Russia's Nuclear Entrepreneurs," *New York Times*, 7 November 1991; William Burrows and Robert Windrem, *Critical Mass* (New York: Simon and Schuster, 1994), pp. 233–71.

15. Mikhailov reportedly has since disavowed his support of CHETEK.

16. There are unconfirmed reports that Russia may have canceled the sale because Iran cannot finance the purchase. See Elaine Sciolino, "Iran's Problems Raising Doubts of Peril to U.S.," *New York Times*, 5 July 1994.

17. The signers were Armenia, Belarus, Kazakhstan, Kyrgyzstan, Russia, Tajikistan, Turkmenistan, and Uzbekistan; Tajikistan signed with reservations.

18. Recent developments in Belarus are discussed in Ural Latypov, "Export Control in Belarus" (Center for Nonproliferation and Export Control, Minsk, March 1994).

19. These figures are cited by Elina Kirichenko, "Export Control Policy of Russia as Nuclear Weapons Successor States" (CIS Nonproliferation Project, Monterey, CA, March 1992). It is estimated that one hundred thousand scientists, engineers, and officials in the former Soviet Union have nuclear clearances equal to the U.S. Department of Energy "Q" clearance. Of those, three thousand to five thousand are believed to have direct work experience in plutonium production and uranium enrichment activities.

20. For more detailed information on the nuclear assets of the non-Russian successor states, see William Potter, Eve Cohen, and Edward Kayukov, *Nuclear Profiles of the Soviet Successor States* (Monterey Institute of International Studies, Monterey, CA, 1993).

21. The failure to include non-Russian NIS representatives in the NSG is a consequence of both the lack of interest on the part of some relevant post-Soviet states and the lack of unanimity on the issue of new NIS members on the part of the current NSG parties.

22. A large number of NPT parties outside the NIS also are in violation of the eighteen-month requirement for safeguards.

23. A contentious issue between the IAEA and Ukraine has been the status of one nuclear reactor and research facility at Sevastopol that the IAEA was prevented from visiting due to its alleged military nature.

24. *IAEA Newsbriefs* (July/August 1994), p. 7.

25. This section draws on testimony presented by William Potter to the U.S. House of Representatives Committee on Foreign Affairs, Subcommittee on International Security, International Organizations, and Human Rights, 27 June 1994.

26. U.S. Office of Technology Assessment, *Nuclear Proliferation and Safeguards*, vol. 1 (New York: Praeger, 1977), p. 194.

27. See, for example, Oleg Bukharin, "The Threat of Nuclear Terrorism and the Physical Security of Nuclear Installations and Materials in the Former Soviet Union," *Occasional Paper*, no. 2 (Monterey Institute of International Studies, Monterey, CA, August 1992).

28. Ibid., p. 3

29. Russia stopped production of highly enriched uranium in 1989, but ten gas centrifuge enrichment plants may still be in operation at four sites in Russia: Verkh-Neivinsk, Angarsk, Krasnoiarsk, and Tomsk. Plutonium production and separation activities continue at Krasnoiarsk–26 and Tomsk–7. See Potter, *Nuclear Profiles of the Soviet Successor States*, pp. 63–64; and "Nuclear Successor States of the Soviet Union: Nuclear Weapon and Sensitive Export Status Report," no. 1 (Carnegie Endowment for International Peace and Monterey Institute of International Studies, May 1994), pp. 13–14.

30. Tomas Ries, "Russian Nuclear Reactors in the Nordic Region," *Jane's Intelligence Review* (August 1993), p. 360. In his chapter in this volume, Oleg Bukharin cites the smaller figure of 324 naval reactors.

31. The most detailed analysis of the decommissioning of Russian nuclear vessels is provided by B. Makeev, "Problemy utilizatsii atomnykh podvodnykh lodok" (paper prepared for the CIS Nonproliferation Project, Monterey Institute of International Studies, Monterey, CA, June 1994). See also Ries, "Russian Nuclear Reactors," pp. 360–64; Joshua Handler, "The Northern Fleet's Nuclear Submarine Bases," *Jane's Intelligence Review* (December 1993), pp. 551–56; idem, "Russia's Pacific Fleet: Submarine Bases and Facilities," *Jane's Intelligence Review* (April 1994), pp. 166–71; and "Facts and Problems Related to the Dumping of Radioactive Waste in the Seas Surrounding the Territory of the Russian Federation" (Greenpeace translation of materials from a report on the dumping of radioactive waste commissioned by the president of the Russian Federation, Moscow, 1993).

32. Slides presented by Academician Aleksei Iablokov during a Workshop on Nuclear Safety in the Former Soviet Union, Monterey Institute of International Studies, Monterey, CA, 11 April 1994.

33. Interviews in Moscow, 3–4 June 1994.

34. Interviews in Minsk, June 1994.

35. This point is also noted by Oleg Bukharin, "Soft Landing for Bomb Uranium," *Bulletin of the Atomic Scientists*, vol. 49, no. 7 (September 1993), p. 46.

36. See Vladimir Sukhoruchkin, quoted by Edith M. Lederer, "Russian-Nuclear Safeguards," Associated Press, 28 April 1994.

37. Reported in testimony by Leonard Spector before the U.S. House of Representatives Committee on Foreign Affairs, Subcommittee on International Security, International Organizations, and Human Rights, 27 June 1994.

38. Interviews in Minsk, 9–10 June 1994.

39. Burrows and Windrem, *Critical Mass*.

40. Ibid., pp. 246–50.

41. See, for example, the 1992 report from the U.S. House Republican Research Committee's Task Force on Terrorism and Unconventional Warfare; and "Tactical Nukes from Kazakhstan," *Mednews*, 8 June 1992, p. 7.

42. Thomas B. Cochran, testimony before the U.S. House of Representatives Armed Services Committee, Military Application of Nuclear Energy Panel, 19 April 1994, p. 2.

43. Ibid.

44. See Aleksei Lebedev, quoted in "Russian Weapons Plutonium Storage Termed Unsafe by MINATOM Official," *Nucleonics Week* (28 April 1994), p. 1

45. See Bukharin's chapter in this volume. Bukharin refers specifically to an internal directive passed by MINATOM in 1993.

46. Ibid.

47. The last two preparatory meetings are scheduled for September 1994 and January 1995.

48. For an excellent review of these issues, see John Simpson and Darryl Howlett, "The NPT Renewal Conference: Stumbling Toward 1995," *International Security*, vol. 19, no. 1 (summer 1994), pp. 41–71.

49. The main differences at present between the U.S. and Russian positions on a CTB concern U.S. preferences for a more extensive and costly system of verification.

50. See *An Annotated Bibliography of Soviet and CIS Studies on Nuclear Nonproliferation* (Monterey, CA: Center for Russian and Eurasian Studies, Monterey Institute of International Studies, 1992).

51. These aid programs are discussed at length in Potter, "The Soviet Union and Nuclear Proliferation."

52. The most comprehensive Russian analysis of contemporary proliferation threats, including country profiles, is provided in "A New Challenge After the 'Cold War': The Proliferation of Weapons of Mass Destruction" (report by the Foreign Intelligence Service of the Russian Federation, Moscow, 1993).

53. Russian aid was halted only in 1992.

54. See, for example, Janet Guttsman, "Russia Says North Korea Still Far from Nuclear Bomb," Reuters, 18 June 1994.

55. See "Kozyrev Accepts Korean Sanctions as Last Resort," Reuters, 15 June 1994.

56. No persuasive reason was given for the decision to exclude Ukraine as an observer at the 1994 Nuclear Suppliers Group (NSG) meeting in Madrid.

3

Technical Aspects of Proliferation and Nonproliferation

Oleg Bukharin

The control of weapons-usable fissile materials and the denial of these materials to a potential proliferant are foundations of the international nonproliferation regime. Indeed, the acquisition of weapons-usable fissile materials is a crucial step in a program of nuclear weapons. Their production requires the development of a modern industrial infrastructure and research base, trained personnel, and unique equipment. Indigenous development of any of these components is time-consuming and costly. In addition, such activities are difficult to conceal; and if discovered, they trigger immense international pressure. At the current level of technologies, production of weapons-usable fissile materials is virtually beyond the reach of a subnational group.

The importance of Russia and other former Soviet republics for the global fissile material control regime is twofold. First, the many thousands of nuclear weapons and sprawling nuclear establishments in combination with the political instability and economic crises make the former Soviet Union a potential source of proliferation. Second, the republics, especially Russia, can play a crucial role in enforcing the international fissile material control regime by participating in global nonproliferation efforts, mainly by negotiating and implementing a ban on the production of fissile materials for weapons. These issues are discussed below.

The Security of Weapons-Usable Fissile Materials

All nuclear weapons contain fissile materials—plutonium (Pu), highly enriched uranium (HEU), or both. The uniqueness of these two materials is in their ability to sustain a nuclear chain reaction. A design of a relatively crude implosion-type fission bomb may rely on a solid sphere of plutonium or HEU (six kilograms of plutonium or twenty-five kilograms of HEU). When compressed by conventional high explosives, the sphere would achieve criticality, which would lead to a nuclear explosion. In an alternative gun-type design, criticality is achieved through rapid collision of two separate pieces of HEU. The total amount of HEU required in a gun-type explosive device might amount to as much as fifty kilograms. The design of most advanced multistage thermonuclear weapons is based on a combination of a fission component (also called a primary) and a fusion/fission component (known as a secondary). A typical primary is a three- to four-kilogram hollow plutonium pit, which is designed to ignite a thermonuclear secondary. To increase the yield of explosion through additional fission reactions, a secondary may contain HEU (fifteen kilograms on average).

Typically, plutonium is produced in a uranium-fueled nuclear reactor. In order to extract plutonium from irradiated uranium fuel, the fuel is reprocessed at a chemical separation (reprocessing) facility. The plutonium isotope Pu–239 is most useful in weapons applications. It is produced by neutron capture in U–238 followed by two beta decays. The isotopic composition of plutonium depends on the length of irradiation of the fuel. Weapons-grade plutonium, containing more than 93 percent Pu–239, is produced by relatively brief irradiation; reactor-grade plutonium is produced in commercial power reactors and contains 75 to 80 percent or less Pu–239. It is important to note that plutonium of both grades can be used in a nuclear explosive device.

Weapons-grade HEU is uranium containing approximately 90 percent of the fissile isotope U–235 (natural uranium consists of 0.7 percent U–235). A technology of isotope enrichment is based on the mass difference between U–238 and U–235. Most countries rely on either gas centrifuge (for example, Russia and Western Europe) or gaseous diffusion (for example, the United States) isotope separation technologies.

The inherent proliferation danger of weapons-usable plutonium and uranium makes them a security problem in any country anywhere in the world. A diversion of weapons-usable fissile materials or their purchase on the black market may allow a would-be bomb maker to leapfrog over the most precarious and expensive part of the weapons project. It would save at least eight to ten years and would increase the probability of keeping the program secret. In Russia (and to a lesser extent in Belarus, Ukraine, and Kazakhstan) the problem is aggravated by very large inventories of weapons-usable materials and the inadequacy of the existing nuclear safeguards systems in deteriorating security environment.

Materials and Facilities

The exact figures for the Russian plutonium and HEU inventories remain a closely kept secret. HEU was produced between 1949 and 1989 by the integrated uranium enrichment complex, which consisted of four enrichment plants. According to publicly available estimates, the Russian HEU inventory ranges between 800 and 1,300 metric tons. Production of plutonium started in 1949. As much as 210 tons of plutonium may have been produced to date at three plutonium production complexes at Cheliabinsk–65, Krasnoiarsk–26, and Tomsk–7.[1] Production of plutonium continues at a rate of approximately 2.5 tons a year. Approximately 1.5 tons of weapons-grade plutonium is produced annually by the remaining plutonium production reactors (two at Tomsk–7 and one at Krasnoiarsk–26); an additional 1 ton of reactor-grade plutonium is recovered each year from the spent fuel of commercial power reactors at Cheliabinsk–65.

Russia is a major world producer of low- and medium-enriched uranium. More than eight hundred metric tons, or the equivalent of 4.4 percent enriched uranium is produced and used each year. Although low-enriched uranium (LEU) cannot be fabricated into a nuclear explosive device directly, it would be valuable as a feed for an unsafeguarded enrichment facility in a proliferant state: about one-half of the enrichment work required for the production of HEU is done in enriching uranium to the level of reactor fuel (typically 2 to 4 percent U–235).

In Russia, fissile materials are stored, used, or processed in many locations. A large fraction of weapons-usable HEU and plutonium is in deployed nuclear weapons and warheads that are stored at military depots. These materials are in the custody of the Ministry of Defense. Most materials other than nuclear weapons are in the custody of the Ministry of Atomic Energy (MINATOM).[2] These include plutonium and enriched uranium at warhead assembly and component manufacturing plants, enrichment and reprocessing plants, fuel fabrication facilities (fuel for naval, research, and plutonium production reactors), and research centers. LEU is produced and processed at enrichment plants, fuel fabrication plants, and research centers. Table 3.1 lists some of the principal nuclear fuel cycle facilities and research centers processing weapons-usable nuclear materials and large amounts of LEU.

Outside Russia, weapons-usable HEU is located in research centers in Ukraine, Kazakhstan, and Belarus (see Table 3.2). In addition, significant amounts of LEU are processed at the fuel fabrication plant in Ust'-Kamenogorsk in Kazakhstan.

Table 3.1

Nuclear Fuel Cycle Facilities and Research Centers in Russia Processing Enriched Uranium and Plutonium

A. Nuclear Fuel Cycle Facilities

Facility	Location	Fissile material–related activities
Industrial Association "Maiak"	Cheliabinsk–65	• reprocessing • Pu storage and utilization • naval fuel cycle • isotope production • weapon components storage
Siberian Chemical Combine	Tomsk–7	• reprocessing • Pu storage and processing • weapon components storage • uranium conversion • uranium enrichment
Electrochemistry Plant	Krasnoiarsk–26	• reprocessing
Ural Electrochemistry Combine	Verkh-Neivinsk	• uranium enrichment • HEU processing • weapon components storage
Electrolyzing Chemical Combine	Angarsk	• uranium conversion • uranium enrichment
Electrochemistry Plant	Krasnoiarsk–45	• uranium enrichment • fabrication of fuel for naval and fast reactors
Machine-Building Plant	Elektrostal (Moscow area)	• fabrication of fuel for VVER–440, RBMK reactors
Industrial Association "Chemical Concentrates Plant"	Novosibirsk	• fabrication of fuel for material-production, research, and VVER–1000 reactors

B. Research Centers Processing Significant Amounts of HEU and Plutonium

Facility	Location	Fissile material–related activities
Institute of Technical Physics	Cheliabinsk–70	• material research • weapon R&D

(continued)

Table 3.1 *(continued)*

Facility	Location	Fissile material related activities
Institute of Experimental Physics	Arzamas–16	• material research • manufacturing of weapon components
Inorganic Materials Institute (VNIINM)	Moscow	• nuclear fuel cycle technologies • R&D on Pu utilization
Nuclear Reactors Institute (NIIAR)	Dimitrovgrad	• reprocessing technologies • nuclear fuel production technologies • Pu utilization technologies • isotope production
Physics and Power Institute	Obninsk	• Pu utilization technologies
NPO Khlopin Radium Institute	St. Petersburg	• reprocessing technologies and radiochemistry
Research Center "Kurchatov Institute"	Moscow	• nuclear technologies
Production Association "Luch"	Podolsk	• fuel technologies

Source: Author.

Table 3.2

Location of Enriched Uranium in Kazakhstan, Ukraine, and Belarus

Facility	Location	Fissile material–related activities
Kazakhstan		
National Research Center	Semipalatinsk	• research reactors
Ulba Metallurgical Plant	Ust´-Kamenogorsk	• production of uranium oxide powder and pellets for power reactors
Ukraine		
Kharkiv Physical Technical Institute	Kharkiv	• material research
Naval Training Center	Sevastopol	• land-based training reactors
Institute of Nuclear Energy	Kiev	• research reactor
Belarus		
Institute of Power and Engineering Problems	Minsk	• nuclear physics research

Source: Author.

Safeguards

Nuclear material would be relatively easy to hide or smuggle across the border as soon as it was outside the perimeter fence of the nuclear facility. Indeed, conventional techniques of detection of fissile materials are based on a combination of nondestructive assay techniques (passive gamma-ray detection and active neutron interrogation), X-ray radiography, and physical search. Under field conditions, successful implementation of these techniques might be very difficult. For example, an HEU warhead component or a comparable mass of HEU metal could be successfully shielded from detection inside a sufficiently thick metallic container.[3] In the former Soviet republics the inherent technical difficulties of detection are compounded by the lack of trained personnel and detection equipment, as well as the increased transparency of state borders. Under these circumstances, a facility-level system of nuclear safeguards is a primary barrier against diversion.

A modern safeguards system consists of the following important elements.

A Physical Protection Program

A program of physical protection is designed to deter and repel a forcible seizure of nuclear materials and retrieve nuclear material should it be stolen. An effective program of physical protection incorporates a barrier system, an array of detection devices for timely detection of an intruder, a trained guard force (including a program of training and qualification), a system of communications, and entry and exit control systems.

In the Soviet Union, physical protection was the backbone of nuclear safeguards. The system, however, may have become inadequate. A credible threat to nuclear materials is conceivable in light of the growing technical, organizational, and human resources capabilities of criminal and terrorist groups in the former Soviet republics. In addition, the system relies on the numerical strength of the guard force. Low and irregular pay and reduced motivation may have lowered the morale of the troops and degraded the effectiveness of physical protection.

A Material Control and Accountancy System

The objective of a material control and accountancy (MC&A) system is to deter and detect an "inventory shrinkage"—a stealthy removal of nuclear materials by an insider—and provide continuing positive control of amounts and locations of nuclear materials. The principal elements of MC&A include a system of surveillance and a program of measurements capable of determining the weight and chemical and isotopic compositions of nuclear materials; a measurements control program; bookkeeping and reporting programs; a program to control the procedure of shipping and receiving nuclear materials; and measures to control materials in scrap and waste.

MC&A has never been a strong element of the Soviet nuclear safeguards. In the past the military nature of nuclear activities, the isolation of the society, and the lack of economic motivation made theft of nuclear materials unlikely. As a result, the MC&A system was designed and implemented to assure the quality of the product and support material planning and financial accounting. Accounting was based on the personal responsibility of a designated individual, and only a minimal number of material measurements were employed.

A Human Reliability Program

A human reliability program is designed to increase the responsibility of the personnel who have access to nuclear materials and prevent collusion of employees. Typically, such a program is based on background checks and a system of clearances. The Russian human reliability program is likely to be of a similar design. Its present status and effectiveness, however, are difficult to evaluate.

In addition to these three basic elements, an integrated national system of nuclear safeguards must include a centralized technical and training support system, effective regulatory oversight, and a computerized nationwide system to track nuclear materials. In Russia these components are either weak or nonexistent. There is still no national nuclear energy law. The regulatory agency, Gosatomnadzor, is only beginning to establish a foothold as a regulator of nuclear activities. A national material tracking system and a technical support program are still on paper or in the early stages of development.

The Soviet/Russian system of nuclear safeguards has been based on the "human factor." The economic, political, and social crises in the society have eroded this foundation and made obvious the inadequacy of the current technical and organizational procedures to safeguard nuclear materials. According to an analysis by MINATOM's experts, the principal deficiencies of safeguards in Russia include the lack of qualified personnel and equipment (including measuring equipment and portal monitors), the lack of adequate shipping and receiving control procedures, and the inadequacy of storage and processing facilities. According to U.S. experts, the list of deficiencies also includes a limited legal basis and regulatory structure and the lack of a safeguards community. Similar problems exist in Kazakhstan, Ukraine, and Belarus. The size of the Russian nuclear industry and its inventories of weapons-usable fissile materials, however, makes Russia a special problem.

These deficiencies of safeguards, combined with degraded morale in the industry, a blossoming black market in the country, and the increased transparency of Russian borders, have resulted in a wave of diversions of fissile materials from MINATOM's and the Ministry of Defense's facilities. Among documented cases are thefts of uranium from a metallurgical facility in Glazov and research centers in Moscow and Podolsk, as well as thefts of uranium fuel rods from a naval base at Murmansk and from the Chernobyl nuclear power plant in Ukraine. Some of these cases (for example, naval reactor fuel) involved uranium of high levels of enrichment. No case has been reported in which stolen material has not been retrieved.

The Russian authorities—MINATOM and Gosatomnadzor, which as the principal executive and regulating agencies[4] are responsible for the bulk of nuclear materials—are aware of the problem. In 1993 MINATOM adopted a resolution related to nuclear safeguards. The resolution stressed the urgency of beefing up security of HEU and plutonium. Also, it called for a comprehensive policy to improve safeguards in the industry and create a nationwide system of nuclear safeguards. The original effort would be focused on the weapons production and nuclear fuel cycle facilities processing weapons-usable fissile materials and large amounts of LEU in bulk form (including conversion, enrichment, reprocessing, and fuel fabrication plants). The program outlined in the resolution contains a number of useful measures. Financial problems and institutional inertia, however, have been stalling its implementation.

Western Assistance in the Area of Material Control

The development of safeguards in the republics of the former Soviet Union is being assisted by Western countries. In Russia the bulk of safeguards-related technical assistance is planned to be provided by the United States under the Cooperative Threat Reduction (CTR) program (Nunn–Lugar legislation). The proposed program would assist in the development of a regulatory oversight program and the establishment of model safeguards systems at the LEU fuel fabrication plant at Elektrostal. After that, MINATOM would be expected to replicate this model system at other nuclear fuel cycle facilities. Similar activities are planned in other former Soviet republics.

The U.S.-Russian CTR program is complemented by safeguards-related technical exchanges between national nuclear weapons laboratories and by cooperative projects at the International Science and Technology Center. Recently, the United States has put forward an "extended" proposal. Under this proposal the Russian authorities would compile a list of the most acute safeguards problems at HEU- and plutonium-handling facilities. After that, the United States would assist in developing "quick fixes" to address these problems.

In general, the implementation of the safeguards assistance program in Russia is painfully slow. This inefficiency is rooted in the tremendous bureaucratic inertia of the governmental agencies of both countries, the historical lack of trust, and the sensitive nature of many nuclear facilities in Russia.

The former Soviet republics are also assisted by other Western nations and international organizations. For example, Russia is working with Euratom in developing a national information system to track nuclear materials. Ukraine and Kazakhstan are receiving significant assistance from Sweden, the United Kingdom, and the International Atomic Energy Agency (IAEA).

Fissile Materials from Weapons

Warhead dismantlement places an additional burden on the system of nuclear safeguards in Russia. The warhead elimination process may have already yielded on the order of two hundred metric tons of HEU and forty metric tons of plutonium. Another three hundred metric tons of HEU and sixty metric tons of plutonium will be released in the coming decade. Control of these materials during storage and disposition is difficult because of their large quantities, the high rates of recovery from weapons, and the lack of adequate storage facilities.

MINATOM's intermediate strategy is to place the materials in long-term (at least twenty years) secure storage. Two central storage facilities are planned to be brought into operation before the end of this century at Cheliabinsk–65 and Tomsk–7.[5] The facilities are designed as modern high-security underground installations, capable of withstanding aerial bombing and most conceivable natural disasters. A security system in each of the facilities will be based on several layers of physical protection barriers (a site-protected area, a perimeter antiterrorist barrier, and barriers inside the facility and inside material vaults), a guard force, and a system of control and accounting.

Additional assurance of the security of fissile materials will be achieved through increased transparency and international cooperation. Design assistance is currently provided by the United States under the CTR program. The parties have agreed on the "General Safety Criteria for the Russian Fissile Material Storage Facility," which codify safeguards requirements for future central storage facilities. Also, the agreement envisages that the United States would receive some level of access to the facilities and would be able to observe material control practices. The United States and Russia may initiate transparency measures with regard to materials from weapons much sooner. At a meeting in March 1994, the parties tentatively agreed to start bilateral inspections of plutonium pit storage facilities at Tomsk–7 and Rocky Flats by the end of 1994. Also, the Russian and U.S. governments have stated their intention to place a fraction of fissile materials released from weapons under IAEA safeguards.

Final disposal options are different for HEU and plutonium. Some of the HEU will be fabricated into the fuel of naval and research reactors. The rest will be diluted to low-enriched uranium to fuel commercial power reactors. The process will be facilitated by the U.S.-Russian HEU agreement. Under the agreement, in the next twenty years the United States will buy at least five hundred metric tons of HEU from Russia and fifty metric tons of HEU from Ukraine. It is expected that the material will be converted from metal to uranium hexafluoride and blended down to LEU at the Russian plants at Verkh-Neivinsk (near Ekaterinburg) and Tomsk–7 and shipped to the United States for fabrication into fuel for power reactors.[6]

The HEU agreement will have an important nonproliferation function. It will facilitate the dismantlement process in Russia by providing funding (about $11.9 billion at initially negotiated prices) and reducing HEU storage requirements. In the long term it will eliminate a potential source of materials for proliferation by transferring a significant part of the HEU inventory out of the Russian weapons program. The implementation of the agreement, however, will increase the risk of diversion of HEU in the course of its conversion and blending. The security of HEU may be compromised by large throughputs of HEU at the conversion and blending facilities (ten metric tons per year for the first five years and thirty metric tons per year for the subsequent fifteen years),[7] direct access of workers to HEU (HEU metal or oxide is not self-protected by radiation or toxicity), and poor detectability of shielded HEU.

The problem of plutonium disposition requires an in-depth study of different options. The Russian nuclear industry favors utilization of plutonium in power reactors. The main proposal includes fabrication of plutonium into plutonium–uranium "mixed oxide" (MOX) fuel for sodium-cooled fast-neutron reactors; research has also been initiated on use of plutonium in conventional light-water VVER–1000 reactors. These approaches emphasize utilization of the energy potential of plutonium.

From a security standpoint, recycling plutonium in power reactors involves substantial diversion risks. Indeed, large-scale processing of plutonium at a fuel fabrication facility would place a burden on safeguards, which even if in place would not be able to guarantee that no diversion has occurred. In addition, a large-scale plutonium recycling program would increase the risk that MOX fuel would be hijacked en route to or at a reactor site. (In order to minimize the risk of hijacking, MINATOM proposes utilizing plutonium in a small number of defense centers. The first such center is planned at Cheliabinsk–65. It would include a chemical separation facility, a plutonium storage facility, a fuel fabrication plant, and BN–800 fast reactors.)

Alternative approaches suggest treating plutonium as waste because of the high costs of fabricating plutonium into reactor fuel and because of associated safety, health, and security problems. The most prominent alternative to the option of burning plutonium in power reactors is to mix it with high-level radioactive waste and to vitrify the mixture before final disposal. Vitrification of plutonium would also involve plutonium processing (conversion to oxide) and, therefore, would involve a security risk. The operation, however, would be relatively simple, and the burden on safeguards would be minimal.[8]

In light of the problems associated with the disposition of plutonium from retired weapons, there is little sense in the ongoing plutonium production program at the RT–1 reprocessing plant at Maiak (Cheliabinsk–65). Some thirty metric tons of reactor-grade plutonium have been accumulated at the facility to date. Similar to the plutonium programs in Western Europe and Japan, the program of commercial reprocessing at Maiak is tied to contractual obligations, management of spent fuel, and the future of nuclear power. Its termination would require the resolution of a number of economic, technical, and social issues.

The Security of Nuclear Weapons

A diversion of a nuclear weapon from the Russian military would be the ultimate disaster. A vivid scenario was suggested by T. Cochran, a scientist at the U.S. Natural Resources Defense Council:

> Some Special Operations *(Spetsnaz)* units of the Russian military are trained in how to use atomic demolition munitions (ADMs) and have the knowledge, skills, and in some cases access to nuclear weapons storage depots. Current and former Spetsnaz soldiers, either for profit or political reasons, could steal ADMs or other easily transportable tactical nuclear weapons. It would be rather easy to smuggle stolen weapons from a storage depot, e.g., the

Kaliningrad naval base area, across the border, e.g., into Poland or Lithuania, and from there via third parties to anywhere in the Middle East.[9]

There are no atomic demolition munitions stored in the Kaliningrad area. The case for maintaining the highest possible security of nuclear weapons, however, is impossible to overstate. Tactical weapons (artillery shells, mines, etc.) are easy to hide and transport and, under certain circumstances, are directly usable. Indeed, although tactical weapons are protected by mechanical locks and require special equipment to use them, a group of terrorists, never mind a state, is likely to be able to overcome associated difficulties given the time and resources. Direct use of a strategic warhead might be much more difficult, if not impossible. (Even for a weapons expert familiar with advanced warhead designs, it would be close to impossible to derive useful design information from studying a modern multistage thermonuclear warhead.) A bomb maker, however, may benefit from a strategic warhead by recycling fissile and other special materials.

Russia has been successfully guarding many thousands of nuclear weapons for more than forty years. Deployed weapons are guarded by special units of the General Staff and units of the armed forces that are responsible for the use of weapons. When weapons are withdrawn from the armed forces for retirement or maintenance, responsibility for weapon security is transferred to the Twelfth Main Directorate of the Ministry of Defense (Main Administration of Nuclear Weapons). The directorate safeguards weapons during transportation and storage at central weapons depots. At dismantlement plants safeguards responsibility is transferred to MINATOM; the military, however, continues warhead bookkeeping until the warheads are disassembled into individual components.

The general principles and main components of safeguards systems for weapons in Russia are roughly equivalent to those used in the United States. Tactical weapons are kept separate from associated delivery systems in specially designed storage depots. The depots, usually underground bunkers, are located inside heavily guarded exclusion areas that are surrounded by several layers of engineering barriers and are equipped with special access control systems. Strategic warheads are more difficult to steal. Warheads on deployed missiles are incorporated into multiton delivery systems. In addition, most missiles are kept in protected underground silos and are virtually inaccessible from the outside. Vulnerability of weapons increases during transportation. As a part of the warhead maintenance and elimination programs, thousands of warheads are routinely shipped each year by rail between warhead assembly plants, the General Staff's central depots, and troops in the field.[10] The principal threat during transportation is sabotage and/or a

Table 3.3

Dismantlement Plans in Russia

Category of weapons	Target date	Fraction of weapons to be dismantled
Mines	1988	all
Artillery shells	2000	one-third
Naval tactical	1995	one-third
Air-defense	1996	one-half
Tactical aviation	1996	one-half

Source: General V. Yakovlev, presentation at a workshop organized by the Federation of American Scientists and the Natural Resources Defense Council, Washington, D.C., 18 December 1993.

direct attack on the warhead train, possibly with the help of corrupted guards.

The weapon security system was designed to thwart an attack by North Atlantic Treaty Organization special operation forces on the eve of the Third World War. Weapon security relied on the strength of the guard force and conventional physical barriers; use of modern Western-type electronic protection systems was minimal. Under these circumstances a principal risk of diversion is a corrupted insider (or group of insiders) in the security force. Crisis in the society may have made this threat credible.

The Elimination of Nuclear Weapons

The insider threat has been significantly reduced by the program of consolidation and dismantlement of nuclear weapons. The program of dismantlement was initiated in 1986.[11] Since then the arsenal, which peaked in the early 1980s, has been reduced at a rate of fifteen hundred to two thousand warheads per year. According to a recent Central Intelligence Agency estimate, in 1993 the Russian nuclear stockpile numbered approximately twenty-seven thousand warheads.[12] It appears that the present dismantlement effort is focused on tactical warheads (the targets of the dismantlement program are indicated in Table 3.3). In addition, Russia continues to dismantle on a priority basis the warheads returned from Ukraine: some fourteen hundred Ukrainian warheads were eliminated in 1993.

The dismantlement has been accompanied by a major program of consolidation of nuclear weapons. The removal of tactical warheads from the territory of Warsaw Pact allies started in 1989 and was completed in December 1991. In parallel, nuclear weapons were removed from the territory of non-Russian republics: as of the end of 1991, tactical nuclear weapons remained only in Ukraine and Belarus. The last shipment of tactical warheads from

Ukraine took place in May 1992. Finally, following the unilateral initiative announced by President Mikhail Gorbachev in October 1991, the Ministry of Defense started transferring tactical weapons from frontline units to central depots on the territory of Russia. This effort was largely completed by the end of 1993.

Warhead elimination involves several steps. From the sites of deployment warheads are shipped by rail to central storage sites that are operated by the Twelfth Main Directorate of the Ministry of Defense. In the past, there were twenty-five weapon storage sites. The location of these is not publicly known. Some of them have been lost as a result of the dissolution of the Soviet Union. Warhead dismantlement takes place at four assembly/disassembly plants at Nizhniaia Tura (Sverdlovsk–45), Iuriuzan' (Zlatoust–36), Kuznetsk (Penza–19), and Arzamas–16.

Dismantlement operations repeat the process of warhead production in reverse order. Warheads are taken apart at the facilities where they were assembled. Principal individual components are shipped (possibly after a period of on-site storage at dismantlement sites) to the facilities where they were manufactured. Reportedly, HEU components are shipped to the Ural Electrochemistry Plant at Verkh-Neivinsk, plutonium components to the Siberian Chemical Combine at Tomsk–7, and hydrogen components to the Production Association Maiak at Cheliabinsk–65.

While reducing long-term concerns about security of nuclear weapons, dismantlement may have increased near-term danger. First, the loss of weapon storage facilities in the non-Russian republics and the mass withdrawal of weapons from frontline units and from non-Russian republics have created a deficit of storage facilities. As a result, some warheads may have been stored at less secure facilities and under unsafe conditions. Second, the security of weapons might be compromised by their massive movement to central storage facilities and dismantlement plants. Finally, the process of dismantlement raises the issue of the security of the components of dismantled warheads in the process of their storage and transportation. The lack of adequate storage capacity to accommodate fissile materials was repeatedly cited as a principal bottleneck in the dismantlement process in Russia.

Western Assistance

The bulk of Western assistance in the safe and secure elimination of nuclear warheads has been channeled through the CTR programs. Relevant agreements signed by United States and Russian agencies include the following issues:

1. Armored blankets. Armored blankets are used to protect warheads from small-arms fire during their transportation. Approximately twenty-five hun-

dred blankets have been transferred to the Russian Ministry of Defense.

2. Railcar security. In order to increase the security of warhead transportation, the Sandia National Laboratory has developed and been manufacturing special conversion kits. The kits are designed to assist Russian car builders in installing fire and security alarms and enhance the thermal insulation of warheads inside railcars.

3. Accident response equipment. Under this agreement Russia has received U.S. equipment that would be used to diagnose and stabilize a damaged warhead and remove it from the scene of an accident. Ukraine, Belarus, and Kazakhstan have also signed emergency response agreements with the United States. Each of them will receive protective clothing and equipment needed to conduct on-site radiological monitoring. No "hands-on" equipment will be provided to the non-Russian republics.

4. Containers for storage and transportation of fissile materials from weapons. The containers are similar to new U.S. Department of Energy (DOE) containers for storage of weapon components.

5. Design of and equipment for central storage facilities for fissile materials from retired weapons.

Additional assistance is provided by other Western countries. France is providing radiological equipment to assure the safety of workers carrying out actual dismantlement, some accident response equipment, warhead containers, and some disassembly-related machine tools.[13] A similar program of cooperation exists between Russia and the United Kingdom.

Control of Fissile Materials: The Role of Security Agencies

The Ministry of Defense, MINATOM, and Gosatomnadzor have principal responsibility for the containment and control of nuclear materials within authorized locations. Their activities, however, must be supported by nuclear safeguards and nonproliferation programs of other security and intelligence organizations. Responsibility for securing nuclear installations, fighting nuclear terrorism, carrying out background investigations and security clearances, and developing physical protection technologies has been traditionally assigned to the Ministry of Security and other security agencies. In addition to these traditional tasks, the security organizations must develop the following nonproliferation programs.

Threat Assessment

A threat assessment program is part of a regulatory oversight program that defines safeguards requirements at a nuclear facility. Generally, the program is based on periodic interagency review of domestic and foreign information with regard to potential threats to nuclear installations and materials. It is not known if there is a formal threat assessment program in Russia.

Identification and Control of Potential Smuggling Routes

Organized crime is on the rise in Russia. A major source of income for criminal organizations is illegal export of strategic materials (cadmium, rare earth metals, etc.) and other goods. As a result, they have developed sophisticated networks for illegal shipments of goods and materials across the border. These networks include secret storage/transit points, people and technical means to conduct shipments, connections at border checkpoints, and cooperation with criminal organizations abroad. Fissile materials, should they be stolen, are likely to be shipped out of the country via these established criminal routes. Therefore, monitoring and disrupting smuggling routes are major nonproliferation tasks of the security and law enforcement agencies. Russian agencies are cooperating with police organizations in other countries and with Interpol. One example of such cooperation is the interception of an illegal uranium shipment at the Belarus–Poland border (the uranium was stolen from a facility at Glazov in Russia). The special services of some of the Commonwealth of Independent States (CIS) countries have agreements to exchange information related to illegal nuclear trafficking. The formal mechanism of cooperation is still weak on the level of police organizations. The ministries of interior of the CIS countries have set up the Bureau for Coordination of Activities Against Organized Crime (based in Moscow). However, it does not address the issue of nuclear materials explicitly.[14]

Control of the Demand-Side

The monitoring of demand for weapons-usable fissile materials is a principal task of the nonproliferation group in the Russian Foreign Intelligence Service. The group analyzes information on nonproliferation developments and fledgling nuclear programs in foreign countries.

Little is made known to the public about the nonproliferation role of the Russian security agencies. Because of that, any public analysis of the effectiveness of the nonproliferation activities of the security agencies is bound to be sketchy and speculative at best.

A Halt on the Production of Fissile Materials for Weapons

On 27 September 1993, U.S. President Bill Clinton announced a nonproliferation initiative by the United States. The centerpiece of the initiative was the proposal to negotiate a ban on the production of plutonium and highly enriched uranium for weapons. A production cutoff would cap existing stocks of unsafeguarded fissile materials and subject relevant production facilities to international safeguards. Thus it would make universal the basic commitments already undertaken by the non-weapon states that have signed the Nuclear Nonproliferation Treaty. A cutoff would facilitate arms reductions in the nuclear weapon states (the United States, Russia, France, Great Britain, and China) by making irreversible any transfer of weapon materials from military programs. Also, it would limit the development of incipient weapons programs in the de facto nuclear weapon states (India, Israel, Pakistan), whose stocks of fissile materials are still relatively small.

The cutoff idea dates back to the 1950s. A bilateral U.S.-Soviet production cutoff was an important component of U.S. arms control policy between 1956 and 1969. At that time, the Soviet Union had just started large-scale production of HEU and plutonium for weapons. Fearing that an agreement would lock it into a position of inferiority vis-à-vis the United States, whose stockpile was considerably larger, the Soviet Union rejected the cutoff idea. In the late 1980s the Soviet Union terminated production of HEU and drastically reduced the production of plutonium. Simultaneously, the Soviet Union declared its support for a production cutoff.[15]

A production cutoff would be of significant strategic advantage to Russia. Indeed, deep cuts in its nuclear arsenal have eliminated the strategic need for new fissile materials. An active position on the issue would strengthen the political and diplomatic position of Russia and would help in persuading the other former Soviet republics to become responsible members of the international nonproliferation community. Also, a cutoff would facilitate improvements in nuclear safeguards in Russia.

There are, however, several technical problems that the Russian nuclear complex must resolve before joining a cutoff agreement. Probably the most serious problems are the ongoing operation of plutonium production reactors and verification at sensitive defense sites.

Plutonium Production Reactors in Russia

To implement the fissile cutoff, Russia will have to terminate the production of plutonium for weapons and place its plutonium production reactors and chemical reprocessing plants under international safeguards. As of today, the production of weapons-grade plutonium continues at three (out of thirteen) reactors: two at Tomsk–7 and one at Krasnoiarsk–26. The reactors are dual-purpose reactors supplying heat and electricity to the local population, as well as producing plutonium for weapons. Each of them is a graphite-moderated, pressure tube reactor with a capacity of approximately two thousand megawatts thermal (MWt). The reactors are fueled with low burnup (up to eight hundred MWday/MT) aluminum-clad natural uranium fuel with HEU "spike" fuel assemblies.[16] Irradiated natural uranium fuel is reprocessed at the colocated chemical reprocessing plants. The reactors produce a total of one to two metric tons of weapons-grade plutonium per year.

In the past, freshly produced plutonium was blended with plutonium recovered from recycled warheads. The purpose of the blending, part of a stockpile maintenance program, was to prevent a buildup of americium–241 above a certain level. Americium–241, the product of beta-decay of Pu–241, emits high-energy gamma rays and thus is a health hazard; also, its presence reportedly degrades the mechanical properties of plutonium.[17] The rationale to continue the production of fresh plutonium for blending, however, has been eliminated by the recent stockpile reductions, the retirement of some americium-sensitive categories of weapons, and the development of a sufficient capability to remove americium from plutonium chemically.

At present, the principal mission of the reactors appears to be the production of residential heat and electricity for the associated nuclear sites and for 100,000 and 200,000 to 250,000 residents in Krasnoiarsk and Tomsk, respectively. The reactors cover a substantial part of the heat requirements and are absolutely essential for the cities to survive the severe Siberian winters. The problem is especially acute in Tomsk, where the heat deficit already amounts to about 15 percent, and the reactors produce approximately 30 percent of the required heat.[18]

Nevertheless, the reactors are to be shut down by the year 2000. An internal decision to this effect was made by the Soviet government in 1988; it was subsequently announced by Gorbachev in October 1989 and affirmed by Yeltsin in January 1992. The decision was driven by the economic need to scale down the Soviet program of nuclear weapons (the decision was part of the national program of conversion of 1988) and by concerns about the safety of the operating reactors. The reactors, designed in the early 1950s, are vulnerable to potentially severe accidents and lack modern safety features.[19]

To compensate for the anticipated loss of electricity and heating capacity, Tomsk and Krasnoiarsk have been constructing coal-fired power plants. The construction, however, has been slowed down by economic difficulties and environmental concerns. MINATOM has suggested to the Tomsk administration that it construct two district-heating AST–500 nuclear power reactor units. This proposal has been derailed by a lack of finances and public distrust of the nuclear industry. MINATOM has studied the possibility of conversion of the reactors to increase their safety and to stop the production of weapons-grade plutonium.[20] This project also has been paralyzed by financial problems.

In July 1992 the issue of reactor conversion and identification of alternative sources of heat and electricity for Tomsk and Krasnoiarsk became a subject of U.S.-Russian intergovernmental discussions. Its priority increased as a result of the United States' fissile cutoff initiative and implementation of the program of technical assistance to Russia under the Nuclear Threat Reduction Act.[21] The discussions culminated in a government-to-government agreement in December 1993. Specifically, the parties agreed to conduct "a study on replacing plutonium production reactors with alternate energy sources to provide electricity and heat in a clean and safe manner."[22] In the follow-up agreement in March 1994, the United States agreed to help Russia "obtain ... the finances ... and to move forward quickly with the options ... to replace the power now produced by the Tomsk and Krasnoyarsk reactors."[23] In addition, the United States proposed to help assess the potential for energy conservation technologies in the two cities. Another intergovernmental agreement was signed in June 1993. The agreement commits the parties to shut down irreversibly all plutonium production reactors by the year 2000 and to enter into a mutual verifiable agreement to stop the military use of produced plutonium.[24]

The proposed replacement options include the construction of four new gas-turbine power plants at Tomsk and a coal-fired plant at Krasnoiarsk. The projects are hoped to be completed by 1997–98. The Russians agreed to discontinue the production and chemical separation of plutonium within a year after startup of replacement capacities.

Thus the reactors are likely to continue the production of plutonium at least through 1997. From the viewpoint of the production cutoff, solutions appear possible to assure that the reactors are not an obstacle to implementation of an agreement. The progress of the proposed power replacement programs may, however, determine the complexity and intensity of verification inspections. Shutting down the reactors would simply require assurances that the reactors and reprocessing plants do not operate. If the reactors continue to operate, it would be necessary to apply IAEA-type safeguards to the reactors, spent fuel, reprocessing plants, and produced plutonium.[25] This measure would require complicated verification arrangements. These arrangements, however, would benefit significantly from suggested compliance schemes that will have been developed on a bilateral basis by the United States and Russia according to the 1994 agreement to stop the use of freshly produced plutonium for military purposes.

Verification at Sensitive Defense Sites

Implementation of a fissile cutoff in Russia could be seriously complicated by the presence of defense-related activities at the fissile material production sites that would have to be monitored under an agreement. In Russia plutonium and HEU production sites have historically been developed as large multipurpose complexes. In addition to reprocessing and uranium enrichment, the Tomsk–7 and Verkh-Neivinsk production sites are involved in plutonium and HEU metallurgy, stockpile maintenance programs (removal of americium, reliability assurance, etc.), and production, assembly, and storage of HEU and plutonium weapon components. The Maiak complex produces tritium and other nonfissile weapon components; also, it has an important naval fuel-cycle function.

Russia is likely to have a problem with international intrusive inspections because of the sensitivity of its facilities. Classification and security concerns include the possibility that sensitive national security information (weapons-related, proprietary, and naval reactor information) might be revealed through visual observation or environmental sampling by international observers. (This alleged threat to classified information may become a convenient argument for the opponents of an agreement in internal debates.)

The problem is site specific. There are, however, the following generic approaches to deal with it.

Declassification

Much of the existing classified information has been classified in the past under the Soviet rules of classification, which today appear excessive and redundant. Some information could be declassified with no damage to national security.

Managed Access Inspections

Under managed access inspections, international inspectors would have access only to selected material production areas within a larger weapons production site. Such an arrangement is likely to be acceptable when material production and weapons-related facilities, colocated within the same site perimeter fence, are separated physically. Nevertheless, additional security measures to mask sensitive equipment and information might be required. The feasibility of managed access inspections at colocated facilities is demonstrated by expected IAEA safeguards at an HEU storage vault at the Y–12 plant at Oak Ridge in the United States.[26] The plant is involved in most sensitive weapons fabrication and dismantlement activities.

Remote Sensing and Environmental Sampling Techniques

Remote sensing includes visual and infrared overflight data collected by satellites and airplanes. Environmental sampling includes the sampling of air, soil, and water on-site or in the vicinity of the site. Detection of specific radioactive or chemical elements would indicate that reprocessing or enrichment might be taking place at the facilities. Both techniques are currently used by the IAEA for detection of clandestine materials production activities. In general, they do not result in an appreciable interference with facility operations or reveal classified information.[27] Remote sensing and environmental sampling are especially effective in verifying facilities that have been shut down.

Separation of Defense and Materials Production Activities

Challenge inspections at closed facilities, IAEA-type safeguards at operating facilities, and, in some cases, environmental monitoring will have an inherently intrusive nature. They are likely to be acceptable if sensitive defense facilities and a safeguarded facility are separated physically. Therefore, consolidation of classified defense-related activities in separate exclusion areas should be a priority in preparations for a cutoff at a site level. In some cases separation of defense and materials production activities might not be feasible. For example, at the Maiak site the RT–1 reprocessing plant separates plutonium from the spent fuel of power reactors and also is involved in defense-related naval fuel cycle activities. Intrusive safeguards might not be possible under such circumstances. Removal or relocation of sensitive defense activities or convincing transparency measures demonstrating that no production of fissile materials takes place might be required.

Thus a verifiable production cutoff in Russia is feasible. Its implementation will have to be based on a vigorous effort to develop appropriate schemes of safeguards, conduct advance preparations at sites and facilities, and change the deep-rooted and in many respects obsolete culture of secrecy within the nuclear weapons establishment. This effort will require time and resources and will have to be carried out in a step-by-step fashion.

The Need for a System of Nuclear Safeguards

There are many hundreds of tons of weapons-usable fissile materials in Russia. The possibility of their diversion might be unacceptably high in light of the economic crisis, corruption, the surge in economic crimes, and the lack of an adequate system of nuclear safeguards. The country must quickly develop a robust system of national safeguards, the primary barrier to diversion of nuclear materials. As a first and urgent step, MINATOM and Gosatomnadzor must establish and implement a modern and thoroughly integrated system of material control and accountancy and physical protection at HEU and plutonium facilities. The system must be supported by strong programs of technical support and regulatory oversight. After that, a comprehensive national system of nuclear safeguards must be developed.

There is no reason to believe that safeguards of nuclear weapons are inadequate. The long-term security of nuclear weapons is further enhanced by their consolidation and dismantlement. It is important, however, to provide adequate storage facilities for warheads and fissile materials and to assure the security of warheads in transit.

Although the Ministry of Defense and MINATOM are the principal agencies in developing and implementing a system of nuclear safeguards, other federal agencies have an important role with regard to control of fissile materials. Specifically, an input from intelligence and other security agencies is vital for the programs of threat assessment, control of potential smuggling routes, and control of the illegal international demand for weapons-usable fissile materials.

A halt on the production of fissile materials for weapons is an important component of the international nonproliferation regime. As a nuclear weapon state, Russia can play an important positive role in negotiations and implementation of such an agreement. To be in a position to do so, the Russian nuclear complex must resolve the problem of the plutonium production reactors and prepare its nuclear facilities for international inspection.

The Russian government has the ultimate responsibility for the protection of its fissile materials and weapons. The Western countries, however, may provide seed money and assistance to facilitate the development of a coherent fissile material control policy in Russia.[28] So far this effort has not been particularly successful because of both the natural sensitivity of these issues and bureaucratic momentum in the respective governments. In order to make the assistance more effective, the parties have to undertake new transparency measures, including declarations of their weapons stockpiles and fissile material inventories, exchanges of dismantlement-related data, and mutual access to nuclear facilities.

Notes

1. It is estimated that the USSR and subsequently Russia have separated 177 metric tons of weapons-grade plutonium and about 30 metric tons of reactor-grade plutonium. T. Cochran and S. Norris, *Russian/Soviet Nuclear Warhead Production*, NWD 93–1 (Washington, DC: Natural Resources Defense Council, 1993).

2. Some materials are owned by other agencies and by research centers. For exam-

ple, the Ministry of Shipbuilding owns naval reactor fuel. Large amounts of fissile materials are owned by the Kurchatov Institute.

3. A three-centimeter-thick layer of tungsten shield surrounding an HEU weapon component would not be detectable by practical gamma-ray monitoring means. See Steve Fetter et al., "Detecting Nuclear Warheads," *Science and Global Security*, vol. 3, nos. 3–4). Effective shielding against active neutron interrogation would be provided by twenty centimeters of dense borated polyethylene with a thin cadmium layer between the polyethylene layer and HEU metal.

4. The Ministry of Atomic Energy was created by presidential decree by Boris Yeltsin in January 1992. Its predecessors have been the USSR Ministry of Medium Machine-Building (prior to 1989) and the Ministry of Atomic Power and Industry (1989–92). The ministry is responsible for the entire nuclear fuel cycle, generation of nuclear power, and nuclear weapon design, testing, manufacturing, and disassembly. As of 1992, MINATOM operated 151 research institutes and production facilities and employed about 100,000 personnel.

The State Committee for the Supervision of Nuclear and Radiation Safety (Gosatomnadzor) is responsible for the development of state regulations and control of their implementation in the area of production and use of nuclear materials and energy. The committee is charged with the development of nuclear and radiation safety rules and standards, supervision of nuclear safeguards and physical protection, and compliance with international obligations, licensing, inspections of nuclear installations, and coordination and support of safety-related research. Gosatomnadzor supervises both military and civilian nuclear activities and reports directly to the president of the Russian Federation.

5. It is expected that both facilities will be built in two phases (twenty-five thousand fissile material containers each phase). At Maiak, site preparation will start in July 1994; the first phase will be operational in 1997, and the second phase will be operational in 1999. In Tomsk, site preparation will start in the summer of 1995; the rest of the schedule will shift accordingly.

6. Some material might be shipped to the United States for blending as HEU oxide or hexafluoride.

7. This corresponds to the throughput of 50 kilograms of HEU per day during the first five years and 150 kilograms of HEU per day thereafter. Such throughputs are typical for large reprocessing plants.

8. Currently, vitrification of high-level waste is carried out at Maiak. There is a plan to build a vitrification plant at Krasnoiarsk–26.

9. T. Cochran (a scientist at the U.S. Natural Resources Defense Council), testimony to the U.S. House of Representatives Armed Services Committee, 19 April 1994.

10. Assuming the Soviet arsenal in the late 1980s and early 1990s of twenty-five thousand warheads and the average warhead lifetime of fifteen years, some sixteen hundred to seventeen hundred warheads have been replaced annually. *SIPRI Yearbook 1991: World Armaments and Disarmament* (Oxford: Oxford University Press, 1992), pp. 18–21. As of January 1991, the arsenal included about eleven thousand strategic and fourteen thousand nonstrategic warheads.

11. Warheads have been assembled and disassembled routinely in the past.

12. CIA Director J. Woolsey, testimony before the U.S. Senate Armed Services Committee, 25 January 1994. In the past, CIA estimates have had a margin of uncertainty of about five thousand warheads, mostly owing to uncertainties about the inventory of tactical weapons.

13. D. Yost, "Nuclear Weapons Issues in France," in *Strategic Views from the Second Tier: The Nuclear Policies of France, Britain, and China*, ed. J. Hopkins and W. Hu (San Diego: Institute on Global Conflict and Cooperation, University of California,

1994), p. 39. A framework agreement between France and Russia was signed in November 1992. It envisages five technical agreements totaling 400 million francs.

14. Discussions with representatives of the Ministry of Interior and KGB of the Republic of Belarus, Minsk, 8 June 1994.

15. Foreign Minister Eduard Shevardnadze, speech to the United Nations General Assembly, 26 September 1989.

16. A ring of HEU "spike" fuel assemblies is designed to level the power output throughout the core.

17. In the United States, americium was removed from plutonium chemically at the Rocky Flats plant until the plant was shut down in 1989.

18. Sixth International Workshop on the CTB and Nuclear Warhead Elimination, Washington, DC, 15–17 December 1993.

19. Among the safety design problems are the low temperature of melting for fuel and fuel channels, the potential severity of an accident as a result of fuel channel rupture, the positive reactivity coefficient in the event of a loss-of-coolant accident, the lack of containment, and some others.

20. Production of plutonium for weapons can be terminated by conversion of reactor fuel. The goal of conversion would be to increase fuel burnup and extend the storage of the fuel without reprocessing. At present, burnup is limited by radiation and temperature effects in aluminum; also, fuel must be reprocessed within six months after irradiation because of the limited on-site storage capacity and the high rate of corrosion of aluminum cladding. An increase in burnup would shift plutonium from weapon to reactor grade and would reduce the amount of discharged fuel.

21. In fiscal year 1994, the U.S. Congress passed the Markey Amendment, tying the release of Nunn–Lugar funds for the construction of a plutonium storage facility in Russia to presidential certification that Russia is committed to terminating the production of weapons-grade plutonium.

22. "Report on the Sixth International Workshop on the CTB and Nuclear Warhead Elimination" (Washington, DC, 15–17 December 1993).

23. "Protocol of Meeting Between the United States and Russian Federation on the Replacement of Russian Plutonium Production Reactors" (Washington, DC, 16 March 1994).

24. In principle the U.S.-Russian agreement allows MINATOM to convert the reactors and continue their operation without production of weapons-grade plutonium. The United States, however, indicated that it would not support such a project.

25. Verification of the reprocessing plants might be avoided by calculating the mass balance between plutonium in spent fuel and in safeguarded storage.

26. IAEA inspectors are to inspect the Vault–16 building at Y–12, containing some thirty metric tons of HEU, by the end of 1994; they have already visited the location.

27. Environmental sampling potentially can put classified information at risk.

28. Assistant Secretary of Defense Ashton Carter, at a 9 March 1994 hearing before the U.S. House of Representatives Defense Appropriations Subcommittee, formulated the goals of assistance as follows: "The FSU [former Soviet Union] governments must commit their own policies and their own resources to accomplishing the bulk of these tasks. What the United States can do, through constant diplomatic urging and by providing seed funding, is to draw these governments into programs through which they will ultimately allocate their own resources to accomplish these tasks themselves." Quoted in *Post-Soviet Nuclear Complex Monitor*, vol. 1, nos. 20, 21 (18 March 1994), p. 6.

4

Russian Control of Nuclear Weapons

Bruce G. Blair

The Specter of Nuclear Anarchy

With cruel irony, the geopolitical revolution that dissolved the Soviet empire and defused the confrontation between the nuclear superpowers also strained Russia's ability to maintain firm control over its far-flung nuclear arsenal, heightening the world's fear of nuclear catastrophe. As the nuclear command and control system of the former Soviet Union (FSU) came under unprecedented stress from several angles, projections of an imminent or eventual catastrophic breakdown shaped worldwide public opinion and the security policies of many governments around the globe.

Among the forms that nuclear anarchy in the FSU might take, the following ranked high on most lists: (1) the unauthorized use of nuclear weapons by rebellious weapons commanders in the field; (2) loss of control caused by political incoherence at the top of the chain of command in Moscow; (3) a Ukrainian grab for independent launch control over nuclear weapons stationed on its territory; and (4) the leakage of nuclear bombs, fissile materials, and expertise onto the global black market.

A preexisting condition was the source of a fifth nuclear danger. The long-standing Soviet practice of maintaining vast and dispersed nuclear forces in a launch-ready configuration posed a danger of inadvertent attack. Launch-on-warning—that is, disseminating firing orders after detecting an enemy nuclear missile strike but before the missiles reach their targets—was and still is a core element of Russian nuclear strategy. In consequence, this rapid reaction posture carried a significant risk that nuclear missile forces would be fired on the basis of a false warning. The breakup of the former Soviet Union increased this risk by politically dismembering the missile attack early-warning network.[1]

This chapter examines and assesses these five strains on the Russian system of nuclear command and control. The wisdom of Western policy responses to the dangers depends on our ability to distinguish fact from fiction and to gauge the relative magnitude of these problems.

Rogue Commanders in the Field

The danger of unauthorized use of strategic forces by local rogue commanders of land-based rockets, submarine missiles, and bombers is lower than commonly alleged. Moscow micromanages the field operations of these forces to such an extent that subordinates down the chain of command have little discretionary authority, or physical ability, to do anything without explicit permission from the center.

Technical safeguards are stringent. For instance, to fire their weapons, the local commanders need unblocking codes held in Moscow by the General Staff.[2] In the case of silo-based missiles, any attempt by a local launch crew to pick the lock would be automatically reported to the war rooms of the General Staff and the headquarters of the strategic rocket forces (SRF), both in greater Moscow. These central control posts could then send special commands that would isolate the deviant launch center, severing its communications links and transferring launch control to neighboring regimental launch posts. If the lock were somehow picked, the General Staff could transmit a command called a "zero flight command" that would restore the blocking function. If despite all these safety precautions a land-based intercontinental missile were fired without proper authorization, rocket guards units equipped with machine guns could disable the missile during liftoff.

Technical safeguards are less extensive for ballistic missile submarines because of a crew's autonomy during its long combat patrols at sea.[3] The boats do not maintain continuous two-way communications with higher authority, and the General Staff cannot continuously monitor their status or electronically override the actions of their crews.

This relative freedom of operation during a crew's seventy-eight-day cruises raises the specter of a renegade crew taking matters into their own hands—à la *Hunt for Red October*. The safety of submarine operations compared to other strategic forces clearly depends more heavily on crew loyalty and discipline, even though Russian submarines are equipped with blocking devices of the sort described earlier. The crew normally must receive unblocking codes from the General Staff (or other high authority) to activate the boat's fire and missile control systems. Still, it is impossible to know based on available public information whether a renegade crew could take advantage of its autonomy and defeat this safeguard. The Soviets imposed additional organizational safeguards on board undersea vessels to compensate for this potential weakness in the technical safeguards, but their effectiveness also remains open to question.

The weakest technical safeguards are found on the gravity bombs and cruise missiles for strategic bombers. The locks on the bombs are not sophisticated, and the cruise missiles lack adequate technical protection.[4] To compensate, the Russians store these payloads in depots (a mile or so from the airstrips and bombers), where special custodial troops of the General Staff guard them.[5]

In the event of a nuclear crisis, the Russians plan to load the payloads onto the bombers, at which point the main safeguard against unauthorized use consists of a blocking device on the bomber (similar to the coded switch devices on U.S. bombers that require receipt of codes from a higher authority to unlock the bomb racks in the bomb bay) that only special codes held by the General Staff can remove. A bomber's flight pattern must also conform to preplanned operations prior to weapon release, a criterion enforced electronically by onboard navigation equipment.

Despite these safeguards, the Soviets always kept nuclear payloads separate from bombers during daily operations. With the possible exception of crisis circumstances, they never put bombers loaded with nuclear weapons on strip alert.[6] The Russians have upheld this tradition. Also, remember that Presidents Bush and Gorbachev declared in October 1991 that strategic bombers would be taken off alert and their nuclear armaments put in storage. Both nations continue to abide by this zero-alert pledge for bombers.

This safeguards regime for Russian strategic forces is of course far from ironclad. The blocking devices, for example, are really just gimmicks designed to buy time. In the event of a serious breach of safeguards in the field, the Russian military establishment would need to promptly dispatch personnel to suppress the disobedience and restore physical control. If social and political circumstances weaken the cohesion of the military, then its ability to deal with such violations would obviously be diminished.

Short of an acute domestic crisis that destroys military cohesion, the prospect of an unauthorized attack by strategic forces is so remote as to be negligible. The risk is being unintentionally driven up, however, by a deep-seated bias in U.S. arms control strategy. The American obsession with Soviet counterforce capabilities resulted in the reduction of the forces that happened to have the strongest safeguards (the silo-based missiles) and in greater Russian reliance on weapons with relatively weaker safeguards—submarines, bombers, and mobile land-based missiles.

Political Incoherence at the Apex

Moving from the lower to the upper rungs of the command ladder, Russian control of nuclear weapons is threatened by political incoherence in Moscow. To be reliably effective at the top, the control system must meet two conditions so basic we usually take them for granted. First, the civilian leadership must be competent and virtuous. Second, the military must be thoroughly subordinated to civilian authority. Unfortunately, these conditions cannot be taken for granted in Russia today.

Regarding military subordination, there is a genuine lack of clear civilian authority.[7] President Boris Yeltsin has not created new institutions for civilian control to replace the old Communist Party apparatus. His authority rests mainly on personal loyalties, leaving him at the mercy of power struggles at the center of the political system that imperil civilian control in an institutional sense and invite the military to intervene in politics. Although the armed forces feel bound by a norm of professionalism that rejects such intervention, this norm is not a sufficient basis for civil–military relations over the long term. It is inevitably strained by political crises such as the 1991 coup attempt and the constitutional crises of 1993. Declining defense spending in Russia aggravates the stress. The deputy minister of defense, Andrei Kokoshin, recently warned that plans to halve the defense budget put control over the military in jeopardy: "It's clear we are heading into a situation where we will be losing control over the armed forces."[8]

Within the nuclear chain of command, the significance of tenuous civil–military allegiances is underscored by the fact that although only the civilian leadership—namely, the president and the defense minister—has the right to order nuclear launches, top Russian military leaders have the technical ability to carry them out. The civilian authorities have the right to decide, but the Russian military, just like the U.S. military, holds all the unblock and launch codes necessary to launch a strategic attack. As a technical matter, the Russian General Staff also controls the transfer of nuclear authority to the president's successors and the activation of their famous nuclear suitcases, although these suitcases are technically superfluous to the launch process. They transmit a so-called permission command to the senior nuclear commanders, a command that only authorizes a launch; it does not enable it.[9] The General Staff sends a different message containing different codes—the so-called direct command—that actually authorizes and enables the dispersed forces to fire.

The essential role that key military officers play in nuclear weapons control arrangements thus gives them an inherent ability to determine who in fact is in power, at least in terms of who commands the nuclear forces.

The military's obedience to legitimate civilian political authority is thus crucial. Anything that undermines this allegiance would threaten the entire control system.

During the 1991 coup this allegiance of course partially broke down. The defense minister, General Yazov, was one of the major conspirators; the chief of the General Staff was also implicated. Gorbachev loyalists in the General Staff, however, evidently decided against activating the nuclear suitcase held in reserve for Vice President Ianaev (Gorbachev's legal successor, who was illegally declared acting president during the coup). Furthermore, the senior nuclear commanders in the field—the commanders of the strategic rocket forces (SRF), navy, and air force—secretly formed a pact to disobey any nuclear orders sent by the coup plotters. They remained loyal to Gorbachev, a political alignment backed up by the technical wherewithal to severely impede, if not completely block, the dissemination of launch orders from the General Staff through the normal channels of communications down the chain of command.[10]

The abortive coup underscores the other essential precondition for reliable nuclear control: competent leadership. We too often take for granted that top leaders have political aims that coincide with the national security goals of the state, especially when it comes to matters as grave as nuclear security.[11] The matter of devious intrigue in high places and its effects on nuclear control became very relevant during the coup. The plotters' political aims clearly diverged from the goals of the state, and on top of that they became desperate, exhausted, and sometimes intoxicated. Besides becoming prone to bad judgment, these self-anointed leaders sowed some confusion within the nuclear chain of command, and de facto nuclear authority partially devolved to military leaders of the General Staff and the nuclear branches of the armed forces.

Russian nuclear control remains susceptible to such lapses of legitimate civilian leadership and, given Russia's failure to thoroughly subordinate the military to civilian authority, to lapses of strict political control from the center. An internal Russian proposal floated after the coup indicates just how far they had to go to create institutional safeguards. The idea was to assign representatives of parliament to the war room of the General Staff to guard against any mishandling of the nuclear launch codes. Whatever its merit on narrow technical grounds, the idea was overtaken by larger political events. Yeltsin dissolved the parliament and the old constitution, and along with them went the president's immediate legal successor (Vice President Rutskoi) and another successor two notches down the line of succession (parliamentary speaker Khasbulatov). Yeltsin subsequently declared that the prime minister (Chernomyrdin) would succeed him in the event of his incapacitation, a pronouncement that underscores the dubious legitimacy and inadequate institutionalization of mechanisms for controlling nuclear operations.

Ukraine's Bid for Nuclear Status

Turning now to Ukraine, we have another tottering state with a nuclear arsenal. Its leaders fortunately do not have their fingers on the nuclear "button" and almost certainly do not intend to pursue that option. A political consensus exists to retain possession and block the relocation of at least some weapons back to Russia until the issues of compensation and security guarantees are fully resolved. But no consensus exists to seize operational control.

Russian-Ukrainian interdependence ameliorates nuclear tension between them. Ukraine's nuclear weapons establishment, while inclined by pragmatic self-interest to align itself politically with the pronuclear Ukrainian nationalists, is ideologically pro-Russian and cooperates with Russia in maintaining and modernizing the forces in both countries. This cooperation is indispensable, because each state produces vital parts of almost all missile systems deployed throughout the former Soviet Union. For instance, Ukraine builds the guidance systems for the SS–18 missiles deployed in Russia and Kazakhstan. Ukraine also builds the SS–24 missiles deployed in Ukraine and Russia, but Russia has the design bureau and supplies the guidance system for the SS–24. Ukraine builds the blocking devices for all the strategic missiles in the FSU, but the devices are designed and put on line ("booted up") by a design bureau based in St. Petersburg.

Russia is nonetheless hedging its bets on future cooperation; for instance, it terminated joint development with Ukraine of the only land-based missile currently under development (the follow-on mobile SS–25). In the recent past, Moscow also blamed Kiev for difficulties in maintaining missile and warhead safety. But although Ukraine was not blameless, it had not systematically interfered with SRF maintenance activity in the silos or warhead storage sites. Both nations bore some responsibility for the poor record of maintenance and the attendant safety hazards—Russia for neglecting on-site maintenance and Ukraine for delaying the repatriation of nuclear warheads in need of repair at Russian facilities. As a consequence, there were credible reports of radiation leakage (from tritium bottles?) equivalent to forty rads per hour at one local storage facility (Pervomais´k) brimming over with defective missile warheads. Neglect of the chemical high explosives in warheads also increased the risk of an accidental conventional explosion that would release toxic plutonium into the environment (a Chernobyl-class catastrophe in Russia's view). Moscow exaggerated such dangers and played on international fear, however, in order to exert pressure on Ukraine to relinquish its arsenal. The defense minister even threatened to disavow Russia's responsibility for nuclear safety in Ukraine because of alleged Ukrainian interference with safety programs and maintenance schedules.[12]

Ukraine's renewed pledges of disarmament under the Trilateral Agreement, signed in January 1994, and the parliament's November 1994 vote giving overwhelming approval to join the NPT dramatically improved the prospects for nuclear cooperation with Russia. An encouraging sign was the transfer in 1994 of 360 SS–19 and SS–24 warheads from Pervomais´k back to Russia.[13] Another is that Ukraine's avowed interest in operational control still remains confined to a desire for a technical veto that would physically prevent Russia from unilaterally launching Ukrainian missiles. In talks in late 1991, Marshal Shaposhnikov of the Commonwealth of Independent States pledged to devise such a veto and implement it sometime in 1993. The system surely never materialized, leaving President Kravchuk no worse off, however, than President Yeltsin, who also lacks a technical veto (over his own military). Since Ukraine actually builds the blocking devices for Russian missiles, the government may well be investigating veto options on its own.

Blocking devices unfortunately do more than just prevent unauthorized launches; they are also integral to the launch process. If Kiev decided to pursue positive launch control, it could take a major step toward it simply by replacing the Russian-keyed devices with its own. Ukraine would then be able to activate the flight plans on the missiles and fire them at their predesignated targets. Once Ukraine had the devices in hand, it would take only a few weeks to install them.[14]

Ukraine's ability to fire the missiles, however, assumes that Russia had not earlier stripped out the flight plans and targeting information from the missiles, something the SRF maintenance teams could have easily accomplished already.[15] Recent statements by the commander of the Russian SRF in fact assert that all Russian strategic land-based rockets have been stripped of target data in conjunction with implementing the U.S.-Russian agreement now in effect obliging the parties to stop targeting each other in peacetime.

A seizure of positive launch control also assumes that local missile crews are unable or unwilling to prevent the substitution of blocking devices and that Russia would acquiesce in the face of Ukraine's grab for operational control—major assumptions indeed. With the notable exception of the commander of the Forty-third Strategic Rocket Army (located at Vinnitsa), under which all Ukrainian strategic missiles are subordinated, and the commander of one of the two missile divisions in Ukraine, none or almost none of the SRF officers in Ukraine have renounced their allegiance to Russia, and their willing participation in any Ukrainian takeover seems very unlikely.

If Ukraine seeks a credible missile deterrent aimed at Russia, furthermore, it would face the daunting task of programming new target sets for the missile computers. This would pose extreme difficulty for the Ukrainian-built SS–24 missiles, because the guidance for them is built in Russia. Ukraine perhaps could eventually build the guidance system and match it with the blocking devices, but this could take upwards of a year (a very rough estimate).

The implausibility of this course of action is underscored by the fact that thirty-seven SS–24 missiles had already been deactivated by the end of September 1994; all will be deactivated by November 1994 if the Trilateral Agreement stays on schedule. Furthermore, Ukraine's confidence in its launch capability would depend on flight-testing. Ukraine lacks the requisite test facilities, not to mention permission from surrounding countries to overfly their territory. Another impediment concerns the silo launchers for the SS–24 (and SS–19) missiles. Their configuration apparently precludes rotating the missile azimuth to the extent necessary to fire at Russia. Finally, the SS–24 is a solid-fuel missile that cannot be fired at short range. The shortest range in its testing history is about seventeen hundred miles, which is eleven hundred miles greater than the distance to Moscow from the Ukrainian missile fields. It could still threaten Russia from Novosibirsk eastward, however.

The ongoing deactivation of SS–19 missiles (forty, by the end of September 1994) also constrains the Ukrainian nuclear option. Ukraine builds the SS-19 missile guidance system and could possibly aim the missiles at Moscow, because this missile type was evidently designed for short-range theater missions against Western Europe as well as intercontinental missions against North America. The SS-19 has been routinely tested at ranges just over six hundred miles and could be tested over the Black Sea if necessary. On the other hand, its silo is not configured for firing at Russia, Ukraine does not build the missile itself, and its service life ends in 1998. Ukraine would have to cannibalize the existing inventory of increasingly decrepit missiles in order to keep diminishing numbers in launch-ready condition.

A Ukrainian nuclear option may be more feasibly based on air-delivered weapons. Their safeguards are more primitive, they require less maintenance (although Ukraine's Bear-H and Blackjack bombers are severely under-maintained), and they can be employed more flexibly. Also, the bombers and cruise missiles have fallen under the operational control of the Ukrainian air force, though Russia probably removed the targeting tapes from the cruise missiles. Ukraine lacks the geodetic data needed to produce guidance tapes with the requisite detail of the terrain over which cruise missiles would fly to attack Russia.

The status of the warheads is less clear. It is believed that they were separated from the cruise missiles and placed in depots near the two bomber airstrips and that Ukrainian conscripts guard the perimeter of the depots. There may also be some gravity bombs in the depots, though American officials appear to believe otherwise. Ukrainian sources say that some of the officers managing the depots have taken oaths to Ukraine but remain operationally subordinate to the Russian General Staff. Russian military sources say that Russia has effectively surrendered custody. In any case, Ukraine could readily overrun and capture the payloads there. Unlike the strategic rockets, stolen bomber payloads could easily and quickly slip into the countryside and elude recapture by Russia.

A narrow cost-benefit analysis of these nuclear options is very unlikely to encourage nuclear ambition in Ukraine, but such an assessment is not absolutely conclusive. The initial direct costs of cobbling together a deterrent force out of inherited or seizable assets would be relatively small. Ukraine's actual and potential inventory of missiles, aircraft, and nuclear warheads is huge and paid for. Even though the assets are wasting away and Ukraine can ill afford to maintain them, let alone support the establishment of a new nuclear infrastructure to produce indigenous nuclear self-sufficiency, Ukraine has a relatively cheap short-term nuclear option at its disposal.

Part of the appeal of this option is of course its potential to offset the imbalance of conventional military strength favoring Russia over Ukraine.[16] This imbalance poses a deep and long-term structural obstacle to denuclearization in Ukraine. It complements the other more immediate security problems that also might inhibit denuclearization, particularly the dispute over the Black Sea fleet and the threat to Ukrainian territorial integrity posed by the Crimean secession problem.

These and other sources of Ukrainian insecurity have the potential to unravel Ukraine's recent accession to the NPT. Although it appears that the Rada's demands for security guarantees from the nuclear powers (except China, whose participation is not demanded and whose nuclear doctrine already eschews the first use of nuclear weapons) are being met to its satisfaction,[17] the Rada voted to join the NPT on the condition that the nuclear states refrain from using economic coercion such as embargoes or blockades against Ukraine. It reserved the right to reconsider its adherence to the NPT if any of the nuclear states exerts economic or military pressure, though such a right of withdrawal inheres in the treaty in any case. Ironically, the day before the vote, Russia reportedly announced it would stop supplying nuclear fuel for Ukrainian nuclear power plants until Ukraine joined the NPT.[18]

A pessimistic scenario would thus have Ukraine reneging on its denuclearization commitments if, for instance, Russia coerces it economically or threatens to annex the Crimea to protect the interests of ethnic Russian inhabitants. No prognosis is offered here, but it seems very plausible that Ukraine will at least prolong denuclearization as long as possible to test the reliability of Russia's commitments. Keep in mind that the schedule for warhead withdrawal under the Trilateral Agreement is missing from the public agreement, and that the secret withdrawal terms allow Ukraine another two years to eliminate the last remaining weapons. Ukraine could receive virtually all the compensation it has been promised so far, while preserving a nuclear option, simply by pulling up short on the last delivery of the last installment of warheads.

Those warheads would be the bomber payloads whose transfer to Russia is reportedly the last to occur under the secret three-year withdrawal schedule. Control over these warheads is precarious compared to the missile warheads, and they offer the cheapest and most versatile nuclear capability. Ukraine might in the end withhold a portion of this inventory and obtain full-fledged nuclear status even after receiving the bulk of the compensation for its nuclear arsenal.

For this deviation, it would lose the reaffirmation of the CSCE security reassurances by the other parties and obviously pay a heavy price in other political and economic terms. The scenario thus seems unlikely.

Nevertheless, there continue to be undercurrents in Ukraine that support keeping a nuclear option open as long as possible. Former Defense Minister Morozov, who authored the original draft of the Ukrainian military doctrine that rejected nuclear status, now reveals in his memoirs that he consciously tried to keep a nuclear option open for Ukraine. Since this position could still gain momentum in the event of a deterioration in Ukrainian-Russian relations, the United States should at least prepare a contingency plan to deal with it.[19]

The optimistic view sees the Crimean problem, and the vulnerability of Ukraine generally, as motivating Ukraine's recent accession to the NPT in order to activate the big power security assurances predicated on such ratification (as stipulated in the Trilateral Agreement). This view also emphasizes the enormous liabilities of nuclear status. Pursuing the nuclear option would not only incur severe political and economic costs but might even provoke an aggressive Russian reaction. If Kiev were to renege on its trilateral commitments and seek nuclear status after all, it is not implausible that Russia might take the drastic step of cutting off oil, gas, timber, or nuclear fuel supplies in order to coerce Ukraine to surrender the nuclear arms. Its economy paralyzed, Ukraine might well succumb to the pressure. Or it might view the nuclear option as its last desperate hope to preserve its sovereignty. Whether Ukraine would be driven to seize operational control, and whether this would beget a hostile Russian military response to preserve its nuclear control are open questions, but in all likelihood a Ukrainian grab for control would trigger a military fight over nuclear weapons custody. Russia's new military doctrine appears to carry exactly this warning by saying that any interference with Russian strategic nuclear command and control would constitute an immediate military threat to Russia.

In sum, Ukraine's alleged drift toward nuclear status has been arrested and, in all likelihood, permanently reversed. In late 1992, a U.S. national intelligence estimate reportedly reflected "a broad consensus among government analysts that Ukraine is now as likely to keep the nuclear weapons as it is to give them up."[20] My view at the time was that "This prediction is debatable and probably wrong. The Ukrainian government—the executive branch and the vast majority of the legislators—still subscribes to its early and bold declaration of intent to become a non-nuclear state."[21] Ukraine's commitment to denuclearization appears even stronger today, though doubts linger that will take another couple of years to dispel.

Nuclear Leakage

Economic, social, and political conditions within the FSU seem conducive to nuclear smuggling and an exodus of nuclear expertise to proliferant states. Both the supply and demand sides of the picture point up serious difficulties in preventing the leakage of nuclear materials or brainpower onto the black market.

Many thousands of nuclear weapons have been shuttled around in recent years. How many thousands is uncertain, as are their storage locations. The Russians have not disclosed the size of their total nuclear inventory, and U.S. estimates of weapons at various field and storage sites rely heavily on indirect evidence, for instance, the apparent storage capacity of suspect bunkers detected through surveillance from space.

In recent years, official U.S. intelligence estimates put the inventory of strategic and nonstrategic nuclear weapons at about thirty thousand, but Russian sources have indicated a much higher number. The highest reported figure was forty-seven thousand as of 1992.[22] Russia has agreed to supply aggregate numbers of nuclear weapons in its stockpile, but as of the time of this writing the numbers, particularly of nonstrategic weapons, remained uncertain. In late September 1994, the Pentagon estimated the then current stockpile of nonstrategic warheads to be somewhere between six thousand and thirteen thousand.[23]

Although the consolidation of previously dispersed inventories surely enhanced their security, central depots have probably been overfilled, and ill-designed facilities by the dozens have likely been tasked to handle the excess.

Many thousands of weapons have also been dismantled, and many more thousands are slated for disassembly. Compared to the weapons at military central depots, which fall under the custodial jurisdiction of a special branch of the armed forces, the weapons transferred to disassembly plants and the plutonium pits recovered during dismantlement lend themselves more readily to theft and diversion because of their smaller size and because primary responsibility for their security belongs to a civilian agency (the Ministry of Atomic Energy). MINATOM appears to be somewhat less strict in managing nuclear stockpiles than its military counterpart, although this relative laxity applies more to nuclear materials outside the nuclear weapons complex—that is, nuclear materials under MINATOM control produced for and by nonweapons activities in the research, commercial power, and military sectors.

Another factor is the declining state of morale and well-being of nuclear custodians at all levels. In the current economic climate, the temptation to sell expertise or stolen nuclear materials for large sums of money surely is irresistible for some. The decline of discipline, law and order, and central authority, combined with the rise of organized crime, weakens the barriers to the diversion and smuggling of nuclear contraband. Bureaucratic infighting among the key entities responsible for ensuring safeguards—the ministries of defense and atomic energy, intelligence and police organizations, and a newly formed state nuclear oversight committee—exacerbates the problem.

And the demand for nuclear components and materials has presumably grown in this era of global nuclear proliferation. One can only presume that potential buyers of weapons-grade nuclear materials are plentiful.

The combination of these factors partially explains the rampant speculation in the press and even the scholarly literature that a hemorrhage of illicit nuclear materials from the FSU is occurring. Given current conditions, one can readily accept the judgment of a recent report by the National Academy of Sciences that the problem of plutonium storage and disposition in the FSU is a "clear and present danger."[24] A spate of recent incidents of nuclear smuggling appears to provide concrete evidence that a trickle of illicit trade may be turning into a flood.[25]

But with a single exception, the nuclear weapons complex, as opposed to other sectors of the FSU nuclear infrastructure, does not appear to be implicated in these incidents. Various government officials and outside experts who track this issue have found no evidence of significant diversions of nuclear contraband from the weapons complex.[26] A possible exception concerns the pure plutonium seized by German authorities in Tengen.[27] This material, which amounted to a few grams, may have been originally produced at one of the two main nuclear-weapon design bureaus (the research institute at Arzamas–16) as part of a plutonium enrichment experiment conducted decades ago. But the plutonium apparently was not produced for nuclear weapons, and specimens of it were widely distributed in small allotments to civil and military research facilities throughout the FSU. The Tengen incident presumably began as a theft from one of these facilities.

The evident effectiveness of safeguards on nuclear weapons and their ingredients reflects the high priority of nuclear command and control in the Russian political and military culture. The Soviets went to extraordinary lengths to ensure strict central control over nuclear force deployments, and this obsession with control ran through the entire weapons cycle—from production and assembly to operational deployment to dismantlement. The Russians show no signs of relaxing the traditional standards.

Looser security within the nonweapon nuclear infrastructure reflects the widespread misconception that proliferant states or terrorists would seek only weapons-grade nuclear materials because of the difficulty of making a bomb from the less pure fissile materials that circulate within the nonweapon sectors. The Soviets, like Japan and other states, have been slow to recognize the inherent danger posed by reactor-grade plutonium, for example, and by uranium enriched to suboptimal levels for bomb-building purposes. Material that is not weapons-grade often is weapons-usable in that it could be fashioned into a nuclear bomb, albeit a more unwieldy one with less explosive power.

The nuclear material at most risk falls under this category of "weapons-usable." The risk derives from its widespread dispersal throughout the FSU—many hundreds of sites—and from the relative laxity of safeguards over its disposition. The largest cache of material smuggled into Germany—hundreds of grams of plutonium 239 enriched to about 87 percent—probably leaked from MINATOM's commercial sector, particularly facilities such as the fuel fabrication plant at Novosibirsk or the reactor research institute at Dmitrovgrad.[28] Similarly, relatively lax safeguards over a huge cache of enriched uranium, enough to make twenty or more nuclear bombs, at a fuel fabrication site in Kazakhstan impelled the United States to transport the material to Tennessee.[29] Although the bulk of the material consisted of nuclear waste and alloys not readily usable for bomb making, a significant fraction was fuel for naval nuclear reactors, uranium 235 fuel so highly enriched as to be weapons-grade and thus usable in bomb making without further enrichment (the Kazakh plant mainly fabricates fuel for commercial reactors, which do not use such pure uranium 235).

The Kazakh episode illustrates that large quantities of weapons-grade material, and not just lower-grade but weapons-usable material, circulate outside the nuclear weapons complex. That such material could be stolen with relative ease is more than hypothetical. A successful theft of naval reactor fuel actually occurred in late 1993. Three fresh fuel rods for nuclear submarine reactors disappeared from storage in Murmansk. Thieves cut through a padlock, detached a door latch, and removed the fuel rods without detection; the rusty alarm fixtures designed to alert a nearby guard post of intrusion failed to do so.[30]

By all accounts, the Russian mafia has not been behind any of the incidents of nuclear diversion. The culprits have been "small-time" opportunists outside the extensive web of organized crime in the FSU. While bracing for the eventuality, the FBI has not detected any involvement of FSU organized crime groups in any actions or plots to obtain and profit from the sale of nuclear contraband.[31]

In sum, the risk of nuclear smuggling varies according to the category of material in question. While the risk appears to be low for intact weapons and their fissile components, because security within the nuclear weapons complex is tight, the risk appears to be high for nonweapon nuclear material circulating within the commercial nuclear power sector, research institutes, and parts of the military. This author's assessment in late 1992 still stands: "Russia especially needs to ensure the security of fissile materials, given that the illicit diversion of even small amounts could result in the spread of nuclear weapons around the world. . . . The military custodians of nuclear weapons pose a smaller security risk than the custodians in charge of safe-keeping plutonium and highly enriched uranium (HEU)."[32]

Because the nonweapon sector of the FSU nuclear infrastructure is the most vulnerable to illicit diversion, Western assistance should be concentrated less on securing FSU nuclear weapons and their components than on improving safeguards at MINATOM facilities and stockpiles. The current U.S. policy reverses these priorities and in this respect is misguided.

Russia's Unsafe Strategy of Launch-on-Warning

Like America's operational strategy for strategic nuclear forces, Russia's strategy features rapid reaction. Launch-on-warning has long been the primary retaliation plan for the land-based strategic rocket forces and ballistic missile submarines on pier-side alert.[33] The Soviet command and force structure was all geared to this concept, a posture characterized by Aleksei Arbatov as "the one-sided Soviet strategy which relied exclusively on the launch-on-warning principle."[34]

This rapid reaction strategy falls between two alternative options: preemption and retaliation after ride-out. The former option has played little or no role in strategic nuclear operations during the last decade and a half.[35] The latter option has been technically demanding and practically infeasible because of the acute vulnerability of the Russian nuclear command and control system.[36] One credible recent assessment by a Russian analyst asserts that "at present, none of the command posts of the highest echelons in Russia could reliably survive a nuclear strike and retain the capability to transmit orders for retaliation."[37] The Soviet military has indeed performed classified computer simulations that have produced the worst possible results: decapitation and total paralysis of the Soviet strategic forces. Statistical artifact or not, the prospect of wartime decapitation has deeply concerned Soviet planners.

To compensate for this vulnerability, the Soviets relied on launch-on-warning and, to a lesser extent, on launch-under-attack, using the "dead hand" system discussed later. The Russians continue to depend on these options while striving to shift to a strategy of delayed second strike—that is, a posture that relies more on classical second-strike retaliation by a force structure composed increasingly of mobile ICBMs and SSBNs, especially the former. To this end, the Russians are building a superhard, more survivable underground command post in the southern Urals and plan to equip it with a buried low-frequency to extremely-low-frequency (LF-ELF) antenna (conceptually similar to the ELF Sanguine program abandoned by the United States in favor of a "soft" [vulnerable] ELF Seafarer grid deployed in Wisconsin and Michigan to communicate with deeply submerged U.S. SSBNs) for disseminating launch orders to Russian missile submarines and SS–25 mobile ICBMs. Other command bunkers may be under construction in Siberia and elsewhere.

Until the shift toward a strategy of delayed retaliation is confidently established, which is unlikely to happen anytime soon, if ever, launch-on-warning will remain the predominant option. The Soviets (and Russians) have deployed and thoroughly exercised all the warning and command-control systems necessary to support this rapid reaction plan.[38]

The Hair-Trigger Timeline

After receiving positive attack indications from their infrared satellite and ground-radar early-warning sensors, the Russian counterpart to the U.S.

missile attack warning center at North American Aerospace Defense Command (NORAD) warns the General Staff and strategic rocket force (SRF) headquarters of an imminent enemy missile strike.[39] Within about four to six minutes after liftoff, the top leadership, including the Russian president and defense minister, should be notified of the attack by the General Staff.[40] The General Staff, together with certain senior nuclear commanders, especially the SRF commander in chief, transmits a "preliminary" command that activates the special communications links used to disseminate any subsequent launch orders.[41]

The Russian national command authority (president and defense minister) then deliberates under a strict time limit—no more than about three minutes. Using their famous nuclear suitcases, if they are not already ensconced in the wartime command bunkers, the national decision makers would give (or withhold) permission (a "permission" command) to launch a retaliatory strike to the General Staff and three senior nuclear commanders (the commanders in chief of the SRF, navy, and air force) in the field.[42] This permission must be obtained within about ten minutes after enemy missile liftoff in order to launch-on-warning successfully. Then the General Staff forms and disseminates the launch order replete with unblock codes; this procedure takes about two or three minutes.[43] By this time, about twelve to thirteen minutes have elapsed since enemy missile liftoff.

The General Staff can elect to disseminate launch commands by either of two methods.[44] One method is to pass the unblock and launch codes directly to the individual launch crews, who then carry out the order. For the ICBMs, the General Staff can deliver the launch order to the regimental launch posts in fifteen seconds. The crews require three minutes to receive, verify, and confirm the dispatch and another few minutes to implement it. Russian ICBMs would thus fire out of their silos in under twenty minutes from the time of the initial enemy missile launch.[45]

The second method is to bypass the subordinate command posts and deliver the launch order directly to the launch platforms, for example, the launch equipment in the unmanned silos (e.g., SS–18s) or on the mobile transport erectors (SS–25s). This direct, robotic like launch from the center bypasses the launch crews in the field. From its war room, the General Staff (or the SRF commander in chief in some circumstances) literally can turn the launch keys that signal the unmanned rockets to fire from their silos or truck launchers. The rocket equipment can process the unblock and launch signals and ignite the booster within about five minutes after receiving the command. Using this method, which became operational in 1976, the General Staff can thus trigger a mass retaliatory salvo in less than twenty minutes from the onset of an enemy missile strike.

Both of these launch methods support launch-on-warning. Both timelines beat the arrival of incoming U.S. ICBMs by about ten minutes. Yet the Russians lack confidence in these methods for a host of reasons.[46] The West could beat the timeline using forward-deployed submarine missiles with flight times as short as ten to twelve minutes. The Russian early-warning system has gaping holes in its coverage of SSBN launch areas. Precursor strikes by nuclear bombers or submarines against critical nodes in the Russian command system could escape unnoticed until it was too late. Attack indications from the early-warning network, which has been put in jeopardy of being splintered by the breakup of the Soviet Union, could be absent, ambiguous, or false. Political leaders could hesitate too long before authorizing retaliation. The list goes on.

"Dead Hand" on the Trigger

This state of affairs inspired the development of another method of strategic launch that has been dubbed the "dead hand" by Russians familiar with it. Developed during the 1970s and fully operational about 1985, this last-ditch method of launch dissemination has been described in considerable detail elsewhere.[47] Suffice it to outline the main features.

After detecting nuclear missiles headed in the direction of Moscow or in anticipation of a possible decapitation strike, the Russian leadership could opt to activate a reserve command system designed to ensure massive Russian retaliation if the expected attack actually materializes. This "dead hand" reserve system would be activated by a "fail deadly" message sent by the General Staff from its main war room to a more survivable underground command node outside Moscow (duplicate nodes were built between 1985 and the early 1990s). This message contains a component of the unblocking codes necessary to launch the strategic forces. If after receiving this message the node subsequently experiences a complete break in communications with the General Staff and if sensors ringing the node detect nuclear explosions,[48] the team assembled there will be automatically enabled to form and distribute a complete launch message to the dispersed strategic forces.

This team consists of a small skeleton staff in residence under normal peacetime conditions. If time and circumstances permit, senior officials of government (at the level of deputy defense minister, for example) could relocate there under emergency conditions. Whatever its composition, however, the team lacks the discretionary authority to make the retaliatory decision; that is the point of the three requirements noted above. At the same time, the team must perform certain tasks for the "dead hand" system to work as designed. If they fail to carry out these duties, the system remains dormant.

Once all the technical prerequisites are satisfied, this special node uses a colocated underground low-frequency antenna to radio a launch order with unblock codes. The order is received by command rockets in silos (special SS–17s) or on trucks (special SS–25s, formerly SS–20s) within range of the LF radio signal, or about six hundred miles. The special command rockets then automatically launch (after a short delay) on different trajectories and relay the order from space to the dispersed nuclear-armed strategic forces— bombers, ICBMs, and submarines (the latter via naval shore transmitters such as the Kola ELF station serving the northern fleet SSBN force).[49]

In the case of mobile or silo-based nuclear ICBMs, the signals from the command rockets trigger an automatic launch unless the individual missiles are still connected to their parent regimental launch control centers. If the local links remain intact, the command rocket signals are received by the regimental posts, which then perform the launch procedures. If the links have been severed by enemy strikes, the missiles in the unmanned silos receive the launch order directly from the command rockets and automatically fire after a short delay. If the nuclear-tipped mobile SS–25 missiles with local firing crews have lost contact with higher authority, the missiles receive the launch order directly and automatically fire from their transport erector launchers at presurveyed sites.[50]

The rationale for this "dead hand" system is evident. It backs up the two main methods of launch discussed earlier, in which the national command authorities and General Staff attempt to authorize retaliation and disseminate the order before incoming enemy missiles wreak havoc on the command system. A backup arrangement was deemed necessary because the main methods might not work under a wide range of plausible adverse conditions. The idea was to transfer the executive function to more survivable elements of the command system in anticipation of a decapitation strike so that fairly prompt retaliation could be ensured even if the top leadership perished before it could personally order retaliation using the two main methods. Under this scheme, retaliation would take a few minutes longer than launch-on-warning.

The principle of the "dead hand" would thus imply that the General Staff would activate it at the critical moment in the launch-on-warning cycle. Recalling the earlier timeline, the critical moment occurs between six and ten minutes after enemy missile liftoff. If by ten minutes after enemy liftoff the top leaders still do not have a clear enough picture of the attack, or if the civilian leadership fails for any reason to give timely authorization to retaliate, the General Staff can resort to the "dead hand" system to ensure quasi-automatic retaliation in the event of their own annihilation. Approval to activate could be obtained from the president before any final decision on retaliation has been rendered and before any damage has been sustained from enemy submarine missiles. Approval might be given earlier in a nuclear crisis if Russia suffers a degradation of its early-warning or command system performance due to conventional hostilities or other strains. In any case, presidential approval is not technically essential; the General Staff evidently could activate the "dead hand" on its own accord.

Launch-on-Warning, "Dead Hand," and Safety

The Russian strategic posture is clearly geared to rapid retaliation in response to positive attack indications from early-warning networks and nuclear explosion sensors. It is impossible to precisely gauge the adverse effects on nuclear weapon safety, but the crisis preparations undertaken to ensure prompt retaliation surely increase the risk of inadvertent or unauthorized launch. In broad outline, the two main methods of nuclear release appear to run a greater risk than the backup "dead hand" method, because the former impels decision makers to make the fateful decision in a few minutes on the basis of sensor reports of imminent attack. Given the many imperfections of warning systems and other strains on the decision process, launch-on-warning is not an option that meets high standards of nuclear weapon safety.

It would be more prudent for the Russians to withhold a launch decision and activate the "dead hand" in response to tactical warning. The "dead hand" at least imposes a set of objective conditions—especially, nuclear detonations—that supposedly must be satisfied before launch authorization is disseminated. Its design and functioning remain too obscure, however, to evaluate its safety and reliability (indeed, some skeptics doubt its very existence).[51]

But all these arrangements sustain alert practices and emergency procedures that emphasize deterrence over safety. If these priorities were reversed, none of these arrangements would survive evaluation. The operational posture would have to undergo fundamental change to eliminate its dependence on strategic and tactical warning and replace prompt retaliation with delayed retaliation at its core. Strategic forces would be dealerted and the "hair trigger" removed from the nuclear command system.

A symbolic step in this direction has been taken. In the afterglow of the Vancouver summit between Presidents Bill Clinton and Boris Yeltsin in early 1993, the White House announced that the United States had begun "a comprehensive review of measures that could enhance strategic stability, including the possibility of each side reprogramming its nuclear missiles so they are not routinely aimed at each other."[52] By late 1993, the Defense Department and strategic command had closely examined the idea of detargeting and prepared an option called "broad ocean area" targeting for consideration by President Clinton.[53] An agreement was struck at the Clinton–Yeltsin summit in January 1994 to implement such a scheme by 30 May 1994.

Both sides thus aimed their missiles away from their wartime targets and pointed them at the oceans. This agreement applies only to those strategic missiles that must have target data in their computer memory to maintain launch readiness: Minuteman III and older classes of Russian ICBMs. The MX Peacekeeper missiles (and U.S. SLBMs, as well as some of the newest classes of Russian ICBMs) do not normally hold target data even when they maintain a high level of launch readiness, and hence this scheme does not apply to them. In any case, the United States, and doubtless Russia, too, has the ability to restore the wartime targets in seconds, and both continue to rely on postures of rapid reaction that pose very demanding problems of safety for the nuclear command and control systems.[54]

Conclusion

An assessment of the various risks examined above must take into account both their probabilities and consequences. An integrative judgment that combines these components is intrinsically difficult, but certain tentative conclusions emerge from the exercise. The events of lowest probability are the unauthorized use of nuclear weapons by rogue field commanders and the seizure of operational control of nuclear weapons by Ukraine. The events of highest probability are nuclear smuggling, particularly the illicit diversion of material from the civilian sector under MINATOM control, and the sudden breakdown of nuclear control at the top levels of command in Moscow. The event of intermediate probability is the inadvertent launch of nuclear missiles on hair-trigger alert during a crisis, the risk of which varies according to the state of nuclear tensions between Russia and its potential nuclear adversaries, particularly the United States.

Combining the potential consequences of these events with their probabilities leaves little doubt that political upheaval in Moscow poses the gravest overall danger. As argued in an earlier analysis, the multitude of nuclear control problems in the FSU "are overshadowed by a weakness inherent in any nuclear command system but one of particular concern in the Russian system at this juncture: the potential unreliability of the apex of nuclear command. No command and control system can stand apart from the foibles and mischief of persons who hold, or seize, the top positions of leadership. The system reflects their virtues or lack thereof; and its effectiveness depends on their legitimacy, loyalty, and competence. These are the guardians of the nuclear arsenal. The malevolence, corruption, or greed of a few of them could sweep aside a regime of safeguards."[55]

This theme and its variations underlie the current U.S. nuclear policy and its goal of "hedging" against the seizure of power by reactionary leaders who would set off a new cycle of nuclear confrontation with the West. The United States nonetheless has not pushed for changes in the arena of nuclear operations that offer the greatest relief from all the problems of control that afflict the Russian system.

Taking all nuclear weapons off alert so that none remain poised for immediate launch—"zero alert"—is the single most promising remedy for the entire range of existing and prospective dangers. A reciprocal agreement among the nuclear weapon states to adopt "zero alert" for all nuclear forces would provide the best hedge against a breakdown of nuclear control in all its forms.[56]

Notes

1. As of February 1994, the network of the former Soviet Union continued to operate as an intact system with functional radar sensors in Latvia (Skrunda), Ukraine (Mukachevo and Sevastopol), and Azerbaijan (Lyaki), as well as Russia. Plans to modernize the Skrunda radar have been canceled, however.

2. The headquarters of the strategic rocket forces at Perkhushkovo can also assume custodial responsibility for the unlock codes (and launch authorization codes) needed by all three legs of the Russian strategic forces. This headquarters, near Moscow, is not normally assigned this role, although provisions were made for this just after the 1991 coup attempt. Because the General Staff, including its chief, was implicated in the coup, the SRF headquarters became the primary executive agent for strategic attack operations, and the General Staff headquarters was assigned a reserve role. The primary and reserve statuses of their communications nets were switched accordingly. The SRF commander in chief was given the requisite codes. He also was given a nuclear suitcase used for disseminating launch authorization to senior nuclear commanders (a procedure separate from the dissemination of unlock and launch authorization codes to the individual weapons commanders). Those responsibilities were again reversed within a year, and the General Staff reassumed custody of the unlock and launch codes and other paraphernalia.

3. Current patrol rates are very low because of material and maintenance shortages. The Russians keep only one or two SSBNs at sea on combat patrol at any time, compared to about ten boats on alert at sea just a few years ago. However, the Russians keep additional SSBNs on launch-ready alert in port. Their SSBNs were designed to allow for quick surface-launch from pier-side (routinely exercised under launch-on-warning time constraints), and historically SSBN crews spent more alert time in port than at sea. This alert practice obviously reduces crew autonomy and strengthens safeguards.

4. According to Russian sources, a captured cruise missile armed with its nuclear payload could be readily launched from a variety of planes and would produce a nuclear detonation.

5. These troops belong to the Twelfth Main Directorate of the Defense Ministry and operate under the direction of the General Staff. The arrangement is very similar to the separate custodial chain of command in Europe, in which the Fifty-ninth Ordnance Brigade managed U.S. army tactical nuclear weapons in the theater.

6. Unbeknownst to the West at the time, the Soviet Union raised its nuclear alert level many times during the Cold War, including in 1960, in 1962 (the Cuban missile crisis), in 1968 (the Czech crisis and the Soviet invasion), and in 1973 (the Arab-Israeli war). On some of these occasions, Soviet long-range bombers were alerted along with the strategic rocket forces. See Bruce G. Blair, *The Logic of Accidental Nuclear War* (Washington, DC: Brookings, 1993). Bruce Menning of the U.S. Army Command and General Staff College recently unearthed another alert episode from the General Staff archives in Moscow. During the Berlin crisis in 1961, the Soviets raised the nuclear alert level for the SRF, Long-Range Bomber Forces, Air Defense Forces, and fighter aviation assets of the military districts and groups of forces. This alert ran from 13 October to 8 November 1961. See Bruce W. Menning, "The Berlin Crisis from the Perspective of the Soviet General Staff" (unpublished manuscript).

7. This paragraph draws heavily on the comments of David Holloway in "One Year After the Collapse of the USSR: A Panel of Specialists," *Post-Soviet Affairs*, vol. 8 (October–December 1992), pp. 318–22. See also Mikhail Tsypkin, "Will the Military Rule Russia?" *Security Studies*, vol. 2 (Autumn 1992); John W.R. Lepingwell, "Soviet Civil-Military Relations and the August Coup," *World Politics*, vol. 44, no. 4 (July 1992); and Stephen M. Meyer, "How the Threat (and the Coup) Collapsed: The Politicization of the Soviet Military," *International Security*, vol. 16, no. 3 (winter 1991/92).

8. Marcus Warren, "Russia Risks Mutiny Over Defense Cuts, Says Minister," *London Daily Telegraph*, 11 March 1994, p. 18.

9. The suitcases are little more than high-tech versions of the presidential identification codes carried by the U.S. national command authorities and certain successors. These U.S. codes are not the ones used in launch messages to enable and authorize nuclear strikes by U.S. forces. However, the permission command issued by the Russian suitcases may be organizationally and even technically essential, under certain circumstances, for subsequent dissemination of launch authorization and enabling codes by the General Staff. But there is little doubt that the General Staff could work around the established safeguards under a range of conditions and trigger the launch of strategic forces on their own accord.

10. The SRF commander in chief, for example, could send either a zero flight command restoring the blocking function or a cancel launch command terminating the launch authorization on the heels of a General Staff order to fire. However, the ability to completely stymie the General Staff would depend on extraordinary effort by the SRF to sever communications links and disable equipment, an effort that would take many days to complete.

11. A rare exception on the U.S. side concerns an episode during the last year of President Nixon's tenure. At the time there was widespread suspicion—unfounded suspicion—that the global nuclear alert declared during the 1973 Arab-Israeli war was meant as much to distract public attention from Watergate as to deter Soviet military intervention in Egypt. A related anecdote, proffered for illustrative purposes only, has it that Nixon's despair over his impending impeachment drove Defense Secretary James

Schlesinger to instruct the Pentagon to contact him before carrying out any unusual orders from the president.

12. According to a Russian military officer familiar with the situation, Defense Minister Grachev seriously considered cutting the communications links between Moscow and the blocking devices on Ukrainian strategic missiles to force Ukraine to bear responsibility for safety and answer to the international community. Advisors dissuaded him from taking this extreme step. Interview by author.

13. Robert Seely, "Perry Visits Ukraine's Deadliest Missile Sites," *Washington Post,* 23 March 1994, p. A24; and William Perry, "Gambling on Ex-Soviet States," interview, *USA Today,* 15 March 1994, p. 9. The transfer of 360 warheads was accurate as of 4 October 1994; interview by author of U.S. government official.

14. A Russian expert in this particular technology estimates that Ukraine would need at most one or two months to install the devices and upload the software.

15. A capability may also exist for removing this vital data by remote command from the local launch center or higher command posts; the United States can perform this function with an "overwrite" computer command sent by local launch centers in the ICBM fields. At any rate, the process of deactivating missiles and off-loading warheads is probably further along than commonly believed. Russia has apparently taken all Ukrainian strategic forces out of the Russian war plan, reason enough to have dealerted all of the missile forces. Any efforts at maintaining them probably are devoted largely to ensuring a controlled and safe deactivation, rather than keeping them combat ready.

16. The conventional balance is lopsided in favor of Russia for five reasons. First, Ukraine's army is malpositioned under CFE flank limits. Only a small fraction of its Treaty-Limited Equipment of tanks, armored combat vehicles, and artillery can be forward deployed to defend its borders and the Crimea against Russian aggression. Obviously, from Ukraine's vantage point, forward deployed today means the opposite of what it meant when the treaty was negotiated. Although the flank limits also constrain Russia's ability to threaten Ukraine, the net effect is adverse to Ukraine. Since 1991, Russia has built up a force of fifteen ground divisions and thirteen brigades along its previously undefended western borders running from the north through Moscow to the North Caucasus military districts.

Second, the state of operations and maintenance of forces in Ukraine is miserable. This is most evident in the Ukrainian air force, which simply does not fly for want of spare parts. The planes are underserviced and the pilots are rusty. Although former Defense Minister Morozov deserves credit for organizing the remnants of the Soviet forces into a coherent and independent force, its combat readiness must be rated very low. Russian combat readiness has of course also declined very sharply, but it is still probably an order of magnitude better than Ukraine's.

Third, Ukraine depends heavily on its potential adversary Russia for critical materials like oil and gas for its military, and Ukraine's strategic reserves of these materials appear to be nonexistent. It doubtless has plenty of ammunition, but its logistics train for supporting the deployment of forces in wartime has to be extremely short.

Fourth, the large fraction of ethnic Russian officers in the Ukrainian military raises the question of motivation and morale in the event of conflict with Russia. Despite a concerted effort to indoctrinate and convert this corps, its loyalty to Kiev has to be questioned. We hear a great deal about Russian officers in the strategic rocket forces switching allegiance to Ukraine, but this has been greatly exaggerated. The loyalty problem is just the opposite from the one advertised, and one suspects that deep-seated resistance to fighting Russia under Ukrainian command permeates the regular army officer corps as much as the SRF.

Fifth and last, Ukraine's economy cannot sustain an effective military. The economy's downward spiral bodes ill for building up and modernizing the army over the next decade.

On the other side of the ledger is Ukraine's huge inventory of weapons inherited from the Soviet Union (for instance, it received about one-third of the tanks compared to Russia's one-half as a result of the CFE split), the large size of its army (about half a million strong), the tremendous decline in Russian military strength, and the intrinsic advantage of a defensive versus offensive strategy. But the net balance still strongly favors Russia. These assessments are tricky, but most likely Russia could successfully grab the eastern portion of the country, including the Crimea. Ukraine might well be able to mount a successful defense of the western portion, given the current weakness of Russia's military.

17. The United States, Russia, France, and Great Britain are giving both positive and negative security assurances to Ukraine. The "positive" assurance pledges that they will go to the United Nations Security Council on behalf of Ukraine if the latter is threatened or attacked by a nuclear-armed state. The "negative" assurance pledges that none of them will use or threaten to use nuclear weapons against Ukraine as long as the latter remains a non-nuclear party to the NPT and refrains from allying itself with a nuclear state threatening action against the state offering the assurance. Furthermore, President Kuchma announced that Ukraine had received official confirmation from the United States, Russia, and Great Britain that they would "respect Ukraine's independence, sovereignty, and integrity within its existing borders."

18. Doug Clarke and Ustina Markus, "Ukraine Accedes to NPT," *RFE/RL Daily Report,* 17 November 1994.

19. An element of that plan would anticipate the potential diversion of some bomber payloads and try to head it off by providing technical assistance and economic incentives soon to consolidate the entire inventory at a central depot and place it under joint U.S.-Russian-Ukrainian monitoring.

20. R. Jeffrey Smith, "Officials See Shift in Ukraine's Nuclear Position," *Washington Post,* 19 December 1992, p. 10.

21. Blair, *Logic of Accidental Nuclear War,* p. 261.

22. This figure was given to the author by a Soviet military officer in 1992. According to this source, the inventory peaked at fifty-five thousand in about 1985. See Blair, *Logic of Accidental Nuclear War,* pp. 106, 306, 315.

23. Press Conference with Secretary of Defense William J. Perry, 22 September 1994.

24. National Academy of Sciences, Committee on International Security and Arms Control, *Management and Disposition of Excess Weapons Plutonium* (Washington, DC: National Academy Press, 1994).

25. A good overview and reasoned perspective on this spate of incidents is Spurgeon M. Keeny Jr., "Nuclear Smugglers Spark Worries Over Russian Safeguards," *Arms Control Today,* vol. 24, no. 7 (September 1994). Detailed press reports include William J. Broad, "Russians Suspect 3 Sites as Source of Seized A-Fuel," *New York Times,* 19 August 1994, p. A11; Lee Hockstader, "Russia Announces Probe Into Origins of Nuclear Material," *Washington Post,* 19 August 1994, p. A32; Daniel Williams and John F. Harris, "U.S. Uncertain About Origin of Seized Nuclear Material," *Washington Post,* 18 August 1994, p. A28; Steve Coll, "Stolen Plutonium Tied to Arms Labs," *Washington Post,* 17 August 1994, p. A1; William J. Broad, "Experts in U.S. Call Plutonium Not Arms-Level," *New York Times,* 17 August 1994, p. A1; idem, "Germans Suspect Russian Military in Plutonium Sale," *New York Times,* 16 August 1994, p. A1; Craig R. Whitney, "Germans Seize 3d Atom Sample, Smuggled by Plane From Russia," *New*

York Times, 14 August 1994, p. A1; and idem, "A Second 'Sample' of Atomic Material Found in Germany," *New York Times*, 12 August 1994, p. A1.

26. William C. Potter, while judging the danger of illicit exports of weapons-grade material from the former Soviet Union to be "great," conceded in early 1993 that "To date, there is no solid evidence of the illicit export of any nuclear weapons, nuclear weapon components or militarily significant quantities of weapons-grade material." William C. Potter, "Nuclear Exports from the Former Soviet Union: What's New, What's True," *Arms Control Today*, vol. 23, no. 1 (January–February 1993), p. 3. The director of the CIA testified in February 1993 that although Russia's ability to maintain control of its nuclear weapons and technologies had been "somewhat weakened," "So far, we have detected no transfers of weapons-grade material in significant quantities. We have no credible reporting that nuclear weapons have left CIS territory, and we do not believe that nuclear weapon design information has been sold or transferred to foreign states." James Woolsey, testimony before the U.S. Senate Governmental Affairs Committee, 24 February 1993. More recently, an official of the U.S. Defense Intelligence Agency reiterated Woolsey's assessment: "We have no convincing evidence that any weapon-grade nuclear materials have been sold or transferred to third parties." This official further noted that "While many scientists have emigrated, very few, if any, have detailed knowledge of nuclear weapons designs." Citing Russian estimates that only two thousand to three thousand scientists possess such knowledge, the official asserted that these scientists are located in a few institutes, where they remain closely monitored by Russian authorities. William Grundmann, Statement for the Record to the Joint Economic Committee of Congress, 15 July 1994. Last, a U.S. intelligence official privately reported in late October 1994 that all evidence as of then indicated that no nuclear material produced for former Soviet weapons, or taken from such weapons, had leaked out of the former Soviet Union. Private conversation with author.

27. This discussion draws heavily on Mark Hibbs, "Plutonium, Politics, and Panic," *Bulletin of the Atomic Scientists*, vol. 50, no. 6 (November–December 1994), pp. 24–31.

28. Ibid., p. 31.

29. Michael R. Gordon, "Big Cache of Nuclear Bomb Fuel Found in an Ex-Soviet Republic," *New York Times*, 23 November 1994, p. A1; Stephen Erlanger, "Kazakhstan Thanks U.S. on Uranium," *New York Times*, 25 November 1994, p. A10; and Bill Gertz, "U.S. Defuses Effort by Iran to Get Nukes," *Washington Times*, 24 November 1994, p. 1.

30. I thank Joshua Handler for information on the Murmansk robbery.

31. Louis J. Freeh, speech at the Ministry of Internal Affairs Academy, Moscow, 4 July 1994. This ministry, referred to as the MVD, had major custodial responsibilities for nuclear weapons during the early years of the Soviet nuclear program.

32. Blair, *Logic of Accidental Nuclear War*, pp. 259–60.

33. Ibid., especially pp. 202–16; and Alexei Arbatov, ed., *Implications of the START II Treaty for U.S.-Russian Relations*, report no. 9 (Stimson Center, October 1993), pp. 65–67.

34. Arbatov, *Implications of the START II Treaty*, p. 66.

35. The totality of evidence since the late 1970s—heavy Soviet investment in launch-on-warning and "dead hand" schemes, heavy Soviet emphasis on launch-on-warning in strategic exercises and training—strongly indicates a Soviet preoccupation, if not obsession, with scenarios in which the West initiates a strategic nuclear attack. The dominant, perhaps exclusive focus of Soviet strategic doctrine and operations throughout the 1980s and 1990s was to achieve the capability to retaliate in the event of a

U.S.-Western first strike. Russian sources, including all former SRF and SSBN officers interviewed by Blair, considered Soviet strategic nuclear preemption an obsolete (though still technically available) option by the late 1970s, and all emphasized the central role of launch-on-warning in Soviet strategic planning during the 1980s and 1990s.

Many U.S. government analysts contest this interpretation of the evidence on several grounds. First, although the analysts appear willing to concede that the Soviets emphasized retaliatory operations (launch-on-warning and classical second strike) in strategic exercises during the 1980s, they almost invariably argue that retaliation is a far more demanding option than preemption, that retaliation thus requires far more training and exercise than preemption, and that this emphasis in the operational arena does not reflect underlying predilections and preferences in the actual strategic command system. But this view is not accurate; preemption is in many respects more difficult than dumb retaliation. It requires extraordinary coordination and smooth execution under conditions of extreme secrecy (launch orders usually must be encrypted to preserve secrecy in this situation, whereas retaliatory orders can be disseminated in plain language, for instance). One of the U.S. analysts' favorite scenarios of Soviet preemption features an orchestrated attack by SSBNs from both fleets (northern and Pacific) and ICBMs that produces a precisely timed sequence of high-altitude electromagnetic pulses (approximately twenty-four HEMP bursts spaced ninety seconds apart) over the continental United States (CONUS) starting in the center of CONUS and working outward. This extraordinary feat of command and control is way beyond the capability of the Soviet (and Russian) system, however. And it is more demanding than simply disseminating orders to retaliate. If the Soviets did not practice these feats under realistic exercise conditions, which they did not, then they simply could not have had confidence in such hypothetical preemptive options.

Second, U.S. analysts have identified a class of strategic exercises that many of them claim features a preemptive option. In these cases (one of which is described by Blair, *Logic of Accidental Nuclear War*, pp. 128–30), a strategic exchange begins with an SLBM launch at a time designated in advance (see Blair, *Logic of Accidental Nuclear War*, index entry "launch at designated time"). The SSBN receives the launch order several hours prior to launch time. Shortly after this launch, Soviet ICBMs fire en masse, followed by additional SLBM and other force strikes, creating the impression of a coordinated Soviet preemptive strike led off by a precursor SLBM strike. The most recent exercise in this class occurred around the spring of 1993. An SSBN in the Pacific fired an SLBM at a designated time and set off a chain of events that culminated in the real or simulated launch of SLBMs deployed in the northern fleet as part of a strategic exchange with the United States. U.S. government analysts again are portraying this exercise as featuring preemption.

But this interpretation is easily refuted. A superior alternative explanation (see Blair, *Logic of Accidental Nuclear War*, p. 347 n. 85) is that the initial SLBM launch represented the leading edge of a Western first strike; the SSBN was playing "blue" not "red" in the exercise. This becomes clear because the initial SLBM launch triggers events and timelines that clearly represent a process of Soviet (now Russian) retaliation. The initial launch activates the Russian early-warning network, which feeds information to the top-level commanders, who conduct deliberations and authorize a nuclear response, which is disseminated down the chain of command and then carried out by the weapons commanders. Such procedures are undoubtedly associated with retaliation, not preemption. In a preemptive strike, the decisions affecting the SSBNs, the SRF, and others would have been rendered and disseminated earlier and simultaneously. It is unreasonable to suppose that the Russians would launch a preemptive SSBN strike and only then (after break-water) would they reach and disseminate authorization to fire the ICBMs. The spring 1993 exercise of the northern fleet SSBN force was surely a test of its ability to receive and carry out retaliatory orders in the face of a U.S. first strike paced by a U.S. SSBN strike launched from the Pacific Ocean.

Third, many U.S. government analysts would contest this assessment of the negligible role of preemption in Russian strategic planning because of sensitivity to the implication that they have exaggerated the importance of Soviet preemption and in doing so grievously distorted the debate over the Strategic Defense Initiative and strategic force modernization. U.S. offensive and defensive programs like SDI rested squarely on the premise of a coordinated Soviet first strike. Unfortunately, during the professional and public debate over the programs, the intelligence community did not weigh in with its abundant evidence that the Soviet nuclear planning system was almost totally preoccupied with scenarios in which the West strikes first. The intelligence community in effect repressed a competing view of Soviet strategic motivations and activities and as a result of this bias the United States pursued what could be considered a dangerously misguided nuclear policy.

36. Blair, *Logic of Accidental Nuclear War*, especially chap. 5.

37. Arbatov, *Implications of the START II Treaty*, p. 66.

38. Blair, *Logic of Accidental Nuclear War*, especially chap. 6.

39. The early-warning satellites are focused on U.S. and Chinese ICBM fields and could detect a missile launch in about one minute after liftoff. The data are downlinked at site E21 near the Moscow beltway (E-ring) and automatically forwarded via cable links to the Russian NORAD equivalent (the Center for Analysis of Missile and Space Situation) at Veniukovskii inside the beltway. Over-the-horizon ground radar can detect and report to the Veniukovskii center a mass ICBM liftoff almost as rapidly. The Veniukovskii center then forms a missile attack warning message and sends it over cable links to the General Staff main war room in Moscow and the SRF main war room near Perkhushkovo, as well as to designated alternate wartime command posts.

40. At this time, the political leadership of Ukraine, Belarus, and Kazakhstan are also supposed to be tied into the emergency decision-making conference over a special telephone communications system (called KAVKAZ, which is part of the KAZBEK network) installed for this purpose.

41. The preliminary command also initiates a host of precautionary alert steps—for instance, bombers take off, submarines hide in depth, mobile ICBMs in transit scurry to the nearest presurveyed or other launch sites, and units adopt cover and concealment practices. The actual steps taken depend on the prior readiness of the forces, which in turn depends on prior alert declarations. Four alert levels for Soviet (and Russian) strategic forces exist: constant, increased, military threat, and full. The normal peacetime level is constant. For the ICBMs in silos, this puts them only a few minutes from full alert status, at which point their launch reaction time would be 1.5 minutes. For mobile ICBMs, constant alert means that about 20 percent are deployed in the field (one regiment out of a given division) and the remainder are in garrison. At increased alert (the level usually declared during past crises), the bombers would be loaded with nuclear weapons and the mobile ICBMs in garrison would be primed for launch-on-warning. If military threat is declared, the mobile ICBMs leave their shelters and travel to preset hide or launch sites. At full alert, the mobile ICBMs achieve a launch reaction time of 2.5 minutes.

42. The nuclear suitcase is called CHEGET, which is part of the KAZBEK network.

43. The formation and dissemination of this launch order normally requires the active participation of the commander in chief of the nuclear forces to be launched. To

launch ICBMs, for example, the General Staff sends the launch code to the SRF commander in chief, who processes it electronically and then transmits it back to a node of the General Staff, where the two inputs are combined, encrypted, and disseminated over the Basic Automated Command System (BACSAN), another integral element of the KAZBEK network. If the SRF headquarters is destroyed beforehand, the General Staff working alone can send the codes that trigger launch. The BACSAN is tied into large computer centers that modify attack plans and if necessary compute new flight trajectories for missiles. BACSAN employs primary and reserve communications using cable, radio, satellites, troposcatter, and other links, and it automatically switches from damaged to reserve channels in seconds. All channels are encrypted. In addition, BACSAN is integrated with a backup system known as the duplicating radio command system (DRCS). This system consists of one-way radio channels linking the nuclear commanders in chief to the ICBM regiments, the bombers, and submarines. It uses primarily satellites, high-frequency radio, and very low-frequency to extremely-low-frequency radio stations. A common center manages the many transmitters to choose the optimum frequency for the conditions in various regions and to ensure that the different frequencies work synchronously.

44. Both methods use BACSAN, which employs terminals placed on all strategic command posts as well as all launch platforms—bombers, submarines, and ICBMs in silos or on mobile transport erector launchers.

45. These estimates come from Russian experts. The West has monitored Soviet strategic exercises in which Soviet ICBMs lifted off twenty-one minutes after the simulated onset of Western missile attack. In the event of an enemy strike that hits the Russian missile fields and disrupts local launch procedures before Russian missiles can be fired, provisions have been made to switch to backup launch centers and communications channels.

46. See Blair, *Logic of Accidental Nuclear War*, for a longer discussion of this issue.

47. Bruce G. Blair, "Russia's Doomsday Machine," *New York Times*, 8 October 1993, p. A35; and William J. Broad, "Russia Has Computerized Nuclear 'Doomsday' Machine, U.S. Expert Says," *New York Times*, 8 October 1993, p. A6.

48. The communications outage must persist for a certain period of time, and the sensors detect nuclear detonations using visual, seismic, radiation, and overpressure instruments.

49. The SS–25 and SS–17 command rockets transmit for about twenty and fifteen minutes, respectively, over ultra-high-frequency channels to all the regions of strategic force deployment in the former Soviet Union. The range constraint of UHF is limited only by line of sight.

50. After receiving the command rocket signal, the TELs automatically level themselves and raise and fire the missile.

51. In addition to Blair's original sources, several (at least four) knowledgeable Russian sources (formerly, if not in some cases currently, highly placed) have in the recent past provided pertinent information that bolsters Blair's contention that the Soviets developed and deployed a "dead hand" system to ensure nuclear retaliation.

It seems that the U.S. intelligence community's latest position is that the "dead hand" was developed but perhaps never deployed operationally (except for the command rockets). Considering its original skepticism, which basically dismissed the whole story, and considering its lack of knowledge about the command rocket system (it did not know that these rockets could directly fire the fixed and mobile ICBMs without any assistance from launch crews in the missile fields), the intelligence community bears the burden of proof that the "dead hand" never became operational.

52. "Statement by the President on Advancing U.S. Relations with Russia and the

Other New Independent States" (Office of the Press Secretary, the White House, 23 April 1993), p. 1.

53. Michael R. Gordon with Eric Schmitt, "U.S. Is Considering Aiming Its Missiles Away From Russia," *New York Times*, 6 December 1993, p. A1.

54. For a technical explanation of the capabilities for retargeting missiles against wartime targets in seconds, see Bruce G. Blair, "Global Zero Alert for Nuclear Forces" (Washington, DC: Brookings, forthcoming). Basically, the launch crews enter a single number into the launch control computer prior to launch, instructing missiles to change their trajectories in flight so that their warheads land on wartime targets instead of nominal ocean targets.

55. Blair, *Logic of Accidental Nuclear War*, p. 260.

56. For a detailed analysis of this proposal, see Blair, "Global Zero Alert for Nuclear Forces."

Russia's Nuclear Weapon Infrastructure

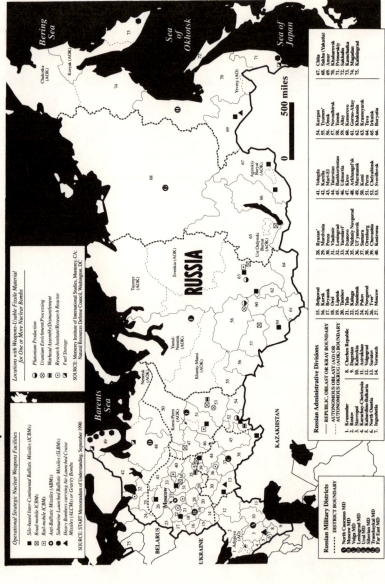

Operational Strategic Nuclear Weapons Facilities

- ■ Silo-based Inter-Continental Ballistic Missiles (ICBMs)
- ▣ Road-mobile ICBMs
- ◈ Rail-mobile ICBMs
- ◐ Anti-Ballistic Missiles (ABMs)
- ● Submarine Launched Ballistic Missiles (SLBMs)
- ▲ Heavy Bombers carrying Air-Launched Cruise Missiles (ALCMs) or Gravity Bombs

SOURCE: START Memorandum of Understanding, September 1990.

Locations with Weapons-Usable Fissile Material for One or More Nuclear Bombs

- ◖ Plutonium Production
- ⊗ Uranium Enrichment/Processing
- ■ Warhead Assembly/Dismantlement
- ◉ Research Institute/Research Reactor
- ● Fuel Storage

SOURCE: Monterey Institute of International Studies, Monterey, CA; Natural Resources Defense Council, Washington, DC

Russian Administrative Divisions

— REPUBLIC, OBLAST OR KRAY BOUNDARY
···· AUTONOMOUS OBLAST (AO) OR AUTONOMOUS OKRUG (AOK) BOUNDARY

1. Krasnodar
2. Rostov
3. Stavropol'
4. Karachay-Cherkessia
5. Kabardino-Balkaria
6. North Ossetia
7. Ingushetia
8. Chechen Republic
9. Dagestan
10. Kalmykia
11. Astrakhan
12. Volgograd
13. Saratov
14. Voronezh
15. Belgorod
16. Kursk
17. Bryansk
18. Orel
19. Lipetsk
20. Tambov
21. Tula
22. Kaluga
23. Smolensk
24. Pskov
25. Novgorod
26. Tver'
27. Moscow
28. Ryazan'
29. Mordvinia
30. Penza
31. Vladimir
32. Leningrad
33. Yaroslavl'
34. Ivanovo
35. Nizhniy Novgorod
36. Ul'yanovsk
37. Kirov
38. Samara
39. Chuvashia
40. Kostroma
41. Vologda
42. Karelia
43. Mari-El
44. Tatarstan
45. Bashkortostan
46. Udmurtia
47. Kirov
48. Arkhangel'sk
49. Murmansk
50. Komi
51. Perm
52. Chelyabinsk
53. Sverdlovsk
54. Kurgan
55. Tyumen'
56. Omsk
57. Novosibirsk
58. Tomsk
59. Altay
60. Kemerovo
61. Gorno-Altay
62. Khakasia
63. Krasnoyarsk
64. Tuva
65. Irkutsk
66. Buryatia
67. Chita
68. Sakha (Yakutia)
69. Amur
70. Khabarovsk
71. Primorskiy
72. Sakhalin
73. Kamchatka
74. Magadan
75. Kaliningrad

Russian Military Districts

···· DISTRICT BOUNDARY

- ❶ North Caucasus MD
- ❷ Moscow MD
- ❸ Volga MD
- ❹ Leningrad MD
- ❺ Ural MD
- ❻ Siberian MD
- ❼ Transbaykal MD
- ❽ Far East MD

Source: Carnegie Endowment for International Peace and the Monterey Institute for International Studies.

5

Russia and Nuclear Weapons

Steven E. Miller

Russia inherited the Soviet Union's status as a recognized nuclear weapon state under the Nuclear Nonproliferation Treaty (NPT). It inherited as well the lion's share of Soviet nuclear assets, including nuclear weapons and delivery systems, nuclear weapon production facilities, command and control arrangements, and the organizational infrastructure for nuclear custodianship. Alone among the Soviet successor states, Russia possesses a full and coherent nuclear capability: it can produce, deploy, maintain, and modernize a substantial nuclear arsenal; and it can, therefore, attempt with some confidence to gain the benefits of nuclear deterrence.[1]

No doubt the legacy of Soviet nuclear policy, doctrine, and practice will also cast a shadow on Russian efforts to fashion its own nuclear policy,[2] but the Soviet doctrinal inheritance will not suffice to provide all the answers for Russia's nuclear policy. Russia is a new state, with different borders, distinctive problems and constraints, and different security challenges. It inhabits a new world in which the familiar structuring features of the Cold War are almost entirely absent and patterns of alignment and diplomatic interaction are dramatically different. Hence, despite the inevitable influence of the Soviet nuclear past, Russia will have to craft its own nuclear policies, responsive to its own needs and circumstances. While it is premature to assume that durable nuclear policies have emerged, the effort to create a Russian approach to nuclear weapons is clearly under way. In what follows, I will sketch the main features of Russian nuclear policy that seem to have appeared so far.

Several characteristics of the new international landscape might suggest that it is possible for Russia to consider diminishing the role of nuclear weapons in its security policy. In the first place, its relationship with the United States has been transformed. Even if the bright hopes of early 1992 for "strategic partnership" have proven overly ambitious, Moscow's relaions with the United States are no longer deeply and inherently adversarial. Indeed, substantial levels of comity and cooperation have been evident in U.S.-Russian relations,[3] and Russia's struggle for political and economic reform proceeds with American sympathy and support. Accordingly, in stark contrast to the Cold War, with its clearly drawn lines of antagonism, even the military doctrine document promulgated in November 1993 states that the new Russia "regards no state as its enemy."[4] Thus, one of the primary motivating forces behind the Soviet Union's intense strategic nuclear rivalry with the United States is absent in the Russian case.

Second, Russian estimation of the likelihood of war is quite low—again in contrast to the Cold War, when (at least in certain periods) the possibility of war was taken quite seriously. As the military doctrine document puts it, "the immediate threat of direct aggression being launched against the Russian Federation has considerably declined."[5] The prospect of large-scale nuclear war is regarded as even more remote. For example, the chief of Russia's 12th Main Directorate, Colonel General Maslin, has stated, "A world nuclear war, it has to be thought, is unlikely."[6] Hence, not only does the primary adversary no longer exist, but the primary nuclear contingency for which the Soviet Union prepared has faded as well.

Third, the Russian nuclear arsenal is going to shrink substantially. In START I and particularly START II, Russia has committed to reduce its strategic nuclear forces to a level roughly one-third to one-fourth of its Cold War peak (as well as to reconfigure its arsenal with less emphasis on ICBMs). Even if these agreements never enter force or are never implemented, Russia's nuclear capabilities will contract due to financial constraints. Moscow simply cannot afford to maintain and modernize the large force it inherited from the Soviet Union.[7]

In short, Russian attitudes and policies toward nuclear weapons are developing in a vastly different context than that which shaped Soviet nuclear attitudes and policies, and Russia will face the future with a nuclear arsenal that is much smaller, and differently structured, than that possessed by the USSR. These considerations notwithstanding, indications are that nuclear weapons will play a prominent role in Russia's security policy for the foreseeable future—arguably more prominent than in the Soviet period. This is true for both political and military reasons.

Nuclear Weapons and Russia's International Status

Russia's nuclear capability is thought to serve at least two significant political purposes for Moscow. First, it buttresses Moscow's claim to great power status. Having lost both its external and internal empires, experienced protracted economic crisis, and witnessed the dislocation and deterioration of its military capabilities, Moscow is acutely aware of its diminished international standing; Sergei Karaganov has written, for example, that except for its nuclear weapons and extensive territory, Russia is a medium power.[8] Moreover, it is understood that Russia is not merely weakened, it is still declining.[9] But whatever its other problems and limitations, Russia remains one of two superpowers in the context of nuclear weapons. Alexander Pikayev captures the point nicely: "The problem of status is especially acute for Russia. A unique strategic arsenal represents Moscow's sole claim to superpower status. It is still seen as an important factor in the country's influence in the world."[10]

The second related point is that Russia's nuclear capabilities give Moscow a unique place on the foreign policy agenda of the United States. Nuclear weapons provide each with a powerful interest in engaging the other and, because of their nuclear superpower status, a set of bilateral issues that are distinctive to their relationship. Sergei Rogov writes, for example, that "Russia will retain the condition of mutual assured destruction with the United States which will provide the Russian-American relationship with a special character, which might move from regulated rivalry to limited partnership. The precarious strategic balance needs a very delicate joint management."[11] Pikayev puts the point even more directly: "Strategic parity with the United States affords Moscow a special place in U.S. foreign policy and a means of gaining Washington's support in areas vital to Russia's interests."[12] In short, Russian analysts see Russia's nuclear superpower status playing an important political role in Russian grand strategy, bolstering its international standing and giving it a much needed source of diplomatic influence. These concerns about status undergird the emphasis of many in the Russian debate on preserving nuclear parity with the United States. Over time, they could well result in Russian resistance to post-START II reductions that would lessen the distinction between the two nuclear superpowers and other nuclear-armed states.

Russian attitudes toward nuclear weapons will not be purely political in orientation. It is clear that nuclear weapons are expected to play a major role in the country's security policy. Official statements and associated public commentary suggest that Russia's nuclear posture is meant to serve at least four purposes.

The first is to deter American nuclear capabilities. Just as the United States maintains nuclear deterrent forces to safeguard against the residual Russian nuclear threat, so Russia must also preserve nuclear deterrent capabilities against the residual American threat. Perhaps in the long run, this mission will wither away if political relations between Moscow and Washington evolve in a positive direction. But in the short run, it is both inevitable and necessary. As Alexei Arbatov puts it, mutual deterrence "is the only feasible mode of relations between nuclear powers who are not full-scale allies and are within each other's range."[13] Evidence of this mission can be seen in the growing Russian discussion about the vulnerabilities of Russia's nuclear arsenal and the possibility that it lacks an adequate deterrent force; there is only one state that can possibly attempt to threaten Russia with a disarming strike. Russian officers and analysts have openly worried that Moscow's land-based forces (including mobile missiles) are vulnerable to attack, that its sea-based nuclear forces are jeopardized by U.S. antisubmarine warfare (ASW) capabilities, and that its early-warning systems are insufficient.[14] Russian critics of START II complain that it will leave Russia in an inferior and vulnerable position, undermining rather than enhancing strategic stability. Some have even worried that Russian strategic nuclear assets will be vulnerable to American high-technology conventional weapons;[15] indeed, Russia's military doctrine document specifically singles out conventional attacks on nuclear assets as a potential trigger of nuclear escalation.[16] These issues matter only in the context of the U.S.-Russian nuclear relationship.

Second, the doctrine specifies the need to deter other nuclear powers. The United States is the largest, but not the only, nuclear threat faced by Russia. It must concern itself as well with Britain, France, and China. To some extent, these are lesser cases: any deterrent posture sufficient against the United States will be adequate to deter lesser nuclear powers. But Russia has explicitly reserved the right to use nuclear weapons against any nuclear power.

Third, Russia must hedge against nuclear proliferation. Russia has a powerful interest in preventing further nuclear proliferation (and the proliferation of other weapons of mass destruction) because many potential proliferators inhabit the periphery of Eurasia—that is, the periphery of Russia and its FSU neighbors. Russian security policy must take into account the possibility that nonproliferation efforts may fail; in the worst case, in which the NPT regime is substantially breached, Russia could be nearly encircled by nuclear powers, a number of whom could be rivals, if not adversaries. These possibilities influence Russian thinking about nuclear weapons.[17]

The fourth need is to deter a major conventional attack on Russia. The Soviet Union and its Warsaw Pact allies possessed enormous conventional military capabilities and were widely presumed to possess conventional military superiority in Europe; in the West, it was believed (or feared) that, in the event of war, NATO would need to compensate for its conventional inferiority by threatening or executing nuclear strikes. The situation for Russia is much different. It is a much smaller state than the USSR, with half the population and a considerably reduced territorial expanse (however vast it remains). Its former allies are at best buffers against potential threats from the West, and at worst willing participants in hostile coalitions. The substantial quantitative advantages once possessed by Moscow now lie with NATO. Further, the war in the Persian Gulf vividly demonstrated the technological superiority of U.S. and Western equipment against Soviet-produced arms.

Compounding this picture are three further factors. First, China's rapid economic growth and equally rapid investment in improved military capabilities (with significant contributions from Russia in the form of military sales) raise a potential conventional military challenge of formidable dimensions along Russia's lengthy Far Eastern frontier. Second, the rapid collapse of the USSR and the subsequent ongoing political and economic crisis in Russia have produced a substantial deterioration of the conventional capabilities Russia inherited from the Soviet Union. And finally, Russia's severe economic and budgetary difficulties greatly circumscribe the resources it can invest in restoring its conventional combat power.

None of this matters greatly so long as relations with China and NATO remain reasonably good and the likelihood of war seems low. But Moscow has a long history of hostile relations with both, and it is unlikely to rest its security on the assumption that relations with NATO or China will remain forever harmonious. As the military doctrine document puts it, the immediate threat of war is low, but "the danger of war does remain."[18] Even a healthy Russia, though powerful, would be weak relative to its most powerful potential challengers. But in current conditions Russia is particularly weak and, at least for some considerable time to come, lacks the resources to dramatically improve its conventional forces.

Hence, it is hardly surprising that many Russian officers and analysts have concluded that Russia must rely on nuclear weapons to compensate for conventional weakness, that nuclear threats will be the ultimate deterrent of major conventional war. Some seem to regard this as a temporary (and, in some instances, a not particularly desirable) state of affairs, pending the revival of Russia's conventional capability. Others embrace it as an affordable long-term strategy, akin to the "massive retaliation" policy of the United States in the 1950s, that obviates the need to spend heavily on conventional forces.

Nuclear Weapons in Russia's Military Doctrine of November 1993

The military doctrine adopted by Russia in November 1993 is couched in broad, general, and often vague terms. Its treatment of the nuclear issue is not found in a single, coherent discussion. Rather, brief, often cryptic references to nuclear weapons are scattered throughout the published document. Nor does it provide specific guidance or clarification of nuclear force requirements or employment preferences. But the doctrine does indicate, either directly or implicitly, that nuclear weapons are meant to serve the four purposes described above. In some ways, the Russian view of nuclear weapons is less ambitious than was the Soviet Union's for most of the Cold War. There is no reference to winning nuclear war and no emphasis on massive strikes and maximum blows. Rather, there is a clear emphasis on deterrence and "ensuring guaranteed intended damage to the aggressor."[19] On the other hand, the emerging Russian conception envisages using nuclear weapons not only to deter nuclear attacks on itself and its allies, but to deter conventional attacks on nuclear forces and other sensitive installations and to be the primary deterrent of major conventional aggression by large potential adversaries. In this sense, Russia is relying more on its nuclear deterrent than did the USSR.

Russia's Nuclear Policy Agenda

If the broad political roles and military purposes of Russia's nuclear forces seem fairly well established, the more specific contours of its nuclear policy are less well settled. Over the last several years, several issues have been prominent on the nuclear policy agenda.[20]

Dealerting and Detargeting

During the Cold War, both the United States and the Soviet Union maintained substantial portions of their nuclear arsenals on high alert, ready for rapid response—the so-called cocked gun posture. The Soviet Union, in particular, emphasized launch-on-warning and therefore maintained forces in what Bruce Blair describes as a "launch-ready configuration."[21] As Blair notes, preoccupation with high readiness and rapid reaction raises destabilizing dangers.

Starting in late 1991, both sides have since made strides in the direction of uncocking the gun, taking various components of their arsenals off alert or otherwise relaxing their Cold War nuclear postures.[22] This has occurred primarily through a series of reciprocal unilateral measures rather than by formal agreement—not least because many of the steps taken are both reversible and difficult or impossible to verify. The latest step in this direction was announced during the U.S.-Russian presidential-level summit between Bill Clinton and Boris Yeltsin in January 1994: both sides promised to stop targeting their missiles against one another. This means that the guidance instructions of deployed missiles will not automatically steer the missiles to targets in the other country in the event of launch. Because this is another measure that is easily reversible and impossible to verify, it is somewhat symbolic in nature—a confidence-building measure.[23]

Nevertheless, this step and similar measures serve two practical purposes. First, they reduce the risk of accidental or unauthorized launches; dealerted missiles cannot be readily fired, and detargeted missiles will not strike the other's home territory if launched. This matters particularly because both

Washington and Moscow have been concerned, in this period of turbulence and instability in Russia, about the heightened risk of an unsanctioned launch. Second, dealerting measures reduce concerns about preemption and inadvertent escalation, enhance stability, and thereby detoxify the U.S.-Russian nuclear relationship. This addresses the awkward tension between efforts to promote political rapprochement, on the one hand, and efforts to maintain a nuclear deterrent posture, on the other. Low or zero alert postures allow the maintenance of deterrent capabilities in their least threatening manifestation.[24] As Sergei Rogov has commented in suggesting dealerting as a central element of cooperative U.S.-Russian management of the strategic nuclear balance:

> The new [dealerted] nuclear postures of Russia and the USA will not permit many of the previous nuclear escalation scenarios and will deny the advantages of preemption. That means that the United States and Russia will shift to a much more stable relationship. Although mutual nuclear deterrence is maintained, it will become a different form of deterrence, aimed at the prevention of nuclear war, and not at escalation control.[25]

In short, dealerting measures can both reduce the risks of inadvertent or unauthorized use and facilitate a cooperative U.S.-Russian strategic relationship.

Denuclearization in the Former Soviet Union

Nuclear diplomacy in the post-Soviet period has focused on preventing the non-Russian states of the former Soviet Union from exploiting the Soviet nuclear arsenal to gain a nuclear capability of their own. In the first half of 1992, Soviet tactical nuclear weapons were withdrawn back into Russia, but strategic nuclear deployments remained in Belarus, Kazakhstan, and Ukraine (as well as Russia). The subsequent two years have witnessed a persistent melodrama, centered on the problematic case of Ukraine, in which the United States, Russia, and other members of the international community have attempted to encourage, cajole, pressure, bribe, or otherwise press Kiev to proceed with the denuclearization of its territory. For its part, Ukraine has repeatedly promised, with varying degrees of formality and legality, to become a non-nuclear weapon state and to join the NPT. However, the fulfillment of these promises still lies more in the future than in the past, and there has been mounting concern in Washington and elsewhere about both Kiev's apparent unwillingness to accept the prompt and uninterrupted denuclearization of its territory and the evident growth in Ukraine of sentiment favoring the retention of a nuclear weapon capability. This has led to doubts about Ukraine's ultimate intentions, which Kiev regards as unfair, unpleasant, and exasperating. Nearly three years after the collapse of the Soviet Union, the issue remains unresolved, and some sixteen hundred strategic nuclear warheads remain on Ukraine's territory.

What is Russia's stake in this issue? In the immediate aftermath of the demise of the USSR, Moscow's goal was not consolidation of the strategic arsenal on its own territory but the preservation of a unified command structure over inherited Soviet strategic deployments, wherever they might be. This approach reflected Russia's initial conception of what the CIS should be and what role it should play in preserving a single "security space" in the former Soviet Union; it may also have reflected the reluctance of the Russian military to dislocate nuclear deployments that included some of the most modern systems in the Soviet arsenal, including SS–25s in Belarus, SS–24s in Ukraine, and modernized SS–18s in Kazakhstan. Thus, in the first half of 1992, Russia—the designated nuclear successor to the Soviet Union—did not make vigorous efforts to pull strategic deployments out of Belarus, Kazakhstan, and Ukraine. Rather, it attempted to breathe life into CIS command arrangements that had been agreed upon in Minsk and Almaty in December 1991. Only when it became apparent that the CIS command structure would not play the central role that Moscow intended, that other CIS members were determined to possess national military capabilities and command structures, and that Ukraine would claim ownership of the nuclear weapons on its territory, did Russia abandon its initial approach.

But Russia has no interest in seeing independent nuclear capabilities established along its borders. As noted, it fears that nuclear proliferation may cause it to live in a "zone of nuclear risk." Hence, it has a strong interest in the denuclearization of all the other newly independent states of the former Soviet Union—more so since nuclear acquisition by Ukraine could spark additional proliferation within or outside the FSU. Moscow has sought to achieve this goal in part by pressuring Ukraine, and at least equally by pressing the United States to pressure Ukraine. Moscow's own foreign policy behavior has not been particularly helpful in promoting the resolution of the issue, since its friction-laden relations with Kiev and its apparent assertiveness toward other FSU neighbors have fueled pronuclear sentiments in Ukraine.

However, Russia does not necessarily have an interest in the rapid resolution of the denuclearization issue, provided Ukraine, Kazakhstan, and Belarus eventually end up as non-nuclear states. Ukraine's nuclear policy has proven a blessing for Moscow. It has given the United States and Russia a powerful common interest while impeding the development of closer relations between Ukraine and the United States. It has given Russia an issue on which it has the high ground and has deflected attention from some of its own foreign policy blemishes. It gives Moscow a chronic opportunity to criticize Ukraine and to raise the alarm about its behavior. In short, a continued stalemate on Ukrainian denuclearization has its advantages, at least in the short run, for Russia. This may explain why Russia has seemed no more eager than Ukraine to resolve bilateral differences that have blocked progress toward denuclearization.

What are the implications for Russia if Ukraine becomes a nuclear power? First, this will put preemptive and preventive war on the agenda of Russian nuclear planning, putting the Russian retreat from no first use in a more ominous context. This will mean that Russian-Ukrainian confrontations will be nuclear crises, in conditions where stability does not obtain, because Russia will have disarming options against a smaller and vulnerable Ukrainian nuclear force and Ukraine will face "use them or lose them" pressures. This world is so unattractive that Russia may consider war to prevent Ukraine's attainment of nuclear status.[26] Second, under most circumstances (except the case in which Ukraine opts for the nuclear path in reaction to the emergence of a truly ugly and menacing Russia), it would consign Ukraine to a position of international troublemaker. This would give Russia an international political advantage, Ukraine having opted for nuclear status and isolation. However, the security disadvantages of this outcome would significantly outweigh any political advantage. Third, this would scuttle the START I and START II agreements, since the entry into force of the first and the ratification of the second are dependent on Ukraine's accession to the NPT as a non-nuclear state. Those in Russia who are critical of aspects of START II might see benefits in this development. But it would mean the end of the agreed road map for the next decade of strategic nuclear relations between the United States and Russia and would thus introduce a large complication in U.S.-Russian relations. Moreover, the emergence of a nuclear Ukraine could well alter Russian calculations about desirable force levels and capabilities and render existing negotiated levels unattractive.

No First Use in Russian Doctrine

The feature of Russian nuclear doctrine that has attracted the most comment and controversy so far has been its modification of the Soviet commitment to no first use of nuclear weapons. While maintaining its pledge not to use nuclear weapons against non-nuclear members of the NPT who are not allied to a nuclear power, the Russian doctrine statement suggested that Moscow might use nuclear weapons first against four categories of states: nuclear powers; allies of nuclear powers that joined in aggression against Russia; other states that acted in concert with a nuclear power in attacking Russia; and states that are not members of the NPT.[27]

What explains this retreat from no first use? Several considerations seem to have been at work. First, using nuclear weapons to deter conventional attack implies nuclear first use; the logic is that conventional advantages on the other side will be neutralized by nuclear escalation. It is for this reason that throughout the Cold War and beyond, NATO refused to commit to no first use. Russia finds itself in a similar position today. Second, first use is an answer to mounting concerns about the vulnerability of Russian nuclear forces and strategic command and control. If one's ability to strike second is in doubt, striking first is an obvious remedy (dealerting may contribute here by removing launch-on-warning as a solution to Russia's real and perceived strategic vulnerabilities). Third, Russia's new policy seems clearly (if implicitly) constructed to give Ukraine incentives to give up nuclear weapons and to join the NPT. Doing otherwise, Moscow explicitly warns, leaves Ukraine vulnerable to Russian first use. Similarly, states of East-Central Europe pursuing NATO membership are given to understand that allying with a nuclear power has the price of exposing them to the possibility of Russian first use.[28] Finally, Moscow may have judged that the political costs of this move would be manageable because the Soviet no-first-use pledge was commonly dismissed as propaganda in any case and because most of the other nuclear powers (China notably excepted) have similarly avoided commitment to no first use and hence will have little grounds for criticism.

Notes

1. It is worth noting, however, that significant elements of the Soviet nuclear infrastructure are located outside Russia, including early-warning radars in Latvia and elsewhere, ballistic missile production sites in Ukraine, and the nuclear test facility in Kazakhstan. Despite Russia's extensive nuclear inheritance, the "missing pieces" can be problematic for Moscow and have influenced Russia's relations with other states of the former Soviet Union.

2. Emphasizing this point is Alexei Arbatov, "Evolving Russian Nuclear Doctrine," in *Revising the U.S.-Russian Nuclear Relationship*, eds. Alexei Arbatov and Steven Miller (forthcoming, 1995).

3. Harmony in U.S.-Russian relations, however, has increasingly lessened because of Washington's unease about assertive Russian activity in the former Soviet Union.

4. "Basic Provisions of the Military Doctrine of the Russian Federation," reprinted in *FBIS Daily Report: Central Eurasia* (FBIS-SOV–93–222-S), 19 November 1993, p. 1.

5. Ibid., p. 2.

6. Colonel Oleg Falichev, "Who Has the Keys to the Nuclear Arsenal?" *Krasnaia zvezda*, 26 November 1993, p. 1, in FBIS-SOV–93228, 30 November 1993, p. 41.

7. For more on these points, see John W.R. Lepingwell's chapter in this volume.

8. Sergei Karaganov, "Russia and Other Independent Republics in Asia," in *Asia's International Role in the Post–Cold War Era,* Adelphi Paper no. 276 (London: IISS, 1993), p. 22: "By the majority of parameters (excluding territory and nuclear potential) Russia has moved to the category of a medium-sized power."

9. See, for example, USA and Canada Institute, "The Position of Russia and Its National Interests: Yearning for an Unattainable Future," *Rossiia* (Moscow), 4 January 1994, p. 5, in FBIS-USR–94–005, 26 January 1994, p. 51, which comments that "Russia is in a state of decline," and notes incredulously that U.S. President Bill Clinton's administration had classified Russia as a developing state for the purposes of providing aid, asking plaintively whether Russian politicians understand that "the results of the government's activity as of the present are, truly, putting Russia in the category of a poor developing country?"

10. Alexander Pikayev, "Russia, the CIS, and Minimum Nuclear Deterrence," in *Minimum Nuclear Deterrence in a New World Order,* ed. Peter Gizewski, Aurora Papers, no. 24 (Canadian Centre for Global Security, 1994), p. 40.

11. Sergei Rogov, "The Prospects for a Russian-American Strategic Relationship" (unpublished manuscript, 1993), p. 3.

12. Pikayev, "Russia, the CIS, and Minimum Nuclear Deterrence," p. 40.

13. Arbatov, "Evolving Russian Nuclear Doctrine," p. 48.

14. These concerns are very usefully distilled in Konstantin E. Sorokin, "Russia After the Crisis: The Nuclear Strategy Debate," *Orbis*, vol. 38, no. 1 (winter 1994), especially pp. 20–24.

15. See, for example, "Conventional Counterforce Impact," in *Implications of the START II Treaty for U.S.-Russian Relations,* ed. Alexei Arbatov (Washington, DC: Stimson Center, 1993), pp. 59–61.

16. "Basic Provisions of the Military Doctrine of the Russian Federation," pp. 6, 8

17. Lepingwell's chapter in this volume touches on this issue. See in particular his quotation from Pavel Grachev, to the effect that nuclear proliferation may confront Russia with a half-circle "zone of nuclear risk." Also noting Russia's concern with proliferation is Sorokin, "Russia After the Crisis," p. 31.

18. "Basic Provisions of the Military Doctrine of the Russian Federation," p. 2.

19. Ibid., p. 6. This somewhat awkward formulation appears to be a restatement of the notion of assured destruction.

20. In the absence of Lepingwell's chapter in this volume, I would have included here brief treatments of the START II debate and the force posture controversy. As these topics are well covered in Lepingwell's chapter, they are omitted here.

21. See Bruce G. Blair's chapter in this volume.

22. For details, see Steven E. Miller, "Dismantling the Edifice: Strategic Nuclear Weapons in the Post-Soviet Era," in *American Defense Annual, 1994,* ed. Charles Hermann (New York: Lexington Books, 1994), pp. 65–83.

23. And it was so described by U.S. officials at the time. See Mary Curtius, "Two Sides Likely to Announce a Change in Nuclear Targets," *Boston Globe,* 14 January 1994.

24. The logical endpoint of the dealerting process is zero alert. With respect to land-based forces, for example, this could be achieved by removing warheads from delivery systems. Zero alert is advocated most prominently by Bruce Blair. See Blair's "Global Zero Alert for Nuclear Forces" (PRAC Paper, Center for International and Security Studies, University of Maryland, April 1994).

25. Rogov, "Prospects for a Russian-American Strategic Relationship," p. 6. On the "gap" between rapprochement and strategic deterrence, see Pikayev, "Russia, the CIS, and Minimum Nuclear Deterrence," p. 37.

26. In discussions in Moscow in January 1994, I asked about the implications for Russian military planning of a nuclear Ukraine. I was told that Russian planning focuses on only two scenarios: a non-nuclear Ukraine or war.

27. The relevant passage can be found in "Basic Provisions of the Military Doctrine of the Russian Federation," p. 2, but it is hardly a paragon of clarity and was subsequently embellished in official commentary on the document. A very useful interpretation, much more accessible than the original, is Arbatov, "Evolving Russian Nuclear Doctrine," pp. 50–51.

28. For similar interpretations, see Dunbar Lockwood, "U.S., Russia Revamp Nuclear Strategies," *Disarmament Times,* 21 December 1993, p. 4; and Lepingwell's chapter in this volume.

6

Is START Stalling?

John W.R. Lepingwell

In the immediate aftermath of the Cold War, it appeared that the old approaches to arms control had become irrelevant and that the problems associated with large inventories of nuclear weapons had disappeared. These assumptions were only partly justified. Certainly, debates over strategic stability and the finer points of deterrence theory are now no longer very widespread or compelling. Nevertheless, the arms reduction process still has far to go. The culminating achievements of the "traditional" approach to arms control, the Strategic Arms Reduction Talks (START) treaties, remain in an uncertain state. The question is, has the START process stalled? Will the reductions envisioned by the START treaties be implemented by the end of the decade, or will nuclear inventories in the Commonwealth of Independent States (CIS) slowly disintegrate in an uncontrolled and potentially dangerous way? Despite recent progress in the removal of nuclear weapons from Belarus, Kazakhstan, and Ukraine, there is also cause for concern that the denuclearization process outside Russia may grind to a halt, causing further tensions and dangers. Thus, while many of the traditional issues of arms control may now be irrelevant, the nuclear danger still remains, albeit in a different form.

This chapter addresses some of the issues concerning the prospects for Russian implementation of the START treaties. In doing so, it first surveys the status of the former Soviet Union's nuclear forces and then turns to the doctrinal, political, and economic issues associated with the problem. Scenarios for the possible development of the denuclearization process are then sketched and assessed, together with an analysis of strategies for speeding the process. Overall, it appears that the prospects for full implementation of START II within the specified time frame are not promising. It is likely, however, that Russian strategic nuclear forces will nonetheless undergo a significant restructuring and reduction over the next decade.

The Strategic Legacy

The collapse of the Soviet Union left Soviet strategic forces scattered across the newly independent states. Not only were missile and bomber bases distributed across Russia, Ukraine, Belarus, and Kazakhstan, but so were parts of the early-warning system and armament plants. Initial attempts to maintain a unified strategic command and control system under the CIS military command soon began to fall apart as Ukraine moved rapidly to assert its independence in all military areas. While Ukraine did not, and continues not to assert the right to operational control (positive control) over the nuclear weapons on its territory, its extension of control over logistics and personnel, together with its claim to the material in the warheads, has precipitated a long struggle with the CIS command and Russia over ownership and control issues.[1]

In 1994, substantial progress began to be made in the arms reduction process outside Russia. The signing of the Trilateral Agreement in January 1994 by the U.S., Russian, and Ukrainian presidents appears to have solved many problems concerning Ukrainian denuclearization, but the implementation of the accord may take until at least early 1996.[2] By September 1994, Ukraine had already transferred over three hundred warheads to Russia, more than meeting its obligation to transfer two hundred warheads in the first ten months of the accord.[3] However, despite this encouraging trend there remains the danger that the accord may prove vulnerable to other political developments, such as increased tension in the Crimea. The slow delivery of Western financial aid for Ukrainian disarmament has also been a point of contention between the United States and Ukraine and may also lead to delays.[4] Belarus has transferred a substantial portion of the SS–25 Topol intercontinental ballistic missile (ICBM) force located there to Russia. Similarly, bombers have been transferred from Kazakhstan to Russia, as have at least a few ICBMs. A treaty governing the transfer of all nuclear warheads by 1995 was signed by Kazakhstan and Russia on 28 March 1994 and apparently specifies a timetable for the removal of nuclear warheads from Kazakhstan by May 1995.[5] Outstanding issues concerning Western funding for weapons dismantlment and compensation for the highly enriched uranium removed from the warheads are being negotiated.

This optimistic overview must be tempered with a closer look at the status of the forces both within Russia and outside it. While the denuclearization process is under way, it is proceeding more slowly than desirable, particularly given the deteriorating conditions within the strategic forces. The strategic rocket forces (SRF) were an elite force during the Soviet period, receiving the first pick of both material and personnel. While the SRF appears to have retained this priority in Russia, it is far from immune to the negative trends that have swept through the Russian military over the past few years. Indeed, in many respects the SRF may be more vulnerable than other services to these trends because the SRF must maintain a technologically advanced service deployed in some of the remotest regions of Russia.

One of the Russian military's, and the SRF's, most pressing problems is the shortfall in personnel due to declining draft intakes. While the SRF is an officer-heavy service, this shortfall is hitting it as well, perhaps because many midlevel officers have technical qualifications that allow them to make the transition to the civilian economy. Given that many SRF units are deployed in remote areas where housing is poor or unavailable, there are strong incentives for officers to leave.[6] According to SRF Commander Igor Sergeev, missile combat crews are staffed at only 50 to 60 percent of their required level. At the same time, however, combat alert shifts have apparently been reduced from one week to three to four days, apparently compensated for by increasing the number of combat shifts per month.[7] To compensate for these personnel shortfalls the SRF is increasing its intake of volunteers, with some fifty-three hundred serving in mid-1993.[8] In addition, some units are being dissolved as weapons are retired, with officers being assigned to new units, and some SRF officers are being repatriated from Belarus, Kazakhstan, and Ukraine.[9]

As with all other branches of the Russian armed services, SRF officers must adapt to a seemingly chaotic new economy. Salaries within the military have been increased over time, but pay does not appear to have kept up with the rapid inflation of 1992–93. In 1994, there were reports that units, especially those in remote areas, were not receiving their pay on time or were being only partially paid.[10] The combined trends of erratic pay, poor housing, and a disappearing sense of mission (especially in view of the cuts envisioned under START) have undoubtedly had a negative impact on the morale and performance of the SRF, despite official protestations to the contrary.

Two dramatic incidents in early 1994 underlined the dangers inherent in declining morale and living conditions. The first took place at an ICBM base in the Altai region in March 1994, when an enlisted man in a guard detail went berserk, killing two soldiers and seriously wounding another two. The local SRF command tried to cover up the incident, but it leaked to first the regional and then the national press.[11] While the incident apparently did not directly endanger any nuclear weapons, it is a troubling reminder of the potential for such danger. Nor can it be dismissed as a totally isolated incident, for just a month later a serviceman in a counterintelligence unit in the Russian northern fleet stole some weapons and opened fire in a barracks of submarine officers, killing one and seriously injuring another. In the ensuing chase, a total of three more people were killed before the attacker was seized after taking sailors hostage onboard a torpedo boat.[12] These dramatic incidents (which followed one in March in the border guards and thus may have been "copycat" killings) suggest that if crazed troops can create mayhem in high-security facilities, rather more sane criminals could perhaps wreak even more havoc.[13]

The SRF is also experiencing problems with deteriorating equipment. One of the reasons for the Russian Defense Ministry's endorsement of the START II Treaty was that many of the production facilities for ICBMs lay outside Russia, and thus Russia was left with only the capability to produce the SS–25 (RS–12) Topol missile at a plant in Votkinsk. Plants for both the SS–18 and SS–24 missiles were located in Ukraine, as were some plants producing electronics and guidance systems. While Ukraine's difficulty in maintaining both warheads and delivery systems has been a subject of much concern, there are some indications that Russia has also had difficulty supporting all its systems. Thus, the Massandra protocols, signed in September 1993 by the Russian and Ukrainian governments, include an agreement on supply and maintenance that provides for Ukraine to supply parts to Russia, as well as vice versa.[14]

In the submarine and bomber legs of the Russian nuclear forces, the situation appears no better. Alert rates for Russian SSBNs have plunged, while many of the Soviet Union's newest bombers were deployed in Ukraine. Russia has only a few Tu–160 Blackjack bombers, with the rest located in Ukraine, apparently in unserviceable condition.[15] There are no plans to produce more of the aircraft, the performance and safety of which were criticized by articles in the military press.[16] Similarly, most of the latest models of the Tu–95 Bear strategic bomber were located in Ukraine, as were many of the tankers required for aerial refueling.[17] As a result of the decline in readiness and capability of the other two legs of the strategic forces, the long-standing predominance of the SRF in the Soviet Union has been reinforced in the Russian armed forces.

Finally, an essential component of the strategic forces, the early-warning system, has also been hard hit by the disintegration of the Soviet Union. Early-warning radars are located in Azerbaijan, Belarus, Kazakhstan, Latvia, and Ukraine, as well as Russia.[18] While the CIS strategic forces were initially supposed to operate these facilities, the failure to create a real CIS force has resulted in Russia's attempting to maintain control of the radars. So far, Russia has apparently succeeded in keeping the stations operational.[19] (These facilities are operated by the Russian Air Defense Force [VPVO], which is also experiencing personnel and budgetary problems.) Furthermore, most of the radars in operation are not the relatively new Pechora class systems but older systems (the "Dnieper" or Hen House) based on technology from the 1960s and 1970s. Russian military commentators estimate that these systems may remain serviceable only for another few years at most. Construction of new systems is apparently hampered not only by a lack of funds but also by the fact that one of the main electronics factories for radar systems is located in Ukraine.[20] The very structure of the air and space defense system may also be subject to change, as the Ministry of Defense has publicly announced plans to dissolve the VPVO, incorporating its forces into the army and air force, probably by the end of the decade. While there has been extensive discussion of the need to create new "rocket-space troops" that would integrate air defense, early-warning, anti-satellite, and antiballistic missile (ABM) systems in one service, this may be more a bureaucratic attempt to rejuvenate the VPVO rather than a concrete plan for a new service. Over the longer term, even the possibility of dissolving the SRF and transferring the ICBM force to the air force is being discussed, a move that would reduce administrative overhead and leave Russia with a three-service structure, down from the current five.[21]

Thus, Russia's strategic forces have not escaped the disruption and decay that have affected the rest of the Russian military. This fact makes their restructuring and reduction a pressing task, even in the absence of the START treaties. Indeed, the need to create a new post–Cold War rationale for the strategic forces has become one of the key tasks in the formulation of the new Russian military doctrine.

Doctrine and Force Restructuring

The speed with which the negotiations over START II were completed meant that for once arms control outstripped debates over doctrine and force structuring, at least within Russia. After START II was signed in early 1993, however, the political intrigues within Russia pushed consideration of nuclear issues toward the bottom of the political agenda, even though there were studies and debates among the military and foreign policy elites. Public discussion of the new Russian stance on nuclear weapons and force structure increased substantially in 1994, however, as the political situation stabilized. The treaty may be submitted to the State Duma for ratification in 1995.

The approval of the Russian military doctrine in November 1993 codified Russia's policy on nuclear weapons, and is hence worth examining. The "basic tenets" of the military doctrine were published, and while they are incomplete, together with other public statements by military figures they provide some insights into the new policy.

The key nuclear element in the new doctrine is the renunciation of the policy of no first use, first enunciated under Leonid Brezhnev in 1979. While this change attracted much attention in Western news reports, it was often dismissed as a largely rhetorical shift, since Soviet force planning had already incorporated first-use options.

To be precise, the new doctrine does not explicitly eliminate the no-first-use pledge. Instead, it defines so many exclusions that almost all states near Russia, including all North Atlantic Treaty Organization (NATO) states, are excluded from the pledge's provisions.[22] Thus, while no first use formally remains a part of the doctrine, it is circumscribed in a manner intended to have both military and political dimensions. The rationale behind this shift appears to have been twofold.

First, there is growing concern that the conventional strategic balance has shifted against Russia. Even though NATO does not have large conventional forces bordering Russia, many commentators have pointed to the fact that Russia is increasingly threatened by conventional precision-guided munitions (PGMs). This capability could, in turn, theoretically allow NATO to destroy a significant fraction of Russian nuclear forces with conventional weapons. As the doctrine states when discussing the possibility of escalation, "Deliberate actions by the aggressor that aim to destroy or disrupt the operation of strategic nuclear forces, the early-warning system, or nuclear power and atomic and chemical industry installations may be factors that increase the danger of a war using conventional weapons systems escalating into nuclear war."[23] The doctrine goes on to note that even limited use of nuclear weapons could lead to massive use and "catastrophic consequences." This point was driven home by Russian Defense Minister Pavel Grachev in an article apparently intended to clarify and defend some doctrinal points, where he stated,

> It is necessary to take into account that, with the current development of means of armed combat, including high-precision weapons, even in a war with the use of conventional arms our nuclear potential might be reduced to a level at which it could not fulfill its deterrent role.[24]

While Grachev does not spell out the threat to go nuclear in such a case, it is clearly implied. Thus, the doctrine is intended to widen the policy of deterrence to include conventional attacks not only against nuclear forces, but against other sensitive installations (and ones whose destruction could be environmentally disastrous) as well.

Second, there is an important political component to the no-first-use issue. The doctrine does renounce the first use of nuclear weapons against non-nuclear states that are signatories to the Nuclear Nonproliferation Treaty (NPT) and are not allied with a nuclear power.[25] This aspect of the doctrine appears partly directed at Ukraine, which at the time the doctrine was passed had not acceded to the NPT, despite its commitment to do so in the Lisbon Protocol. Furthermore, it raises the stakes for states that are non-nuclear NPT signatories if they are considering joining NATO. Thus, under the current terms of the doctrine, states such as Poland, Hungary, and the Czech Republic are covered by the no-first-use pledge but would not be if they joined NATO as full members. This distinction has not yet been stressed in Russian foreign policy, but if some states do move closer to NATO membership, the implicit threat could begin to emerge more explicitly.

The clause concerning NPT accession may also be aimed against non-European states. Russian analysts have become increasingly concerned about the threat of proliferation near Russia's borders, especially in the cases of Iran, Iraq, Pakistan, North Korea, and even Japan.[26] The emergence of these potential nuclear proliferators has met with mixed reactions in Moscow. While there is substantial interest in continued trade, including arms trade and in the case of Iran nuclear technology sales, there is also a long-term concern about the potential threat they pose. Again, this is more clearly spelled out in Grachev's article on doctrine:

> In this connection, it is necessary to underline that the countries of the unofficial "nuclear club" create almost a complete half-circle, encompassing from the south the geopolitical expanse occupied by Russia and its closest neighbors, creating in this an indeterminate zone of "nuclear risk." Therefore, Russia's policy of nuclear deterrence must in complete measure respond to this situation.[27]

Thus, the no-first-use pledge provides yet another incentive for these states to join the NPT (or to continue to respect its provisions if already a signatory), as well as giving the Russian military more options (such as the use of tactical nuclear weapons) in the unlikely event of a conflict with one of these states.

The new deterrence policy thus extends deterrence down the escalation ladder by attempting to deter conventional threats, and it also is intended to deter states near Russia from crossing the nuclear threshold. A relatively unnoticed clause in the doctrine also provides for "extended deterrence," for *casus belli* is defined to include attacks not only against Russia but also against Russian troops and Russia's allies. By implication, the policy could be extended to include the right to use nuclear weapons (against states excluded from the no-first-use clause) even in the event of a conflict outside the bounds of the Russian Federation or in a conflict involving one of Russia's allies.[28] While it is not clear whether Russia has any allies at present, this clause would seem to hold in the hypothetical case, for example, of a clash between Russian troops in Armenia and Turkish troops in Azerbaijan. Such a clash is highly unlikely, but this example serves to illustrate the lengths to which this concept of extended deterrence could be stretched.

These doctrinal developments have not been without their critics. For example, Sergei Rogov of the Institute of the U.S.A. and Canada has harshly criticized the doctrine for extending nuclear deterrence too far, noting that nuclear weapons are useless in deterring regional conflicts. Furthermore, argues Rogov, the implicit message in the doctrine—that nuclear weapons are an effective deterrent—contradicts the explicit message that nuclear weapons are of limited utility and that the nonproliferation regime must be strengthened.[29] Another reform-oriented military analyst, Alexei Arbatov, has made similar points and has argued that deterring large-scale conventional attacks is irrelevant, since there is no such threat to Russia at present. Arbatov suggests that China might be an exception to this rule only if Russia continues to sell it sophisticated weaponry.[30]

The objections of the reformers appear to have had little influence on the doctrine, however. Rogov notes that few of the suggestions put forward by reformers were incorporated in the final draft.[31] Indeed, it appears that civilian reformers have little more influence in high-level decisions than they did during the late Gorbachev period, and perhaps even less.

While the doctrine lays out the broad terms of Russia's nuclear policy, it does not explicitly indicate what kind of military strategy or force posture Russia is adopting. While Grachev insists that the purpose of nuclear forces is deterrence, this is not a clear indication of how forces should be configured or for what mission.

The key to the force posture and mission question may lie in an argument expounded in the influential military journal *Voennaia mysl'*.[32] The article lays out in some detail the argument that the threat of attrition of nuclear forces by conventional means requires the renunciation of no first use. However, the authors develop the argument further, arguing that an imbalance in nuclear forces might lead to the "attacking" side being able to carry out a first strike that would leave the "defending" side only the options of launching an assured destruction (countervalue) retaliatory strike or capitulating. They argue that the first option would result in the destruction of civilization, since even after the "defender's" counterstrike, the "attacker" would be able to launch a large countervalue second strike. The second option would mean defeat. This situation, they argue, is unstable, for it gives the attacking side the possibility of winning a nuclear exchange. The logic of this argument is strikingly similar to that advanced in the United States during the debate over Strategic Arms Limitation Talks (SALT) II, when Paul Nitze and other critics of the treaty argued that since the Soviet Union was developing a strong counterforce capability they could disarm the United States and then dictate terms.

Indeed, the Russian authors follow the logic one step further, arguing that since the adversary might be committed to flexible, limited use of nuclear or precision-guided conventional weapons, the "defending" side must be similarly prepared to engage in the controlled use of limited nuclear strikes, even in response to conventional attack. Furthermore, strategic systems must be developed that can assure that at no stage in the nuclear escalation process can the adversary gain a decisive advantage or leave only the option of escalation to assured destruction. In short, the proposed strategy is very similar to the "countervailing strategy" advocated by the Carter administration in response to criticism of the SALT II Treaty. The primary difference is that the authors explicitly extend the threshold for escalation downward, so as to deter attacks with precision-guided munitions (PGMs).

This argument, as the authors note, also points to the critical importance of ballistic missile early-warning systems (BMEWS) for attack assessment. Without access to warning and assessment data, the defending side would be unable to judge the scale of the attack, identify intended targets, and select appropriate limited counterstrike options. This argument clearly also indicates that limited agreements for the provision of some U.S. early-warning satellite data will be far from sufficient to assuage Russian concerns—one cannot be dependent on one's possible opponent for crucial strategic information. Furthermore, detailed attack assessment and confirmation would require sophisticated ground-based radars similar to the Pechora class.

These considerations also point to the need to structure Russian forces in a manner that is both survivable and controllable during a period of limited nuclear strikes or conventional strategic strikes. While the authors do not draw direct force structure conclusions from their analysis, the logic of their argument would seem to point directly to the need to provide survivable forces, either through mobility or through hardening. However, the authors do not call for the substantial hard-target kill (HTK) capability stipulated in the countervailing strategy. Indeed, a force structure based largely on the

SS–25 and SLBMs would appear to have relatively little HTK capability unless guidance systems are greatly improved. Furthermore, the "leverage" afforded by multiple independently targetable reentry vehicles (MIRVs) would not be available, making successful counterforce strikes very difficult.

Subsequent discussions of Russian doctrine in the military press have not repudiated the earlier analysis but have tended to stress that the assured destruction (AD) mission remains paramount, at least in terms of the U.S.-Russian nuclear balance.[33] Counterforce missions and first-strike capabilities are far more feasible, however, against smaller nuclear states, and especially states preparing to cross the nuclear threshold. Thus, Russian doctrine and force structure might be developing along two lines: (1) retaining an AD capability against the United States, and (2) ensuring a strong counterforce capability against other nuclear powers, particularly China and near-nuclear states around Russia's borders. The second appears to be a "lesser included case" for Russian force planners, however, since the relatively large force structure required for the AD mission should also be capable of counterforce strikes against smaller nuclear states. This sensitivity to other nuclear powers is also reflected in recent Russian moves to extend the existing strategic arms control limitation regime to the other nuclear powers.

Force Structure Debates

A debate over force structure, with clear implications for the ratification of START II, began to emerge in early 1994. While initial statements concerning START II's impact on force structure had been made throughout 1993, in January 1994 it appeared that a final determination of the nature of the post-START force structure had been made. An article by Lieutenant General Lev Volkov published in *Izvestiia* in February 1994 implied that all the force restructuring decisions had been made, with the new force to be based on the SS–25 Topol, in a mix of 60 to 70 percent mobile and 30 to 40 percent silo launchers. Advocates of this mix do not always give a total number of launchers, but it appears to be close to nine hundred (see Table 6.1).[34] Volkov argued that SS–25s were more economical, survivable, and safer than an equivalent deployment on SSBNs or bombers. (In addition to the SS–25, some SS–19 missiles will be "downloaded" so that they carry just one warhead and will be based in silos.)

The road-mobile missiles will apparently be located on former SS–17 and SS–19 bases, where the necessary road and communications infrastructure exists. Volkov did not make clear how the naval component of the new force would be structured, but he implied that it would be secondary in

Table 6.1

Hypothetical Russian Force Structure Under START II (c. 2003)

System	Number of launchers	Warheads per launcher	Number of warheads	
Typhoon (6) SS-N–20	120	10	1,200	
Delta-IV (7) SS-N–23	112	4	448	
SLBM total			1,648	
SS–19	105	1	105	
SS–25 in SS–18 silos	90	1	90	
SS–25 in other silos	162	1	162	(6 divisions)
SS–25 mobile	600	1	600	
ICBM total			957	
Tu–160 Blackjack	6	12	72	
Tu–95H6	27	6	167[a]	
Tu–95H16	40	16	640[b]	
Bomber total			879	
Grand total			3,484	

Source: Author's estimates.

Note: Assuming that no new SSBNs are built, and that SS–25 production can be increased to approximately fifty to sixty missiles per year. Also assumes no losses to the current bomber fleet and no conversion of ALCM-capable bombers to conventional-only weapons delivery. This table does not take into account bombers in Ukraine that might be sold back to Russia.

[a]From Kazakhstan.
[b]Some from Kazakhstan.

terms of priority. This argument for what amounts to a dyad in which the SRF would have the leading role was seconded by experts from the Arzamas–16 nuclear laboratory.[35]

Arguments in favor of the mobile SS–25 and the START II Treaty have not gone unchallenged. In a direct reply to Volkov's article, Colonel Petr Belov charged that the SS–25 was dangerous, vulnerable, and expensive.[36] According to Belov, the SS–25 has a poor safety record, with up to ten accidents involving the overturning of a launcher since the system's first deployment.[37] Belov also argued that the cost of deploying the system would be substantial and that a preferable option would be to not ratify START II and continue a slow process of restructuring, one that would evidently involve maintaining multiple-warhead (MIRVed) missiles (presumably including the SS–18) and SSBNs. Belov's comments were echoed in an impassioned criticism of the SS–25 by the chief designer of the Typhoon SSBN, suggesting that bureaucratic interests are playing a major role in the debate.[38] (Belov has charged that Volkov and other SS–25 advocates were involved in the development of the system and are therefore biased in its favor.)

Volkov and others have responded to these charges, adding details to their arguments concerning SS–25 survivability against conventional and nuclear attack.[39] A key to the argument, however, is that there is no good alternative to this force structure; as Volkov observes, "ratification or non-ratification of START II will not change the main direction of development of the SRF—the transition from MIRVed missiles to single-warhead missiles. The START II Treaty only shortens the time for the transition to single-warhead structure."[40] Despite this argument, however, Volkov does go on to suggest that some changes be made in the treaty in accord with the economic problems of the country. Presumably this implies a shift in the deadline for full implementation from 2003 to a later date.[41]

Finally, there is a middle ground that accepts many of the criticisms of mobile basing and notes the vulnerability of SSBNs to antisubmarine warfare. Thus, Vladimir Belous has suggested that the ratio of mobile to silo-based SS–25s be reversed, retaining the existing three hundred mobile launchers but putting another four hundred SS–25 missiles into renovated older silos.[42]

Despite the objections to the new emphasis on the SS–25 and the lack of movement on the START II Treaty, the process of deployment appears to be continuing apace. In part this is driven by the deteriorating condition of current missiles and the lack of any realistic land-based alternative to the SS–25. The speed with which old missile systems are being replaced with the SS–25 is difficult to determine. As of mid-1993, there were reportedly some 288 SS–25s deployed, including the forces in Belarus that are being transferred to Russia.[43] The current production rate for the missiles is unclear, but it is probably around twenty missiles per year and at most thirty-five missiles per year.[44] It appears that the current production rate is insufficient to produce the estimated three hundred to four hundred additional missiles required to make a force of six hundred to seven hundred missiles. Thus, the process of restructuring the ICBM force is proceeding, in spite of the fact that neither of the START treaties is legally in force. Whether this process will continue, however, depends both on budgetary limitations and the actions of the Russian parliament in approving or disapproving the START II Treaty.

Will START II Be Ratified?

It initially appeared that START II would be submitted to the Russian Supreme Soviet soon after its signing in January 1993, with ratification perhaps forthcoming by the summer. Because of the ongoing political crisis in the country, however, the issue fell by the wayside. That the Supreme Soviet did not consider the treaty may have been an advantage. While the START I Treaty was ratified in November 1992 on a 157 to 1 vote (with 26 abstentions), the deeper cuts called for by START II were likely to be more controversial.[45] Indeed, one reason for the overwhelming ratification of START I was that it could be used to pressure Ukraine to ratify it and eliminate its nuclear weapons. Prospects for the passage of START II were less clear. An optimistic analysis of the likely outcome of the vote, conducted by Presidential Council member Georgii Satarov and based on past voting patterns, projected that some 60 percent of the deputies would favor the treaty, but he also noted that the outcome would be determined by ten to twenty votes.[46]

Initial discussions of START II began in the Supreme Soviet on 11 January 1993.[47] Questions immediately arose over both the cost of implementing the agreement and its effect on the strategic balance and stability. Formal hearings in the Committee on Defense and Security began on 2 March, with testimony in favor of the treaty presented by Foreign Minister Andrei Kozyrev.[48] The Foreign and Defense Ministries, together with the Russian Security Council, apparently lobbied hard for the treaty but were concerned that treaty opponents were attempting to prolong hearings and were preparing to introduce amendments when the treaty reached the floor.[49] Proceedings ground to a halt when Russian President Boris Yeltsin attempted to bypass the parliament and rule by decree in March, and the treaty became directly entangled in the clash of personalities when Supreme Soviet Chairman Ruslan Khasbulatov stated that the treaty would be endorsed only if it were presented by a foreign minister who enjoyed the respect of the public, a clear and direct attack on Kozyrev.[50] Thus, by April 1993, opposition to the treaty appeared to be intensifying in parliament, and with Khasbulatov blocking action it appeared that governmental pressure for ratification ceased.[51] In part, this may also have been a relief for the government, for Ukraine had still not ratified START I, and that move was becoming an unstated prerequisite for START II consideration.

START II languished throughout the rest of 1993 as the political battles became more intense and the prospects for ratification diminished. With the forceful dissolution of parliament in October 1993 and the election of a new parliament, the State Duma, in December, the stage was set for another round in the ratification debate. According to the new Russian constitution, treaty ratification requires a simple majority in both houses of the Russian Federal Assembly, the State Duma and the Federation Council.[52]

It is not clear, however, whether the treaty stands any better chance of ratification in the new parliament than it did in the old. To win a majority of 226 votes in the Duma would require that Russia's Choice, the Union of 12 December, the Party of Russian Unity and Concord (PRUC), YABLOKO, and the New Regional Policy factions, plus at least three more deputies, all vote in favor of ratification, with no absentees, abstentions, or defections.[53] This prospect appears rather unlikely, for it requires complete support from centrist groups such as the PRUC, which are likely to be split on the treaty. One indication of the difficulty of passing important legislation is given by the vote over the 1994 budget, when on the final reading of the bill the Duma failed to reach a quorum on three attempts to hold a vote. The budget did finally pass, but most of the votes in favor came from more "conservative" factions, such as the Russian Communist Party, the Liberal Democratic Party, and the Agrarian Party.[54] These groups will almost certainly vigorously oppose the START II Treaty, rendering ratification a difficult if not impossible proposition. (Together the three groups, plus the nationalist Russian Way group, control about 188 votes. The party that might hold the balance of power in a conservative versus radical-centrist split might be the Women of Russia faction, with 23 votes.)[55] If the treaty were to pass the Duma, the vote in the Federation Council would appear to be even more uncertain. In the Federation Council regional interests dominate, and the orientation of the deputies may therefore vary more widely from issue to issue.[56] The START II Treaty appears to be "region-neutral", thus making the outcome unpredictable, although the Federation Council is generally considered to be more moderate than the Duma.

If the START II Treaty is submitted to the Duma, a number of issues are likely to be raised by treaty opponents. Principal among these will be the cost of implementation and the danger of Russia losing parity with the United States.

Estimates of the cost of implementing the START treaties vary widely. A semiofficial estimate, published shortly after START II was signed, estimated the total cost of START I implementation at 30 billion rubles (using first quarter 1992 prices), with implementation of START II costing an additional 20 to 30 percent. Costs to the navy of treaty implementation were reportedly nil. This is compared to an annual expenditure on strategic forces of some 20 billion rubles, which could decline to 15 billion rubles after the reductions.[57] Another estimate, apparently one done for the Supreme Soviet, suggests a cost of 80 billion to 90 billion rubles over and above the cost of START I.[58] There may also be some cost savings, since SRF personnel will be trimmed by twenty-five thousand and maintenance and logistics costs will drop, but these are often overlooked during debates on the cost of disarmament.[59]

Some opponents of the treaty are likely to both overestimate the cost of implementation and use this overestimate to demand large contributions from the United States and other Western states in order to subsidize denuclearization. As in the Ukrainian case, some supporters of the treaty may indeed accept these estimates, while treaty opponents may simply advance financial demands in order to defeat the treaty or make its implementation conditional on unrealistic levels of Western funding. Substantial Western aid has been made available, including approximately $400 million committed under the U.S. Nunn–Lugar denuclearization program, although delivery of the aid has been slow.[60] Yet even this amount may not be sufficient to meet the demands of many treaty opponents who propound high estimates of disarmament costs. Indeed, many opponents are likely to oppose the treaty whatever the level of funding out of fundamental opposition to and distrust of the West and the arms reduction process—many members of the Liberal Democratic Party (LDP) and the Communist Party of the Russian Federation (CPRF) might fall into the latter category.

In terms of force structure, opponents of the treaty have been arguing that it forces Russia to give up its great advantage in heavy MIRVed ICBMs while allowing the United States to retain its predominance in bomber and SSBN systems. They argue that START II, taken together with the conventional threat, is dangerous to Russia's security.

A new source of opposition to the treaty may also be emerging. While in the past the Russian military leadership has been supportive of the treaty, in part because it may free funds for conventional forces, the recent passage of a much lower defense budget than the military had requested may jeopardize this support. One apocalyptic report by ITAR-TASS claimed that "military experts" estimated that given the budget approved by the State Duma, Russian strategic forces would be funded at only 10 percent of their requirements, and the forces would deteriorate so rapidly that by the year 2000 only ninety launchers would remain.[61] While such a report is hard to take seriously, it suggests a deep concern within the military concerning the defense budget. A few days after the report appeared, the chairman of the Federation Council, Vladimir Shumeiko, traveled to an SRF regiment in order to determine the budget's impact on the forces. While SRF Commander Sergeev did not repeat TASS's forecast, he did express concern about the SRF's ability to implement the treaties and carry out combat alerts within the proposed budget.[62] The military's financial problems were highlighted when the local electricity company suddenly cut off power to one of the SRF's main strategic command posts in September 1993 because of an unpaid 2.5 billion ruble electricity bill.[63] The command post was able to continue operation on its backup generators until power was restored, and the control of nuclear weapons was not threatened. However, the incident certainly did reemphasize the difficulties the military has had in adjusting to the new economy and triggered a new round of complaints concerning the inadequacy of the defense budget.

There are therefore many reasons for being pessimistic concerning the likelihood of START II being ratified by the Russian parliament. So far the Yeltsin administration does not appear to be pushing hard for the Duma to act on the treaty. Yeltsin may be waiting for the United States to ratify the agreement first (as it did with START I). Even if the treaty does come before the Federal Assembly, it is quite possible that deputies may adopt the approach used by Ukraine—conditional ratification with a number of requirements (such as increased financial assistance) that must be met before full implementation. Such a move could delay full implementation even further and might reopen negotiations on a number of potentially contentious issues. Even if the treaty is finally ratified in 1995, implementation of START II could not begin until late 1995 at the earliest, making the meeting of the treaty's implementation timetable unlikely.

Implementation Without Ratification?

It is possible that nuclear arms reductions in Russia will continue even without ratification of START II. In such a case, however, the drawdown of forces might be slower, and Russia might choose to retain a number of MIRVed ICBMs. If the reduction occurs without ratification, questions of stability and warhead security will remain. Indeed, many of these issues may be exacerbated by a failure to ratify the treaty, since political support in the United States for financial assistance to the denuclearization program might be weakened.

A precedent for such implementation without ratification has been set by START I, which, even though ratified by all parties, had not formally entered into effect as of September 1994.[64] By then the United States had already reduced its nuclear weapons to within treaty limits, a reduction to about eighty thousand warheads.[65] Russian reductions in nuclear weapons have also been proceeding, although Russia has not yet reduced its warhead total to within START I limits. By September 1994, warheads had been removed from approximately four hundred ICBMs within Russia and some twenty bombers, while between ten and twenty older SSBNs had been retired.[66] Yet, while many ICBMs may be deactivated, it appears that their destruction is lagging—an article in *Izvestiia* reported that in 1993 some thirty-two ICBMs had been dismantled at a special facility, with another forty-four scheduled for 1994.[67]

Indicating his support for continuing implementation of START I, Yeltsin asserted after the Washington summit in September 1994 that Russia was not lagging behind the United States in the pace of disarmament and that the two sides were "keeping to within a couple of missiles of schedule."[68] Even if there have been some reductions in weapons in Russia, however, the total number of strategic nuclear warheads in the CIS may still total some ten thousand to eleven thousand.[69] It is unlikely that warhead dismantlement will be able to keep pace with the reduction of launchers, as the Russian dismantling system must already cope with a large number of tactical warheads, and there may be increasing difficulties reaching or maintaining the planned two thousand warheads per year dismantlement rate. Indeed, even in the United States, planned dismantlement rates have not been achieved, and there have been shutdowns at disassembly sites due to safety violations.[70] Some steps have been taken toward speeding the implementation of START II, but it remains unclear whether they will have a significant effect. Shortly before the September 1994 summit meeting the U.S. Department of Defense concluded a nuclear policy review that did not endorse moves to reduce U.S. forces to START II levels unilaterally but did allow for a further reduction in the number of platforms (SSBNs and bombers) on a unilateral basis while retaining the number of warheads allowed under START II.[71] At the summit itself, the two presidents agreed that immediately after START II ratification, the two sides would move rapidly to remove warheads from launchers, so that launchable weapons would be reduced to START II limits well before the 2003 implementation deadline.[72] Since ratification of START II still appears unlikely, the value of this agreement remains unclear.

While nuclear weapons were not a major item of discussion at the Washington summit, Yeltsin did make proposals at the United Nations for follow-on talks on arms reduction with the other nuclear powers, and the issue of interpretation of the Antiballistic Missile (ABM) Treaty was discussed. These two issues may become crucial in debates over START II, since many critics of the accord point out that a reduction to three thousand or thirty-five hundred warheads would leave Russia at a disadvantage, since Russia's nuclear force should be compared to the British, French, U.S., and Chinese forces combined, as they are all potential opponents. Similarly, reductions in nuclear forces increase the risk of "breakout" from the ABM Treaty, and with the United States pursuing an ambitious program to develop a theater defense system, Russian analysts are increasingly concerned that the ABM Treaty be strictly observed.[73]

Thus, the prospects for implementation without ratification remain unclear at best. Perhaps even more likely, however, might be a process of partial implementation. Many of the current generation of Russian ICBMs are nearing the end of their service life and must be retired within the next decade. However, a reduction plan based on necessity, rather than treaty obligations, might proceed more slowly and might not incorporate one of the most important features of START II: the elimination of MIRVed ICBMs. Given the intensity of the arguments against a rapid transition to the SS–25, the SRF could under these circumstances attempt to maintain the SS–24 and SS–19 force for a much longer period, particularly if service agreements, or even new production agreements, could be forged with Ukraine for either whole SS–24 missiles or spare parts. Russia might also attempt to develop a new ICBM based on its MIRVed sea-launched ballistic missile (SLBM) designs, an approach that might allow the deployment of a replacement for aging systems without a long design phase.

Over the longer term, the direction of Russian strategic policies and force structure may be determined by broader political developments rather than the narrower considerations of nuclear planning. Two potential developments stand out here: (1) a victory by nationalist or communist parties in either the parliamentary elections scheduled for late 1995 or the presidential elections in 1996;[74] and (2) a confrontation or possible conflict with Ukraine. These two contingencies, while not highly probable, are certainly within the bounds of possibility and would have a decisive impact on the development of Russian forces.

In the first case, implementation of START II would likely be halted. Even with a conservative government, however, it is unclear how a substantial increase in funding for strategic forces could be achieved. It is more likely that rather than increasing strategic force size, such a government might act to preserve existing forces via refurbishment programs. A key factor under this scenario might be Ukraine's position concerning Russia. A rapprochement between the two states could lead to Ukraine's again providing modern missiles (such as the SS–24) to Russia, allowing it to continue to modernize its MIRVed ICBM force. Even after the election of Leonid Kuchma to the position of Ukrainian president, however, the prospects for such a close strategic cooperation between the two states appear dim.

A more dangerous scenario would entail a Russian *anschluss* of the Crimea, and possibly parts of eastern Ukraine, by force or by threat of use of force. The worst-case version of this scenario could include a war between the two states. If such a scenario came to pass before Ukraine completes its denuclearization process, it would obviously result in its termination. In this worst case it is clear that the strategic situation would change completely and all forms of U.S.-Russian strategic cooperation would be suspended. Rearmament, the extension of NATO eastward to Poland, Czechoslovakia, and possibly Hungary, and the imposition of sanctions could all become top strategic priorities under a new policy of containment. Under this scenario, START II implementation would undoubtedly be halted on both sides.

Conversely, any breakdown in the denuclearization process in Ukraine could result in the suspension of START implementation. While that process does appear to be proceeding fairly smoothly, it would not be surprising if further delays occurred. Under some circumstances, such as increased political instability in Russia or the election of a new Russian government with revanchist aims, Ukraine might reconsider its decision to become non-nuclear.

The uncertainty surrounding Russia's political evolution and its relations with neighboring states thus heightens the uncertainty surrounding the START II Treaty's implementation. The best case, ratification and implementation, appears the least likely outcome. The next-best case, implementation without ratification, appears more likely. Perhaps most probable, however, is a slower reduction than foreseen under the treaty, with the possible retention of at least some MIRVed ICBMs past 2003. The worst-case outcome would now appear to be Russia suspending the implementation altogether and attempting to maintain a force near the START I limits. Further buildups in strategic offensive or defensive weapons would seem to be highly unlikely, however, even under a highly conservative nationalist government.

Conclusions

The arguments for nuclear weapons reduction in the post–Cold War era are compelling, but since the nuclear danger has receded, so has the urgency attached to the destruction of nuclear weapons. In Russia, pressing economic and political problems have diverted attention from the nuclear issue, while the polarization of politics has reduced chances for the early ratification of START II. Indeed, the continued mistrust of the West among conservative circles, combined with the cost of disarmament, has given rise to a strong lobby for retaining nuclear weapons. Thus, a continuation of current Russian policies—implementation of START I and destruction of many tactical nuclear weapons—may be the best short-term outcome.

Over the longer term, the implementation of START II depends primarily on long-term political trends between Russia, its neighbors, and the United States, which are increasingly difficult to predict. While the dissolution of the old Supreme Soviet led to a less confrontational relationship between the president and parliament, it is likely that either new confrontations will develop or Yeltsin will move to co-opt some of the positions of the opposition. In either case, a tougher line in foreign policy toward Russia's neighbors and with the West could lead to further delays or abandonment of the START II implementation.

Given these considerations, Western policy makers might well press for rapid, informal implementation of START II, offering additional financial incentives to Russia to do so. Reciprocal moves to reduce weapons even before the treaty is ratified might well be necessary to keep the process on track. Failure to move with all due haste may well result in the failure to implement these far-reaching disarmament treaties and the growth of new tensions in Russian-U.S. relations.

Notes

1. For an overview of the Ukrainian nuclear weapons issue, see the articles in the "Negotiating Nuclear Disarmament" special issue of the *RFE/RL Research Report*, 19 February 1993; and Sherman W. Garnett's chapter in this volume.

2. See Garnett's chapter in this volume; and John W.R. Lepingwell, "Ukrainian Parliament Removes START 1 Conditions," *RFE/RL Research Report*, 25 February 1994, pp. 37–42; idem, "Russian-Ukrainian Negotiations Over Nuclear Weapons: The Past as Prologue?" *RFE/RL Research Report*, 28 January 1994, pp. 1–11; idem, "The Trilateral Agreement on Nuclear Weapons," *RFE/RL Research Report*, 28 January 1994, pp. 12–20.

3. Interfax, 11 August 1994.

4. Reuters, 28 June 1994; Interfax, 8 September 1994.

5. At least twelve SS–18s in Kazakhstan had been deactivated by early 1994. Agence France Presse (AFP), 20 March 1994. The report on the Russian-Kazakh treaty appeared in Interfax, 29 March 1994, although details were not revealed until an interview with the SRF commander aired on Russia's NTV network, 28 April 1994.

6. On junior officer retention problems, see *Syn otechetstva*, no. 47 (November 1993), p. 4.

7. *Krasnaia zvezda*, 9 July 1993, pp. 1–2; 13 November 1993, pp. 1–2. Sergeev claims that even the SRF leadership now stands combat alert duty, although this would seem insufficient to meet the necessary levels. Increased shifts are discussed in *Krasnaia zvezda*, 4 March 1993, p. 1; and *Syn otechetstva*, no. 47 (November 1993), p. 4.

8. Igor' Sergeev, "Raketnye voiska strategicheskogo naznacheniia: Problemy stroitel'stva i reformirovaniia," *Voennaia mysl'*, no. 6 (1993), pp. 12–18; *Syn otechetstva*, no. 47 (November 1993), p. 4.

9. *Krasnaia zvezda*, 14 May 1994, p. 3.

10. Interfax, 29 March 1994.

11. The most detailed accounts of the incident may be found in *Izvestiia*, 26 March 1994, pp. 1–2; and 14 May 1994, p. 4. The latter article points out that security procedures at the base were very lax, and the soldier had previously been disciplined for attempting to strike an officer.

12. Interfax, 9 April 1994.

13. On the border guard shootings, see ITAR-TASS, 9 March 1994.

14. A summary of the provisions of the Massandra protocols is provided in Lepingwell, "Russian-Ukrainian Negotiations Over Nuclear Weapons."

15. Some Russian sources claim that there are only two operational Blackjacks. One

well-informed Western source reports, however, that there may be "less than a dozen" in Russia. See Craig Covault, "Russia Launches Exercise of Composite Strike Force," *Aviation Week and Space Technology*, vol. 139, no. 20 (15 November 1993), p. 51. A report on a recent large-scale strategic force exercise mentions that a "group" of Tu–160s took part and launched a long-range ALCM. See *Izvestiia*, 24 June 1994, p. 1. Training flights in the Tu–160 are reportedly very limited; see Craig Covault, "Russian Bomber Force Seeks Tactical Role," *Aviation Week and Space Technology*, vol. 139, no. 20 (15 November 1993), pp. 444–49.

16. 2x2 TV, Moscow, 3 June 1994, as cited in *BBC Summary of World Broadcasts, Former Soviet Union, SU/2015*, p. 2.

17. Russia reportedly retains some twelve tankers, see Covault, "Russian Bomber Force Seeks Tactical Role."

18. For a discussion of the early-warning problem and its implications for ballistic missile defense, see John W.R. Lepingwell, "U.S.-Russian Cooperation in Missile Defense," *RFE/RL Research Report*, 21 August 1992, pp. 49–56.

19. *Krasnaia zvezda*, 10 January 1994, p. 2. The Skrunda radar in Latvia was a contentious item in troop withdrawal talks, but an agreement was reached allowing Russia to operate the radar for four years, after which it will be dismantled. See Dzintra Bungs, "Troop Withdrawals from the Baltic States," *RFE/RL Research Report*, 3 June 1994. Similarly, reports indicate that Russia has also reached a deal to continue to operate the facility in Azerbaijan. Interfax, 10 April 1994, reported that Russia was still operating the radar. Grachev visited the facility during his visit to Azerbaijan in June 1994 and reportedly reached at least an informal agreement on its continued operation. See ITAR-TASS, 11 June 1994; AFP, 13 June 1994. The status of the radar at the Sary Shagan test site in Kazakhstan is still under negotiation, but it is also under Russian control. See Interfax, 10 April 1994 and 5 May 1994. Perhaps least clear is the status of the facility in Mukachiv in Ukraine. Public protests resulted in the abandoning of plans to open a new Pechora-class radar there, and it is uncertain whether the older radar located there is still operational. For a discussion of the protests, see John W.R. Lepingwell, "Soviet Early-Warning Radars Debated," *Report on the USSR*, vol. 2, no. 33 (17 August 1990), pp. 11–15. The controversial radar station near Krasnoiarsk, Russia, never became operational and is being dismantled, leaving another gap in Russian early-warning coverage.

20. *Krasnaia zvezda*, 10 January 1994, p. 2.; D.A. Afinogenov, "Voennye voprosy bezopasnosti Rossii," *Voennaia mysl'*, no. 2 (1993).

21. The proposal to dissolve the VPVO is not new; it was first made by Soviet President Gorbachev in late 1991 but then languished. See John W.R. Lepingwell, "Gorbachev's Strategic Forces Initiative: Dissolving the Air Defense Forces," *Report on the USSR*, vol. 3, no. 49 (6 December 1991), pp. 4–9. For discussions of the new plans, see VPVO Commander Viktor Prudnikov's comments in *Krasnaia zvezda*, 9 April 1994, p. 3; G.S. Dement'ev, "Vozdushno-kosmicheskaia oborona: Problemy i suzhdeniia," *Voennaia mysl'*, no. 2 (1994), pp. 12–16; *Segodnia*, 20 July 1994; and *Krasnaia zvezda*, 13 July 1994.

22. For an insightful and critical discussion of the doctrine, particularly its nuclear aspects, see S.M. Rogov, "Novaia voennaia doktrina Rossii," *SShA*, 1994, no. 4, pp. 3–10, and no. 5, pp. 3–10. The latter part of the article treats the issue of exclusions in great detail.

23. *Rossiiskie vesti*, 18 November 1993, pp. 1–2.

24. *Nezavisimaia gazeta*, 9 June 1994, p. 1.

25. *Rossiiskie vesti*, 18 November 1993, pp. 1–2

26. While Japan is a non-nuclear state under the NPT, Russian commentators have

expressed concern over Japan's plans to recycle plutonium for nuclear reactor fuel and have pointed to the potential for using such material to develop a bomb.

27. *Nezavisimaia gazeta*, 9 June 1994, p. 1.

28. *Rossiiskie vesti*, 18 November 1993, pp. 1–2; Rogov, "Novaia voennaia doktrina Rossii," no. 5, p. 7.

29. Rogov, "Novaia voennaia doktrina Rossii," no. 5, pp. 6–8.

30. *Nezavisimaia gazeta*, 3 December 1993, pp. 1, 3.

31. Rogov, "Novaia voennaia doktrina Rossii," no. 5, p. 10.

32. V.F. Grinko and S.I. Kokhan, "Kontseptsii sderzhivaniia i strategicheskaia stabil'nost' v sovremennykh usloviiakh," *Voennaia mysl'*, no. 4 (1993), pp. 14–23.

33. See V.Ia. Savchenko, A.S. Pis'iaukov, and S.V. Vasil'ev, "Predotvrashchenie iadernoi voiny v izmeniaiushchemsia mire: Metodicheskii podkhod k obosnovanomu putei obespecheniia iadernogo sderzhivaniia," *Voennaia mysl'*, no. 4 (1994), pp. 6–11; V.M. Zakharov, "Iadernoe sderzhivanie v sisteme voennykh mer predotvrashcheniia voiny," *Voennaia mysl'*, no. 2 (1994), pp. 6–11.

34. The debate over these issues appears to have been conducted in more restricted circles during 1993. See Konstantin E. Sorokin, "The Nuclear Strategy Debate," *Orbis*, vol. 38, no. 1 (winter 1994), pp. 19–40, for an insightful discussion of these issues and the number of SS–25s likely to be deployed. Volkov's article appeared in *Izvestiia*, 9 February 1994, p. 1. Mobile missiles are controlled from a fixed command post. Presumably old Launched Control Centers (LCCs) from previous missile units can be renovated for the SS–25. One article notes that it takes some six months for missile crews to complete retraining for the new system. See *Izvestiia*, 21 April 1994, pp. 1–2; *Moskovskii komsomolets*, 24 May 1994, p. 2.

35. *Moscow News*, no. 11 (13–20 March 1994), pp. 6–7. The SS–25s to be deployed in silos may be a new variant of the mobile missile.

36. *Segodnia*, 19 March 1994, p. 10.

37. Ibid.

38. *Rossiiskaia gazeta*, 1 April 1994, p. 2, in JPRS-UMA–94–013, pp. 7–8.

39. An unusually detailed discussion of mobile versus silo-based vulnerability may be found in *Rossiiskie vesti*, 11 May 1994, p. 5, in *FBIS Daily Report: Central Eurasia*, (FBIS-SOV–94–092), 12 May 1994, pp. 27–30. See also Volkov's article in *Segodnia*, 1 June 1994, p. 9.

40. *Segodnia*, 1 June 1994, p. 9.

41. The treaty allows for moving the deadline earlier (to 2000) if financial assistance for weapons destruction is provided. Most Russian commentaries, however, assume 2003 is the deadline to meet.

42. *Segodnia*, 9 February 1994, p. 9. For a more detailed argument against mobile ICBMs, see V.S. Stepanov, "K voprosu o destabiliziruiushchikh faktorakh SNV," *Voennaia mysl'*, no. 3 (1994), pp. 10–15.

43. Some eighty-one SS–25 mobile launchers were deployed in Belarus in early 1992. By September 1994, some forty-five of them (five regiments) had been transferred back to Russia and deployed at bases at Ioshkar-Ola and Vypolzovo. See *Moskovskii komsomolets*, 24 May 1994, p. 2; *Nuclear Successor States of the Soviet Union,* project report (Monterey, CA: Monterey Institute of International Studies and the Carnegie Endowment for International Peace, 1994), p. 7. *Izvestiia*, 17 March 1994, p. 2, is perhaps the most detailed source. The total number of SS–25s deployed in Russia and Belarus is taken from a report in *Izvestiia*, 20 November 1993, p. 8, based on official figures for May 1993 released by the CIS Joint Armed Forces Command. An independent Western source places the number at 378 at the end of 1992. See "Russian (CIS) Strategic Nuclear Forces, End of 1992," *Bulletin of the Atomic Scientists* (March 1993), p. 49. The usually well-informed

International Institute for Strategic Studies, *Military Balance 1993–94* (London: Brassey's, 1993), p. 99, gives a figure of some 340, including 80 in Belarus.

44. According to Defense Intelligence Agency testimony before the U.S. Congress, Russia produced only thirty-five strategic ballistic missiles in 1993, presumably some of which were SLBMs. See Dunbar Lockwood, "Russian Defense Budget Continues Downward Spiral, Says CIA, DIA," *Arms Control Today* (September 1994), p. 27. The lower figure is consistent with an article on inspectors at the Votkinsk missile plant, where the SS–25 is manufactured, which reports that the output rate for the SS–25 is one or two per month; *Wall Street Journal*, 2 November 1993. ITAR-TASS reported on 20 May 1994 that four regiments of SS–25s (thirty-six launchers) would be deployed in 1994. This number may include the planned transfer of regiments from Belarus.

45. *Washington Post*, 5 November 1992. The U.S.-Russian agreement concerning the safe and secure dismantling of nuclear weapons ran into opposition in the Supreme Soviet in December 1992, and was not voted on because of concerns over clauses limiting the United States' liability for accidents. The opposition to this treaty, which had to be passed to start U.S. disarmament assistance, may have indicated a shift in sentiment within the Supreme Soviet. See Interfax, 9 December 1992; *Krasnaia zvezda*, 10 December 1992, p. 3. Indeed, the agreement appears to never have been formally ratified, although Yeltsin did pass a special decree enabling the assistance after the forcible dissolution of the Supreme Soviet in October 1993.

46. Ostankino television, 11 January 1993.

47. *Kommersant*, 12 January 1993, p. 11.

48. *Rossiiskie vesti*, 27 February 1993, p. 2.

49. *Izvestiia*, 24 March 1993, p. 3.

50. Hearings on the treaty were prepared for the week after Yeltsin issued his statement concerning his intent to rule by decree. See Interfax, 15 March 1993. On Kozyrev, see Interfax, 13 April 1993.

51. The committee on defense reportedly presented a number of (unspecified) conditions that would have to be met before ratification to a group of visiting U.S. senators. It appears that the committee chairman, Sergei Stepashin, was not a strong advocate of the treaty. See his interview in *Nezavisimaia gazeta*, 2 July 1993, pp. 1, 3. Stepashin was subsequently appointed to head the new Russian Federal Counterintelligence Service, one of the successor organizations of the KGB.

52. Article 106 of the constitution provides for the Federation Council to conduct "compulsory examination" of laws adopted by the Duma in certain areas, including the ratification of treaties. See *Rossiiskaia gazeta*, 10 November 1993, pp. 3–6.

53. This vote count is based on the faction sizes given in Wendy Slater, "Russian Duma Sidelines Extremist Politicians," *RFE/RL Research Report*, 18 February 1994, pp. 5–9. The size of the factions varies in published estimates and may change over time.

54. *Izvestiia*, 16 June 1994.

55. Slater, "Russian Duma Sidelines Extremist Politicians," pp. 5–9.

56. One count analysis suggests that the Federation Council may be more reformist, possibly with a majority of moderate and reformist deputies. See Vera Tolz, "Russia's New Parliament and Yeltsin: Cooperation Prospects," *RFE/RL Research Report*, 4 February 1994, pp. 1–6.

57. The estimate, while unattributed, appears in an article written by two officials from the disarmament department of the Russian Foreign Ministry. See Oleg M. Sokolov and Iurii P. Kliukip, "K bezopasnomu budushchemu: Start dogovora SNV–2," *Mezhdunarodnaia zhizn'*, March 1993, p. 5.

58. *Rossiiskie vesti*, 27 February 1993, p. 2. Presumably this estimate also uses first-quarter 1992 prices.

59. One estimate suggests savings of 80 to 90 billion rubles (in 1992 rubles) due to START II cutbacks. See Sorokin, "The Nuclear Strategy Debate," pp. 29–30.

60. See Oleg Bukharin's chapter in this volume for a discussion of some plans for distributing the aid. Much of the delay in disbursing Nunn–Lugar funds is due to the slow responses from various Russian bureaucracies. For a summary of Western denucle-arization aid to Russia, see *Nuclear Successor States of the Soviet Union*, pp. 19–21.

61. ITAR-TASS, 16 May 1994.

62. ITAR-TASS, 20 May 1994. At the time, Shumeiko was calling for the Federation Council, which he chairs, to greatly increase the government's proposed defense budget, an effort that failed.

63. Interfax, 22 September 1994; *Segodnia*, 23 September 1994.

64. While the treaty was approved by all parliaments involved, full ratification remains conditional on Ukraine's acceding to the Nuclear Nonproliferation Treaty (NPT), as required by both Russian and United States ratification resolutions.

65. Associated Press, 20 September 1994. The number of deployed warheads is higher than the seven thousand "weapon" ceiling of START I because of counting rules that discount bomber loads.

66. The ICBM and bomber figures are from "U.S. and Soviet/Russian Strategic Nuclear Forces: Past, Present and Projected," *Arms Control Today* (December 1994), p. 29. Strategic rocket forces Commander Sergeev stated in April 1994 that some 302 launchers and 403 missiles had been destroyed (presumably he meant deactivated) in accordance with START I, including missiles deactivated in Ukraine. See *Segodnia*, 29 April 1994. On SSBNs, see Robert S. Norris, "Estimated Russian (CIS) Nuclear Stockpile, September 1994," *Bulletin of the Atomic Scientists*, vol. 50, no. 5 (September/October 1994), pp. 61–63. The treaty requires not just the removal of warheads, but the destruction of launchers such as silos.

67. *Izvestiia*, 20 August 1994.

68. Russian television, 28 September 1994.

69. See Norris, "Estimated Russian (CIS) Nuclear Stockpile, September 1994," p. 63.

70. For details on the warhead dismantlement process, see Bukharin's chapter in this volume. On the United States' problems, see *New York Times*, 4 October 1994.

71. *New York Times*, 23 September 1994.

72. Associated Press, 28 September 1994.

73. *Washington Post*, 2 July 1994. For a detailed discussion of these issues, see Spurgeon M. Keeny Jr., "The Theater Missile Defense Threat to U.S. Security," *Arms Control Today* (September 1994), pp. 3–7; Jack Mendelsohn and John B. Rhinelander, "Shooting Down the ABM Treaty," in ibid., pp. 8–10.

74. Under the terms of the new Russian constitution adopted in December 1993, the current Federal Assembly was elected only for a two-year transitional period. However, there is increasing debate in Moscow about the possibility of extending the term of the Federal Assembly so that simultaneous presidential and parliamentary elections would be held in 1996.

UKRAINE: Nuclear Weapons and Other Sites of Proliferation Concern

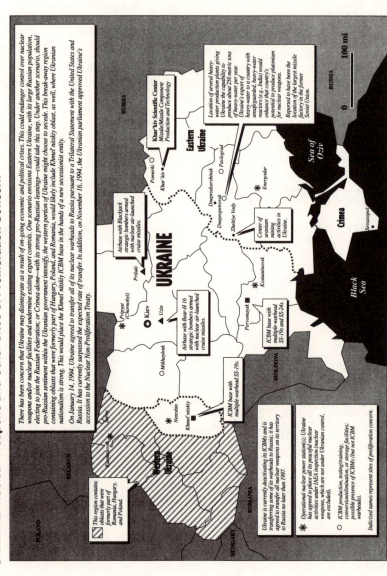

Source: Carnegie Endowment for International Peace and the Monterey Institute for International Studies.

7

The Sources and Conduct of Ukrainian Nuclear Policy

November 1992 to January 1994

Sherman W. Garnett

With the collapse of the Soviet Union, the United States rightly saw the fate of the Soviet nuclear arsenal as a core strategic concern. However, Washington tended to view this problem almost exclusively through the lens of nuclear proliferation and arms control. This perspective—in which nuclear matters occupy a central and autonomous role—has never been sufficient to understand Ukraine's policy on nuclear weapons and disarmament, particularly in the year and a half leading up to the signing of the Trilateral Agreement in Moscow in January 1994.

For Ukraine, nuclear matters have always been subordinate to the larger question of strengthening Ukrainian statehood. This question has an internal and external dimension. Internally, Ukrainian statesmen have sought to create a nation on the basis of conflicting political, economic, and cultural interests. Externally, Ukraine is part of the new geopolitical environment in Eurasia, which will be determined in large measure by the character of the relationship between Ukraine and Russia.

This perspective on nuclear weapons has led to friction and misunderstanding with the West. At times, the actions of the Ukrainian government have complicated the process of negotiating the dismantlement and transfer of nuclear weapons. Policies such as administrative control over missile bases, seen in Ukraine as supporting national control over forces stationed on Ukrainian territory, appeared in the West as a step toward operational control.

In hindsight, it is clear that the Kravchuk government came to view the nuclear weapons on its soil as leverage with the United States and Russia in order to obtain a strategic deal that would address its concerns. That deal was directly related to pressures Ukraine experienced, both internally and externally, to disarm and to address economic and political problems, but it is not simply explained by those pressures. During the course of 1993, as economic conditions deteriorated, Ukrainian President Kravchuk and the senior leadership came to see the need for such a deal. In the months ahead, any nuclear danger in Ukraine will arise more from the impact of the economic crisis on the stability of the government in Kiev and its consequences for stability throughout the region than from alleged nuclear ambitions in Kiev.

Washington's early focus on these ambitions obscured or distorted the real security problem, which is to ensure Eurasian stability in a time of great turmoil and transition. It is the breakdown of stability within and between countries like Ukraine and Russia that threatens the region as a whole, as well as existing nuclear command and control structures and the security of nuclear technology and know-how in Eurasia.

This chapter will attempt to describe Ukrainian nuclear policy from late 1992 to January 1994. This period was marked by the deepening of Ukraine's internal crisis, continued friction with Russia over a range of issues, and the negotiation and conclusion of the Trilateral Agreement by Presidents Clinton, Kravchuk, and Yeltsin on 14 January 1994 in Moscow. The first section will provide an overview of the main sources and orientations of Ukrainian security policy. The second section will focus specifically on the Ukrainian government's nuclear policy, both how it was fashioned within Ukraine and how it was negotiated with Russia and the United States.

The Sources and Orientations of Security Policy

With the exception of a small Green Party, there are no advocates within Ukraine of a pro- or antinuclear policy apart from the larger debate over Ukraine's basic security orientation. For the first years of independence and for the immediate future, that debate will be shaped largely by how statesmen define the conditions for preserving the Ukrainian state. Scholars have debated whether primacy should be given to internal or external factors or a mixture of both.[1] For the purposes of this chapter, it is enough that Ukrainian statesmen have recognized that the two are interrelated.

Domestic Factors

In the West, national security debates assume that a functioning domestic political structure already exists. Ukraine's is still in the making.[2] The legacies of history, of Ukraine's inexperience with statehood, and of the old

Soviet system in politics, law, and economics cannot be overestimated. A new nation must be built that can overcome the habits and conflicts these legacies have left behind. This process will likely take decades. The crucial test for Ukraine is whether it can fashion a stable nation-state on the diversity of economic, political, regional, and ethnic interests bequeathed to it by history and Soviet policy.[3]

At critical junctures, President Kravchuk and other political leaders have argued that compromise on key foreign economic and security issues is necessary as an alternative to the emergence of "two Ukraines."[4] These "two Ukraines" are in fact two orientations on political, economic, and foreign policy questions that have often been described as an ethnic division between the Russian and Russified "left bank" and the ethnically Ukrainian "right bank." Like all such generalizations, it expresses and distorts an important truth. Contemporary Ukraine is a divided society, but its division is not simply an ethnic one.

Rather, for Ukrainian statesmen trying to build and maintain a state, the crucial divisions are over political and economic policy, with the main orientations being those who favor national/reform-oriented approaches and those who favor integrationist/state-oriented approaches. These divisions in places overlap and reinforce the ethnic patterns of settlement (for example, the large socialist and subsidized enterprises and mines are concentrated in the heavily Russian and Russified Donbas).[5] The great danger is not that Russians and Ukrainians cannot live together, but rather that conflicting economic and political interests will politicize ethnicity and bring an ethnic dimension to the current internal crisis. Such an event would have profound consequences for the stability of a multiethnic Ukrainian state.[6]

It should also be noted that these basic political and economic orientations are inextricably bound to the problem of Ukraine's relationship to Russia. Once again, the tie here is not simply an ethnic one, though an ethnic dimension exists for exploitation. The integrationist/state-oriented forces look to Russia for subsidies, markets, the restoration of old economic ties, and an integrationist organizing principle, often with imperial or authoritarian overtones. Ukrainian national and nationalist trends—the two are by no means synonymous—want to break traditional ties with Russia or at least establish countervailing ties with the West.

This basic divergence of views and interests has shaped every political and economic step taken by the Ukrainian state. This divergence cannot be resolved through the triumph of one view or the other without changing the nature of the Ukrainian polity. The Ukrainian leadership, regardless of its party or orientation, must fashion basic policies with a view to balancing these interests, a task made increasingly difficult in the period under review and for the foreseeable future by the economic free fall, the growing regional challenge from the Crimea, and the still incomplete framework of laws and regulations that would regulate these conflicting interests.

External Factors

The external issue that looms largest in the security debate is the problem of Russia. Russia's overwhelming power and historical dominance over much of the territory of present-day Ukraine for the past three centuries have divided opinion over the kind of policy necessary to ensure Ukraine's continued survival. Traditionally, Ukrainian national opinion has been shaped by two basic schools of thought: those who advocated accommodation with Russian power and those who sought national or international alternatives to that power.[7] There is a strong but not absolute overlap between accommodationists in foreign policy and integrationist/state-oriented forces on domestic policy. A similar overlap exists between nationalists in foreign policy and national/reform-oriented forces on the domestic front. Maintaining a balance between these forces has been the essence of the government's policy.

Present-day Ukraine exhibits the clash of these basic orientations. Rough sketches of the two basic orientations follow, with a third—the Kravchuk government's attempt at compromise—described in the following section. These descriptions must of necessity simplify complex positions and ignore nuances of view. The basic orientations are also rather fluid, with adherents often shifting ground on some issues or combining elements of what would seem to be antagonistic positions. The current economic crisis and the lack of solid political institutions help explain this fluidity.[8]

Accommodationists

This group is especially strong in eastern Ukraine, where regional economic ties to Russia are the strongest. Industrial managers, miners, and representatives of labor dependent on the large, heavily subsidized enterprises of the Donbas are the strongest advocates of this orientation. Its major concerns are economic. It believes Ukraine's present crisis will be resolved only through the reestablishment of links with Russia. This approach is not indifferent to Ukrainian statehood, but like its intellectual predecessors, this group believes that Ukrainian statehood depends on accommodation with Russia and that Russia is a power with which accommodation is possible.

The most visible advocate of this position is the president of Ukraine and former prime minister under Kravchuk, Leonid Kuchma. In the period under consideration, particularly from his resignation as prime minister in

September 1993 to his election as president in July 1994, Kuchma emerged as a leading critic of Kravchuk from the accommodationist perspective. Kuchma summarized Ukraine's plight as one of severed connections from the common economic space of the past: "Many of Ukraine's problems are offshoots of the Belovezhskaia Forest," that is, of the December 1991 meeting between the heads of state of Ukraine, Belarus, and Russia that led to the breakup of the USSR and the disruption of the economic ties that supported Ukrainian prosperity.[9] As prime minister and subsequently as head of the Interregional Reform Bloc, Kuchma sought to encourage the revival of regional economic linkages between Ukrainian eastern regions and the neighboring oblasts of Russia.

This trend takes a favorable view of the Commonwealth of Independent States (CIS) and would have Ukraine adhere to the CIS charter and deepen its security cooperation with Russia. On a whole host of issues, from the division of the Black Sea fleet to oaths of loyalty, this trend urges pragmatic compromise with Russia, recognizing that Ukraine's future security policy must work with, not against, Russia. Kuchma took an active role at the Massandra summit in supporting the controversial notion of a swap of Ukraine's share of the Black Sea fleet for debt relief.[10] On nuclear issues, there is little in this view that would pose an obstacle to the return of nuclear warheads to Russia. Kuchma described the series of agreements on the transfer of nuclear warheads to Russia reached at Massandra as "a victory for our state."[11] He supported the Trilateral Agreement in general terms, though doubting whether the compensation and security provisions offer enough to Ukraine—proof that supporters of the accommodationist trend do not simply embrace whatever Russia and the United States have put on the table. As president, he has reaffirmed this support, though again stressing Ukraine's desperate financial situation and the need for additional compensation.

A strong missile lobby forms part of this orientation's support. Defense industrialists, such as Kuchma himself, seek to preserve large-scale industrial enterprises such as the SS–24 production facility. This group is interested less in the nuclear warheads than in the SS–24 and related technologies, which were manufactured in Ukraine. It has heavily influenced government policy, particularly in Ukraine's search for space cooperation and Defense Minister Radets'kiy's apparent embrace of the need to develop a conventionally armed missile.[12] The missile lobby is unlikely to create permanent obstacles to the nuclear disarmament process, though it will be tempted (as have other elements of the Ukrainian government), to link the dismantlement and transfer of nuclear warheads to satisfaction on other issues. In particular this group seeks to participate in space launch and other U.S.-Russian or worldwide efforts that would permit them to keep their missile and defense industrial base intact. In the long run, despite the recent Ukrainian agreement to abide by the provisions of the Missile Technology Control Regime, it is in areas such as missile technology that future troubles might emerge, particularly if economic reform and national defense conversion efforts lag.

Nationalists

Ukrainian nationalist opinion is not easily summarized.[13] Its stronghold is western Ukraine, in regions that remained outside of Russian and Soviet domination until World War II. Culturally, the movement is strong in Kiev, represented in the thinking of a number of political parties, including Rukh, the Ukrainian Republican Party, the Ukrainian Conservative Republican Party, and others.

The nationalists are themselves internally divided over a number of issues. Rukh split over Kravchuk's performance, especially whether support for him or any president, is essential for preserving Ukrainian statehood or whether he was engaged in concessions that will inevitably undermine it. In essence, the division reflects a deeper split within the nationalist movement that pits advocates of the primacy of the state against those who see as the first task the necessity of economic and political reform. The rivalry among various nationalist strands was intense in the March 1994 elections, leading to a competition in some western Ukrainian districts that left many prominent nationalists out of the new parliament.

The orientation does share basic assumptions that underlie its approach to security issues, particularly regarding the long-term threat of Russia. The nationalist view begins with the notion that Russia's size, historical legacy, and present-day intentions pose a long-term threat to the survival of Ukraine. Russia cannot be accommodated, precisely because Russia will eventually pursue a policy that is inimical to Ukrainian independence.[14]

Nationalists have sought Ukraine's immediate withdrawal from the CIS, which Rukh cochairman Viacheslav Chornovil described not long after its creation as "an enormous moral and psychological blow against the recently won independence."[15] In opposition to the accommodationists, nationalists tend to view attempts to restore economic ties between Russia and Ukraine in political, not economic, terms. They argue that Ukraine's economic collapse is the result of a failure to "decommunize" personnel and regulations. Efforts to restore economic links between Ukraine and Russia will inevitably lead to Russian actions that will curtail Ukrainian sovereignty. The example often cited is Belarus. Chornovil characterized proposals for Belarusian-Russian monetary union as a loss of Belarus's independence:

In my opinion, Belarus has been too oriented toward Russia, instead of trying to create a certain counterbalance. If Belarus is too attached to one partner, it will never become an independent state.[16]

To prevent a similar fate for Ukraine, nationalists have advocated various strategies to counterbalance Russian power. These include a cultural policy supporting re-Ukrainization of Ukraine; unwavering support for the army (among certain strains of nationalist thought, an ethnic army); a variety of plans for alliances with near neighbors or the West; and, for some, the advocacy of the long-term or permanent retention of nuclear weapons. Each will be considered briefly below.

Nationalists see in the revival of the Ukrainian language and culture a powerful bulwark against Russia, and nationalist organizations have pushed for the revival of Ukrainian schools and for the "Ukrainization" of the army. Their influence was strongly seen in the first acts of the Rada, particularly in making Ukrainian the state language.

The nationalists are strong supporters of the national military. There were strong ties between the Socio-Psychological Service, headed by General Muliava under Defense Minister Morozov, and the Union of Ukrainian Officers and other nationalist groups. These groups supported the loyalty oath and advocated a much greater purge of the ranks of the officer corps than actually took place.[17] The nationalist orientation would like to see personnel policies favoring ethnic Ukrainian officers, an approach rejected by Morozov and Radets'kiy. The most extreme nationalist organizations, such as the Ukrainian People's Self-Defense Forces (UNSO), are forming their own paramilitary forces, a problem that increasingly worries the Ukrainian leadership at a time when they would like to deal with regional challenges to Kiev peacefully.[18]

The nationalist orientation also places great stress on a foreign policy that would strengthen Ukraine's ties with the West and with other states of the region likely to fear the revival of Russian power. In particular, representatives of the nationalist orientation have argued that Ukraine's geographical importance as a bulwark against Russian expansionism in Europe makes Ukraine the natural ally of the United States and Western Europe. The early nationalist penchant for neutrality—probably reflecting the priority given to nation building—has given way to an urging for deeper and more explicit security ties with the West and evident frustration that the West does not see its own interest in developing a strategic relationship with Ukraine.

The strongest advocates of slowing or halting the process of nuclear disarmament in Ukraine are nationalist. Rukh member and former Minister of the Environment Iurii Kostenko has contributed a number of articles, speeches, and statements on the nuclear question. Kostenko's basic argument returns again and again to the problem of Ukrainian security. In a speech in Washington in the fall of 1992, Kostenko said, "Speaking frankly, the final strategic missile deployed on Ukrainian territory should be destroyed only when any likely aggression against Ukraine will automatically threaten the interests of many other European states."[19] It is this search for security in the face of what the nationalists view as a resurgent, imperial Russia and an indifferent West that drives the argument that Ukraine's nuclear disarmament must be slowed or stopped altogether.[20]

The advocates of retaining at least some nuclear weapons for at least an extended period focus almost totally on the symbolic, not the operational, aspects of nuclear weapons.[21] In discussions with nationalist parliamentarians, issues like secure command and control or the lack of an early-warning system rarely arise. There is little reflection on Russia's likely response to a nuclear Ukraine. Indeed, most appear to regard even a single nuclear weapon in Ukrainian hands as an effective deterrent.[22] One of the chief legacies of the nationalist orientation in the current security debate—and there are many—is to have made it an article of faith that nuclear disarmament must be linked to specific, concrete security commitments from both Russia and the West. The nationalists see the package of security assurances contained in the Trilateral Agreement as inadequate and will try to influence the new Rada, despite the preeminence of the communist and socialist factions, to continue to delay action on the Nuclear Nonproliferation Treaty (NPT).[23] They may succeed in forming at least temporary coalitions with those who want to see if they can raise the amount of compensation for Ukraine for nuclear disarmament. The accession to NPT as a non-nuclear state remains the Rada's last piece of leverage, after the ratification of START I without conditions in February 1994.

The Government's Compromise

The Ukrainian government regularly walked a fine line of compromise between the two dominant political orientations on foreign and domestic policy. In essence, Kravchuk governed by balancing the conflicting interests and orientations described above. His policy reflected to a greater extent the accommodationist and integrationist agenda on economic matters and the national and nationalist agenda on security matters. However, in nuclear matters during the period under study, the government's policy has been accommodationist in aim (disarmament) but nationalist in implementation (for a price).

Though Kravchuk was famed for his ability "to walk through raindrops without getting wet," it is probable that this was a rational (and perhaps the only possible) strategy for giving Ukraine time to consolidate its state. However, this balancing act was inherently fragile, especially as economic conditions worsened. In 1993 and the first half of 1994, there was a general shift toward the accommodationist and integrationist orientations, a move accelerated by the results of the March parliamentary elections and ultimately capped by the defeat of Kravchuk himself. Kravchuk's movements in late 1993 toward a nuclear deal had a great deal to do with his desire to address the increasing weight of the accommodationist orientation and the demands of Russia by bringing the United States into a trilateral strategic framework.

With regard to Russia, Kravchuk pursued the same policy of compromise. He argued that Ukraine and Russia must "live on the same planet, live and be friends, as the saying goes." However, relations between the two must be put "on a new basis, on new principles."[24] This new basis must be a genuine respect for Ukrainian sovereignty. On such a basis, deeper ties between the two states, particularly in the economic sphere, are inevitable. Kravchuk linked this approach to renewed emphasis on developing Ukraine's national military forces and expanding Ukraine's ties with its neighbors, the West, and the world at large.

Kravchuk's policy began by acknowledging Russia's relative strength and Ukraine's relative weakness, particularly on crucial economic questions. He sought to resolve the questions he had to address and was content with putting off matters that could wait. He often achieved this latter aim through the diplomatic method of agreement in principle at the highest level. At times, both Ukraine and Russia have appeared to be pursuing a pattern of diplomatic engagement in which basic principles are ironed out at the highest level, with little or no practical follow-through. For a time, this pattern served Kravchuk well, allowing him to defuse tension with Russia with an agreement, but leaving the issue open as this initial agreement faltered in technical negotiations. Kravchuk and Yeltsin repeated this pattern throughout 1992–94 in attempts to resolve the issues of Ukraine's indebtedness to Russia, the Black Sea fleet, and nuclear weapons.

Kravchuk also avoided entanglements in integrationist political and security schemes that would rob Ukraine of its basic freedom to maneuver. Though Kravchuk supported various economic aspects of the CIS and signed the Russian-Belarusian-Ukrainian economic union, he refused to sign the CIS charter, kept Ukraine in an associate status in the organization, and remained aloof from CIS collective security and peacekeeping arrangements.

This combination of compromise, recognition of Ukraine's economic dependence on Russia, and refusal to permit that dependence to limit political and security options served Ukraine well in the initial period of consolidating the state. However, Ukraine has steadily grown weaker since independence. Its economy has continued to decline, increasing the requirement of compensation for nuclear materials and of general technical and financial assistance to carry out disarmament obligations. Political divisions have increasingly made a coherent compromise more and more difficult to fashion. Indeed, it might be argued that Kravchuk's basic political approach of great tactical maneuvering was well suited to security policy but not to the economy, where real steps had to be taken to avoid pauperization.

Ukraine's growing weakness vis-à-vis Russia was brought home at the September 1993 Russo-Ukrainian summit in Massandra. At this summit, both sides actively explored a compromise in which Ukraine would sell its portion of the Black Sea fleet for debt relief. Interpretations vary over whether Kravchuk actually intended to follow through, whether such a formula was linked to basing rights in Sevastopol, or even whether portions of the Ukrainian government worked out this arrangement with the Russians in secret in advance.[25] Nevertheless, the fallout from this near agreement in Kiev, including the resignation of Ukrainian Defense Minister Morozov, demonstrated to Kravchuk that the policy of delicate compromises and agreements in principle was running up against increasing divisions at home, Russian impatience, and issues that would have to be decided. Kravchuk's experience at Massandra probably played a key role in his decision to accelerate negotiations with the United States and seek a trilateral framework for nuclear and security issues.

In parallel to its Russian policy, the government sought to build and strengthen its own armed forces. From the first days of independence, Ukraine insisted on the right to such forces. Kravchuk avoided any limitation on that right by opposing Ukrainian participation in CIS security structures. Kravchuk remained insistent on Ukrainian freedom of action in the military and security sphere, agreeing only to CIS control over "strategic forces" and defending Ukraine's right to national control over at least a portion of the Black Sea fleet. Yet the Kravchuk government's support for the military must be distinguished from the nationalist position. The government's policy reflected greater flexibility, not simply on nuclear matters but also regarding the willingness to divide the Black Sea fleet and swap at least a portion of Ukraine's share for debt relief. Further, the Kravchuk government had to implement its military and defense policies in a time of great resource constraint. To underscore the resource crisis in the Ukrainian military, the Ukrainian government has repeatedly pressed U.S. officials to implement economic and disarmament-related assistance programs to alleviate the housing shortage for Ukrainian officers.

Ukraine has also sought and received formal diplomatic recognition from the outside world. The Ukrainian leadership looked on this recognition, particularly its scope and speed, as a confirmation of independence. However, the Ukrainian leadership also sought to support its independence and to balance the power and influence of Russia by establishing deeper political, economic, and security ties with its immediate neighbors and with the Western world and its institutions. It did so with only limited success.

With regard to its immediate neighbors, particularly Poland, Ukraine has set aside old enmities that could easily have led to friction between the two states.[26] A regular political and military dialogue between presidents, prime ministers, and defense and foreign ministers has been established. For its part, Poland has recognized the importance of Ukrainian independence for regional stability. However, Ukraine's immediate neighbors face problems similar to Ukraine's own. These states cannot be the source of economic aid or investment. They themselves are searching for greater security integration with the West and must balance their interests in Ukraine with those in Russia. Many fear that the inclusion of Ukraine in the Visegrad Group or other regional structures would hamper their individual progress toward NATO membership. Thus while Poland, the Baltic states, and other neighbors have spoken forthrightly about the importance of Ukraine, they have understandably had little economic or security sustenance to offer. They have also responded correctly but cautiously to Ukraine's Central European Initiative, which sought to establish a forum for consultations among states of the region.[27] Regional initiatives of this type, though useful, do not offer the kind of political and economic benefits Ukraine seeks.

With regard to the West, Ukraine found that these countries have linkages of their own that have prevented the swift development of normal relationships. The economic conditions attached to bilateral and multilateral assistance are beyond the scope of this chapter, though they are very real and frequently misunderstood in Ukraine and throughout the former USSR. What surprised many Ukrainians, however, is the seriousness with which the United States and its allies viewed the problem of nuclear weapons. Many Ukrainians assumed that the West would pursue a much less rigid policy toward Ukraine, recognizing the geopolitical value of Ukraine's independence and thereby lessening the pressure somewhat on nuclear matters. They were wrong. The reestablishment of a single command and control over the nuclear arsenal of the former USSR remained a core strategic concern for the United States and its allies. Ukraine came to understand that to open up a window to the West, it would have to take steps to demonstrate it understood the West's security concerns; in its turn, Ukraine decided that if the West were to obtain what it wanted, it would have to understand Ukraine's concerns.

Nuclear Policy, Nuclear Diplomacy

Ukrainian nuclear policy in the last half of 1994 can be explained by Kravchuk's need to balance the conflicting interests and orientations that define Ukrainian political life. Nuclear weapons represented real Ukrainian negotiating leverage. Kravchuk and his government could exchange Ukrainian nuclear disarmament for real gains, including economic benefits and security guarantees. Of greater importance, however, is that the interest of the United States in nuclear disarmament could be used to draw Washington in on other economic and security problems. As pressure from Moscow increased, Kravchuk could maintain his fragile coalition by bringing in Washington.

The history of Ukrainian nuclear policy and diplomacy of the past few years has yet to be written.[28] From late 1991 to 1993, the Ukrainian government passed from a stage of romanticism about nuclear disarmament to a stubborn insistence that steps toward disarmament be linked to Ukraine's broader security agenda and economic needs. It is my belief that the Kravchuk government—as opposed to various parties and individuals within Ukraine—never seriously contemplated permanent retention of nuclear weapons, particularly after the withdrawal of tactical nuclear weapons in the spring of 1992. Disruptions in the negotiation and implementation of agreements on nuclear disarmament, steps to assert administrative control over missile bases in Ukraine, and other statements and actions that increased anxiety in Washington may be directly traced to the broader security agenda described above, as well as the search for a broad strategic deal on nuclear matters and the rough-and-tumble of Ukraine's internal political process. Such assertions oversimplify a complex reality but go farther to explain events than the view that Ukrainian policy has been a perpetual battle between nuclear hawks and doves.

In late 1992, the Ukrainian government, prodded by critics in the Rada, moved away from its earlier stress on "negative control" and dismantlement within Ukraine in favor of the notion that nuclear disarmament in Ukraine should be linked to specific economic and security conditions. President Kravchuk stated during a November 1992 press conference that Ukraine should have "appropriate compensation" for nuclear disarmament and that, in return for nuclear disarmament, Ukraine should also have "certain guarantees" for its security. These two basic categories—security guarantees and financial compensation and assistance—determined the diplomatic rhythm of 1993 in two ways: first, the Ukrainians themselves had to define those conditions; second, Ukraine, Russia, and the United States had to fashion a framework for Ukrainian nuclear disarmament that incorporated those conditions.

Defining the Conditions

Even while it was negotiating with Russia and the United States on a basic framework, the Ukrainian government was engaged in a half-struggle, half-conspiracy with the Rada to define Ukraine's bottom line on security and financial assistance.[29] For the West, the Ukrainian Rada has played only the role of the villain in the nuclear disarmament process. After the early period of antinuclear declarations, the Rada began raising doubts about the pace and even the wisdom of disarmament. The Rada essentially served in 1993 as the "bad cop," increasing the executive branch's leverage in negotiations with Russia and the United States. However, the Rada also helped define the basic conditions that Ukraine sought and authorized the executive's pursuit of an agreement to obtain them. This is a complex matter, for many within the Rada wanted nothing more than to halt the process altogether, or at least until the more exorbitant demands for security and financial compensations were met. However, with at least the leadership of the Rada, including the speaker, Ivan Pliushch, and the chairmen of key committees, there appeared to be a regular and sustained strategy of cooperation.

To the eternal frustration of Russian and Western diplomats, the Rada repeatedly delayed action on START and the NPT, despite Kravchuk's agreement to language in the Lisbon Protocol that required early action. The Ukrainian government's repeated promises of action throughout the end of 1992 led to U.S. expectations that the Rada would finally address at least START I in January 1993.[30] However, January came, and the Rada postponed consideration until February. On 10 February 1993, the speaker of the Rada stated that START ratification was "not a priority."[31] On 18 February 1993, the Rada formally postponed consideration altogether. The Rada's unwillingness to move on the treaties brought home to many in the West the complexity of Ukrainian politics.

At least the Rada's senior leadership envisaged something more for itself than the role of spoiler. It used its leverage to help define the basic conditions under which the Ukrainian government negotiated with Russia and the United States. Throughout 1993, various members and coalitions spoke out on the question of nuclear disarmament. In April 1993, 162 deputies signed an open letter "on Ukraine's nuclear status." The letter underscored Ukraine's status as a successor to the USSR, including "as a nuclear power." It confirmed Ukraine's "right of ownership of the nuclear weapons on its territory" and underscored the importance of compensation and of "state independence, national security and territorial integrity."[32] This letter, noted more in the West for its strident assertion of Ukrainian ownership of nuclear weapons, nevertheless served to make plain to Washington that a more comprehensive framework than the Lisbon Protocol would have to be found. Throughout 1993, the U.S.-Ukrainian dialogue broadened to include the Rada, even though these meetings often left both sides exasperated at the other's lack of understanding of its concerns.

In August 1993, a group of parliamentarians, led by Deputy Speaker Durdynets and including key members of the foreign and defense committees, visited Washington. This group reflected the divisions within Ukraine itself, leaving U.S. interlocutors with conflicting observations: first, that Ukraine would not push ahead with full nuclear disarmament without a comprehensive framework that addressed its security concerns and requirements for assistance; second, that there were nevertheless differences of opinion within the Rada, with only the nationalist-oriented members setting conditions that could not be met; and, finally, that the senior leadership of the Rada wanted U.S. involvement in a negotiated package that reflected Ukraine's conditions.

The specifics of these conditions remained undefined until November 1993, when the Rada ratified START I.[33] The resolution defined, through specific reservations, the Rada's requirements. Some of these reservations, if permanent, certainly went beyond merely defining the Rada's requirements. Further, the prompt Western negative reaction to the more extreme claims of the document regarding ownership and eliminating Ukraine's obligations with regard to NPT accession also served to shape the Ukrainian executive branch's own interpretation of what the Rada had done. (Kravchuk and other senior officials quickly reassured the United States, Russia, and the world that the Rada's action was not the final word on the matter.) However, it would be wrong, in light of what in fact transpired in the following eight weeks, to see the Rada's action solely as an act of defiance. Further, the links between the senior levels of the Kravchuk government and the Rada ensured that, whatever the Rada as a whole had originally intended, the November 1993 ratification became a basis for the January 1994 Trilateral Agreement.

However, for the West, the resolution presented problems that obscured its value. The resolution could not be taken by the United States or Russia as a legally acceptable ratification of START I. The Rada's resolution declared that Ukraine was not bound by Article 5 of the Lisbon Protocol, which committed Ukraine to becoming a party to the NPT as a non-nuclear weapon state "in the shortest possible time." It reasserted Ukraine's claim to ownership of the weapons and set forth a series of conditions that would have to be met before it would agree to exchange instruments of ratification. These conditions included an interpretation of START I that did not obligate Ukraine to dismantle all nuclear systems on its territory. Yet the document also defined the basic requirements for security guarantees, technical assistance, and financial compensation. It also requested the president of Ukraine to negotiate with other parties on these and other issues and to confirm and control the schedule for elimination of the nuclear systems in Ukraine.[34]

The dilemma in Washington was clear. Should this text be read as shutting the door or opening it? A case could be made that the Rada had finally gone too far, overturning the Lisbon Protocol and seeking the right to retain under START a significant portion of the nuclear warheads on its territory. However, the text also contained specific conditions that could be read as a formal negotiating proposal on security assurances, compensation, and other key issues.

In addition, in several places it either made plain that these conditions were not final or gave the president of Ukraine latitude to negotiate further: first, even in point 6 of the resolution, which claims Ukraine is bound by START to eliminate only a portion of the weapons on its territory, there is language stating that this formulation "did not preclude the possibility of the elimination of additional delivery vehicles and warheads according to procedures that may be determined by Ukraine." Second, points 5 and 11 explicitly asked the president of Ukraine to negotiate with other parties. Finally, point 12 asked the president to confirm the schedule and control over the elimination of nuclear systems to be dismantled by this resolution. These points were important in Washington's assessment of the resolution.

Washington could never accept the Rada's explicit rejection of Article 5 of the Lisbon Protocol as a permanent statement of Ukraine's obligations, but it could explore the basis of an interim deal that would lead to a reconsideration of this statement. In essence, Washington acknowledged that START and the NPT had been temporarily delinked and that an interim agreement might be required for that linkage to be restored. It is clear from subsequent negotiations and the conclusion of the Trilateral Agreement that Washington, in the end, chose to interpret the Rada's action as at least something that could be overcome and perhaps an opening of the door. The key to sustaining the United States' response proved to be the actions of Kravchuk and his government, which led to the Trilateral Agreement in January 1994 and to the Rada's rescinding its November 1993 resolution and ratifying START without conditions in February 1994.

With the March 1994 elections, the Rada continues to reflect the divisions within the country as a whole. However, the largest factions are those of the communist and socialist orientation, which support closer ties with Russia and nuclear disarmament. The largest bloc remains the uncommitted. It is thus likely that the Rada as a whole will continue to delay NPT accession, as well as keep a close and critical watch on the implementation of the Trilateral Agreement to ensure that Ukraine is getting what it was promised.

The Diplomatic Response

Throughout 1993 and until Kuchma's victory in July 1994, decisions within the Ukrainian leadership regarding negotiations on nuclear disarmament with Russia and the United States, as well as other matters of nuclear policy, rested with Kravchuk himself and a small group of senior leaders and advisors.[35] This group included Deputy Prime Minister Valerii Shmarov, Deputy Foreign Minister Borys Tarasiuk, and presidential advisor Anton Buteiko. To this group fell the task of negotiating the Trilateral Agreement.

Though much criticism could be directed at the Ukrainian leadership's lack of energy and persistence on economic policies, the Ukrainian executive showed considerable energy and skill in pursuing a trilateral settlement that reflected, if only imperfectly, its basic conditions. Kravchuk took unilateral steps to begin deactivation of SS–19 warheads in the summer of 1993 and to extend the procedure to SS–24 warheads at a crucial stage of the trilateral negotiations at the end of 1993. In fact, it was Ukrainian executive action in the aftermath of the Rada's November 1993 START ratification that helped solidify the view in Washington that negotiations would continue.[36]

To reach agreement in January, it was necessary to construct a diplomatic framework for negotiations. However, to construct this framework, relations between Washington and Kiev, which had steadily become more tense on account of the nuclear issue, had to be improved. In May 1993, U.S. Ambassador-at-Large Strobe Talbott visited Kiev to discuss a "turning of the page" in U.S.-Ukrainian relations. U.S.-Ukrainian discussions focused not simply on outstanding nuclear matters but also on economic assistance, expanded military and defense ties, and a renewed political relationship between the United States and Ukraine. In essence, the U.S. side sought to sketch the kind of relationship Washington and Kiev could have once the nuclear problems were removed. This initial visit could not possibly reverse months of mutual suspicion, but it did begin a process of negotiation that brought senior levels of both governments together.

This visit was immediately followed by Secretary of Defense Aspin's visit to Kiev. Secretary Aspin came directly from a meeting with Russian Minister of Defense Pavel Grachev, in which the two sides discussed U.S. proposals for early dismantlement of nuclear systems in Ukraine. These proposals included arrangements for international monitoring designed to meet Kiev's concerns about the actual dismantlement, transfer, and final dispensation of the warheads. Ukrainian Minister of Defense Morozov continued these discussions during his visit to Washington in July 1993. Regular diplomatic consultations and correspondence continued, including U.S.-Ukrainian discussions on economic and politico-military matters and defense relations in October 1993. By the visit of Secretary Christopher to Kiev at the end of October 1993, it could be said that the U.S.-Ukrainian dialogue had been restored and a genuine trilateral negotiating process including Russia, Ukraine, and the United States was in existence.

Thus, by the time of the Rada's ratification of START in November 1993, the basic diplomatic structure for negotiation was in place and many of the proposals that eventually found their way into the provisions of the Trilateral Agreement had been tested.

In Ukraine, the growing sense of crisis, brought on by the economic and political demands of striking miners in June 1993 and the Massandra summit in September 1993, made the need to strike a deal more pressing. Washington began to see in Ukraine's latest actions an opportunity to move forward. The announcement on 20 December 1993 that Ukraine would deactivate twenty SS–24s was seen in Washington as a clear signal that Kravchuk and his government had found a way to complete negotiations and deal with the Rada. Indeed, without some prior understanding with at least the senior leadership of the Rada, Kravchuk would not have risked taking such a step. Moscow was also interested in a deal that would preserve the basic framework of Massandra and begin the process of nuclear disarmament in Ukraine.

The Ukrainian Military

A few words should be said at this point about the Ukrainian military. In the period under consideration, the military played a key role in nuclear issues in at least three ways: (1) the military's preoccupation with building a national army under severe resource constraints made it a consistent force for nuclear disarmament; (2) the policies designed to establish control over military facilities and personnel within Ukraine have at times appeared to conflict with the single, secure command and control over nuclear forces;

and (3) Ukraine's deepening defense and military dialogue with the United States made former Minister of Defense Morozov an important conduit for ideas that eventually broke the negotiating logjam.

Though Ukraine inherited some of the best Soviet units and equipment, this inheritance could in no way be regarded as a national military force. The Ukrainian leadership regarded the creation of such a force as a national priority. Kravchuk defended Ukraine's right to establish such a force in late 1991 and early 1992, insisting that nonstrategic forces remain outside CIS command and control. But the creation of this national force had to be carried out under adverse economic and political conditions.

Former Defense Minister Morozov has stated that he worked throughout his tenure without a budget, having to operate on month-to-month, sometimes day-to-day, financing. Social support for officers and enlisted personnel remains inadequate. Over seventy thousand Ukrainian officers and their families lack housing. It was not until March 1994 that Ukraine held its first large-scale field exercise, with most of the first class of draftees passing through without adequate training. That the building of this national force remains unfinished is the single most important determinant in the senior military leadership's perspective on nuclear weapons. These weapons are an unwanted competitor for extremely scarce defense resources. When pressed about military-technical aspects of nuclear weapons, a range of senior Defense Ministry and Main Staff officers stated simply that nuclear weapons were not a military issue but a political matter debated by civilian politicians.[37] In fact, the most difficult struggles between the military and civilian leadership have occurred over resources, military doctrine, and the disposition of the Black Sea fleet.

To construct a national military force, the Ukrainian military leadership has to create loyal and effective officers and enlisted personnel.[38] Ukraine inherited large numbers of Soviet tanks, aircraft, and other equipment, organized into Soviet units, trained in the Soviet manner, and deployed according to Soviet policies and plans. This inheritance had to be transformed, beginning with national control over units and personnel. The policies of acquiring administrative control and administering the loyalty oath to all personnel in Ukraine, including strategic rocket forces (SRF) personnel, brought the imperative of national control into conflict with the need for single command and control of nuclear weapons. In the West, these policies were seen as a potential prelude to the seizure of operational control over nuclear systems. Russia's regularly expressed fears for the safety and control of nuclear warheads added to Western anxiety. However, these policies have to be seen in the context of the collapse of CIS command over strategic forces.[39] Further, as Secretary Perry's party saw in March 1994, Ukrainian administrative control and the administration of loyalty oaths to SRF personnel at Pervomaisk had little or no impact on the dismantlement and transfer of nuclear warheads there.

The Ukrainian military played an important role in the diplomatic dialogue on nuclear disarmament. The United States decided early on in the Clinton administration to pursue a broader policy toward Ukraine, which was announced by Ambassador Strobe Talbott during his visit to Kiev in May 1993. For a variety of reasons, the military and defense relationship developed faster than other aspects of this policy. Secretary Aspin visited Kiev in June 1993, where he discussed a plan for early dismantlement of nuclear warheads as a way of sustaining momentum until the Rada acted on START and the NPT. Morozov visited Washington in July 1993, signing the first Memorandum of Understanding on Defense and Military Relations between the United States and a newly independent state of the former USSR. During these discussions in Washington, the two sides focused on options for early dismantlement. Morozov took a personal interest in bringing proposals back to President Kravchuk, although, as we have seen, the ultimate task of negotiating a deal remained with Kravchuk and a small group of civilian advisors. The military leadership also provided policy and technical support for Kravchuk's decision to begin early dismantlement of SS–19 warheads in the summer of 1993 and the extension of the procedure to SS–24s in December 1993.

The Trilateral Agreement

It is appropriate to turn now to the Trilateral Agreement itself. On 14 January 1994, in Moscow, Presidents Clinton, Kravchuk, and Yeltsin signed the Trilateral Agreement. This agreement represents an explicit linkage of Ukraine's nuclear disarmament to its broader economic and security conditions, though opinion in Ukraine is divided over whether the agreement goes far enough. The Trilateral Agreement most assuredly does not resolve all issues, and its basic provisions remain to be implemented. It significance lies, however, in the strategic framework it provides to address a wide range of issues likely to confront Ukraine. That framework will be tested by coming crises.

The nuclear portions of the agreement commit Ukraine to the "elimination of all nuclear weapons, including strategic offensive arms, located on its territory in accordance with the relevant agreements and during the seven year period as provided by the START I Treaty." Ukraine agreed in particular that "all nuclear warheads will be transferred . . . to Russia" and that "all SS–24s on the territory of Ukraine will be deactivated within 10 months by having their warheads removed." Within the same time period, "at least 200 nuclear warheads from RS–18 (SS–19) and RS–22 (SS–24) missiles will be transferred from Ukraine to Russia for dismantling." Ukraine is guaranteed compensation for the highly enriched uranium, beginning with one hundred tons of low-enriched uranium underwritten by a U.S. advance payment of $60 million.[40] These provisions reaffirm Ukraine's commitment to complete nuclear disarmament over the period of START implementation by transferring nuclear warheads to Russia. Kravchuk also agreed to keep the pressure on the Rada to accede to the NPT as a non-nuclear state. Of greater immediate significance, however, is that the sides agree on concrete interim steps that will lead to the early deactivation of all SS–24s and require a good faith beginning on the transfer of warheads to Russia and Russian compensation for Ukraine. Unlike previous agreements, the Trilateral Agreement provides performance standards against which Ukrainian (and Russian) behavior can be judged. As of July 1994, 240 warheads had already been transferred to Russia.

Three additional elements distinguish the Trilateral Agreement from previous Russo-Ukrainian agreements or even the Lisbon Protocol. First, both in principle and practice the agreement establishes a truly trilateral framework in which to address future issues. It is obvious that Russo-Ukrainian negotiations to date have at best reached agreements in principle, only to founder in the technical follow-up. U.S. involvement brings needed financial resources and technical expertise, of course, but also important experience in seeing agreements implemented. The U.S. side stressed to both sides that its involvement demanded a change in this pattern. The U.S. presence adds a force for balance in a situation which, if it remained bilateral, could easily be derailed. However, the United States is also being tested through its involvement, precisely because Ukraine expects the United States to act as a balancing force, not only on nuclear issues but across the board. The test of U.S. engagement could come early, either on the Black Sea fleet or the Crimea.

Second, the agreement provides for security assurances that will be extended to Ukraine by the United States, Russia, and the United Kingdom once Ukraine has acceded to the NPT as a non-nuclear state.

These assurances fall far short of the kind of guarantees Ukrainian negotiators and parliamentary leaders regularly demanded. Yet they provide the strongest language on the recognition of existing borders to which Russia has ever agreed. Both the RSFSR-Ukrainian SSR Treaty and the Minsk Agreement speak of the recognition of territorial integrity "within the framework of" the USSR or the CIS.[41] These assurances, based on existing language in CSCE documents and the NPT, provide basic pledges that the powers will refrain from the threat or use of force against Ukraine, not employ measures of economic coercion, and not use nuclear weapons against Ukraine. These assurances are political, not legally binding. For Ukraine, they probably represent the best deal obtainable. Once again, their real worth will be determined in the months ahead, as Ukraine tests their efficacy—and particularly U.S. willingness to engage on issues outside nuclear disarmament.

Finally, the agreement pledges the United States to expanded technical and financial assistance.[42] President Clinton promised "to expand assistance" beyond the minimum of $175 million already envisaged. During a subsequent visit of economic experts from Ukraine to Washington in January 1994, the groundwork was laid for an expansion of dismantlement assistance to $350 million. The agreement also provided important momentum to the U.S.-Ukrainian economic relationship. Kravchuk's visit to Washington in March 1994 led to an agreement to double economic assistance to $350 million.

The Trilateral Agreement is not the final settlement of the nuclear question in Ukraine. Much will depend on whether the framework and linkages it establishes hold up to the challenges that lie ahead. Ukraine will seek to apply the framework to looming problems, such as the Crimea. Ukrainian Defense Minister Radets'kiy already invited the United States to mediate in Russo-Ukrainian negotiations on the division and basing of the Black Sea fleet.[43] If Ukraine believes that the broad framework established by the agreement is not working, Ukraine will have few scruples in backtracking on its nuclear obligations. It is both the promise and uncertainty of the agreement that has marked subsequent Ukrainian debate on the agreement and the government's first positive steps to uphold its part. The government did not formally present the agreement to the Rada for ratification; rather, the Rada debated the agreement and then, on 3 February 1994, proceeded to ratify START without reservations, in effect repealing the November 1993 resolution and making the tentative judgment that the Trilateral Agreement met the basic conditions laid out in the original resolution.[44]

Conclusion

This chapter has argued that Ukrainian nuclear policy from late 1992 to the signing of the Trilateral Agreement in January 1994 can be understood only by examining the conflicting domestic and foreign policy interests and orientations that the Ukrainian leadership confronted in its attempt to build and secure the Ukrainian state. In particular, as economic and political pressures mounted, the senior leadership negotiated a deal that linked nuclear disarmament to economic benefits and a strategic framework that would include the United States. This framework would help to provide additional support for the delicate balance internally between integrationist and national orientations and externally between accommodationist and nationalist orientations.

In essence, Ukraine sought to change the American perception of the problem from one of nuclear disarmament and nonproliferation to one of the stability of the emerging geopolitical environment in Eurasia. The United States has agreed to the linkage between nuclear disarmament and security, but questions remain. There is a very real chance that the two sides, not to mention Moscow, harbor different understandings of the nature of this linkage and the obligations it imposes. There are voices in Washington and Moscow that would prefer to seal off the process of nuclear disarmament from the domestic and foreign challenges Ukraine must address. How these differences of view will be reconciled as the United States is called upon to deepen its political and economic relationship with Ukraine and to address problems such as the Black Sea fleet or the Crimea remains to be seen.

In retrospect, the United States probably placed too much emphasis on the problem of a nuclear Ukraine. The real dangers in the region arise from domestic economic and political troubles and quarrels among the states of Eurasia, not a deliberate search for a nuclear deterrent. If the United States now understands these sources of danger and is prepared to address them, future historians will regard the Trilateral Agreement as a crucial turning point in establishing the basic framework for constructive involvement in the region.

Finally, though this chapter has focused on security matters and trilateral diplomacy, it is plain that Ukraine must take economic and political steps of its own. Without such steps, it is likely that the government will not be able to maintain the balance between conflicting forces within Ukraine. The election of Kuchma—essentially on a platform to take such steps and pursue a more accommodating foreign policy with Russia—creates the possibility for greater energy and focus on the economy, though in no way does it remove from the Ukrainian leadership the basic constraints and influences imposed by the political, economic, and regional divisions within the country. If Ukraine does nothing and the crisis deepens, though it might attempt to reconfigure its nuclear policy and squeeze additional leverage from it, this leverage will prove to be less and less useful. In the near term, Ukraine is threatened by its internal economic failures, something for which a nuclear deterrent of any size is useless. The time to act to address its failing economy and permit the deepening of U.S.-Ukrainian political, economic, and security cooperation is now.

Notes

1. For a review of the debate over the factors affecting the failure of Ukrainian statehood earlier this century and its possible relevance to the current Ukrainian state, see Mark von Hagen, "The Dilemmas of Ukrainian Independence and Statehood, 1917–1921," *Harriman Institute Forum*, vol. 7, no. 3 (January 1994), pp. 7–11.

2. Russia, though also a new state, inherits basic institutions and personnel from the USSR that, in matters of arms control and national security, make it an old and experienced state. In Moscow, American diplomats encountered a common language and experiences, often even familiar faces from the Soviet Ministries of Defense and Foreign Affairs. In Kiev, U.S. delegations found everything new, with many senior Ukrainian officials and parliamentary leaders knowing little of START and the NPT. This generalization, though accurate, should not obscure the small cadre of real experts at work in Kiev from the beginning nor the rapid development of additional personnel in the Ministries of Defense and Foreign Affairs and on the president's Security Council. This generalization about Ukrainian officials should also be linked to another about most of their American counterparts: they knew next to nothing about Ukraine.

3. The problem of nation building in Ukraine is extensively treated by Alexander J. Motyl in *Dilemmas of Independence: Ukraine After Totalitarianism* (New York: Council on Foreign Relations, 1993); and idem, "Will Ukraine Survive 1994?" *Harriman Institute Forum*, vol. 7, no. 5 (January 1994), pp. 3–6. The best summary of Ukraine's inheritance from the USSR is in Taras Kuzio and Andrew Wilson, *Ukraine: Perestroika to Independence* (New York: St. Martin's, 1994), pp. 18–41.

4. For example, on the CIS charter and Economic Union, Kravchuk spoke of the danger of "the creation of a situation in which Ukrainian society is divided into two defined groups" and of the need to avoid the emergence of "two Ukraines." See *Holos Ukrainy*, 20 January 1993; *FBIS Daily Report: Central Eurasia*, 22 September 1993, pp. 26–27.

5. According to the 1989 Soviet census, over eleven million ethnic Russians live in Ukraine, though there is some controversy as to the reliability of the figures. The Russian population is concentrated in the eastern regions (Donets′k, Luhans′k, Kharkiv, Zaporizhzhia), the Crimea, and Odessa. Compare Motyl, *Dilemmas of Independence*, pp. 6–7; Ian Bremmer, "The Politics of Ethnicity: Russians in the New Ukraine," *Europe-Asia Studies*, vol. 46, no. 2 (1994), pp. 261–83.

6. For a view that the March parliamentary election reflected economic and political policy differences, not ethnicity, see Roman Szporluk, "Reflections on Ukraine After 1994: The Dilemmas of Nationhood," *Harriman Review*, vol. 7, nos. 7–9 (March–May 1994), pp. 1–10, especially pp. 1–2. For studies of regional differentiation regarding political issues and voting in the Rada, see Serhii Pyrozhkov, "Ukraine: Where Are We Heading? Whom Do We Support? What Do We Expect? Regional Cross Section of Public Opinion," *Demokratychna Ukraina*, 17 August 1993; Dominique Arel, "Voting Behavior in the Ukrainian Parliament: The Language Factor," in *Parliaments in Transition*, ed. Thomas F. Remington (Boulder, CO: Westview Press, 1994), pp. 125–58. On the problem of center–periphery relations, see Roman Solchanyk, "The Politics of State Building: Center–Periphery Relations in Post-Soviet Ukraine," *Europe-Asia Studies*, vol. 46, no. 1 (1994), pp. 47–68. On the problem of Russians in Ukraine, see Bremmer, "Politics of Ethnicity"; Andrew Wilson, "The Growing Challenge to Kiev from Donbass," *RFE/RL Research Report*, 20 August 1993, pp. 8–13. On the confessional tension between the Uniate Church and the two branches of the Orthodox Church, particularly in western Ukraine, see David Little, *Ukraine: The Legacy of Intolerance* (Washington, DC: U.S. Institute of Peace, 1991).

7. In the early 1900s, Ukrainian intellectuals were divided into two main orientations: the federalists, who saw the solution of the Ukrainian problem in the Russian Empire in the framework of a federation; and the independentists, who supported the idea of national independence for Ukraine. (Jaroslaw Pelenski, "Introduction," *The Political and Social Ideas of Vjaceslav Lypyns'kyj*, in *Harvard Ukrainian Studies*, vol. 9, nos. 3–4 (December 1985), pp. 238–39.

8. Other orientations also exist, particularly at the extremes, such as regional separatists who do not accept Ukrainian statehood, or the radical fringe of the Ukrainian nationalist movement. So far, these orientations have not exerted a decisive influence over Ukrainian security policy. However, their influence could be felt in times of great crisis, especially through their use of violence, which could completely transform a conflict such as that between the Crimea and the Ukrainian government.

9. *Izvestiia*, 23 March 1994.

10. Morozov's recent memoirs of Massandra accuse Deputy Prime Minister Shmarov of secretly previewing the idea in Moscow and complains of Kuchma's support for the idea at Massandra. Morozov's memoirs were circulated as a campaign pamphlet in Kiev and published in *Ukrains'ka hazeta*, 1994, vols. 1–4.

11. *FBIS Daily Report: Central Eurasia*, 23 September 1993, p. 28.

12. *Izvestiia*, 25 January 1994.

13. For a broad background on Ukrainian nationalism, see John A. Armstrong, *Ukrainian Nationalism* (Littleton, CO: Ukrainian Academy Press, 1980).

14. On the variety of nationalist and other Ukrainian views of Russia and their policy toward Ukraine, see Roman Solchanyk, "Ukraine's Search for Security," *RFE/RL Research Report*, 21 May 1993, pp. 2–5.

15. *Vysokyi zamok*, 8 December 1992.

16. *Ziazda*, 17 February 1994.

17. Former Ukrainian Minister of Defense Morozov stated that the thousand officers refused to take the oath of loyalty to Ukraine and were permitted to leave Ukrainian service. Draftees from outside Ukraine were also permitted to leave. Six thousand political officers and party secretaries "were not assigned to posts in the Ukrainian armed forces." See Konstantin Morozov, "Theses" (presented to the conference on "The Military Tradition in Ukrainian History: Its Role in the Construction of Ukraine's Armed Forces," Cambridge, MA, 12–13 May 1994).

18. On right-wing extremism in Ukraine, see Bohdan Nahaylo, "Ukraine," *RFE/RL Research Report*, 22 April 1994, pp. 42–49.

19. Iurii Kostenko, "Ukraine's Nuclear Weapons: A Political, Legal and Economic Analysis of Disarmament." This text was distributed during Kostenko's visit to Washington in the fall of 1992.

20. There has been a pronounced shift in nationalist opinion on security issues, particularly on the nuclear questions. Rukh leaders were crucial to the Rada's drafting and adoption of its original antinuclear policy. Many nationalists cared more about policies that would ensure the revival of Ukrainian language and culture than national security issues. They shared with the bulk of the population a revulsion toward nuclear issues brought on by the Chernobyl disaster. Over time, as Russian reform appeared to falter, the Russian parliament asserted territorial claims on the Crimea and Sevastopol; since the response from the West was less than expected, they adopted greater interest in national control over nuclear weapons, even if only to extend the period of disarmament or control the process. A similar shift is under way regarding association with Western security institutions, with the Trilateral Agreement's security assurances raising renewed interest in stronger security options, such as eventual membership in NATO. See Bohdan Nahaylo, "The Shaping of Ukrainian Attitudes Toward Nuclear Arms," *RFE/RL Research Report*, 19 February 1993, pp. 21–45.

21. An exception is the writings of former Soviet SRF General Vladimir Tolubko, who has taken up a "nationalist" position on nuclear weapons but is not regarded by many of the nationalists themselves as one of their own. Tolubko argued forcefully that Ukrainian nuclear disarmament was premature and that what was needed beforehand was a European collective security system that would eventually provide a framework for nuclear disarmament pursued in an "even and equal" fashion. See *Holos Ukrainy*, 10, 20, 21 November 1992. Tolubko has also claimed that Ukraine's military-industrial complex was capable of supporting Ukraine as a nuclear state. See *Kyivs'ki vidomosti*, 6 November 1992. Tolubko lost his seat in the Rada in the March 1994 elections.

22. Former Minister of Defense Morozov, himself now a political figure of the nationalist orientation, recently argued that nuclear weapons have a deterrent value even though they are outside Ukraine's control: "It becomes clear when one analyzes the situation that the very presence of these dangerous weapons on the territory of our state is a factor of deterrence to those wishing to create conflicts in Ukraine." See Morozov, "Theses."

23. Indeed, on 16 May 1994, Chornovil urged that measures to implement the Trilateral Agreement be halted.

24. *FBIS Daily Report: Central Eurasia*, 21 March 1994, pp. 40–45.

25. Morozov, memoirs, in *Ukrains'ka hazeta*, 1994, vols 1–4 (see note 10).

26. On the historical background of Ukrainian-Polish relations, see Ivan L. Rudnytsky, "Polish-Ukrainian Relations: The Burden of History," in *Poland and Ukraine Past and Present*, ed. Peter J. Potichnyj (Edmonton, Canada: The Institute of Ukrainian Studies, 1980), pp. 3–31. For an extended discussion of recent Polish-Ukrainian relations, see Ian Brzezinski, "Polish-Ukrainian Relations: Europe's Neglected Strategic Axis," *Survival*, vol. 35, no. 3 (autumn 1993), pp. 26–37; Stephen R. Burant, "International Relations in a Regional Context: Poland and Its Eastern Neighbors—Lithuania, Belarus, Ukraine," *Europe-Asia Studies*, vol. 45, no. 3 (1993), pp. 395–418.

27. "To Strengthen Regional Security in Central and Eastern Europe: Initiative of Ukraine" (press release, Embassy of Ukraine to the Republic of Poland, 22 April 1993).

28. The best analysis and reporting has been by the staff at Radio Liberty. See particularly the following articles in special issues of *RFE/RL Research Report* devoted to nuclear disarmament issues: John W.R. Lepingwell, "Ukraine, Russia and the Control of Nuclear Weapons," and idem, "Beyond START: Ukrainian-Russian Negotiations," *RFE/RL Research Report*, 19 February 1993, pp. 4–20 and 46–58; idem, "Negotiations Over Nuclear Weapons: The Past as Prologue?"; and idem, "The Trilateral Agreement on Nuclear Weapons," *RFE/RL Research Report*, 28 January 1994, pp. 1–12 and 12–20; Nahaylo, "Shaping of Ukrainian Attitudes Toward Nuclear Arms," pp. 21–45.

29. It remains an intriguing question as to what extent the Rada's role in the nuclear debate reflects genuine institutional conflict with the government. Some senior diplomatic observers in Kiev have suggested that, at least in terms of the senior leadership of both the Rada and the executive branch, a large amount of orchestration occurred.

30. Members of the Rada repeatedly argued that the two treaties should be treated separately, despite the Lisbon Protocol. Washington opposed such separation but was also interested in actions that would give the process of disarmament some forward momentum. By mid-1993, Washington had resigned itself to the prospect that the treaties would be treated separately and hoped to use pressure to ensure that action on the NPT followed START ratification as soon as possible.

31. Ostankino Television, 10 February 1993.

32. The letter reads in part: "[E]ven prior to the ratification of START I, a whole complex of problems needs to be resolved. This applies in particular to the question of compensation for the nuclear materials that were taken out of the warheads of the

tactical nuclear weapons that had been transferred from Ukraine to Russia in the spring of 1992, to the guarantees of destroying these weapons by Russia, and to the enormous financial expenditure on the reduction of the nuclear potential. At the same time it would be a mistake to agree to promises of insignificant monetary compensation in exchange for Ukraine's immediate nuclear disarmament. The question of nuclear disarmament, state independence, national security, and territorial integrity cannot become an object for bargaining or 'monetary compensations.' " The text may be found in *FBIS Daily Report: Central Eurasia*, 30 April 1993, p. 51.

33. Lepingwell has a different view. He states that "none of the conditions [in the Rada's START I resolution] is particularly surprising: the Ukrainian government had been articulating its position for about a year." Lepingwell, "Negotiations Over Nuclear Weapons: The Past as Prologue?" p. 9. This is not quite the way Washington saw the problem. It is true that Ukrainian officials had been talking about security guarantees and technical and financial assistance and compensation for about a year; it is also true that the categories that appeared in the Rada's resolution did not surprise anyone. However, the resolution did put to rest the debate within Ukraine—often reflected in the shifting positions of Ukraine's negotiators—about what specifically Ukraine required from its negotiating partners to meet its conditions. For example, before this resolution, there were a number of proposals from the Ukrainians as to both the form and the substance of security guarantees. The resolution laid out the direction eventually followed in the Trilateral Agreement.

34. The text of the resolution may be found in *Holos Ukrainy*, 20 November 1993. The Rada's action resembles the approach it took to the ratification of the 1991 Minsk Agreement. In this case, the Rada also ratified the document with substantial amendments to the text itself (i.e., on the question of the recognition of borders, the Rada struck language placing such recognition "within the framework of the CIS").

35. On key policy matters—and these include nuclear policy—it is right to speak as many Ukrainian commentators do, of a "Party of Power," understood as key government officials, industrial managers, military leaders, parliamentarians, and outside specialists who influence and make decisions. This group shares basic assumptions and cooperates actively, making it difficult to speak of the parliament or the military or other institutions as wholly separate actors. It would also be wrong, however, to ignore the emergence of real institutional interests and their interplay.

36. Ukrainian executive action on the trilateral negotiations intensified as policy makers' recognition of the broader political and economic crisis within Ukraine deepened. In particular, the lesson of the Russo-Ukrainian summit at Massandra in September 1993 was not lost on Kravchuk. If Ukraine attempted to solve the nuclear question bilaterally, it would face an increasingly assertive Russia seeking to exploit Ukraine's weaknesses. A similar conclusion about the need to move swiftly to complete a trilateral framework was being reached in Washington, as the consequences of an increasingly troubled Ukraine locked in a prolonged leadership crisis came to be recognized. Kravchuk listed the Massandra summit as one of the two major unpleasant problems he faced during 1993: "[At Massandra] Russia then saw how hard the strikes were hitting Ukraine, and it was brought to its knees by internal problems. On top of that there was external pressure, and people were taking advantage of our weakness." See *Izvestiia*, 31 December 1993.

37. These responses could also be consistent with highly compartmentalized efforts to pursue a genuine nuclear option. Observers in Kiev have suggested that senior civilian and military officials were presented with a variety of options in 1992 and ultimately decided on the option of using the nuclear weapons to obtain security guarantees and compensation from Russia and the United States. In addition to the military's over-

whelming resource constraints, the importance of the withdrawal of tactical nuclear systems in 1992 in shaping Ukrainian perceptions of basic options probably was crucial.

38. John Jaworsky, "The Transition from a Soviet Military in Ukraine to a Ukrainian Military" (paper delivered at the conference on "The Military Tradition in Ukrainian History: Its Role in the Construction of Ukraine's Armed Forces," Cambridge, MA, 12–13 May 1994).

39. On administrative control and operational control, see Lepingwell, "Ukraine, Russia and the Control of Nuclear Weapons," pp. 11–14. The loyalty oath was extended to SRF units only after Ukraine perceived that the units had passed from CIS to Russian national control. Former Ukrainian Minister of Defense Morozov said recently that, during the initial administration of the loyalty oath to general purpose, air force, and naval personnel, ten thousand officers chose to return to Russia. Morozov, "Theses." The interaction between Ukrainian and Russian policies and statements was exceedingly complex. Recall the debate in the Russian press in the autumn of 1992—to which CIS Commander Shaposhnikov contributed—claiming that CIS-controlled nuclear weapons nevertheless had Russian statehood. See *Krasnaia zvezda*, 30 September 1992. The maneuvering over compensation, particularly that resulting from the sale of highly enriched uranium to the United States, played an important role in Russian and Ukrainian claims and counterclaims over "ownership" of the nuclear weapons and their components.

40. The text of the Trilateral Agreement may be found in *RFE/RL Research Report*, 28 January 1994, pp. 14–15.

41. The existing agreements on territorial integrity amount to conditional recognition of the existing frontiers, and are premised on Ukraine's continuing participation in the CIS. That point was made clear in Russian Foreign Minister Andrei Kozyrev's discussion of the CIS language before the Russian parliament in April 1992: "Esteemed People's Deputies, as far as the Crimea is concerned, we proceed on the basis of the agreement signed in Minsk on 8 December 1991, on the formation of the CIS, which envisages mutual recognition and respect for the territorial integrity of states which are members of the CIS and the inviolability of existing frontiers within the Commonwealth framework. I would like to stress these words—within the Commonwealth framework." See *FBIS Daily Report: Central Eurasia*, 22 April 1992.

42. The problem of assistance and compensation deserves its own special study. In essence, the problem covers three separate but interrelated issues: (1) the problem of compensation to Ukraine for highly enriched uranium (HEU) removed from the warheads; (2) assistance for the implementation of the obligations imposed by nuclear disarmament; and (3) broader economic assistance to soften the effects of the dismantlement of Ukraine's nuclear-related industrial complex. It was the large amount of money likely to derive from the U.S.-Russian HEU agreement that provided the financial basis for the agreement.

43. Author's notes from a joint press conference of Ukrainian Defense Minister Radets'kiy and U.S. Secretary of Defense Perry, Kiev, 22 March 1994.

44. The text of the resolution was distributed by UNIAR, 3 February 1994.

BELARUS: Nuclear Weapons and Other Sites of Proliferation Concern

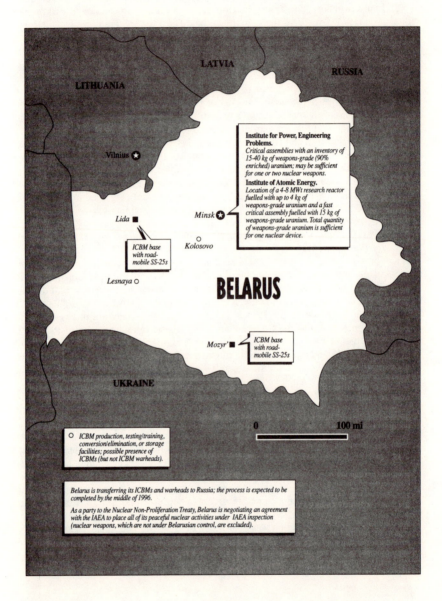

Source: Carnegie Endowment for International Peace and the Monterey Institute for International Studies.

8

Belarusian Denuclearization Policy and the Control of Nuclear Weapons

Vyachaslau Paznyak

In the wake of the dissolution of the Soviet Union, the newly independent republic of Belarus found itself hosting a portion of the former Soviet nuclear arsenal stationed on its territory. This circumstance posed serious questions about the future disposition of these weapons and about future Belarusian nuclear policies. Belarus responded by voluntarily renouncing possession of nuclear weapons and sustaining a positive record of accession to and compliance with relevant international treaties. The road to denuclearization, however, has not been entirely free of obstacles. Belarusian nuclear policy has been unique compared to that of other newly independent states, with its own ups and downs and pitfalls. This chapter explores the major domestic and international aspects of Belarus's nuclear behavior.

Belarus's Nuclear Legacy

During the Cold War, the Belorussian Soviet Socialist Republic (SSR)[1] possessed, according to former republican and Soviet constitutions, the right to pursue foreign policy within its authority. Yet, although it was a founding member of the United Nations, it mainly followed Moscow's lead in foreign policy matters. Needless to say, this subservient role was not always in accord with the republic's national interests. With a few exceptions, Moscow's position on issues ranging from nonproliferation, disarmament, and the positioning of nuclear weapons and nuclear energy were not in accordance with these interests.

Belorussia participated in the international conference in New York in September and October 1956 that founded the International Atomic Energy

Agency (IAEA). It signed and ratified the IAEA statute.[2] In addition, it was also party to the Limited Test Ban Treaty,[3] the Outer Space Treaty,[4] and the Seabed Treaty,[5] and it joined the Conventions on Early Notification of a Nuclear Accident and on Assistance in the Case of a Nuclear Accident or Radiological Emergency.[6]

The republic, however, failed to join the Nuclear Nonproliferation Treaty (NPT), owing to a special decision of the Soviet Politburo directing it not to do so when the treaty was opened for signature.[7] Belorussia's accession to the NPT as a nuclear weapon state would have undermined the broad limiting objective of the NPT and signaled a Soviet violation of Article 1 of the treaty, whereby nuclear weapon parties to the treaty agree "not to transfer to any recipient whatsoever nuclear weapons or other nuclear devices or control over such weapons or explosive devices directly, or indirectly." At the same time, Belorussian accession as a non-nuclear weapon state would have entailed IAEA safeguards on all civilian nuclear activities, which apparently were deemed undesirable then.

During the Cold War, Belorussia also failed to sign or ratify the Convention on the Physical Protection of Nuclear Material. A possible explanation may be that since there was no uranium or other nuclear-relevant natural materials or nuclear power plants in the republic,[8] and the USSR as a convention signatory controlled these matters, there was no need for the republic to sign as well.

There was, however, one four-million-kilowatt research IRT-M pool-type reactor at the Institute of Nuclear Power in Minsk, commissioned in 1962, that was subsequently shut down after the Chernobyl nuclear accident.[9]

From a military point of view, the Belorussian SSR was a huge Soviet military base and, according to Soviet military doctrine and war plans, was to serve as a forward line of defense that included, if necessary, the use of tactical nuclear weapons on its own territory.[10]

Belorussian military and nuclear facilities occupied about 10 percent of the republic, or roughly 2 percent of the former Soviet Union. About 5 percent of all Soviet military forces were stationed in the republic.

After the dissolution of the USSR, Belarus ranked fourth in the "nuclear club" of the newly formed Commonwealth of Independent States (CIS)—after Russia, Ukraine, and Kazakhstan—with about 1,250, or 5 percent, of all the former Soviet deployed nuclear warheads.[11]

There were two operational launch regions for land-mobile RS–12M "Topol" intercontinental ballistic missiles (ICBMs) (U.S. designation SS–25; North Atlantic Treaty Organization code name "Sickle") at Mosyr and Lida, making up 25 percent of their total number in the former Soviet Union, or less than 1 percent of all strategic nuclear weapons.[12] With each equipped with a single nuclear warhead, these ICBMs were deployed in launch groups of nine vehicles. The two bases had six launch groups, or twenty-seven mobile launchers each, for a total of fifty-four warheads.[13] The total number of tactical nuclear warheads in Belarus as of November 1991 was estimated at 1,120: 270 for ground forces, 125 for air defense, 575 for the air force, and 150 for the navy. This total constituted 8 percent of the entire tactical nuclear weapons in the former Soviet republics.[14]

In addition, a phased-array radar of the former Soviet Union's early-warning system has been under construction near Baranovichi and reportedly is nearly 90 percent complete. A radio station at Vileika provides communications for the Russian navy, including vessels carrying nuclear weapons.[15]

Mainstream Nuclear Policies

In the Almaty Agreement on Joint Measures with Respect to Nuclear Weapons, Belarus, Russia, Ukraine, and Kazakhstan confirmed their commitment to the nonproliferation and elimination of all nuclear weapons and pledged "to jointly develop a policy on nuclear issues." In theory, therefore, there would be no sense in talking about these states' separate nuclear policies. However, events took a different direction, especially in the case of Ukraine and Kazakhstan.

Belarus demonstrated its antinuclear stance in its Declaration on State Sovereignty, adopted on 27 July 1990. Article 10 of the declaration set an unprecedented goal of making Belarus a neutral state and its territory a nuclear weapon–free zone.

At the session of the Forty-fifth United Nations General Assembly, Belarus introduced a proposal to create a nuclear-free "belt," which would include Belarus, Ukraine, and the Baltic states, with the possibility of participation at a later date by the countries of Central Europe.[16] Such a zone, according to Belarusian Foreign Minister Piotr Kravchenko, had to be free not only of nuclear weapons but of nuclear power plants as well.[17] Several months later, in January 1992, Kravchenko spoke of a nuclear-free belt including the Scandinavian countries, the Baltic area, and the states of Central and Eastern Europe in the hope that the idea would be discussed within the framework of the Conference on Security and Cooperation in Europe (CSCE).[18]

Even though the narrow objective of a nuclear weapon–free zone comprises only a portion of Belarus's original nuclear-free objective, such a zone would provide enhanced security for its parties through greater mutual confidence, mutual obligations, and credible security assurances. This goal remains as only one component of the broader goal of strengthening the nonproliferation regime.

Nuclear security is indivisible from other security dimensions. An analysis of previous experiences of nuclear weapon–free zones indicates that their feasibility and chances for success depend, in large measure, on the general support they receive from the states of the region concerned. These states must be engaged in a genuine search for common interests and committed to regional stability. Finally, nuclear weapon–free zones must enjoy the relative absence of superpower competition and confrontation.[19] The creation of a nuclear weapon–free zone in Eastern Europe and its expansion in all directions would provide a historic opportunity for the denuclearization of this densely weaponized continent. Unfortunately, this important initiative has not been further elaborated on or pushed forward by Belarus through diplomacy or otherwise.

After the failed August 1991 coup, the Declaration on State Sovereignty was accorded the status of constitutional law on 25 August 1991 until the constitution itself was adopted. The goal of denuclearization has remained unchanged ever since and has been incorporated into all major foreign policy declarations and documents. Article 18 of the newly adopted constitution of the Republic of Belarus reaffirms this goal.[20]

On 2 October 1991, the Belarusian Supreme Soviet adopted the text of the Declaration on the Foreign Policy Principles of the Republic of Belarus, in which CSCE participants were invited to open talks on the elimination of nuclear weapons and declare Europe a nuclear-free zone.[21] Furthermore, at the Forty-sixth United Nations General Assembly session, the Belarusian delegation spoke in favor of concluding a treaty banning all nuclear weapon tests.[22]

Another major step in the establishment of Belarus's nuclear policies was the adoption of its military doctrine in mid-December 1992. While continuing to reflect the state's preference for a non-nuclear and neutral status, the military doctrine also conceptualized the presence of Russian strategic nuclear weapons on Belarusian territory.

The doctrine has two aspects: military-political and military-technical. Whereas the former is represented by the concepts of preventing war and stopping aggression, the latter is represented by the concepts of deterrence and active defense.

In the military doctrine, the concept of deterrence addresses the status of the nuclear weapons of the strategic forces of the Russian Federation temporarily stationed on Belarusian territory and the procedure for their use. The overarching principles that inform the doctrine are stability and reciprocity. Military-strategic stability is ensured by Russian strategic forces as well as by Belarus's veto power over the use of the nuclear weapons stationed on its territory and its right to take part in decision making on or banning their use. Once the withdrawal of Russian strategic forces from the republic's territory is complete, the deterrence concept is to be radically revised or abandoned altogether.[23]

Besides Russia, Belarus became the first of the newly independent states to incorporate the concept of deterrence into its military doctrine. This measure received little attention from analysts, however.[24] Rather, instrumental interpretations of the meaning of Russian nuclear forces for Belarus have been proposed. Roy Allison, for example, concludes that the fact that Belarus formally renounced nuclear weapons and acknowledged Russian possession of them "places Minsk under a de facto Russian nuclear umbrella, covered by a form of 'extended deterrence', with or without specific nuclear guarantees from Russia."[25] Indeed, there can be no Belarusian nuclear deterrence if Belarus does not also possess and control these forces autonomously.

It seems that the drafters of the military doctrine were doing their best to build an all-embracing concept of the military forces on Belarusian soil, even if some of them had little to do with the Belarusian military itself. In addition, this could be an implicit political attempt to reconcile the formation of national armed forces, the consolidation of independence in the context of close military-strategic relations between Belarus and Russia, and the presence of Russian troops on Belarusian territory. Judging by the declared non-nuclear and neutral foreign policy priorities and the corresponding transitory character of the military doctrine, one can see the residual, inescapable, and transient quality behind the post-Soviet deterrence.[26] On the other hand, military agreements between Belarus and Russia were not designed to be, and have not formally become, akin to a military alliance, although some individuals both in Minsk and Moscow regard them as such. (In these agreements, Russia does not pledge to provide Belarus with any special security guarantees that would imply the existence of a military bloc.)

Under the Almaty agreement, Belarus committed itself to accede to the NPT as a non-nuclear state and conclude with the IAEA the corresponding safeguards agreement. The existence of nuclear weapons on Belarusian territory does not violate the treaty as long as Belarus does not own or control them. Hence, there were no legal obstacles that delayed Belarusian accession to the NPT.

According to the former foreign minister, Piotr Kravchenko, in signing the Almaty agreement the Belarusian government wanted Belarus to be the first nuclear weapon–free member of the CIS.[27] Article 6 of the Almaty agreement provided for the withdrawal, by 1 July 1992, of tactical nuclear weapons from Belarus, Ukraine, and Kazakhstan to bases in Russia "for dismantling under joint control." The last train with tactical nuclear weapons left Belarusian territory on 27 April 1992 and marked the first step toward Belarus's nuclear weapon–free status.[28] However, according to the former minister for defense matters, Piotr Chaus, and the former defense minister, Pavel Kazlouski, although Belarusian representatives were supposed to be present in the course of tactical nuclear weapons elimination,[29] there were no reports that they were present for this event.

The CIS agreements had set the end of 1994 as the deadline for the dismantlement of nuclear weapons on Ukrainian territory,[30] but no specific timetable was set in the CIS agreements for the removal of strategic nuclear weapons from Belarus.[31] Indeed, the schedule for strategic nuclear weapons transfer from Belarus was constantly changing and controversial. The CIS military command's plan reportedly provided for the complete withdrawal of strategic nuclear weapons from Belarus by 1995–96.[32] However, Leonid Privalov, the deputy chairman of the Commission on National Security of the Belarusian parliament, indicated that Belarus would be free of its long-range missiles by 1996 or 1997.[33]

Although Belarus has indeed intended to withdraw all strategic nuclear weapons from its territory at an early date, with or without formal decisions,[34] this complicated operation turned out to be more protracted. As Stanislau Shushkevich, then chairman of the Supreme Soviet of Belarus, revealed, economic difficulties within the CIS and the considerable expense involved in the transfer of nuclear weapons slowed down the realization of plans for disarmament. At the same time, Belarusian leaders reportedly advised U.S. officials that all strategic nuclear weapons were to be disabled or removed within three years and eliminated within seven years.[35]

There is the superficial impression that mobile RS–12M ICBMs stationed in Belarus, unlike the silo-based ICBMs in other republics, can be moved to Russia relatively easily. Yet one of the main reasons for this array of dates is the real and time-consuming technical and material problems involved in relocating several divisions of the strategic rocket forces.

Although, prima facie, Belarus did not in any way regard the nuclear weapons on its territory as bargaining chips, its seemingly circumspect position on the issue of their removal has been explained by several other considerations in addition to economic constraints.

First, as stated by Shushkevich, non-nuclear status was made contingent on diplomatic recognition of the republic by the West.[36]

Second, for related reasons, the new Belarusian government was apprehensive about a decrease in the republic's international profile following the weapons' withdrawal. In addition, keeping these weapons for an extended time could provide some sense of security amidst the uncertainties of the CIS.[37]

Third, no legal framework, aside from the most general commonwealth documents and the unratified Strategic Arms Reduction Talks (START) Treaty, provided Russia or any multinational entity with a legal guideline as to how to promptly withdraw these weapons from Belarus. Dismantlement and disposal issues are also not informed by any specific multinational rules and procedures.

Fourth, much depended on Russia's technical, financial, and military-political preparedness for an early withdrawal of great numbers of these weapons.

Fifth, efforts by the United States and other Western states to engage in a direct and productive dialogue with Belarus and provide incentives for denuclearization were viewed as inadequate by many in the Belarusian government. Such shortcomings, however, did not delude it into taking thoughtless steps and creating even more problems.

And sixth, as some individuals have suggested, the value of these weapons could make it advantageous to attempt to sell them for destruction to the United States.[38]

Two other important considerations were voiced in the early months of independence by some government officials. One was economic, the other security-related. The newly appointed minister for defense affairs, Piotr Chaus, stressed that "so long as the property of the former Soviet Union has not been apportioned, [nuclear] weapons must stay in the territory of Belarus. Transferring them to another state is out of the question. In the longer perspective, according to the proclaimed Declaration of Independence, the Republic of Belarus must become non-nuclear. But this must be done simultaneously with the neighboring nuclear powers. Unilateral disarmament should be stopped."[39] These considerations were later overridden by the government's greater political compliance with Russia and disregard for national interests. Accordingly, Chaus and some other figures were moved to less responsible positions.

According to the Lisbon Protocol to the START Treaty signed on 23 May 1992, the three non-Russian states pledged that all strategic nuclear weapons would be eliminated by the end of 1999 and that they would join the NPT as non-nuclear weapon states in the shortest possible time.[40] In October 1992, the republic's Council of Ministers, after approving Foreign and Defense Ministry initiatives, adopted a decree on Belarus's accession to the NPT. It was then decided to make the relevant proposals to the Supreme Soviet.[41] On 4 February 1993, the Belarusian parliament ratified the Strategic Arms Reduction Treaty (START I), and the Lisbon Protocol thereto, without any reservations and preconditions and carried a decision to accede to the NPT as a non-nuclear state.[42] Following the ratification, Russia, the United States, and Great Britain—the depository states of the treaty—informed the Belarusian government of their security assurances (in fact, slightly modified versions of older documents, including United Nations Security Council Resolution 255 in particular).[43]

In June 1993, the government of Belarus adopted a Decree on Measures to Implement the Treaty on the Nonproliferation of Nuclear Weapons. The decree charged the Belarus Nuclear and Radiation Safety Agency (Gospromatomnadzor) with developing a system for accounting for and monitoring nuclear materials.[44] This agency is currently negotiating a safeguards agreement with the IAEA.

Accession to the Nuclear Nonproliferation Treaty on 22 July 1993[45] and the next stage of its implementation should be regarded as one of the most significant actions taken by Belarus in the international arena.

Belarus has become the first state that inherited its nuclear arsenal ever to renounce its new nuclear weapon status of its own free will. This step has been recognized and highly acclaimed by the world community, and it has promoted the international prestige of the republic. There is no doubt that the responsible and cooperative denuclearization policy of Belarus has facilitated successful U.S.-Russian disarmament talks and resulted in greater security for itself.[46]

The ratification by the parliaments of Belarus (on the same day as START and the NPT) and Russia of the Treaty on the Coordination of Activities in the Military Sphere and the Agreement on the Strategic Forces Temporarily Stationed on the Territory of Belarus has further legally fixed the status of the nuclear forces and the further commitments of these parties and has allowed them to coordinate the timetable for the withdrawal of nuclear armaments.[47] Of great importance for the implementation of international agreements was the signing and ratification by the parliament of Belarus (25 November 1993) of the Treaty on the Status of the Military Units of the Russian Federation of the Strategic Nuclear Forces Temporarily Stationed on the Territory of the Republic of Belarus and of the agreement on Russia's military withdrawal to the territory of the Russian Federation. The thirty-five-thousand-strong military unit will be withdrawn by mid-1996, two years ahead of what was previously envisioned by the Lisbon Protocol. Under these agreements, Belarus acquires the entire infrastructure of the military bases; Russia is responsible for the remediating environmental damage on these bases; and ecological safety is to be assured during the withdrawal of the Russian military.

In fact, the withdrawal of SS–25s and their accompanying military contingents was started as early as July 1993, before the agreement between the governments of Belarus and Russia on the Order of the Withdrawal of Military Formations of the Russian Strategic Forces was signed on 24 September 1993. The Agreement on the Conditions of Staying on the Territory of Belarus of Russian Military Units was signed between the two countries, among other agreements on strengthening economic integration, on 3 July 1994. Nothing was reported on its content aside from a provision on the procedure for maintaining Russian military facilities in Belarus.[48]

After the withdrawal of an SS–25 regiment from Postavy during the second half of 1993, the total number of weapons, and thus of warheads, decreased from eighty-one to seventy-two. As of mid-1994, a total of fifty-four warheads and seventy-two weapons were distributed equally between Lida and Mozyr. Thirty-six weapons were to be removed in 1994, and the rest in 1995. By mid-1996, both the Lida and Mozyr rocket divisions will cease to exist.[49]

No dramatic changes were observed in the military-strategic sphere once Aliaksandr Lukashenka was elected as the first Belarusian president. He had made several statements that attracted the attention of military experts, but they implied nothing extraordinary or even different from what the former leadership proposed.[50] A protocol on military and technological cooperation was already signed by the two countries' defense ministries in 1994 to facilitate further steps.[51]

Meanwhile, Lukashenka also proposed to Russia the creation of joint working groups to determine the costs involved in the stationing of Russian military bases on the territory of Belarus.[52] Negotiations are under way with Russia on several military-strategic and nuclear-related issues: among them, the status of the early-warning radar near Baranovichi and the navy communications center at Vileika. Reportedly, Russia proposed an agreement for twenty-five years of free leasing for the Baranovichi radar and the use of the Vileika facility.[53]

With the conclusion of an agreement between Russia, Ukraine, and the United States on the compensation for enriched uranium in the nuclear warheads (January 1994), in which the United States confirmed it would take the interests of Belarus into account, according to a joint Belarusian-U.S. statement,[54] there is greater assurance that Belarus, the Russian Federation, Ukraine, and Kazakhstan will be able to determine each party's share through the mediation of the United States. In fact, the issue was practically dismissed by Shushkevich as early as 1992, when he stressed on several occasions that "nuclear weapons on the territory of Belarus are Russian, they are under the Russian jurisdiction, and the problem of our nuclear disarmament is to repatriate them onto the territory of Russia."[55]

Reportedly, after the issue had been discussed by Belarusian and U.S. officials during 1993, Belarus and Russia began talks. Foreign Minister Piotr Kravchenko disclosed early in 1994 that Belarus was taking part in the negotiating process along with the other four parties to determine the size of compensation to the republic for the fissile material contained in nuclear charges withdrawn from its territory.[56] The talks have been difficult. At first, Russia was reluctant to acknowledge Belarus's rights to its share of the value of the tactical nuclear weapons, all of which had been withdrawn before 27 April 1992. Estimation of the compensation then became a stumbling block. Russia also disputed the right to compensation by Ukraine and Kazakhstan.

The Russian-Ukrainian-U.S. agreement on compensation created a precedent and disentangled a complex problem. According to an agreement between the United States and Russia, the United States will purchase highly enriched uranium (HEU) extracted from Russian nuclear weapons over the course of twenty years at the cost of $12 billion. But, as the U.S. side pledged, this arrangement will come into effect only after the Soviet successor states agree on everyone's share.[57]

Meanwhile, Belarus has a moral right to, and is in need of, substantial material support. Table 8.1 describes the official status (as of March 1994) of U.S. assistance to Belarus under the Nunn–Lugar program for the safe and secure dismantlement (SSD) of nuclear weapons.

The United States has promised to increase its assistance to Belarus to $100 million to assure the safety of nuclear weapons dismantlement, the defense conversion process, environment rehabilitation, and export controls.[58]

These areas of cooperation are a positive result of the development of Belarusian-U.S. relations. The intergovernmental framework agreement signed with Japan with respect to the nonproliferation of nuclear weapons and the establishment of an ad hoc cooperation committee will also promote the solution of denuclearization issues.[59]

As for technical and institutional capabilities to prevent the selling of nuclear weapons or the know-how necessary to produce them abroad, they did not exist as an autonomous system in Belarus before the breakup of the USSR. One can speak, rather, of some peripheral elements of a system with central operational and decision-making bodies stationed in Moscow. Belarus had no need for such a system since it was a republic within the USSR, not an independent state.

After the proclamation of independence, Belarus's domestic needs and international concerns stimulated the creation of an export control system. It was, however, not a restoration of the remains of the old Soviet system, but rather a new construction almost from scratch, although based on the expe-

Table 8.1

U.S. Nunn–Lugar Assistance to Belarus for the Safe and Secure Dismantlement of Nuclear Weapons ($U.S.)

Project	Amount proposed	Amount obligated
Emergency response	5,000,000	3,698,000
Communications link	2,300,000	302,000
Export controls	16,260,000	438,000
Environmental restoration	25,000,000	210,000
Defense conversion	20,000,000	518,000
Missile propellant elimination	6,000,000	—
Military-to-military contacts	1,500,000	—
Total	76,060,000	5,166,000

Source: Nuclear Successor States of the Soviet Union, Nuclear Weapon and Sensitive Export Status Report, no. 1 (Carnegie Endowment for International Peace, Monterey Institute of International Studies, 1994), p. 19.

rience and assistance of Russia and the West.[60] Presently, both technical and institutional capabilities are not yet adequate in Belarus.[61] Technical problems have forced Belarus to make tangible technical assistance a precondition for the conclusion of a viable safeguards agreement with the IAEA, which is required by membership in the NPT.

While recognizing what Belarus has done so far, one should note that the above issues could hardly have been resolved without genuine partnership and mutual understanding, which have not always been easy to achieve with the key players, Russia and the United States.

Denuclearization Determinants and Dissent

The disintegration model of state formation[62] that Belarus has followed puts an analyst into a difficult position with respect to Belarusian nuclear policy. With a naturally emerging nuclear state, acquisition of nuclear weapons is as a rule a lengthy process. It requires the resolution of technical problems, clear perceptions of purposes, dangers, and utility, and some sort of military doctrinal meaning. Such was not the case with Belarus, however, or with the other quasi-nuclear states of the former Soviet Union.

Domestic political players in Belarus did not view the acquisition of nuclear weapons as a means to enhance their power and prestige. Neither the ruling elite nor the opposition seized the opportunity to do so.[63] From the first days of independence, nuclear weapons were perceived to be more a dangerous burden to be addressed. There was no powerful and consistent argument in favor of the political or military value of this weaponry in Belarus. More measured calculations of economic gain and prestige prevailed only some time after the declaration of independence, and only under the influence of debates in Ukraine and Kazakhstan.[64]

Belarus has thus been a unique case in recent nonproliferation developments. Finding itself a quasi-nuclear state quite unexpectedly, not to say against its own will, the republic has had to pursue a quasi-nuclear policy. In fact, it has been a policy of self-denuclearization. Belarus, it seems, has few meaningful precedents upon which to base its policy.

The paradox of Belarus's denuclearization policy and its politics in general consists in the fact that the republic's postcommunist ruling majority has had to perform functions and achieve goals characteristic of more traditional anticommunist, anti-Soviet, and, at times, even nationalist forces. (For a hardline communist or Soviet great power patriot, renunciation of nuclear weapons would generally mean surrender to world imperialism, humiliation, and loss of prestige and influence.) Politically and ideologically, Belarus's antinuclear stance resulted in part from the erosion of the old communist system and the severe criticism of Cold War confrontation, particularly the imperialist and aggressive impulses of the Soviet state (revelations in the mass media about the Cuban missile crisis, statistics on the arms race, environmental hazards of nuclear tests, the Chernobyl legacy, etc.). To sever ties with the vices and dangers of this shared legacy, many had to distance themselves from the means of annihilation. As more and more information surfaced as to the density of Russian weapons on Belarusian soil, these deadly weapons in themselves triggered a negative reaction, despite the fact that, unlike other republics, Belarus did not have any silo-based ICBMs or huge numbers of strategic missiles comparable to other Soviet nuclear successor states to eliminate in the long run.[65]

Despite this desire to break with the past, the situation in Belarus has remained surprisingly stable after its declaration of independence. Unlike trends in Ukraine, for example, radical nationalist and Russophobic tendencies have not been strongly pronounced. Although the old ruling elite safely survived an about-face, it was ideologically disoriented and could not honestly conceptualize any new, original political strategy that might somehow feature a nuclear component. For their part, nationalist forces in Belarus never based their political programs on the nuclear card.

Politically, the nuclear factor was not and could not be neglected. But the nuclearization option, that is, becoming a nuclear weapon state as well as trading off these weapons to some advantage, turned out to be unviable for Belarus. Perhaps this development can be explained, first of all, by the consensus, or the confluence of interests, of the key political players of

Belarus, Russia, the United States, and other Western powers.[66]

Belarus's government had little doubt that retaining nuclear weapons would provide Belarus as a newly independent state with far less security than getting rid of them. Among other reasons, the weapons were a target for foreign nuclear counterforce.[67] Additionally, the postcommunist government majority understood that Belarus would face all sorts of problems and constraints if it attempted to retain nuclear weapons.[68] Besides, enforced possession of these weapons ran counter to Moscow's claims of authority over and possession of the strategic rocket forces.

For the former chairman of the Supreme Soviet, Stanislau Shushkevich, and his supporters, a denuclearization policy that implied the withdrawal of foreign troops was apparently indispensable for fostering independence and bringing about Belarus's declared neutral status. It also seemed to promise the republic prestige and material rewards from the West.

At the same time, for the nationalist opposition, represented by the leaders of the Belarusian Popular Front, Russian troops on the territory of Belarus symbolized foreign imperial domination and the risk of foreign political and military interference. Therefore, the withdrawal of foreign troops along with nuclear weapons would be most desirable primarily for political and military-strategic considerations.[69] It would seem that a broader security approach in relations with Russia had played an important role in Belarus's denuclearization stance.

For their part, Moscow and Washington had their own security interests in the region. Washington has clearly been making its point on nonproliferation to both Moscow and Minsk. Understandably, it would be at least unwise and hardly possible at all for Moscow to remain indifferent to the possibility of a newly independent neighboring state going nuclear. (A case in point is the Russian-Ukrainian nuclear relationship.) Such a stance would have entailed gross complications for international arrangements, violating Soviet successor state commitments, undermining Russian-U.S. plans for further nuclear reductions, and leading to a worsening of the climate in the bilateral relations between Belarus and Russia, Russia and the United States, Belarus and the United States, and so on.

There have been no serious discussions of Belarus's going nuclear either in government or nongovernmental quarters, perhaps because of the realization that, domestically, Belarus lacks the necessary resources to maintain a nuclear weapon status. Belarus possesses no deposits of uranium ore, uranium enrichment capabilities, or plutonium production. It has no nuclear weapon design and production centers.[70] The country not only has no nuclear power plants, it does not have a single element of a nuclear fuel cycle. So there are very limited natural, technological, or engineering resources at hand for retaining nuclear weapons.

Militarily, Belarus has in place only segments of the complete command, control, communcations, and intelligence (or C^{3}I) infrastructure required by nuclear forces, leaving strategic nuclear planning up to Moscow. No one in Belarus has yet to come up with an idea of how best to use nuclear weapons for consolidating its independence militarily.

As for disincentives to the nuclear option, there are quite a few. Inasmuch as Belarus depends strongly on economic and military-logistical assistance from Russia, any decision to go nuclear would have been regarded as anti-Russian, in turn provoking Russia to inflict economic sanctions on Belarus. Such a recourse would seem de facto a deliberate policy of undermining relations with a great power. Costs for not only maintaining the existing elements of the strategic nuclear forces but also building anew the missing ones would be enormous and unaffordable. As Karl-Heinz Kamp rightly stresses:

> In reality, the path to nuclear capability seems to be paved with nearly insurmountable obstacles. All lines of communication to nuclear depots, missile shelters and early warning radars come together in Moscow. To cut this network and redesign it for the individual needs of a single republic could prove to be extremely difficult. It is also reported that the Strategic Rocket Forces have technical procedures to disable strategic nuclear forces regionally, which means "to switch off" these systems in certain areas. In addition, nuclear weapons require periodic inspections to assure their safety and reliability and to replenish their reservoirs of specific substances. This requires hardware and know-how, both concentrated in Russia. Last but not least, strategic nuclear systems are targeted according to the needs of the former USSR. Any retargeting by a single republic is technically hard to achieve.[71]

Also, by violating international nonproliferation arrangements, Belarus would have lost any legitimate claim to substantial Western assistance. In addition, a decision to violate nonproliferation norms would have made Belarus appear aggressive in the eyes of the international community.

Nuclear fears generated by the Chernobyl disaster would definitely have caused mass public protests against a pronuclear weapons decision, which would be amplified by political forces in opposition. The republic incurred enormous health, environmental, and budgetary losses from Chernobyl. The contamination of vast land tracts, which killed people and animals and destroyed agriculture, highlighted the detrimental environmental effects of radioactive releases of any kind. The direct and indirect consequences of the radioactive fallout have affected over 2.2 million people, or one in five residents of the republic. In addition, 18 percent of the most productive agricultural land and 20 percent of all forests were affected. The dosage of accumulated external and internal radiation that had an impact on the Belarusian population is the highest on record. Direct economic damage alone amounted to ten times the republic's budget, in 1990 prices.[72]

This sad reality has engendered a strong psychological backlash. Nuclear power and nuclear weapons have been directly associated in the mass consciousness with devastating danger, diseases, and death. There is a paradox here, however. Because Belarus has no nuclear power plants, and with nuclear missiles and other explosive devices stored in normally inaccessible, guarded locations, nuclear fears have been directed mostly externally, toward other republics. Such fears were recently demonstrated in the panic of people living close to the Ignalina nuclear power plant in Lithuania over civil defense exercises mimicking measurements of radioactive contamination.

Vocal public protests and political campaigning have had some impact on Belarus's nuclear policies. Still, for obvious reasons, political participation in post-totalitarian Belarus is at the early stages of development. Significant openness in Belarusian foreign policy is something yet to be achieved.

Since the Chernobyl accident, nuclear phobia and antinuclear power sentiments have been strongly present in the domestic politics of Belarus. Environmental movements and popular discontent, however, have focused predominantly on state programs for overcoming the deleterious effects of Chernobyl, as well as the related medical, social, and nature conservation problems.

Two more relevant factors must be accounted for here. One is that for the last several years the main preoccupation of the populace has been with economic and physical survival. The other factor is the limited cognition, or even misperception, on the part of the public of the importance of nuclear weapons withdrawal that has contributed to the issue's low salience in relation to other issues of public concern. Until recently, foreign policy priorities, as well as nuclear weapons issues, have not been prominent in the platforms and programs of Belarusian political parties and movements.[73] In addition, nuclear weapons issues have been given relatively little attention in the republic's mass media.

Although no large-scale public opinion surveys on the status of nuclear weapons have been conducted in Belarus to date, there appears to be a remarkable public consensus on and support for the republic's non-nuclear status. Thus, there are no influential political forces calling for playing the nuclear card.

A public opinion survey of Belarusian special and political organizations conducted in 1993 by the Independent Institute of Socioeconomic and Political Studies indicated that the following organizations supported the idea of an unconditional and voluntary renunciation of nuclear weapons by Belarus: (1) organizations advocating capitalist forms of social development and downplaying the reinvigoration of the Belarusian national identity as a priority, such as the Free Democratic Party of Belarus, the Movement for Democratic Reforms, the Union of Entrepreneurs, and independent trade unions; (2) organizations advocating capitalist forms of social development and highlighting the reinvigoration of the Belarusian national identity as a priority, such as the Belarusian Popular Front, the Union of the Poles of Belarus, and the Foundation for Preserving the Jewish Historical and Cultural Heritage; and (3) some organizations advocating socialist forms of development and highlighting the reinvigoration of the Belarusian national identity as a priority, such as the Association of the Belarusians of the World (Bat'kauschyna), the Belarusian Social-Democratic Party (Hramada), the Party of the National Consensus, the Belarusian Association of Servicemen,[74] and the Fellowship of the Belarusian Language.

The idea of renouncing nuclear weapons was disputed by about half of the organizations advocating socialism and downplaying the reinvigoration of the Belarusian national identity as a priority.[75] Allegedly, this group comprised the Party of the Communists of Belarus; the Movement for Democracy, Social Progress, and Justice; the Belarusian Science and Production Congress; the Union of the Youth of Belarus; the Leninist Communist Union of the Youth of Belarus; the Belarusian KGB;[76] and the parliamentary faction "Belarus."[77] According to the survey, all organizations that favor retention of nuclear weapons in Belarus are also in favor of restoring the USSR.

The Pan-Slavic group Belaia Rus' shares the opinion of Russian, Ukrainian, and Polish "Slavic patriotic" organizations to the effect that "a new partition of the world and the expansionist policies of the United States, Germany, Turkey, Iran, and China against the Slavic peoples necessitate the creation of a Great Slavic Commonwealth with the core states comprising Russian, Belarusian, and Ukrainian peoples." Allegedly facing renewed attempts to resort to power politics in international relations, these pro-Slavic organizations are against the withdrawal of nuclear weapons from Belarus and Ukraine.[78]

The official position of Belarus toward the operational control and use of nuclear weapons that it hosts on its territory has been determined in a series of unilateral, bilateral, and multilateral documents and agreements. The decree of the Supreme Soviet of Belarus of 11 January 1992, for example, subordinated all military formations in the country to the Belarusian Council of Ministers. An exception was made for units belonging to the strategic forces, which were subordinated to the CIS Joint Strategic Forces Command. A number of CIS agreements had been relevant provisionally, until the CIS joint armed forces were canceled, and by mid-1993 Russia established clear jurisdiction over the bulk of the former Soviet nuclear arsenal, except in Ukraine.[79] The 1991 Almaty declaration, as well as the Minsk Agreement on Strategic Forces, provided for the unified control of nuclear forces under the Joint Strategic Forces Command of the Commonwealth of Independent States. The decision to use nuclear weapons was vested in the president of the Russian Federation "in agreement with the heads of the Republic of Belarus, the Republic of Kazakhstan, and Ukraine, and in consultation with the heads of the other member states of the Commonwealth."[80] START I and the Lisbon Protocol, as well as the NPT, set the general framework of constraints and commitments in this sphere.

Two intergovernmental agreements have been of special importance for Belarus. Both were signed by Belarus and Russia on 20 July 1992 in Moscow and ratified early in 1993 by the parliaments of both states. They are the Agreement Between the Republic of Belarus and the Russian Federation on Coordinating Activities in the Military Sphere and the Agreement Between the Republic of Belarus and the Russian Federation on Strategic Forces Temporarily Stationed on the Territory of the Republic of Belarus.

In these documents, the two parties reiterated their allegiance to international treaties and documents in the field of disarmament and arms control, as signed by the USSR, and their intention to ensure reliable and sound control over nuclear weapons put under a single command. They pledged "to take concerted measures to rule out the possibility of unauthorized actions by the strategic forces."[81] The system of control of the strategic forces stationed in Belarus was defined as a constituent part of the system of control of the strategic forces of the Joint Armed Forces Command of the CIS and was not included in the system of control of the armed forces of Belarus.[82]

According to the latter agreement, nuclear weapons stationed in Belarus cannot be used without Belarus's consent. Decisions on the necessity of using nuclear weapons were to be taken in line with the procedure on strategic forces envisaged by Article 4 of the agreement of 3 December 1991, which was agreed to by the CIS member states. Mechanisms for control were envisaged that would have made Russian nuclear missile launches from Belarusian territory technically impossible without the consent of Belarusian leaders.[83] The specific means of technical blocking of such a launch were reportedly surveyed, and the period of time for rearranging the existing control system was to be defined in a separate agreement.[84]

Presently, there is no evidence that any technical means of blocking have been developed at all. Formally, Belarus retains the right to participate in decision making on the use of nuclear weapons (the so-called negative control). Nevertheless, in practice it is difficult to imagine, because a "hot line" with Moscow is evidently insufficient, and the real keys belong to Russia.

The only type of control in place today is control over safety at military facilities as well as the safety of nuclear weapons during exercises, relocation, and withdrawal. Reportedly, these controls were introduced in 1993 as a result of the abovementioned bilateral agreements. Additionally, Russia began to provide information on the lifetime of nuclear warheads. Previously, relocations of Russian nuclear forces were not controlled by Belarus.[85]

In charge of these activities is a special body, the Group for the Control Over Nuclear Safety of the National Agency for Control and Inspections (or NAKI, from the Belarusian abbreviation), of Belarus's Defense Ministry. NAKI claims that, owing to regular cooperation with Russian rocket forces units, provision by them of timetables for planned activities, and participation in joint commissions, it exercises control over the safety of nuclear weapons at all stages of their maintenance. Belarus's Defense Ministry is allegedly being apprised of the condition of the nuclear charges, the schedules for their servicing, and storage and custody regimes. Joint actions in case of emergency situations have been thought out and planned.[86]

Cooperation Among Intelligence Agencies on Proliferation Issues

The intelligence agencies of Belarus are practically represented in the nonproliferation field by the Committee for State Security (the Belarusian KGB), which plays a role in the republic's export controls. Among its departments, the Directorate of Economic Security presumably deals with nonproliferation issues on a regular basis. The Belarusian KGB has a seat on the interdepartmental Commission of the Cabinet (formerly Council) of Ministers for Issuing Licenses for External Exchanges of Commodities. The relevant functions of the KGB include providing the government with comprehensive information required for the elaboration and pursuit of export control policies; taking part in the preparation of legal export control regulations; taking part in decision making on deliveries of sensitive items; countering illegal export attempts by foreign intelligence services; and tracing smuggling operations.[87]

Belarus has concluded general agreements on cooperation with its Russian and Ukrainian intelligence counterparts that, aside from pledges not to direct intelligence activities against one another, reportedly included clauses concerning nonproliferation. Although no specific agreements have been concluded so far on nonproliferation issues, these services regularly interact.

Close cooperation on a regular basis between Belarusian and Russian security agencies has prevented several illegal transfers of sensitive materials and equipment via Belarusian territory. One such successful operation, conducted in 1993 by Belarusian and Russian intelligence in collaboration with Polish intelligence, intercepted an illegal transfer of highly enriched uranium from Udmurtiia in Russia to Poland via Belarus.[88]

There are few contacts and no collaboration on a permanent basis between Belarusian and Western intelligence agencies, however, although in 1992–93 working contacts were made by the Belarusian KGB with representatives of foreign security services to determine ways of coordinating efforts to prevent smuggling of fissile materials, illegal trading of arms and dual technologies, and so forth.[89] Some steps have been taken by Belarus's Ministry for Internal Affairs to establish a means of cooperation with Interpol.

Denuclearization: A Case of Lost Opportunities?

For better or worse, Belarus has lacked the resources necessary to form a coherent, effective nuclear policy. On the other hand, there do exist grounds and incentives for the policy of denuclearization. Perhaps in this circumstance lies the principal difference and uniqueness of the Belarusian case. In contrast with the central role that denuclearization has played in Ukraine's and even Kazakhstan's relations with Moscow,[90] Belarusian denuclearization policy has not placed serious strains on Belarusian-Russian relations. On the other hand, to some extent, Belarus's denuclearization policy has played a rather symbolic role in building an independent state and was never turned into its instrument.

A comparison of Belarus's and Ukraine's nuclear policies, as shown in Table 8.2, poses several key questions about largely or even totally different public and political responses and linkages in the two countries.

In Belarus, nationalism and the possession of independent nuclear forces do not go together. Aside from the broad factors presented in Table 8.1, there are different historical experiences and geopolitical roles, as perceived by nationalist forces in the two countries. Taking into account the objective position of the republic, the Belarusian Popular Front (BPF) sees Belarus as a mid-sized European state that should of necessity be neutral, nonaligned, and non-nuclear and should actively build relations with its neighbors while integrating into Western Europe.[91] For this party, the negative meaning of nuclear weapons is not only the dangers that they pose but also their use as an instrument of foreign domination.[92]

Table 8.2

Nuclear Policy–Relevant Factors in Belarus and Ukraine

Factors	Belarus	Ukraine
Resources: natural, political, financial, technological, military	<	>
National self-identity / nationalism / Russophobic trends	<	>
Antinuclear sentiments	>[a]	<

Note: "<": tending to a smaller value; ">:" tending to a greater value. The symbols here stand for relative estimates of the intensity of nuclear policy–relevant factors in each state.

[a]While the Chernobyl disaster affected over 20 percent of Belarusian territory, for Ukraine the figure is 4 percent. As for pronuclear aberrations, there is a curious distinction from the Ukrainian situation, where many supporters of retaining nuclear weapons are nationalists suspicious of Russia. In Belarus a small fraction of the populace that supports the retention of nuclear weapons not only favors close ties with Russia but also very often clings to socialist ideology and memories of a great power past within the USSR. Their motivations are anti-Western and nostalgic.

Table 8.3

Russian Impact on Nuclear Policies of Belarus and Ukraine

	Belarus	Ukraine
Dependence on Russia: economic, military, etc.[a]	>	<
Degree of Russification[b]	>	<
Extent of public opinion favoring closer relations with Russia	>	<
Value attached to nuclear weapons	< (danger)	>[c] (bargaining chip/deterrence)

Note: "<": tending to a smaller value; ">:" tending to a greater value. The symbols here stand for relative estimates of the intensity of nuclear policy–relevant factors in each state.

[a]Clearly, given Belarus's overwhelming dependence on Russia, nuclear independence is a pipe dream.

[b]Conversely, the degree of Russification signifies more or less room for perceiving Russia as an existential threat to a young nation-state.

[c]Some analysts distinguish several schools of thought on the nuclear issue in Ukraine. The consensus view in the Ukrainian parliament has been that Ukraine should eventually remove nuclear weapons from its territory, but they should serve as bargaining chips to obtain security guarantees for state sovereignty and procure Western and Russian financial and technical assistance to help Ukraine implement the START treaty and receive compensation for the material value of HEU in weapons. An overlapping minority view advocates Ukraine as a nuclear state and sees nuclear weapons as the only effective deterrent to Russian aggression. See Bohdan Nahaylo, "The Shaping of Ukrainian Attitudes Toward Nuclear Weapons" *RFE/RL Research Report,* 19 February 1993, pp. 21–45. Cited in Steven Woehrel, Ukraine: Nuclear Weapons and U.S. Interests, Congressional Research Service Report for Congress, no. 94–254 F (Library of Congress, CRS-5–6, 15 March 1994). The influential nationalist Rukh party, though, seems to have the first view, at least on behalf of its leader. See Viachaslau Chornovil, "Helsinkskaie Pahadnenne Vyhadna Usim," *Zviazda,* 17 February 1994.

Ukrainian nationalist forces, for their part, proceed from different realities and geopolitical projections, as shared by various groups in the population. They perceive Ukraine as a regional superpower that is both countervailing Russian imperial encroachments in the southeastern part of Europe and being forced to obtain security guarantees for the purpose of consolidating the independent state.

Table 8.3 offers yet another correlation of Belarusian and Ukrainian positions with respect to relations with Russia and their bearing on nuclear postures.

The nuclear factor has had to be dealt with by all three states (Belarus, Ukraine, and Kazakhstan) in their own way. Eventually all of them settled on the denuclearization option for consolidating their sovereignty.[93] But the big difference is that Belarus was the first among them to opt for and implement denuclearization.

Another interesting feature of Belarus's foreign political strategy is that, among its declared priorities, only denuclearization is coming to fruition so far, whereas others, such as gaining neutral status, overcoming the economic crisis, and instilling a national revival, are yet to be achieved. Thus almost by default, efforts to implement and sustain non-nuclear weapon state status constitute the core of Belarus's foreign and domestic policy. On the domestic front, some have argued that Belarus lost an opportunity to convert its potential nuclear weapon state status into some form of leverage at both the regional and international levels. However, the dictates of political realism would seem to have always worked against such a possibility.

Notes

1. After seventy years, on 19 September 1991, the name was changed officially to the Republic of Belarus.

2. 26 October 1956 and 18 February 1957, respectively. See *Belorusskaia SSR v mezhdunarodnykh otnosheniiakh: Mezhdunarodnye dogovori, konventsii i soglasheniia Belorusskoi SSR s inostrannymi gosudarstvami (1944–1959)* (Minsk: Izdatel'stvo akademii nauk Belorusskoi SSR, 1960), p. 487.

3. Signed 8 October 1963, ratified 26 November 1963. See *Belorusskaia SSR v mezhdunarodnykh otnosheniiakh: Mnogostoronnie mezhdunarodnye dogovori, konventsii i soglasheniia BSSR (1960–1983)* (Minsk: Ministerstvo inostrannykh del BSSR, 1983), p. 12.

4. Signed 10 February 1967 and ratified 23 June 1967. See ibid., p. 260.

5. Signed 3 March 1971 and ratified 6 September 1971. See ibid., p. 17.

6. Both were ratified 26 September 1986. See IAEA documents IN-FCIRC/335/Add.5 and INFCIRC/336/Add.6.

7. Author's interview with a former high-ranking Soviet official, Moscow, May 1992.

8. Since 1992, plans for the construction of nuclear power plants in Belarus, abandoned after the Chernobyl accident, have been revisited. Belarus is importing up to 90 percent of required energy resources. It produces about 75 percent of the consumed

electric energy and imports the remaining 25 percent. These figures served as a basis for concluding that in the near future only nuclear power plants can solve the problem of the energy deficit as well as increase Belarus's economic and political independence. See Stanislau Shushkevich's argument for nuclear power in *Narodnaia gazeta,* 7 October 1992; also *Komsomol'skaia pravda,* 19 November 1992; *Zviazda,* 12 January 1993. The Power Engineering Program for Belarus, adopted by the Presidium of the Council of Ministers, envisaged construction of a nuclear power plant. In 1993, a temporary governmental commission for the organizational work on elaborating the draft of the Governmental Program for the Development of Nuclear Power Engineering in Belarus was established. Reportedly, preparatory work for the construction has been under way. The first power unit will not be ready until after the year 2005. Opponents to these plans stress costs and problems of waste disposal, and they propose alternative energy sources and energy-saving measures. The question, however, remains about how to dismiss the nuclear fears of the populace. See *Sovetskaia Belorussiia,* 25 November 1992; *Zviazda,* 22 December 1992; *Sovetskaia Belorussiia,* 26 February 1993; *Zviazda,* 21 April 1993; *Sem' dnei,* 5 February 1994.

9. *World Nuclear Industry Handbook 1992* (Surrey: Business Press Inernational.) (Special Nuclear Engineering International Publications), p. 126.

10. Belarusian military district commander Colonel General Kostenko's testimony during the republic's parliamentary session. Belarusian television, 15 November 1991.

11. It is ironic that, officially, Moscow kept silent about nuclear weapons in Belarus until October 1991. "For reasons totally unclear, Moscow has stated that there were nuclear weapons only in Russia, Ukraine, and Kazakhstan, but Belarus was thoroughly crossed out from this list in the metropolitan press," commented Iurii Popov, deputy chairman of the Commission on National Security of the Belarusian Supreme Soviet. See *Sem' dnei,* 7–13 October 1991.

12. Wheeled transporter-erector-launchers (TELs) for these missiles have been produced at the Minsk Automobile Plant. *Vo slavu rodiny,* 10 August 1994.

13. See Steven Zaloga, "Strategic Forces of the SNG," *Jane's Intelligence Review* (February 1992), pp. 79–85; Robert S. Norris and William M. Arkin, "Where the Weapons Are," *Bulletin of the Atomic Scientists* (November 1991), pp. 48–49.

14. See William Walker, "Nuclear Weapons and the Soviet Republics," *International Security Information Service Briefing,* no. 23 (18 December 1991), p. 5.

15. *Zviazda,* 29 July 1994.

16. See A. Shal'nev, "Belorussia vydvigaiet predlozheniia," *Izvestiia,* 26 October 1990.

17. Ibid. Plans, however, are being carried out to create nuclear power plants in Belarus itself.

18. *Litaratura i mastatstva,* 29 March 1992, p. 12.

19. See William C. Potter, *Nuclear Power and Nonproliferation: An Interdisciplinary Perspective* (Cambridge, MA: Oeleschlager, Gunn and Hain, 1982), pp. 203–5.

20. See *Constitution of the Republic of Belarus,* adopted at the thirteenth session of the Supreme Soviet of Belarus on 15 March 1994 (Minsk: Polymia, 1994), p. 6.

21. Letter of 18 October 1991 from the Permanent Representative of Belarus to the United Nations addressed to the Secretary General, Annex, Declaration of 2 October 1991 by the Supreme Soviet of Belarus on the foreign policy principles of Belarus, A/46/582, p. 2.

22. Statement by P. Kravchenko, *Sovetskaia Belorussiia,* 2 November 1991.

23. See *Vo slavu rodiny,* 23 March 1993. It seems the government has not yet given thought to the operational implications of abandoning the deterrence concept. After the withdrawal of Russian strategic forces from Belarus, the Russian nuclear umbrella may still be in effect through some new agreement. For the moment it is difficult to suggest what alternative deterrence capabilities the republic could create on its own or procure

on the world market. The present economic crisis leaves a narrow field for speculation here. Meanwhile, attempts are being made to restore military-technical cooperation with Russia.

24. Likewise, little attention was elicited in Belarusian military quarters by the new Russian military doctrine, adopted in November 1993, which abandoned the unilateral no-first-use pledge and expanded the definition of threats to the integrity of Russian systems of the support of its strategic nuclear forces and C^3I infrastructure. The implications of these modifications for Belarus and its military doctrine were never studied or even publicly addressed. Because of the nonadversarial relations, the close military cooperation between the two states, and the continuous maneuvering of the former Belarusian government majority in favor of a further reintegration with Russia, the issue was dismissed as not being of immediate importance.

25. See Roy Allison, Adelphi Paper no. 280 (London: IISS, 1993), p. 46.

26. The author would argue here that practically all CIS and Soviet nuclear successor states' agreements on strategic nuclear forces were aimed not so much at providing deterrence or security guarantees as at stressing nonproliferation commitments as well as reassuring each other and the West that these forces were under joint control and immune from unauthorized use. In fact, the very idea of "collective security" of the CIS member states, found in Article 1 of the Almaty Agreement on Joint Measures with Respect to Nuclear Weapons of December 1991, devolved to the Moscow-controlled CIS Joint Strategic Forces Command, and then to nothing practicable.

27. *RFE/RL Daily Report,* 27 January 1992.

28. *Sovetskaia Belorussiia,* 18 June 1992.

29. *Izvestiia,* 27 January 1992; *Sem' dnei,* 27 April–3 May 1992.

30. Minsk Agreement on Strategic Forces, Article 4.

31. Apparently, the Ukrainian side initially meant to get rid of all implied Russian means of influence over Ukraine as soon as possible. Russia, for its part, was interested in depriving Ukraine of a nuclear card in the shortest possible time. Belarus was hardly prepared for setting any timetable at that moment. Besides, it was not averse to raising apprehensions.

32. *RFE/RL Daily Report,* 10 February 1992.

33. *RFE/RL Daily Report,* 27 January 1992.

34. It was reported that Belarus's Security Council obligated the republic's Council of Ministers and the Defense Ministry to work out the time schedule and determine the term for an accelerated withdrawal of strategic forces from the territory of the republic and draft a corresponding agreement with Russia. See *Izvestiia,* 9 September 1992. According to one such timetable, reportedly to be adopted, the withdrawal had to be completed by 30 December 1994. See *Krasnaia zvezda,* 7 November 1992.

35. *RFE/RL Daily Report,* 7 February 1992.

36. *RFE/RL Research Report,* 10 January 1992, p. 46.

37. This was echoed, in particular, in an interview with the deputy defense minister, Piotr Chaus, who said that Belarus "should not be hasty in the withdrawal of strategic nuclear weapons. The presence of such powerful weapons in our country will at first help Belarus establish itself. The whole world treats us as a nuclear power. We should not be hasty also because with the present situation the course of events in the CIS is simply unpredictable." *Krasnaia zvezda,* 16 July 1992.

38. During a briefing conference in London in January 1992, an advisor to the Belarusian parliament said that for the cost of three missiles everyone from the Chernobyl-polluted area could be resettled on clean land in the north of Belarus. See Vera Rich, "The Great Soviet Divorce," *World Today* (February 1992), p. 19.

39. *Respublika,* 14 January 1992.

40. "Protocol to Facilitate the Implementation of the START Treaty" [Lisbon Protocol], *SIPRI Yearbook 1993: World Armaments and Disarmament* (Stockholm: Wiksen, 1993), p. 575.

41. *Sovetskaia Belorussiia*, 20 October 1992.

42. There were 218 votes for, 1 against, and 4 abstentions on the START Treaty and 220 votes for, none against, and 2 abstentions on the NPT. Interview with a staff member of the Supreme Soviet of Belarus, 10 February 1993.

43. Russia "confirmed its support for the clause contained in the declaration of the heads of state of the CIS of 14 February 1992, to the effect that all possible disputes among CIS member states will be resolved by exclusively peaceful means, by way of negotiations." The United States "reiterated its commitment to refrain from the threat to use force against territorial integrity or political independence and neither kind of armaments in U.S. possession will ever be used, except in cases of self-defense or in accordance with the United Nations Charter." The United Kingdom "joined the United States and Russia in confirming its commitments to seek immediate actions by the Security Council so as to provide assistance in accordance with the UN Charter to any non-nuclear weapon state party to the Nonproliferation Treaty, including Belarus, if it becomes a victim of an act or an object of a threat of aggression in which nuclear weapons are used." See "Rossiia, zeshea, velikobritaniia gotovyia predstavit' Belarusi dadatkovyia harantii," *Zviazda*, 7 April 1993.

44. Press release of the Embassy of the Republic of Belarus in the United States, 21 June 1993.

45. Stanislau Shushkevich deposited the instrument of accession with the U.S. government during an official visit to Washington. On the same day the instruments of accession were also deposited with the governments of the Russian Federation and the United Kingdom—the other two depositaries of the Nuclear Nonproliferation Treaty.

46. The U.S. State Department confirmed on 31 May 1994 that in realization of the intentions of the presidents of the United States and Russia to detarget their strategic missiles by 30 May 1994, as stated in their joint declaration of 14 January 1994, U.S. strategic nuclear missiles would no longer be targeted against territories formerly used for Russian ICBM basing. Press release of the Embassy of the Republic of Belarus in the United States, 1 June 1994.

47. As former Defense Minister Pavel Kazlouski pointed out, negotiations on further agreements with Russia were stalled until these two major accords were ratified and thus came into force. See *Vo slavu rodiny*, 6 February 1993.

48. *Zviazda*, 5 July 1994.

49. For details, see *Sem' dnei*, 26 March 1994.

50. President Lukashenka said that he will not "initiate" the withdrawal of Russian strategic forces from the territory of Belarus (which is difficult to imagine, considering the signed agreements) but would promote the revival of the Belarusian military-industrial complex through Russian orders. See *Narodnaia gazeta*, 14 July 1994.

51. *Vo slavu rodiny*, 18 June 1994.

52. *Zviazda*, 6 August 1994.

53. *Zviazda*, 29 July 1994.

54. The statement was signed during President Bill Clinton's official visit to Minsk on 15 January 1994. In particular, it said, "President Clinton informed Chairman Shushkevich of the 14 January 1994 Trilateral Statement by the Presidents of the United States, Russia and Ukraine. In this connection, he stated that the United States recognized the importance of fair compensation to Belarus for the value of the highly enriched uranium in nuclear warheads located on its territory." On the joint statement, see "Clinton Promises Help for Belarus Before Changing Focus to Mideast," *New York Times*, 16 January 1994.

55. *Nezavisimaia gazeta*, 26 November 1992, p. 1.

56. *Narodnaia gazeta*, 20 January 1994.

57. *Zviazda*, 20 January 1994.

58. *New York Times*, "Clinton Promises Help." 16 January 1994.

59. Japan pledged $8.37 million in disarmament aid to Belarus. *Nuclear Successor States of the Soviet Union*, p. 21.

60. Western assistance to Belarus for the creation of an export control system is being provided almost exclusively by the United States. Other Western countries and multilateral organizations, such as the European Union, have not been involved. Author's interview with an export control official from the Ministry of Foreign Economic Relations, Minsk, 21 November 1994.

61. For the present status of export controls in Belarus, see *Nuclear Successor States of the Soviet Union*, p. 24.

62. Here the author means a particular pattern of independent state formation out of a disintegrating larger entity.

63. As Peter D. Feaver points out, in the "normally" emerging nuclear nations, such weapons tend to be "added to an existing power structure and must be wielded by the existing actors in the political spectrum." See Peter D. Feaver, "Command and Control in Emerging Nuclear Nations," *International Security*, vol. 17, no. 3 (winter 1992/93), p. 177.

64. In fact, Ukraine's nuclear policy has had little influence on official Minsk. The courses taken by the two states were clearly different, and naturally there could hardly be any interaction between them in this field. Of the few instances of Belarusian reaction to Kiev's moves, one can recall Piotr Chaus's often-cited approval of Ukraine's demands that the destruction of tactical nuclear weapons be supervised (*FBIS Daily Report: Central Eurasia*, FBIS-SOV–92–053, 18 March 1992) and Stanislau Shushkevich's criticism of Ukrainian recalcitrance in refusing to ratify START I and repatriate strategic weapons. Cited in Karen Dawisha and Bruce Parrott, *Russia and the New States of Eurasia: The Politics of Upheaval* (Cambridge: Cambridge University Press, 1994), p. 275. More recently and in a relatively positive light, Ukraine has been characterized as "beating money out of the West with the help of a nuclear club." See Valerii Tsepkalo, "Primer Belarusi pokhvalen: No, uvy ne zarazitelen," *Respublika*, 25 August 1993, p. 4. The deputy chairman of the Supreme Soviet Commission on National Security, Leonid Privalov, repudiated some newly voiced doubts about the wisdom of Belarus's renouncing nuclear weapons by reinvoking the republic's technical incapacity to maintain them. See *Vo slavu rodiny*, 26 July 1994.

65. Ukraine, for example, had 1,120 silo-based ICBMs. The total number of nuclear weapons there reached 1,684, or 17 percent of the total CIS warhead deployments, whereas Belarus had around 1 percent. *Arms Control Today* (May 1994), p. 26.

66. An insightful discussion of the overlapping of Russian and Belarusian interests, as well as other aspects of Belarus's nuclear behavior, is offered in Mitchell Reiss, "Belarus: Pushing on an Open Door" (unpublished manuscript presented to the Woodrow Wilson Center, Washington, DC, 1994).

67. Stanislau Shushkevich (former chairman of the Supreme Soviet of Belarus), interview by author, 3 October 1994.

68. Anatoli Novikov (chairman of the Commission on National Security of the Supreme Soviet of Belarus), interview by author, 5 October 1994.

69. See, for example, "Pavedamlenne apazitsii BNF u viarkhounym savete belarusi ab palitytsy urada," *Narodnaia gazeta*, 11 August 1992.

70. William Potter, *Nuclear Profiles of the Soviet Successor States*, Program for Nonproliferation Studies (Monterey, CA: Monterey Institute of International Studies, 1993), p. 6; see table 1.

71. See Karl-Heinz Kamp, "The Role of Nuclear Weapons in European Security," in *The Former Soviet Union and European Security: Between Integration and Renationalization*, eds. Hans-Georg Ehrhart, Anna Kreikemeyer, and Andrei Zagorski (Baden-Baden: Nomos Verlagsgesellschaft, 1993), p. 239.

72. See statement by Viacheslau F. Kebich, chairman of the Council of Ministers of the Belorussian Soviet Socialist Republic in the general debate at the forty-fifth session of the United Nations General Assembly, 26 September 1990, *Sovetskaia Belorussiia*, 29 September 1990, p. 3; "Chernaia byl´ beloi rusi," *Sem´ dnei*, no. 34 (1994), p. 4.

73. See, for example, "Belarusian Popular Front 'Adradzennie' Statute," *Belarusian Review*, vol. 3, no. 3 (fall 1991), pp. 9–11.

74. After the success of Vladimir Zhirinovsky's party in the December 1993 elections in Russia, the Association of Servicemen voiced serious concern that Belarus could be easily drawn into an international conflict sparked off in the former Soviet Union, and it appealed to the republic's Supreme Soviet to speed up the withdrawal of Russian forces from Belarusian soil. See *Zviazda*, 21 December 1993.

75. Their political influence in society has diminished, as was demonstrated by the recent presidential elections. The left-wing presidential candidate, Aliaksandr Dubko, received only 5.98 percent of the electoral vote. *Sovetskaia Belorussiia*, 1 July 1994.

76. It is difficult to judge the scope and accuracy of the survey with respect to the KGB. One would guess that extrapolations were made from a few respondents' opinions (probably not only of those in active service). Belarusian KGB officials have repeatedly claimed that they are not aligned with political forces and are simply performing the functions of an institution in charge of state stability and efficiency of constitutional powers. The main task of the KGB, according to its former chief, Eduard Shirkovski, is "gathering, generalization, and verification of information used for decision making on the macropolitical level." Eduard Shirkovski, "To Be or Not to Be? That is the Question: On Belarusian Security Services" (in Russian), *Sovetskaia Belorussiia*, 14 January 1994. The KGB and other power ministries (i.e., the Defense Ministry and the Ministry for Internal Affairs) have pointedly kept out of politics—or at least they have claimed to. At any rate, compared to their Russian counterparts the Belarusian KGB has kept a very low profile on the country's political scene.

77. *Respublika*, 22 June 1993.

78. *Sovetskaia Belorussiia*, 30 December 1993.

79. For a concise discussion of the transition of command and control from the Soviet Union to Russia, see Alexander A. Pikayev, "Post-Soviet Russia and Ukraine: Who Can Push the Button?" *Nonproliferation Review*, vol. 1, no. 3 (spring–summer 1994), pp. 31–37.

80. Minsk Agreement on Strategic Forces, Article 4.

81. Agreement on Coordinating Activities in the Military Sphere, Article 4, *Vedomost´i viarkhounaga saveta respubliki Belarus*, 1993, no. 15, p. 76.

82. Agreement on Strategic Forces, Article 2, *Vedomost´i viarkhounaga saveta respubliki Belarus*, 1993, no. 18, p. 61.

83. Ibid., pp. 60–61.

84. See Pavel Kazlouski (Belarus defense minister), interview, *Zviazda*, 6 August 1992.

85. *Zviazda*, 30 October 1993.

86. Comments of a NAKI officer at the international conference on "NIS Proliferation Problems," Minsk, 20–22 October 1993.

87. See Ural Latypov, "Export Controls in Belarus" (MIIS CIS Nonproliferation Project working paper, March 1994), p. 18.

88. See Shirkovski, "To Be or Not to Be?"

89. Ibid.

90. It is interesting to note that neither Belarus nor Ukraine had clearly outlined policies toward each other over the nuclear issue. Because of contrasting approaches, both sides were too skeptical of each other to cooperate on denuclearization. At the same time, Belarus tried to gain from some of Ukraine's moves, as in the case of compensation for HEU. Objectively, however, Ukraine's remaining or becoming a full-fledged nuclear power would undermine the international nonproliferation regime, destabilize regional security, complicate Russian-Ukrainian relations, and thus would mean less security for Belarus itself.

91. See, for example, Zianon Paz'niak, "Alternativa vsegda sushchestvuet," *Narodnaia gazeta*, 23–30 October 1990; "Belarus' u dorozhe," *Narodnaia gazeta*, 29 October 1992.

92. "Pavedamlenne apazitsii BNF."

93. Curiously, this idea was sounded already in the autumn of 1991, when Foreign Minister Piotr Kravchenko stated, "One must choose whether to become a nuclear weapon power or an independent state. The United States will never recognize Belarus as a nuclear weapon power." *Sem' dnei*, 9–15 December 1991.

KAZAKHSTAN: Nuclear Weapons and Other Sites of Proliferation Concern

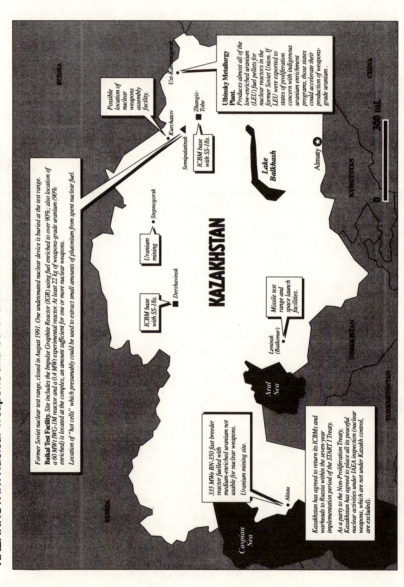

Former Soviet nuclear test range, closed in August 1991. One undetonated nuclear device is buried at the test range.

Baikal Test Facility. Site includes the Impulse Graphite Reactor (IGR) using fuel enriched to over 90%; also location of a 60 MWt IWG-1M reactor and a 0.4 MWt experimental reactor. At least 22 kg of weapons-grade uranium (90% enriched) is located at the complex, an amount sufficient for one or more nuclear weapons.

Location of "hot cells" which presumably could be used to extract small amounts of plutonium from spent nuclear fuel.

Possible location of nuclear weapons assembly facility.

Ulbinsky Metallurgy Plant. Produces almost all of the low-enriched uranium (LEU) fuel pellets for nuclear reactors in the former Soviet Union. If LEU were exported to states of proliferation concern with indigenous uranium enrichment programs, those states could accelerate their production of weapons-grade uranium.

ICBM base with SS-18s.

Uranium mining.

Missile test range and space launch facilities.

335 MWe BN-350 fast breeder reactor fuelled with medium-enriched uranium not usable for nuclear weapons.

Uranium mining site.

Kazakhstan has agreed to return its ICBMs and warheads to Russia within the seven-year implementation period of the START I Treaty.

As a party to the Non-Proliferation Treaty, Kazakhstan has agreed to place all its peaceful nuclear activities under IAEA inspection (nuclear weapons, which are not under Kazakh control, are excluded).

RUSSIA

CHINA

KYRGYZSTAN

TURKMENISTAN

UZBEKISTAN

KAZAKHSTAN

Ust-Kamenogorsk

Zhangi-Tobe

Kurchatov

Semipalatinsk

Stepnogorsk

Derzhavinsk

Lake Balkhash

Almaty

Leninsk (Baikonur)

Aral Sea

Aktau

Caspian Sea

300 mi.

Source: Carnegie Endowment for International Peace and the Monterey Institute for International Studies.

9

Kazakhstan's Nuclear Policy and the Control of Nuclear Weapons

Murat Laumulin

Since 1991, Kazakhstan has had to face some very complicated problems, especially concerning the nuclear heritage of the Soviet Union. For the last forty years Kazakhstan served as one of the strategic bases of the former Soviet Union. The Semipalatinsk test site, where nuclear weapons were tested, is situated there. The Kazakh steppes were transformed into natural sites for intercontinental ballistic missiles (ICBMs). After the collapse of the USSR, Kazakhstan, which possesses vast sources of uranic raw materials, became a nuclear state. But the Kazakh leadership understood that actual control over the nuclear armaments complex belonged to Moscow. That is why Almaty tried to preserve common control over the strategic forces under the command of the Commonwealth of Independent States (CIS). Under pressure from the United States and Russia, however, Kazakhstan signed the Lisbon Protocol to the Strategic Arms Reduction Treaty (START I) and the Nuclear Prolifeation Treaty (NPT), which obliged it to become a non-nuclear state.

It is not unreasonable to suggest that the political leaders of Kazakhstan consider the presence of nuclear weapons on their territory the best safeguard for Kazakhstan's security. Some believe that Kazakhstan should conclude a military-strategic alliance with Russia that would allow it to keep Russian ballistic missiles (of the class permitted by START I and START II) on Kazakh territory; they could be mobile missiles with one nuclear warhead each. But any plan to involve Russia in Kazakh national security seems improbable in the near future. At the time of this writing, too many disagreements remain over who will own the nuclear components of dismantled missiles and which state will inherit the strategic nuclear forces.

Russia insists that there can be only one owner—Russia. In an interview, President Nursultan Nazarbaev pointed out that the plan for a unified Commonwealth of Independent States (CIS) military policy appeared to have been abandoned.

On 13 December 1993, the Kazakh parliament (Supreme Soviet) ratified the NPT. This document formalizes the country's non-nuclear status. It does not, however, establish who owns the nuclear forces in Kazakh territory. Closely watching Ukraine's attempts to bargain with Russia and the United States over compensation for nuclear warheads, Kazakhstan may make similar claims if an agreement is reached. Presently, Kazakhstan has taken a fairly moderate position on the issue of nuclear control; its intentions regarding the NPT and nuclear weapons as a whole have become clear.

Kazakhstan as a Nuclear Successor of the Former USSR

The Soviet Nuclear Weapons Legacy

By the time the USSR broke up, Kazakhstan had become one of its most important strategic regions. It was a nuclear missile bridgehead, the premier site for nuclear testing, and an important source of uranium deposits.

The nuclear infrastructure of Kazakhstan, as assessed by Western experts, is as follows: 104 ICBM SS–18s with 10 warheads each (1,040 warheads total); 40 strategic bombers with 320 nuclear charges; and 650 units of tactical nuclear weapons.[1] Thus the total USSR arsenal of strategic and tactical weapons in Kazakhstan was over 2,000 units.

One of the components of the nuclear infrastructure is the physical presence of power sources used by atomic reactors. One reactor, in Aktau (formerly Shevchenko), in western Kazakhstan, is used for industry. The electric power of this fast-neutron reactor, using concentrated 20 to 25 percent uranium, is 335 megawatts.[2] The main purpose of this reactor, brought on-line in 1973, is to provide Aktau with fresh water (the town is situated in the desert). Furthermore, there are scientific research reactors in Kazakhstan.

The republic's uranium deposits, exploited during the Soviet regime, are found in Aksuek-Kijahty, near Aktau, and in Koktas (here along with copper). One big uranium deposit is on the Mangyshlak Peninsula (Mangistau), another in Stepnogorsk, and two in Tasbulak and Shalgiya. All these deposits are located mainly in western, northwestern, and central Kazakhstan.[3]

The Ulba metallurgical works, in Ust'-Kamenogorsk (eastern Kazakhstan), produces beryllium and pure uranium dioxide (metals used in the eventual production of nuclear warheads). Thus this area provides resources for the production of raw materials used in RBMK- and VVER-type reactors.[4]

As for the facilities needed to handle radioactivity during safety inspection and testing of nuclear weapons, one hot cell is located at the famous Semipalatinsk (formerly Semipalatinsk–21, now Kurchatov) test site.[5] In 1949, the first explosion took place there, followed by eighty-seven atmospheric explosions between 1949 and 1963. Underground testing began in 1961.[6] In all, there were 557 explosions.[7] Several explosions—for "peaceful purposes," as the Soviet mass media defined them—occurred in the Aktiubinsk region during the 1970s and 1980s. As is known from several sources, during the 1950s and 1960s, several surface explosions took place in the deserts of the Mangyshlak Peninsula. In 1991, the test site was closed by a decree of Nazarbaev.

Obviously, at the time of the USSR's collapse, Kazakhstan was a powerful inheritor of the Soviet war arsenal, especially its nuclear potential. This is why the question of the republic's integration into the international security system and nonproliferation regime is now being raised.

Prospects for Kazakhstan's Uranium Trade

In late 1991 and early 1992, it was rumored that the Central Asian republics, including Kazakhstan, could or had just begun to trade in nuclear raw materials, technological components, missiles, and nuclear warheads. Such rumors reflected the political struggle within and outside of the CIS. A deep economic crisis, the political ambitions of the ruling circles, and, finally, a sharp reduction of skilled personnel in the nuclear infrastructure could lead to a chaotic proliferation of nuclear substances and materials.

If we are to proceed from the premise that all these nuclear elements will be transferred legally on the basis of international agreements, it is necessary to study the potential and size of the Soviet nuclear trade during the last years of the USSR. It is also necessary to select such countries as may be of interest to Kazakhstan. Geographical, economic, political, cultural-historical, and religious factors are important here. Moreover, Kazakhstan must also be of interest to such former partners as India, Pakistan, Iraq, Iran, North and South Korea, Libya, Israel, China, and Japan. Almost all these countries are Asian and situated in Central Asia or the Middle East. These are the areas of Kazakhstan's political and economic activity.

The prospect for cooperation in the nuclear field is possible with such countries as India, Pakistan, Iran, and South Korea. The same holds true of Turkey, considering its Western leanings. In spite of the interest of such countries as Iraq, Libya, and possibly Syria in the nuclear legacy of

Kazakhstan and Central Asia, cooperation with them has little chance of success. Presumably, Kazakh-Indian and Kazakh-Pakistani relations would be balanced. Thus it can be seen that the nuclear policy of Kazakhstan does not have a direct Islamic tendency.[8]

At the moment, three departments dealing with production, processing, and proliferation of uranic raw materials have been formed in Kazakhstan: the Atomic Energy Agency, the National Nuclear Center, and the Kazakh State Atomic Energy Industrial Corporation (KATEP). Their functions and authorities have been defined by the government. The Atomic Energy Agency conducts state policy in the field of atomic energy, safety control, regulatory law, and licensing. The National Nuclear Center is an academic institution where scientific and technological research is conducted. KATEP is a corporation formed from all enterprises in Kazakhstan that were part of the USSR's atomic industry.

The Atomic Energy Agency is taking part in the work of the International Atomic Energy Agency (IAEA). Preparatory work and the conclusion of agreements on fulfillment of IAEA safeguards for atomic industrial enterprises require the creation of a national system of control over nuclear materials. The Swedish Nuclear Physics Inspectorate will be giving technical assistance to Kazakhstan. An agreement on cooperation in atomic energy will also be concluded with Russia. Currently the agency has two main aims: control over atomic production and the creation of legislation regulating the activity of the atomic industrial complex.[9]

The efficiency of the agency's control at all stages of the technological process is obvious, and inspectors from Sweden and the IAEA have confirmed it. In the future, all licenses on the export and import of nuclear materials will be issued by the government of Kazakhstan on the basis of examination by the agency.

One of the main concerns about the export of uranic raw materials is the issue of quotas and prices. When Soviet uranium producers entered the world market in 1989, they were accused of dumping by the United States government, which threatened the introduction of a prohibitive tax—116 percent. The uranium producers of Kazakhstan decided to adopt quotas in order to save the republic's atomic industry. The stated price of Kazakh uranium was $21 for one kilogram, a relatively low cost that caused much discussion. An agreement with Russia on coordination of prices and continuation of cooperation was concluded, but in contrast with the Soviet epoch, uranium will be processed not in Russia but in the buyer country.[10]

As a whole, Kazakhstan's prospects for developing atomic energy are assessed as quite good. Undoubtedly, the atomic corporations in the republic are counting on cooperation with the IAEA.

Kazakhstan and the Nonproliferation Regime

With the collapse of the USSR, instead of there being one nuclear state, at a minimum four were created. The United States assessed this situation as a factor for instability and the revival of former threats to its security. The director of the Central Intelligence Agency, Robert Gates, said, "Only China and the CIS have missiles that can directly reach the territory of the United States."[11] Thus, the main aim of United States policy from the end of 1991 became liquidation of this potential threat in the following way: within the framework of the START Treaty, all nuclear weapons were to be transferred from Ukraine, Kazakhstan, and Belarus to Russia for liquidation. These countries also were to become members of the Nuclear Nonproliferation Treaty as non-nuclear weapon states.[12]

The development of nuclear policy in Kazakhstan falls into two stages. The first period, from 1989 to 1991, is characterized by strong antinuclear attitudes, the struggle for a nuclear test ban in Semipalatinsk, and the conversion of Kazakhstan into a nuclear weapon–free zone (Declaration of Independence of 1990) by closing the test site (August 1991). The second period ensues from the end of 1991. It can be characterized by the aspirations of the high echelons of Kazakhstan to stay under the Russian nuclear umbrella and their secret unwillingness to relinquish nuclear weapons. The ruling class of Kazakhstan has striven for partial arms control and maximum use of political and economic dividends from the Soviet nuclear legacy.[13] This contradictory policy was reflected in the official documents signed by Kazakhstan.

Almaty's Declaration of Independence on 21 December 1991 put an end to the seventy-year history of the USSR. Simultaneously, Kazakhstan concluded a treaty with Russia, Ukraine, and Belarus that put their nuclear strategic potentials under physical protection. There are eight articles in this treaty. Article 5 states that three republics have to join the NPT as non-nuclear weapon states. Article 4 states that the leaders of these three non-Russian republics could decide together on the use of these weapons until their total liquidation.[14] Whereas the United States and the West favored the implementation of Article 5, Ukraine and Kazakhstan preferred that Article 4 be implemented. Russian policy toward Ukraine reflected the Western position, the policy toward Kazakhstan was left undefined. The agreement on strategic forces was then signed by the leaders of eleven CIS republics.[15]

The accession of Kazakhstan to the Lisbon Protocol (23 May 1992) was an important event. According to the protocol, Kazakhstan was obliged to join the NPT as a non-nuclear weapon state in the shortest possible time.[16] Simultaneously, the IAEA had to enforce control over the non-nuclear weapon assets of Kazakhstan and sent its experts to the republic in September 1992. On 19 May 1992 Nazarbaev informed U.S. President George Bush of his actions.[17]

Despite these positive processes, Kazakhstan declared that it was not ready to leave the strategic program of the former USSR. Ukraine and Kazakhstan required security assurances from the United States upon their exit from the Soviet nuclear umbrella.[18] Subsequently, Kazakhstan demanded assurances for its security as a non-nuclear weapon state from Russia, the United States, China, Great Britain, and France. The West, however, suspected Kazakhstan, in its apparent unwillingness to relinquish the nuclear weapons of the former USSR, of some ulterior motive. These suspicions became stronger when, in early 1992, Nazarbaev presented his view on how Kazakhstan could obtain nuclear weapons. Hence the ballyhoo surrounding the supposed warheads sale by Kazakhstan to Iran. It was, after all, an example of Kazakhstan's readiness to follow the signed agreements. At the same time, an attempt was made to examine the strength of Islamic attitudes in the republic and its readiness to cooperate with Islamic fundamentalist regimes.

Kazakhstan's diplomatic maneuvers in May and June 1992 continued its former tendencies. During his visit to Washington, Nazarbaev confirmed once again the readiness of Kazakhstan to follow all its signed agreements. But after that, in Moscow, Nazarbaev and Russian President Boris Yeltsin negotiated a continuation of their nuclear-strategic cooperation. It was decided that Russia would "rent" the former Soviet bases in Kazakhstan. Subsequently, Nazarbaev said that Kazakhstan had become a nuclear state against its will, but that Kazakhstan was presently ready to become a non-nuclear weapon state. According to the agreement, Kazakhstan had to remain a member of the joint armed forces of the CIS for seven years. Once the CIS established a Joint Armed Forces Command, all strategic weapons in Kazakhstan would be under its jurisdiction.[19]

Kazakhstan was repeatedly informed, however, that if it failed to join the NPT, the West could not assure any security guarantees.[20] The West is anxious to achieve a political settlement over the Soviet nuclear weapon problem and is particularly concerned with the chaotic and uncontrolled (and possibly, controlled) proliferation of nuclear raw materials, technologies, and exports by the CIS.

Objectively, Kazakhstan has made great strides toward nonproliferation and nuclear disarmament. It is the only country (besides South Africa) to close its nuclear test site and firing grounds (in western Kazakhstan).[21] All military assets of the former USSR on Kazakh territory are now controlled, their functions either limited or completely liquidated. All underground uranium mines in Shalgiya and Tasbulak have been closed.[22]

But at the same time, Kazakhstan faces strong resistance from its military-industrial complex. The Semipalatinsk test site was closed only after the putsch's failure in August 1991, preventing the military from carrying out three planned nuclear explosions. A well-known authority in the field of nonproliferation, William C. Potter, suggested that service personnel in the former USSR were totally against a peaceful nuclear program, and that this opinion held especially true of the military leaders of Kazakhstan.[23]

One more step toward nonproliferation was taken by Kazakhstan. Organizations such as the National Nuclear Center and the Atomic Energy Agency, which control nuclear activity in Kazakhstan, were created by Nazarbaev's decree on 15 May 1992.[24] These organizations will participate in the coordination of scientific nuclear research and industrial uses of nuclear energy in cooperation with the IAEA. Commercial activity connected with nuclear raw materials and technologies lies within the competence of the special Kazakh State Atomic Energy Industrial Corporation. This corporation is engaged in the production of raw materials for the atomic energy industry.[25] Experts assess that Kazakhstan can produce about three thousand metric tons of U–238 annually. All enterprises producing enriched uranium, however, are located in Russia.

Currently, Kazakhstan is not able to conduct an active nuclear material export policy in spite of its great potential. In production, the training of specialists, and communications, Kazakhstan is still dependent on the old infrastructure of the former USSR.

The Nuclear Issue in Kazakhstan's Internal Policy

The Impact of the Antinuclear Movement

The nuclear issue in Kazakhstan has also been linked with some of the country's more serious sociopolitical problems. Health, for example, has become a topical issue. Dozens of atomic and hydrogen explosions in the atmosphere (until 1964) and hundreds of underground explosions contaminated the environment of Semipalatinsk, eastern Kazakhstan, and the Karaganda region, as well as the territories of Altai (in Russia) and probably China. Areas contiguous to the test site suffered the most, as is manifested in the rise in cancerous diseases, the high rate of infant mortality, and the overall genetic damage in the native population. A rise in various deviations and anomalies in the mental and physical development of children has been noticed. As was recently reported, infant mortality in this region is five times higher than in the USSR.[26] The latest scientific studies have attributed the causes of a certain immune deficiency, known as Semipalatinsk AIDS, to the contamination.[27]

The founding of the Nevada-Semipalatinsk movement should be considered in the context of political events in the USSR and Kazakhstan at the end of the 1980s. This movement, at first antinuclear in nature, was extremely centrifugal. The struggle against the Semipalatinsk test site was equivalent to the struggle for Kazakhstan's sovereignty; the movement became representative of a national drive. Later, representatives from Russia, Germany, and other nations joined the movement.

The closure of the Semipalatinsk test site was the main aim of the movement, a goal that was achieved on 29 August 1991, when Nazarbaev issued his decree. By this time, the movement had such branches as the Union of Nuclear Test Victims and the Relief Fund for Nuclear Test Victims all over Kazakhstan and especially in Semipalatinsk. Gradually the force of the antinuclear movement weakened.

An obvious symptom of the antinuclear movement's degradation in Kazakhstan is the current recession of antinuclear attitudes. If policy makers were to legalize Kazakhstan's obtaining of nuclear weapons or trade in nuclear components, or if they were to torpedo the NPT, it is unlikely that there would be much active public opposition. In gauging future policy concerning nonproliferation, this change in attitude ought to be taken into consideration.

In 1993, the antinuclear and ecological Nevada-Semipalatinsk movement once again began trying to attract public attention to the dangers of the former Soviet test sites. It was discovered that since the mid-1960s at least seventeen underground nuclear explosions had taken place in western Kazakhstan. Furthermore, Russian missiles landed in this region (at the Azgir test site). Scientists succeeded in drawing public attention to the fact that this region, for the most part situated in the latitude forty-five degrees north, had received a maximum fallout of radionucleids as a result of tests at Semipalantinsk and other test sites.[28]

The researchers at the Laboratory for Observation of Radioactive Contamination have their own opinion. According to their data, there were twenty-five explosions in seven regions of Kazakhstan (besides the Semipalatinsk test site) from 1966 to 1987. More than half the territory of the Semipalatinsk test site (its total area is 1.8 million hectares) is useless to the national economy. Currently, the test site is under observation by sixteen stations. As for the Lobnor test site, the tests and atmospheric explosions there resulted in insignificant levels of nuclear explosive by-products. By comparison, the researchers at the laboratory came to the conclusion that from 1962 to 1992, the greatest contamination was caused by the Chernobyl accident.[29]

The plans of industrialists to develop an atomic industry in Kazakhstan have increased the anxiety of "green" organizations. Kazakhstan has the world's largest uranium deposits and ranks third in the CIS for the power of its atomic industry and fourth in uranium export. The problem is how and where to bury the radioactive waste (RAW). Currently, there are five classes of RAW in Kazakhstan. In the first group are the radioactive wastes from uranium mining and processing enterprises. More than 200 million tons of RAW from this group have been accumulated (total activity is over 200,000 curies). The second group consists of equipment and wastes from the processing of mined raw materials. The third group is formed by the consequences of nuclear tests at different test sites. The fourth group of RAW consists of 9,000 tons of wastes from energy plants (26,500 curies). The fifth group consists of wastes from enterprises using ampuled (isotope) sources. There are 100,000 sources of this type (25,000 curies). Under such conditions experts suggest that the population's strong fear of radiation will be a serious obstacle to the realization of any future atomic energy programs.[30]

Another issue related to nuclear testing is the lack of a clear state policy toward the test victims. In January 1993, a law was issued in Kazakhstan confirming the readiness of the government to compensate victims for physical and moral losses.[31] This law, however, was criticized by some experts for using quite indefinite criteria to identify affected persons and regions. The negative consequences of tests are thought to be exaggerated, and critics believe the law promotes an intensification of fears about radiation and antinuclear attitudes.[32]

Political Parties and the Internal Struggle

To understand the current political landscape of Kazakhstan, it is first necessary to clarify some terms. According to the classical definition of the word, *radical* is equivalent to "left-wing," *liberal* to "centrist," and *conservative* to "right-wing." These definitions, however, are not valid for describing political realities in Kazakhstan. It is important to remember that the division is only relative, but that without it no analysis would be possible. So, if these classical definitions are put aside, the country's political associations can be divided into the following groups: (1) left-wing parties: the Socialist Party of Kazakhstan (SPK), the Social Democratic Party of Kazakhstan (SDPK), the Communist Party, and small neocommunist organizations; (2) centrists: the People's Unity of Kazakhstan Union (PUKU), the People's Congress of Kazakhstan (PCK), and various small parties; (3) right-wing parties: the National Democratic Party of Kazakhstan (NDPK), the Azat Movement, the Republican Party of Kazakhstan (RPK), and the Alash; and (4) various mixed groups made up of social and ecological movements.[33] Four parties of the current conglomeration of parties, movements, and sections have political weight: the SPK, the PCK, the PUKU, and Azat.

The Socialist Party of Kazakhstan promotes a democratic, market-based economy, the independence of Kazakhstan, the social welfare of the population, and a closer integration into the CIS, with its supranational structure. So far, the SPK has supported the government course but has begun to criticize it for its inability to stabilize the domestic situation, its misguided decisions on the reform model, and the impoverishment of the people.

The People's Congress of Kazakhstan, which considers itself a liberal-democratic party of the center, is likely to be the most active party. It has assumed the role of a constructive opposition whose aim is to create a democratic society and a law-governed and unitarian state. This party is supported by the Nevada-Semipalatinsk movement.

The People's Unity of Kazakhstan Union has put forward a program with a centrist bent in which members of the People's Congress of Kazakhstan see a compilation of their ideas. These ideas have long been propagated by Nazarbaev, who has given the union his blessing. A keen observer would have known that this would happen; Nazarbaev could not afford to be permanently alone. The establishment needs a powerful political organization that is capable of defending its interests. The union has a team of experienced officials, headed by strong leaders, but it lacks outstanding speakers capable of attracting masses of people to its ranks.

The two centrist parties, the PUKU and the PCK, have decided to merge into one party. But it is a marriage of convenience, and each of the parties hopes to take more than it can give.

The national democratic movements (Azat, Alash, and others) criticize Nazarbaev's policy on a number of issues, including the rejection of nuclear weapons, cadre politics, the lowering of living standards of the Kazakh population, the poor status of the Kazakh language, and the pro-Russia orientation of the Kazakh government.[34]

There are prospects for the establishment of a Slavic party by way of uniting the interethnic movement Unity, the Slavic population, and the separatist movements in the north and east of Kazakhstan, and it may become a conspicuous political force that will have to be dealt with.

It is not easy for anyone observing the dynamics of political processes in Kazakhstan to remain optimistic. Kazakhstan's crisis involves all aspects of the life of the state. One of the rays of hope comes from the activities of different political associations. All this is taking place against a very complicated background: the economic crisis, the inability of the government to rule the country, the aftermath of the political struggle in Russia, Russia's high-handed treatment of Kazakhstan, and increasing separatism in some regions.

The Evolution of Kazakhstan's Position on Nonproliferation

Predicting Kazakhstan's policy in the field of nonproliferation is impossible without analyzing the republic's attitude toward START I and START II. The fate of these treaties, after all, will be decided as much by Kazakhstan as by the CIS and Russia.

In Russia, the START II Treaty was criticized immediately after it was signed by the U.S. and Russian presidents for not meeting the interests of Russia. Later, the treaty was criticized for its technical imperfections: the manner of dismantling Soviet ballistic missiles and the terms of and responsibilities for their dismantling.[35] Other experts found arguments against the treaty from the military-strategic and geopolitical points of view, declaring that the nuclear forces of Russia would lose any possibility of striking an efficient retaliatory blow.[36] Serious arguments in favor of START II appeared two months later on the threshold of parliamentary meetings. There the official point of view was affirmed that START II would strengthen the security of Russia.[37]

While Russians debated the merits of the START II Treaty, Ukraine had yet to respond affirmatively to START I. That country's indecisiveness has affected the policy of Kazakhstan. Ukrainian political figures reject all accusations and suspicions concerning any nuclear ambitions of their country and insist on what they suggest are just demands: Ukraine must have security safeguards from the nuclear states; Ukraine has a right to its share of compensation from the sale of highly concentrated uranium from the dismantled nuclear arms;[38] and Ukraine does not need to hurry with ratification of START I, because the program of dismantling nuclear missile complexes is very expensive.[39] Obviously, all these arguments have the same importance for Kazakhstan.

Russian-Kazakh relations in the nuclear field, however, never have been as strained as Russian-Ukrainian relations. This was always emphasized by Moscow.[40] Currently, the main reproof by Russian experts against Ukraine is that the latter cannot ensure the proper level of maintenance, service, and security for the nuclear weapons.[41] Characteristically, Russian-Kazakh relations in the nuclear field have been more loyal, leading some individuals to assert that a new military-strategic alliance was forming between the two countries. Kazakhstan appeared to favor the START I Treaty, and warnings not to rush nuclear disarmament still were ignored.[42]

As is known, Ukraine and Kazakhstan have required security guarantees as one of the necessary conditions for the liquidation of nuclear weapons on their territories. As for Belarus, it was given assurances by U.S. President Bill Clinton—a unique case for the CIS.[43] One has to question whether these states really need American guarantees. Or do they need something more tangible, more effective—maybe nuclear weapons?

Of course, the geopolitical situation of Kazakhstan differs noticeably from the situations of Russia and Ukraine. Central Asia represents an increasingly serious hotbed of instability, lying near the frontiers of Kazakhstan. But the closeness of China is the most important factor for instability. It is said in Western,[44] Russian,[45] and Kazakh[46] sources that China is now actively building up its armed forces. Today, the armed forces of Xinjiang surpass those of the CIS and Russia located in this region in terms of technology, number, and morale. Therefore, it is not unreasonable to suggest that the political leaders of Kazakhstan have considered the presence of nuclear weapons on their territory the best guarantee for Kazakhstan's security.

The ratification of START I by Kazakhstan has two aspects, economic and political. Experts propose considerable economic advantages for Kazakhstan after the liquidation of its nuclear infrastructure, including the use of ballistic missiles for launching satellites; the use of nuclear materials from warheads for atomic energy; the use of deserted mining plants for the development of nuclear energy; the influx of foreign (i.e., American) aid for disarmament; and the rewards from repeated demands for security and international guarantees.[47]

On the other hand, there are great doubts in Almaty about the fate of the NPT after 5 March 1995.[48] Obliged to observe the START I Treaty and, at the same time, assure its own security, which logically dictates the retention of nuclear weapons, Kazakhstan has only one choice: to conclude a military-strategic alliance with Russia that includes placing Russian ballistic missiles (of the class permitted by START I and START II) on Kazakh territory. These would, seemingly, be mobile missiles (SS–25s) with one nuclear warhead.[49] Naturally, the question is how well Russia likes this idea, but there are reasons to suggest that Russia would favor such a proposal. In Kazakhstan, service personnel have long been accustomed to the concept of a defense based on monoblock ICBMs, instead of the SS–18, SS–19, and SS–24, which should be liquidated. Another factor for consideration would be the probable serious weakening of the missile attack warning system. Russia, possessing eight radiolocation stations, but with only three based on its own territory, would need to have a station in Kazakhstan as well.[50] Thus, objective conditions may force Russia and Kazakhstan to the conclusion of a military-strategic alliance, possibly outside the framework of the CIS defense doctrine.

Nuclear Weapons and the Nonproliferation Treaty

Kazakhstan and the NPT

START I and START II appeared ideal if Kazakhstan were to think in terms of definitive disarmament.[51] The reality of the disarmament process has turned out to be somewhat harsher, however. The issues of nuclear disarmament and the nonproliferation of nuclear weapons have now become intertwined, as may clearly be seen from the stance adopted by the United States and Russia. Thus, for Kazakhstan joining the NPT became a decisive factor in the resolution of not only those questions surrounding the implementation of START I but also a wide range of issues concerning Kazakhstan's development as a member of the world community.

An analysis of the existing situation indicated that there were no alternatives insofar as ratification of the NPT was concerned. Kazakhstan would either become a party to the treaty as a non-nuclear state, thereby establishing normal relations with all the major world powers and the world community as a whole, or be drawn into dangerous games with the nuclear weapon legacy of the former Soviet Union. Kazakhstan chose the non-nuclear path even before the collapse of the USSR for a reason that is still fresh in everyone's memory: the fight to close the test site at Semipalatinsk. Kazakhstan has endured a tremendous number of nuclear tests. The consequences of this testing affected the life and health of the local population, as well as the ecological balance of a vast expanse of land. It also made the people of Kazakhstan strongly "allergic" to nuclear issues. The closing of the nuclear test site, the withdrawal of nuclear weapons, and the joining of the NPT—these are all links in the same chain, the final link of which was the actual ratification of the NPT on December 13, 1993.

In addition to the moral aspect of this question, there were also significant economic and political aspects. These issues related to the considerable aid package that Kazakhstan is to receive from the world community, including a number of developed countries, in order to introduce measures for dismantling strategic nuclear missiles, dealing with the aftereffects of nuclear testing, and developing a peaceful nuclear energy program. This aid package hinged on Kazakhstan's unconditional adherence to the NPT as a non-nuclear state. It is common knowledge that Kazakhstan has a tremendous supply of raw uranium at its disposal and, therefore, has great potential for developing its nuclear power industry. But it cannot trade this raw material and effectively develop its own nuclear power industry without IAEA cooperation, which is a condition of its joining the NPT.

For a quarter of a century following the signing of the NPT, the promoters of nuclear nonproliferation experienced both successes and defeats. Despite monitoring by the IAEA, nuclear states, and the United Nations, a number of countries have succeeded in coming very close to creating nuclear weapons. They are known as "threshold" or "nearly nuclear" states. Yet the overall trend in international relations points toward a non-nuclear world. The huge nuclear arsenals of the United States and the former USSR are being cut back; the issue of the remaining nuclear states, France and China, joining the NPT is on the agenda. There have been instances in which countries possessing nuclear weapons have voluntarily given them up (South Africa). Talks are ongoing regarding a comprehensive test ban. Regulations have tightened worldwide in an effort to prevent the proliferation of nuclear components and dual-use materials. Solutions, moreover, are being found for regional conflicts that were once the reason why certain states were developing their nuclear industries. These changes are encouraging, and Kazakhstan has an opportunity to contribute to this increase in world security.

Although there were moral, economic, and political reasons for Kazakhstan's joining the NPT, there were also well-grounded reasons for Kazakhstan's delaying the ratification of the NPT. Nevertheless, certain spokespersons for the U.S. government maintained that Kazakhstan was hiding behind Ukraine in order to drag out the resolution of the nuclear weapons issue. Indeed, there had recently been major changes on the nuclear scene: the Ukrainian parliament ratified the START I Treaty and the Lisbon Protocol, but with amendments that de facto made Ukraine a nuclear state. This development exacerbated tensions between Russia and Ukraine, generating concern in Washington. There could be no talk of Kazakhstan's adopting a wait-and-see attitude, however.

Kazakhstan clearly could not accept the Ukrainian way of solving this problem, as both Moscow and Washington understood full well. It was in Russia's interest not to aggravate already controversial issues, particularly those concerning agreement on compensation for uranium taken from the warheads of dismantled missiles. It was in the interest of the United States (which was now obliged to resolve this Ukrainian crisis) not to let the same thing happen with Kazakhstan, which will need real security guarantees once START I is implemented. This new situation presented an opportunity to raise cooperation between Kazakhstan and the United States to a new level.

Kazakhstan's gradual shift to non-nuclear status has passed a decisive threshold: the country has ratified the NPT and joined the NPT as a non-nuclear state. These actions brought an end to an entire era in Kazakhstan's history, over the course of which its territory has seen atomic and nuclear testing, the stationing of strategic nuclear weapons, and the extraction and export of raw materials for the Soviet nuclear power industry. New choices lie ahead for Kazakhstan, perhaps in connection with the creation and development of its own peaceful nuclear structures, but these choices will be Kazakhstan's to make as a sovereign state.[52]

The Increasingly Contradictory Nature of Nuclear Issues

In the wake of the events in Ukraine, groups in favor of preserving the nuclear status of Kazakhstan formulated their position as follows: when the Supreme Rada of Ukraine ratified the START I Treaty, it introduced a number of changes and stipulations that fundamentally altered the meaning of the treaty and the status of Ukraine. As a result, there was a change in the status of nuclear weapons from the former USSR located in the republic. Ukraine was broadcasting the fact that it is a nuclear state, which renders problematic its fulfillment of START I obligations. This situation is an extreme consequence of the contradiction inherent in the Lisbon Protocol. Three former Soviet republics are required to acknowledge their non-nuclear status, while, at the same time, they appear in the protocol as nuclear entities.

One could have predicted all the potential conflicts surrounding nuclear weapons issues in late 1991. After the actual collapse of the Soviet Union, followed by that of its legal system, Russia and the United States tried to resolve such nuclear issues on an emergency basis, relying primarily on their own conceptions of security. This shared conception may be summarized as follows: the Soviet Union's place as a nuclear state may be occupied by only one country, and that country is Russia. Hence nuclear weapons must be withdrawn from the territory of Ukraine, Kazakhstan, and Belarus.

Events took a different course, however. If it were in fact possible to maintain an integrated structure for CIS strategic forces, under joint command—which is apparently what the leaders of the newly independent states wanted—then the reduction of CIS strategic forces would need to reflect the distribution of former Soviet forces on the territory of the individual republics. The most convenient way to denuclearize these republics now is via START I, which provides for a 50 percent reduction of the former Soviet Union's strategic potential. The Lisbon Protocol of START I states that this 50 percent reduction shall consist of the weapons located on Belarus, Ukraine, and Kazakhstan.

The actions taken by Moscow and Washington demonstrate that they do not trust the remaining republics with nuclear weapons. All important decisions regarding nuclear issues are therefore to be made by Russia and the United States, without the other states' participation. This kind of policy, reminiscent of dictatorship, naturally met with opposition, even from the republics that were loyal to Moscow. Ukraine, with its considerable political, military, and economic clout, spoke out openly against this policy of forcing decisions upon the republics. An analysis of the Russian-Ukrainian conflict over nuclear issues brings one to the conclusion that Russia has no one to blame but itself for what happened. First, Russia's tactic of resolving security issues at the expense of the other republics was shortsighted. Second, Russia's unwillingness to make concessions regarding compensation for the nuclear materials extracted from the warheads has undermined confidence that Russia is capable of being an honest partner. Third, Russia's perpetual threats and underhanded way of dealing with the former Soviet republics give the impression that Russia is returning to its former imperialistic politics.

The Ukrainian parliament's ratification of START I was important because it confirmed the sovereign right of a state to arm itself, even with the nuclear weapons on its own territory.[53] Throughout the disputes between Russia and Ukraine, Kazakhstan has always remained on the sidelines, not openly declaring itself to be on one side or the other. In practice, however, the possibility of Ukraine's withdrawal from START I calls into question the entire structure created by the treaty, including Kazakhstan's participation. The fact that Kazakhstan did not support Russia on this issue clearly demonstrates that both Kazakhstan and Ukraine have had equally negative experiences in holding negotiations with Russia about nuclear issues. Russia has been pursuing only its own selfish interests. All of this goes beyond the framework of conventional political and diplomatic relations among states, because what is at stake is the security and respective national interests of the newly independent states. Taking all these factors into consideration, one cannot help but recognize that the Ukrainian parliament's decision in regard to START I reminds Kazakhstan once again of its own security issues, which will not automatically be resolved simply by adhering to START I and the NPT. The extent to which these issues are interconnected is at least as significant for Kazakhstan as it is for Ukraine.

The entire START I framework and the Lisbon Protocol are based on the mandatory participation of all the former Soviet republics that possess nuclear weapons. Thus, if any one link in the chain (Ukraine, in this instance) were to break, the entire disarmament process would be disrupted. The only way out of such a situation would be through bilateral agreements (for example, between Kazakhstan and Russia or Kazakhstan and the United States).

The changing situation of nuclear weapons in Ukraine has offered Kazakhstan the opportunity to strengthen its position in negotiations with Moscow and Washington. From Kazakhstan's perspective, further development of the negotiations on nuclear issues must proceed within the framework of bilateral relations between Kazakhstan and Russia or Kazakhstan and the United States. Therefore, Kazakhstan's negotiating partners need to understand that it will not accept the Ukrainian method of addressing this issue. Russia should not disrupt the settlement of issues regarding agreement on compensation. Kazakhstan will also need new security guarantees once START I is implemented. This new situation will enable Kazakhstan to take its relations with the United States to new levels. It also needs to be made clear to the leadership in Washington that the ultimate goal of Kazakhstan's policy vis-à-vis the United States is strategic partnership.

The Military Aspects of Current Kazakh-Russian Relations

The Kazakh View of Russian National Interests

Historically, Russia, as a former superpower, thinks of Kazakhstan and the rest of Central Asia as its own national interest zone. No one can presently say exactly whether Russia has surrendered Central Asia for good or whether it intends to reconstruct its rule in this region in the near future.

What kind of interests does Russia have in Central Asia? Analyzing statements made by Russian politicians, Kazakh experts have come to the conclusion that the Russian approach toward Central Asia has not yet taken shape but that there is a framework for its creation.

The most salient points in this analysis are as follows. First, the Russian military estimates the loss of Kazakhstan (and all of Central Asia) as a threat to Russian state security.[54] Second, Central Asia is, and will always remain, a periphery of the world economy. Russian economic interests, however, have to be promoted, especially in Kazakhstan, by the following measures: the end of direct control, but continued preservation of Russian possessions and rights; support of Russian economic interests by ethnic Russians; and the support and conservation of the economic system in the Ural, western Siberia, and northern Kazakhstan regions.[55] Third, in the event of instability and for the sake of preserving Russian national interests, it has been proposed that Kazakhstan be divided into three parts (coinciding with the historical division of Kazakh borders). Western Kazakhstan (the Little Horde), the richest in oil supplies and possessing the best prospects for future development, has to be joined to Russia sine qua non. Central Kazakhstan (the Middle Horde) would remain a buffer security zone, and southern Kazakhstan (the Great Horde) would be incorporated by Islamic Central Asia.[56] Fourth, Russia should not abandon Central Asia so far as to relinquish its place to other states with more dynamic economies and more related (religious) cultures. As usual, the contenders are Turkey and Iran.[57] Fifth, Russia is the last bastion capable of stopping an escalation of Islamic fundamentalism.[58] And sixth, Russia cannot tolerate the reenforcement of China's position in the Central Asian republics, which could be realized through economic pressure, the presence of nuclear weapons, and ethnic infiltration. From the Russian point of view, the demographic factor is the most dangerous.[59]

Russia's approach to Central Asia is twofold. Externally, Russia wants to demonstrate to the world that Central Asia remains a part of the sphere of Russian interests and that it will not allow any power rivalries. Internally, Russia wants to convince the newly independent states of Central Asia (as well as public opinion in Russia) that there is an imminent foreign threat and that only Russia is capable of protecting them from absorption by new leaders.[60]

It is believed in Kazakhstan that this justification will direct Russian foreign policy in the future. One has only to look to the Zhirinovsky phenomenon to reach this conclusion. Vladimir Zhirinovsky's declarations relating to foreign policy, Russian national interests, and the fate of Kazakhstan could be alarming indicators of things to come. Kazakh analysts believe that the demagogy of Zhirinovsky reflects not only his constituency's opinion but also the desires of Russia's ruling elite.

The newest factor is Aleksandr Solzhenitsyn. This modern Russian prophet recently declared that the northern half of Kazakhstan had to belong to Russia, as these territories were colonized and settled by Russians during a long historical period. It would also be foolish to dismiss the point of view expressed directly by the Russian defense minister, Pavel Grachev, in the spring of 1994, when he in essence said that the Commonwealth of Independent States was in fact Russia. Although the concept of Russia's national interests has not yet been officially declared, it can be found in certain documents, the most important being Russia's military doctrine.

The Kazakh View of the Russian Military Doctrine

Kazakh experts have concluded that the new military doctrine of Russia is radically different from that of the former Soviet Union. Whereas the Soviet doctrine had proclaimed that the USSR would never initiate nuclear strikes, the new Russian doctrine allows the use of nuclear weapons in specific situations, such as in the case of a threat toward a state that is party to the Nuclear Nonproliferation Treaty and an ally of Russia. This contingency may be characterized as a policy of nuclear deterrence. It allows support to the parties of the Treaty on Collective Security (signed in Tashkent in May 1992). Kazakhstan, therefore, already has something of a "nuclear umbrella."[61]

Russia's military doctrine, however, could have a reverse effect, and Kazakhstan theoretically could be the object of political, military, and nuclear blackmail. The doctrine considers the subversion of strategic stability in violation of international agreements in the areas of arms reduction and limitation as a source of military danger.

This point is clearly demonstrated in the example of START I, whose parties are Russia, the United States, Ukraine, Kazakhstan, and Belarus. If Kazakhstan had not joined the NPT in December 1993, it could have been considered a military threat. In proclaiming Ukraine de facto a nuclear state, Ukraine's parliament (Rada), according to Russia's military doctrine, made that country a source of military threat.

Russia is said to consider the violation of the rights of Russian minorities abroad as a potential military threat. Since 1993 Moscow, which looks on the Russian (so-called Russian-speaking) population in Kazakhstan (about 50 percent) as Russian citizens, has demanded that Kazakhstan recognize the principle of dual citizenship for Russians. Kazakhstan, hypothetically according to the doctrine, could become a source of threat to Russia.

In such a doctrine, it is impossible to ignore Russia's guarantee and maintenance of governmental and military control over strategic nuclear forces. This aspect of the doctrine has a direct impact on Kazakhstan's space port at Baikonur. Russia could conceivably classify any unilateral activity of Kazakhstan relating to the property it inherited as the sole nuclear successor of the Soviet Union as a military threat, as it could any other state's activity that obstructed the functioning of the Russian system of control over strategic nuclear forces. That is to say, this doctrine proclaims once again that the nuclear weapons of the former Soviet Union belong to Russia.

In addition, the Russian military doctrine supports the continued participation of the Russian Federation in collective security structures such as the CIS and its only treaty, the Treaty on Collective Security, which Russia recently put to the test in the case of Tajikistan. From the view of Kazakhstan, the realization of the treaty demands financial disbursement that Russia cannot now bear.

Thus, one can draw certain conclusions from Russia's military doctrine and its place in Russia's policy. First, in refusing the establishment of a separate, united armed forces contingent under the control of the CIS, Russia reserved the right to follow its own policy in dealing with matters of security. Second, different sources of threat to Russian security will at times appear. For the solution of some problems, Russia can afford to sacrifice the sovereignty of its allies. Third, the solution to the nuclear armaments problem is closely connected to the solution of Russia's economic problems. Fourth, according to the Russian military doctrine, Kazakhstan can be seen either as an ally, a sphere of influence of Russian national interest, or a military threat. In any case, Russia will follow its own interests in dealing with Kazakhstan, even if that means neglecting the interests of its allies.[62]

Prospects for a Kazakh-Russian Military Alliance

Notwithstanding such realities as the differences in national interests and the aggressiveness of the Russian military doctrine, the common security problem of both Russia and Kazakhstan would seem to make these two natural allies. The prospects for a Russian-Kazakh military alliance are therefore held in high regard. In this event there are more common interests than contradictions. For such an alliance to come about, however, Russia and Kazakhstan would first need to come to terms on military strategy, the use of nuclear weapons, the development of conventional armaments, their policy toward other CIS partners, and their collective response to external threats.

Strategic Partnership

The problem of the strategic unity of Russia and Central Asia is confirmed by history, and more recently has been resolved by the domination of one side over the other in tsarist times and under the Soviet regime. Central Asia has historically been the object of Russian colonial expansion. Since the collapse of the USSR, however, a new situation has emerged that calls for collaboration.

Russia needs Kazakhstan to guarantee and develop its strategic forces system. First of all, there is the problem of Baikonur,[63] the radiolocation stations, and the reactivation of nuclear and conventional test sites. Moreover, only through Kazakhstan would Russia be able to influence effectively the other Central Asian republics, China, and the Middle Eastern states. For Kazakhstan, the strategic partnership can be understood as a necessary element of economic security: Kazakhstan's main communications and connections with the outside world are through Russia. More importantly, the political influence of Kazakhstan and its security are dependent on its strategic significance for Russia and other powers.

Nuclear Weapons

The nuclear problem is closely connected with that of strategic partnership, with the additional dimensions of nuclear nonproliferation, nuclear raw materials, nuclear weapons, and nuclear test sites. Kazakhstan, with its vast reserves of uranium, will always be important for the Russian military and peaceful nuclear programs. In addition, Russia, as the successor to the USSR's nonproliferation policy, has to be concerned with collaboration with Kazakhstan to support the nonproliferation policy.

The nuclear weapons problem in Kazakhstan, in its first phase, concentrated on the demolition of Soviet strategic armaments according to START I. The next phase, however, could transform the process altogether; for example, the establishment on Kazakh territory of Russian nuclear weapons of a new generation (not covered by START I and START II) could alter geopolitical positions and pose a real threat to the security of either state. So far, though, Russia and Kazakhstan have yet to sign a formal military treaty on the issue of nuclear weapons. In spite of what the Russian military may design or envisage, Kazakhstan will not jeopardize its security to serve Russian interests merely as a base of military operations.

Conventional Armaments

Kazakhstan cannot develop an effective army without the technical and military assistance of Russia. At present the Kazakh army, a rudiment of the Soviet armed forces (the former Fortieth Army), is very much dependent on Russian technology and equipment. The majority of staff officers are either Russian or of some other Slavic nationality. If ethnic Russian military officers should leave the country, Kazakhstan will have to form a purely national army, whose experience and professionalism will likely be brought into question.

From an economic standpoint, the reduction in the manufacture of armaments is having a direct impact on Kazakh business and industry. Out of hundreds of plants in Kazakhstan that were once involved in the Soviet military-industrial complex, slightly more than forty enterprises currently manufacture military equipment. The factories primarily produced weapons for the Soviet fleet: torpedoes, naval missiles, antitorpedo technology, radio-electronic equipment, guidance systems, and launchpads. Before the disintegration of the USSR, they all took orders from Moscow. But in the current political climate, Kazakhstan's arms industry represents something of a paradox. It has managed to find markets in the countries of Pacific Asia, the Indian subcontinent, Africa, and Eastern Europe. The hard currency profit from arms sales in 1993 could reach $200 to 250 million. Nevertheless, Kazakhstan's weapons production has decreased by more than a third over the past two years.[64]

Policy Toward CIS Partners

As proved when Kazakh President Nursultan Nazarbaev failed in his effort to influence the conflict between Armenia and Azerbaijan in 1992–93, effective joint action by Russia and Kazakhstan in the sphere of security can be realized only in the Central Asian region. The matter of Tajikistan is a case in point. This was a unique occurrence in which, the Central Asian states, following Russia's lead, demonstrated solidarity in stopping the deep military-political crisis in that republic. The net result, however, was Russia's increased military-political influence in the region.

Response to External Threats

Since the obligations of the partners to the Treaty on Collective Security can be realized only under certain conditions, in order to drive the mechanism of this treaty it is necessary to have not only the desire of one party (Russia) and the capacity of the second (Kazakhstan) to carry out these obligations but also the appearance of a potential source of threat. In such an event, the Kazakh-Russian political-military alliance could grow very rapidly. Its dimensions would vary depending on the level of threat; the establishment of conventional or nuclear armaments; the participation of Russia in the formations of the Kazakh army (or its absorption by the Russian armed forces); the allocation of Russian military bases on Kazakh territory; and the involvement of Kazakhstan in the military-strategic structures of Russia.

Nuclear Problems in Kazakh Policy and the Chinese Impact

China's Claims in Central Asia

China's influence in Central Asia has deep historical roots. Today China is actively taking part in the renewal of the "Great Game" in Central Asia with its increasing economic influence. Further political pressure can be expected as a consequence of the power vacuum created by the fall of the Soviet Union.

As is well known, the modern Kazakh-Chinese border is a legacy of the Soviet-Chinese, and before that the imperial Russian-Chinese, frontiers. It is the result of the territorial expansion of the Russian Empire from the west and the Chinese from the east. A compromise for both expansionist powers was fixed in the St. Petersburg Treaty of 1881, with the later provisions of 1883, 1884, and 1885. After the Chinese Revolution, all treaties with European states based on the Peking Treaty of 1860 were denigrated by the new government and considered inequitable to Chinese interests. This attitude continued as official doctrine in communist China. Under Mao Zedong, China tried to change (according to the Chinese ambassador, "correct")[65] the Sino-Soviet border along Kazakh territory in 1968 and 1971. The military confrontations were a failure for China. China has had other territorial and border pretensions toward neighboring countries (seven at a minimum), going so far as to occupy disputed territories in India (1962) and Vietnam (1979).

Contradictions in Chinese policy relating to the border question—official declarations to the world community versus propagandist policy inside China—have instilled distrust in other nations. On 17 August 1992, for example, the foreign minister of the People's Republic of China proclaimed at the United Nations that China had no territorial ambitions on the former Soviet republics, yet public opinion in China seemed convinced that the vast spaces in Central Asia were historically joined to former Chinese empires. China's implicit ambitions are indicated on Chinese maps and in scientific publications.

But there is one more problem connected with China's policy in Central Asia—eastern Turkestan, or Xinjiang. The Tsing empire penetrated into this region in the middle of the eighteenth century, and a final conquest of eastern Turkestan was realized after World War II by communist China. The Turkic Muslim peoples of eastern Turkestan (Kazakhs and Uigurs) had formed their own states in the 1860s to 1870s, the 1930s, and the 1940s, the last one being the so-called Islamic Republic of Eastern Turkestan. In the early 1950s, this region became the object of massive Chinese colonization. According to census data of 1930, 4 percent of the population was Chinese; today the figure is 40 to 50 percent. The "autonomous" status of today's Xinjiang-Uigur Autonomous Region (the official title of eastern Turkestan) is a fiction because of the communist regime's oppressive national policy toward the Muslim peoples of that area, especially the abominable coercive birthrate limitation policy.[66]

Thus, there are serious motivations for Chinese expansion into Central Asia. These are based on historical pretensions of the Chinese empires and depend on the demographic situation in inner China[67] and its economic growth, requiring new space, markets, and resources. From the political point of view, the existence of independent Turkic states is a potential threat to Chinese domination in Xinjiang. In order to keep its western domain, China must find a solution to the Central Asian problem. But from a strategic point of view, these pretensions must and will have to be based on military capability. Does China have this?

Chinese Military Ambitions: Focus on Kazakhstan

Chinese military ambitions have two dimensions: political and military. The political aspect of China's military development is provided by the Communist Party rule over the army. In 1992 the Fourteenth Congress of the Chinese Communist Party devoted strong attention to the army situation. The army, the "battle detachment of the party," was proclaimed a guarantor of the realization of reforms. These changes in military policy in China were a reaction to new realities: the disintegration of the USSR and the winning of the Cold War by the West; the widening of local conflicts, including those in China's areas of interest; and the influence of the newest technologies of modern war.

In regard to the army, the government of China designated several objectives: formation of a strong, modern standing army; coordination of economic and defense developments; absolute rule by the Communist Party over the army; development of new armaments and technologies (technical equipment) for the army; concentration of reserve funds for the needs of the army; maintenance of the army as a politically stable instrument; and development of the reserves according to the conception of "people's war."[68]

China has the largest army in the world: 3.2 million troops. The Lanzhou military district alone, which targets Kazakhstan, has 200,000 troops (and reserves of 400,000 to 450,000). Chinese forces have superiority over the Kazakh armed forces by as much as fifteen to one. The Chinese army in the Xinjiang area has 500 tanks, 5,000 cannons, and 450 bombers. It has artillery supremacy by three times, military planes by two and a half, and antitank systems by seven. Kazakhstan has parity with China only when it comes to tanks.[69]

According to various sources, from 1990 to 1993, China increased its military budget by about 50 percent (in 1991, 15 percent; 1992, 12 percent; 1993, 15 percent).[70] Western experts indicate that China can realize the modernization of its armed forces on the basis of a growing economy, and will thus become more dangerous for its neighbors in Asia. The French sinologist, M. Jean, concluded that, since 1990, the concentration of Chinese armed forces in the northwestern regions (that is, near Kazakhstan and other Central Asian states) has increased, thus escalating the prospect of local conflicts in this area.[71]

Kazakh experts foresee probable Chinese aggression through the following scenario: In the near future China will avoid signing an effective peace treaty with Kazakhstan. After 1999, when the last nuclear ballistic missile will be destroyed, according to START I, China will begin to provoke border problems. A repetition of the 1962 experience is very probable. At that time, the Chinese authorities will send one hundred thousand peoples indigenous to Xinjiang (Kazakhs, Uigurs, and Dungans) over the border into Kazakhstan. If Kazakhstan does not agree to change the border on Chinese terms, China will force a solution to the disputed questions. The Chinese army will move offensively in either of two directions, if not both: through the southern Horgos and Ili Valley to Almaty or via the northern route through the Dzhungarian mountain range to Lake Balkhash. The main objective of these breakthroughs would be to plunder the Turksib railroad. Then a breakthrough in the Altai region would probably follow. The basis for the offensive would be twelve ordinary divisions (Twenty-first and Forty-seventh Armies). The air force and tanks would not figure prominently during the offensive; special troops would play a decisive role. The last factor in the conflict would be four Chinese special storm divisions. According to the estimation of Kazakh military experts, the Chinese army would occupy from one-third to one-half of Kazakh territory (the area from Almaty to Karaganda) within three to four weeks.[72]

China is now actively building up its armed forces. At this time its armed forces in Xinjiang excel in technology, numbers, and morale over those of the CIS and Russia located in Central Asia.

Kazakhstan considers China a communist totalitarian state. The Chinese government of eastern Turkestan (Xinjiang) conducts a repressive policy toward ethnic minorities, such as the Turkic Muslim peoples, which include Kazakhs. Furthermore, Kazakhstan feels threatened by the increasing economic power of China, its tremendous population, and its nuclear weapons. Heightening the alarm are the serious doubts the leadership of Kazakhstan has about the efficiency of the CIS collective security system.

Kazakh-Chinese Relations and the Antinuclear Movement

From the Kazakh point of view, Chinese nuclear activity is considered a potential source of instability. The issue is complicated, not only by virtue of the strategic weapons possessed by China, but also because China continues to develop its nuclear program at the Lobnor test site in Xinjiang. The Kazakh antinuclear movement Nevada (or Nevada-Semipalatinsk), which had demanded and attained the closing of the Soviet nuclear test site in Semipalatinsk, had called for the closing of the Chinese test site, as did the Uigur political lobby. In 1992, the Uigur lobby had tried to influence Kazakhstan's leadership to take up the problem of nuclear tests on Uigur lands in China with the Chinese government. For the past two years, in fact, the Nevada movement has called for the closing of all test sites in the world and the introduction of a global moratorium on all nuclear weapons testing. But the government of the Republic of Kazakhstan understood that such radical demands could destroy the emerging political dialogue with China.

Nevertheless, Kazakhstan's position on nuclear issues became more clearly defined over the course of 1993. An antinuclear conference organized by the Nevada movement was held in Almaty at the end of the summer of that year. This conference was different from its predecessors in that the demand being made—closing the Lobnor nuclear test site—affected diplomatic and intergovernmental relations between the People's Republic of China and the Republic of Kazakhstan. The conference called for the creation of a global antinuclear alliance. It also published data indicating that a zone of ecological danger and radioactive threat to the environment envelops not only the Semipalatinsk region but also southeastern Kazakhstan (the Almaty region).

According to the data, from 1964 to 1992, China had conducted thirty-eight nuclear explosions. Before 1980, all explosions were in the atmosphere. Although Almaty is far from the Lobnor test site (twelve hundred kilometers), the prevailing east wind has borne contaminants to the region. The level of radioactive background in the Almaty region, according to experts, is twice as much as that in Semipalatinsk. Over the last twenty years, mortality has increased by 50 percent; cancer rates have risen as well. Scientists have concluded that, in addition to the Soviet nuclear and industrial activities, there was one more source of the radioactive background in Almaty—China's nuclear explosions.[73]

Kazakh society's longtime mistrust and prejudice toward China only increased after the publication of this information (the Soviet Union held the same information secret) concerning the Chinese atomic program and the nuclear testings in Lobnor. To say the least, China is not looked on favorably at all as a peaceful neighbor by either the Kazakh public, the military, or politicians. Skeptics question the sincerity of China's prime minister, who recently said that his country would endorse a comprehensive nuclear test ban on condition that the nuclear weapon states first conclude a no-first-use agreement.[74]

Russian Interests in Kazakh-Chinese Relations

It is a paradox that no commentators speak as passionately about the friction in Kazakh-Chinese relations as they do about the complicated relations between Russia and Kazakhstan. As for the latter, one is left with the impression that the two states have irreconcilable differences, particularly on the problems surrounding the Baikonur cosmodrome, the development of a standing army, and compensation for enriched uranium from the nuclear missile warheads (not advantageous for Kazakhstan). The Russians are inspiring yet another problem—dual citizenship. Obviously, this issue is connected with the status of Kazakhstan's sovereignty. A more significant issue, however, concerns the viability of a military alliance treaty between Russia and Kazakhstan.[75]

Kazakhstan and Russia have also clashed over the issue of compensation for the dismantling of nuclear armaments. From Russia's point of view, only Russia is entitled to compensation as a nuclear successor to the USSR. Kazakhstan, on the other hand, because of its historical impact on the Soviet nuclear program (uranium deposits, nuclear test sites, etc.), believes it also has a right to compete for a part of the compensation. In February 1994, the Russian official newspaper *Izvestiia* claimed that the condition of, and security over, the nuclear weapons in Kazakhstan was deplorable. The claim was unfounded, according to Almaty, which attributed this démarche to pressure politics and political blackmail on the part of Moscow to force Kazakhstan into surrendering the weapons.[76]

According to Kazakh experts, the strengthening of Russia's uncompromising position on many important issues since 1992 can be ascribed to the military's increased influence in the Russian government. Russia's tactics toward Kazakhstan, particularly in the security sphere, are seen as detrimentally shortsighted. Yet, to maintain a strategic advantage, Russia will have to take more farsighted steps to protect its interests in Central Asia, what with the growing Chinese pressure on the Russian Far East, which is expected to intensify through economic and demographic penetration. China's inroads in Central Asia, especially in Kazakhstan, threaten the very ethnic heart of Russia and make more urgent the need for Russia and Kazakhstan to settle their differences and ally themselves militarily by treaty.

In the coming years, we may well see contradictory developments in the political and economic relations between Russia and China. Moscow could end up selling various armaments, including the newest types, to its eastern neighbor, with the political aim of keeping China from influencing Central Asia and other regions. In addition, the United States, together with Russia, could castigate China for not joining the moratorium on nuclear testing.

Entering into a joint military alliance would be in the best interest of Russia and Kazakhstan. Yet, as Kazakhstan grapples with serious domestic problems (economic, military, and political) that might well be alleviated through such an agreement, Russia bides its time, hoping to gain a tactical advantage by having Kazakhstan agree more readily to Russian terms. On the other hand, Kazakhstan would like more time to garner Western support and procure real guarantees for its security from the North Atlantic Treaty Organization and the United States.[77]

If the Chinese threat became more imminent, however, Kazakhstan would have to put aside its qualms and agree to any Russian conditions if it is to effectively counter the threat. Russia in turn would guarantee to shield Kazakhstan, as its natural ally, with any armaments (up to nuclear deterrence).

Kazakh Nuclear Policy: In Search of Security

During the final months of 1993, the political life of the Republic of Kazakhstan was replete with events concerning nuclear issues. In September 1993, delegations representing the governments of Kazakhstan and the United States held intensive negotiations that resulted in the initialing of a framework agreement on United States participation in, and financing of, the dismantling of Soviet SS–18 ballistic missiles. In Almaty, it was hoped that the signing of this document would signify Kazakhstan's true intention of fulfilling the obligations set forth in the START I Treaty and the Lisbon Protocol. Finally, in early October 1993, Kazakhstan was officially accepted into the International Atomic Energy Agency at its headquarters in Vienna. For the immediate future, all nuclear facilities in Kazakhstan will now fall under IAEA safeguards, that is, the agency's regulations for accounting, information, and monitoring.

Because the Soviet Union was a nuclear state, it had no need of IAEA safeguards. Kazakhstan, however, has had no experience with such safeguards. Now the Atomic Energy Agency of the Republic of Kazakhstan has developed a program for including Kazakhstan's nuclear facilities within the framework of the IAEA. Nevertheless, serious obstacles are being encountered in training personnel and providing technical backup to make sure that Kazakh nuclear facilities are covered by IAEA safeguards. A number of Western states have pledged to cooperate with Kazakhstan in training personnel to work at nuclear facilities. With the passing of time, the level of security in its nuclear industry is certain to improve. In contrast, the level of security in Kazakhstan's military and political spheres, once guaranteed by Soviet nuclear capabilities, remains weak.

Unfortunately, in spite of its ratification of the NPT and START I with the Lisbon Protocol, Kazakhstan still lacks real guarantees for its national security and integrity. That is the reason the Kazakh leadership has initiated the so-called Conference on Interaction and Confidence-Building Measures in Asia, which advocates the creation of a system of security in Asia, in the belief that the states of this region share equal interests in providing stable and long-lasting peace and stability.

In the process of forming a national army, Kazakhstan faces difficult problems. All commanding officers of the former Soviet army in Kazakhstan were supposed to return to Russia by December 1994, according to an intergovernmental agreement. The Kazakh government is greatly concerned about the mass exodus of military staff. Since it is no longer able to select junior officers from other former Soviet republics (Russia, Ukraine, or Belarus), Kazakhstan will have a hard time preventing a military collapse. The obvious decline of Kazakhstan's defense capabilities worries the government and comes at a time when Kazakhstan should be designing its armed forces. Improving army life would require not only radical measures but great expenditures, which Kazakhstan cannot afford.

The harsh debates surrounding the Soviet nuclear legacy, especially between Russia and Ukraine, cannot overshadow the tragic economic legacy of the post-Soviet era. Even if all members of the CIS were to agree to maintain a collective defense system with nuclear weapons, assuming relations among them were to improve and all the contradictions and threats were somehow smoothed over or eliminated, they would still be unable to bear the burden of a "nuclear shield" simply for economic reasons. Clearly, this is the true significance of the disarmament process begun in 1987. The collapse of the Soviet Union in 1991 accelerated this process, and from that time on, policies adopted by the United States and Russia were aimed at making it irreversible.

Yet the issues related to Kazakhstan's national security still remain unresolved. Kazakhstan's signing of the NPT will not require that there be support from the nuclear states in the event of aggression. Only three of these states (the Soviet Union, the United States, and Great Britain) issued special statements in 1967 that addressed acts of aggression using nuclear weapons. Furthermore, the security guarantees that Kazakhstan receives as a member of the CIS are becoming ever more fragile. For that matter, even the very existence of the commonwealth is problematic. Finally, the inclusion of Kazakhstan in START I was accompanied by verbal assurances from the United States and Russia to the effect that they would guarantee the territorial integrity and security of Kazakhstan following the destruction of Soviet ballistic missiles and the elimination of nuclear-armed aircraft on Kazakh territory. These assurances, however, were not backed up by any kind of special written agreements spelling out the obligations of the great powers.

At present, the political configuration in Kazakhstan offers no answers to these questions. Developing these answers is Kazakhstan's real task for the future.

Notes

1. W.C. Potter and E.E. Cohen, *Nuclear Assets of the Former Soviet Union* (Monterey, CA: Monterey Institute of International Studies, 1992), p. 9.

2. V.F. Davydov, *The Disintegration of the USSR and the Nuclear Arms for Non-proliferation* (U.S.-EPI, 1992), no. 3, p. 23.

3. Potter and Cohen, *Nuclear Assets of the Former Soviet Union*, pp. 9–10.

4. Ibid., pp. 10–11.

5. Ibid., p. 11.

6. W.C. Potter, "Exodus: Constraining the Spread of Soviet Nuclear Capabilities," *Harvard International Review* (spring 1992), p. 27.

7. M.C. Escalona, "The Legacy of the Semipalatinsk Nuclear Test Site," *CIS Environmental Watch*, 1992, no. 2, pp. 40–46.

8. M. Laumulin, "The Kazakh Nonproliferation Policy and Islamic Impact" (unpublished manuscript presented to the Monterey Institute of International Studies, Monterey, CA, 1992).

9. *Panorama* (Almaty), 1993, no. 2.

10. *Panorama*, 1993, no. 1.

11. *Arms Control Today* (March 1992), p. 16.

12. Potter and Cohen, *Nuclear Assets of the Former Soviet Union*, p. 13.

13. Davydov, *Disintegration of the USSR*, p. 23.

14. *Izvestiia* (Moscow), 23 December 1991.

15. *Diplomaticheskii vestnik* (Moscow), 1992, nos. 2–3.

16. *Arms Control Today* (June 1992), pp. 34–35.

17. Ibid., p. 36.

18. G. Bunn, "Security Arrangements in Support of Nonproliferation Regime" (unpublished manuscript, 1992), pp. 5–6.

19. *Central Eurasia*, 29 September 1992, p. 38.

20. *Eye on Supply*, 1992, no. 6, p. 70.

21. *Central Eurasia*, 15 October 1992, p. 41.

22. *Nuclear Fuel*, 23 December 1991, p. 13.

23. W.C. Potter, "The New Nuclear Suppliers," *Orbis*, vol. 36, no. 2 (spring 1992), pp. 209–10.

24. *Central Eurasia*, 27 May 1992, p. 24.

25. *Nuclear Fuel*, 26 October 1992, pp. 5–6.

26. *Soviet Environmental Watch*, 1992, no. 1, pp. 50–51.

27. Escalona, "Legacy of the Semipalatinsk Nuclear Test Site," p. 43.

28. *Nezavisimaia gazeta* (Moscow), 19 January 1993, p. 1.

29. *ASIA*, 1993, no. 1, p. 7.

30. *ASIA*, 1993, no. 5, p. 4.

31. *Sovetu Kazakhstan* (Almaty), 7 January 1993.

32. *Express* (Almaty), 4 March 1993, p. 4.

33. *Express*, 6 November 1993; *Kazakhstan*, no. 52 (December 1993), pp. 15, 22.

34. *Kazakhstan*, no. 52 (December 1993), p. 29.

35. *Nezavisimaia gazeta*, 5 January 1993, p. 1.

36. *Nezavisimaia gazeta*, 12 January 1993, p. 2.

37. *Nezavisimaia gazeta*, 5 February 1993, p. 4.

38. *Izvestiia*, 10 April 1993, p. 15.

39. *Nezavisimaia gazeta*, 11 January 1993, pp. 1, 3.

40. *Nezavisimaia gazeta*, 11 February 1993, p. 3.

41. *Nezavisimaia gazeta*, 21 January 1993, p. 2.

42. *Izvestiia*, 7 April 1993, p. 5.

43. *Express*, 19 February 1993, p. 4.

44. *The Military Balance, 1992 to 1993* (London: International Institute for Strategic Studies, 1992), pp. 143–47; *Za rubezhom* (Moscow), 1993, no. 4, p. 4.

45. *Nezavisimaia gazeta*, 21 January 1993, p. 2.

46. *ASIA*, 1993, no. 4.

47. "Why Doesn't Kazakhstan Sign the NPT?" *Express*, 20 April 1993, p. 9.

48. M. Laumulin and K. Abuseitov, "Farewell to Arms?" *ASIA*, 1993, no. 10, p. 3.

49. Ibid.

50. Y.E. Fedorov, "The Nuclear Weapons and the CIS Security Problems," *Policies of Russia, Ukraine, and Kazakhstan Toward Nuclear Armaments* (Moscow: Center for Political and International Studies, 1993), p. 32.

51. This section has been translated by Catherine Boyle and published by the Monterey Institute of International Studies. See M. Laumulin, "Viewpoint: Nuclear Politics and the Future Security of Kazakhstan," *Nonproliferation Review*,vol. 1, no. 2 (winter 1994), pp. 61–65.

52. The author took part in the discussion on this subject before the ratification of the NPT in the autumn of 1993. See M. Laumulin and K. Abuseitov, "Conference on Nuclear Nonproliferation," *ASIA*, 1994, no. 49.

53. A most radical and acidic statement against Kazakhstan's joining the NPT and Nazarbaev's nuclear policy was formulated in *Kazakhskaia pravda*, no. 4 (January 1994), p. 1.

54. *ASIA*, 1994, no. 4.

55. *Mezhdunarodnaia zhizn'* (Moscow), 1993, no. 3.

56. Ibid.

57. *Mezhdunarodnaia zhizn'*, 1993, no. 2, p. 25.

58. *Mezhdunarodnaia zhizn'*, 1993, no. 1, p. 26.

59. *Mezhdunarodnaia zhizn'*, 1993, nos. 5–6, p. 146.

60. *ASIA*, 1994, no. 1.

61. *Panorama*, 1993, no. 45, p. 5.

62. *Panorama*, 1993, no. 46, p. 5.

63. By the end of 1993, the bilateral agreement on Baikonur was signed. It was strongly criticized by Kazakh independence experts because of its pro-Russian character. *Panorama*, 1994, no. 2, pp. 1, 5.

64. *Bulletin of the Atomic Scientists*, vol. 49, no. 8 (1993).

65. *Express-K*, 20 November 1992. China had intended to correct the border during the official visit of Kazakhstan's prime minister in 1992. See *ASIA*, 1993, no. 4.

66. L. Benson and I. Svanberg, eds., *The Kazakhs of China* (Uppsala: Uppsala University Press, 1989).

67. A. Grozin, "A Bridge Between Asia and Europe," *New Generation*, 1993, no. 4.

68. "On Some Trends of Military-Political Developments of the States Around Kazakhstan" (unpublished manuscript presented to the Center for Strategic Studies, Almaty, 1993).

69. Rand Corporation (October 1992).

70. *International Herald Tribune*, 15 January 1993.

71. *Quotidienne de Paris*, 17 December 1992.

72. "How Real Is the Chinese Threat to Kazakhstan?" (unpublished manuscript presented to the Center for Oriental Studies, Almaty, 1993), pp. 13–15.

73. *Argumenty i fakty* (Kazakhstan), 1994, no. 11, p. 4.

74. *Mainichi Shimbun*, 1 March 1994.

75. *Argumenty i fakty*, 1994, no. 7, p. 2.

76. *Panorama*, 1994, no. 7, p. 2.

77. "Why Doesn't Kazakhstan Join NATO?" *Express*, 3 March 1994, p. 3.

10

The Nuclear Problem in the Post-Soviet Transition

Craig Nation

There is still relatively little consensus about the larger meaning of the disappearance of the USSR and the end of the Cold War, or where the events to which they have given rise are leading. By contrast, the "Soviet threat" that preoccupied Western security planners for so long was relatively straightforward. Soviet conventional and nuclear forces in Europe, represented institutionally by the Warsaw Pact, posed a clear and present danger that demanded high levels of readiness on the part of NATO and a steadfast commitment to the defense of Europe by the United States. The Soviet nuclear arsenal was the only existing force capable of wreaking military devastation on North America and had to be thwarted by a robust deterrence. The post–World War II international system was essentially bipolar, and America's Soviet rival was an ideologically driven superpower pledged to shifting the global correlation of forces to its advantage. One might quibble over the Soviets' real intentions, but if for no other reason than the sheer size of their conventional and nuclear arsenal, the logic of the West's identification of Soviet power as its primary security concern appeared to be unchallengeable.

The sudden and unexpected collapse of the Soviet Union and the emergence of fifteen sovereign states upon its ruins have changed the picture almost beyond recognition. Though the Russian Federation inherited the USSR's international status as well as many of its physical assets, and though its armed forces, albeit much reduced, remain impressive on paper, it is clear that the Soviet military threat as traditionally perceived has all but disappeared. Russia has lost the forward positions in the heart of Europe that made its military potential seem so formidable in the Cold War era. It has lost the western borderlands that historically served as a defensive buffer. The non-Russian territories of Eurasia once controlled by the USSR have been torn by a series of armed conflicts claiming tens of thousands of victims. Russia has committed itself to a military build-down along its long common border with China, a region that once absorbed up to 40 percent of Soviet military assets. Its armed forces have been reduced from 4.25 million men at arms in 1989 to fewer than 2 million at present, and the falloff continues. Those forces that remain are riven by major problems, including a declining base for conscription, a collapse in morale, political division and embitterment within the officer corps, the lack of a clear-cut and compelling mission, and significantly reduced budgets.[1] Although the Russian Federation assumed control of most of the USSR's nuclear assets, its strategic force planning was completely disrupted, not least due to the loss of facilities for research, production, and testing now located outside its national borders. The rigors of transition have left all the newly independent states of Eurasia significantly weakened, with no hope for short-term redressment. What kind of military and security concerns do these radically altered circumstances pose for the West?

There is of course no self-evident answer to the question. The breakup of the Soviet Union has given rise to layers of instability—within the Russian Federation, between the fifteen nominal Soviet successor states, and among the international alliances and associations originally drawn together to counter Soviet power—that will take years, if not decades, to resolve themselves. What the West is called on to respond to is not a discrete event, but an open-ended process that is far from having run its course, and whose very essence is radical discontinuity.

Prevailing uncertainties impose caution. They do not preclude reasoned policy choices capable of taking advantage of the potential for positive change that is latent in the new geopolitics of Eurasia. How these policy choices will be determined depends to a large extent on how the dynamic of post-Soviet transition is grasped intellectually. How have Western observers sought to interpret post-Soviet developments; what assumptions about the motive forces underlying change have informed policy; and what kind of opportunities and risks are perceived to be at stake? These are basic conceptual issues that need to be thought through as a basis for evaluating Western responses to the unprecedented challenge of post-Soviet transformation.

Western Images of Post-Soviet Instability

The collapse of the Soviet Union in the final months of 1991, culminating in the series of events that began with the East European revolutions of 1989, came rapidly and with little forewarning. As the result of an embarrassingly ill-conceived and disastrously unsuccessful coup attempt, almost literally from one day to the next, the Soviet Union disappeared, European communism was placed into the ash can of history, and power in the Kremlin was transferred to a group of vociferously pro-Western democratic reformers. The suddenness of the transformation and the mysteries that surrounded it made it almost inevitable that the task of coming to terms with its consequences would be a difficult one.

First, reactions were often triumphant and euphoric. Though a vestige of the old USSR remained in the hastily assembled Commonwealth of Independent States (CIS), this was widely considered to be a transitional body whose major responsibility was to smooth the way to full independence for the former Soviet republics.[2] Gradual democratization, rapid transition to a market economy, demilitarization, and the consolidation of sovereignty among the newly independent states were presented as a blueprint for the creation of a new Eurasian regional order freed from the weight of the Russian imperial tradition. A democratic Russia would in turn become the key to a new era in international relations marked by the triumph of Western liberalism, with Russian-American partnership as its keystone. "The West naturally welcomed this prospect without reserve," writes Rodric Braithwaite, "in the naive belief that the new Russia would be transformed overnight into a democratic, loyal, and above all unquestioning, supporter of Western policy."[3]

For a fleeting moment, the optimistic scenario seemed to be coming true. During the first months of 1992, the post-Soviet republics moved quickly to establish full independence. In the Lisbon Protocol to the START I Treaty, signed by Ukraine, Belarus, Kazakhstan, Russia, and the United States on 23 May 1992, the three non-Russian successor states promised to turn over nuclear weapons on their territory to Russia and to adhere to the Nuclear Nonproliferation Treaty (NPT) as non-nuclear states "as soon as possible." In November 1992, the Russian parliament voted overwhelmingly to ratify the START I accord, and in January 1993 Russia and the United States signed a START II Treaty calling for reductions of up to 50 percent beyond START I levels. Meanwhile, Egor Gaidar's shock therapy reforms were launched with much fanfare, and Russian President Boris Yeltsin and his ambitious young foreign minister, Andrei Kozyrev, went out of their way to adapt their foreign policy to Western tastes. "We resolutely reject a policy of force," Kozyrev wrote in 1992, "and we strive for a qualitative shift in our approach to the problems of humanity. Promotion of political interactions between Russia and the leading countries of the world, the development of partnerships and major progress in disarmament will be the foundation for new global relations characterized by stability and predictability. This will enable us to direct enormous material resources and human potential to raising standards of living and providing social security and health care. It will allow us to undertake significant, urgently needed measures to prevent the imminent environmental crisis; it will pave the way for creative solutions to other global problems—especially those of developing countries: the eradication of mass starvation and poverty, the consequences of overpopulation and natural disasters."[4]

On the strength of such effusive promises, the co-optation of Russia's residual military capacity into the framework of a U.S.-sponsored "new world order" seemed to be a goal that was well within reach.

The rosy picture was of course deceptive, and disappointment was not long in setting in. The breakup of the USSR did not necessarily stimulate democratization. In many of the successor states, the structures of Soviet power gave way almost imperceptibly to new forms of authoritarianism. The manipulation of nationalism as an alternative source of political legitimacy also contributed to the eruption of a series of violent regional conflicts along Russia's southern marches. In Russia itself, Gaidar's reform program failed to achieve its most important goals and led quickly to an unprecedented decline in popular well-being. A swelling sense of disillusionment and national humiliation created a badly polarized political environment, manifested most clearly by a noisy clash between president and parliament. As the confrontation gained momentum from the fall of 1992 onward, the Yeltsin government, perhaps in an effort to co-opt part of its opponents' program, publicly distanced itself from the unambiguously pro-Western stance of its first months in office. Russia began openly to intervene in regional conflicts within the former Soviet territories (now redefined as the "near abroad") on behalf of an ambiguously defined concept of peacemaking, in what were perceived by many observers as "thinly veiled operations intended to protect or advance Russia's strategic interests."[5] It declared all the territories of the former USSR to be an area of vital national interest and sought with some success to reanimate the CIS as a vehicle for Russian leadership. The strategic relationship with the United States also came under strain, as influential voices within the foreign policy establishment began to call into question the logic of an arms control process driven forward by disproportionate Russian concessions. Also, relations between Moscow and Kiev became badly agitated over issues such as control over the former Soviet Black Sea fleet, the fate of the Crimea, and the status of the Russian minority inside Ukraine as a whole. In the Balkans, without breaking altogether with the Western peacemaking effort, Moscow responded to nationalist pressures at home by becoming increasingly assertive as an advocate for the new Yugoslavia of Slobodan Milošević. In response to criticism, Foreign Minister Kozyrev and other high-level spokespersons reiterated the determination to pursue a foreign policy defined by an ambitious assertion of Russian state interests.[6] As a consequence of these developments, Western interpretations of the dynamic of post-Soviet transition moved toward more cautious evaluations emphasizing the threat of a creeping reassertion of Russian imperial prerogatives. Yeltsin's victory of August 1991 was now represented as having been far less than complete. The contest between Yeltsin and his parliamentary antagonists was interpreted as a decisive political struggle pitting democratic reformers against communist restorationists linked to the old Soviet structures of privilege and power. Annoyance with Russian international conduct was not long in making itself felt, and in the United States voices began to urge action to counter what was now described as Russian "neoimperialism." Zbigniew Brzezinski spoke of the dangers of "premature partnership" and urged a shift of emphasis from relations with the Russian Federation to the non-Russian republics, particularly Ukraine.[7] Other analysts urged what amounted to a policy of neo-containment designed to coerce Russian compliance with Western norms.[8] In office from January 1993 onward, the Clinton administration sought to maintain the priorities of partnership with Russia and support for the Yeltsin team, but it was an uphill battle against increasingly vocal criticism.

Even the most pessimistic observers were probably surprised by the viciousness of the clash between Yeltsin and the parliamentary opposition, and its violent resolution in the crisis of 21 September–4 October 1993. These stormy events, including the dismissal of parliament by decree in defiance of the constitution and an attempt to launch an armed uprising in the streets of Moscow, culminated with tanks blasting gaping holes in the walls of the building that housed Russia's only democratically chosen parliamentary assembly. Political violence on such a scale in the heart of the capital, combined with continuing economic disintegration and rampant criminality, produced a considerable shock to popular consciousness. A reckoning of sorts arrived with the election of December 1993. Originally intended as a plebiscite for the "democratic" forces linked to Yeltsin, the results were disconcerting. Yeltsin's new constitution carried the 50 percent majority of votes cast required for passage, but just barely, and in the best of cases it was approved by no more than 25 percent of the eligible electorate. Though a fragmented list of reform-oriented parties attracted a respectable share of votes, the real winners in elections by party list to the new State Duma were the communists (12.3 percent), their agrarian allies (7.9 percent), and most of all the aggressively nationalistic Liberal Democratic

Party of Vladimir Zhirinovsky (22.7 percent). Zhirinovsky's inflammatory rhetoric was a cry of protest against national humiliation; his much discussed book included an elaborate scheme for the assertion of Russian hegemony as a "stabilizing factor" in Eurasia; and he did not shrink from rocket rattling as a means of strengthening his conclusions.[9] A worst-case image of the post-Soviet transition was reinforced by Zhirinovsky's unexpected success. Analysts now spoke of a "Weimar analogy," with a failed democratic experiment clearing the way for a new authoritarianism. If such a turn of events was a real possibility, calls for U.S.-Russian partnership were not only premature, they were positively dangerous. The road from the promise of a new era of reconciliation to what almost seemed to be a reincarnation of the Cold War against an eternal Russian enemy, incapable of extricating itself from the demons of authoritarianism and expansionism, threatened to be short indeed.[10]

The Zhirinovsky phenomenon, despite the burlesque elements attached to the comportment of its inspirer, needs to be taken seriously. The possibility that Russia's agonizing transition might lead it into the hands of a radical extremist cannot altogether be discounted, and Zhirinovsky has succeeded in articulating a volatile amalgam of emotive themes drawn from Russia's rich traditions of conservative and Pan-Slavic thought. Zhirinovsky is a flawed personality whose personal prospects are probably limited, but his political discourse, both potent and dangerous, is certain to exercise an important influence on public policy for some time to come. On balance, however, the Weimar analogy has probably been somewhat overblown. Yeltsin himself helped pave the way for Zhirinovsky's relative electoral success by banning a significant part of the conservative opposition. A portion of the vote was clearly a protest against disintegrating living standards rather than an expression of positive support for the Zhirinovsky program, and the Russian far right, of which Zhirinovsky is an exemplar, remains a distinct minority despite its recent gains.

Perhaps the most convincing images of the challenge of post-Soviet transition have been those that seek a middle ground between the unbridled optimism of the partnership agenda, and the fatalism of neo-containment. Russia has a great power tradition. It maintains the attributes of great power status, whether physical, human, or psychological, and it is unlikely to accept subordination as a permanent condition. But Russia is also in the midst of a deep crisis that seriously constrains its capacity to pursue an aggressive or expansionist foreign policy. No one is better aware of these constraints than the Russians themselves, and despite a continuing debate over foreign policy priorities, a kind of consensus appears to have grown up among elites in power concerning long-term national interests and the way to pursue them.[11]

According to that consensus, Russia's essential security interests in the present transitional phase lie in the accomplishment of domestic tasks: economic development, institutional restructuring, and ideological redefinition. The successful accomplishment of these tasks demands cooperative relations with the West and international peace and stability. The role of the Russian armed forces in this kind of security equation would be considerably reduced. Manpower could be drawn down to a permanent level well below two million, and the armed forces would be restructured to emphasize the development of more technologically sophisticated, lighter, and mobile components. Strategic forces cannot be maintained indefinitely at current levels, and reductions considerably below those defined by START II would not conflict with a basic deterrence core mission for a new nuclear arsenal.[12] Russia would seek to retain and reinforce its status as a dominant power in Eurasia, but reject any attempt to rival the United States as a global power.

The case for accommodation also has an assertive edge. The most immediate threats to the domestic stability required for the pursuit of reform are perceived to be those that emerge from Russia's immediate periphery. "The greatest security threat to the Russian Federation," according to one evaluation, "is a rapid abandonment of the 'outer' empire, leading to agitation in Russia itself."[13] In view of that threat, both for practical reasons and in order to reinforce the legitimacy of the governing authorities, Moscow is urged to reassert its prerogatives in the near abroad, either formally through some kind of confederative association under the auspices of the CIS, or informally by imposing something resembling a classic sphere of influence. The unique historical character of the multinational Russian state, it is argued, makes the term "neoimperialism" inappropriate for characterizing such policies. Furthermore, by providing a new foundation for stability in Eurasia, guaranteed by a Russia pledged to democratization, reassociation under Russian auspices would work in the West's best interests as well.

These arguments have a certain force, and the calm after the storm that followed Yeltsin's October 1993 crackdown encouraged more moderate evaluations of the dynamic of Russian reform. Though Western confidence in Yeltsin was shaken, he appeared to remain firmly in the saddle. Prime Minister Viktor Chernomyrdin, once portrayed as the embodiment of the conservative Soviet establishment, earned praise for his professional comportment and diligence in presiding over economic restructuring. The Russian armed forces benefited institutionally from the critical role they played in resolving the crisis, but strong historical traditions, it was presumed, precluded any risk of Bonapartism. It appeared, in fact, that the armed forces had intervened to restore order on 3–4 October 1993 only with the greatest reluctance and as the result of a direct presidential order.[14] The appointment of Vitalii Radets'kiy as the new Ukrainian defense minister in December 1993, the January 1994 signing of the Trilateral Agreement on nuclear weapons between Russia, Ukraine, and the United States, and the July 1994 election of Leonid Kuchma as Ukrainian president on a platform promising conciliation with Moscow also seemed to drain some of the tensions from the Russian-Ukrainian relationship.

In conjunction with these events, a somewhat chastened, less ambitious, but still guardedly hopeful image of the prospects of post-Soviet transition began to assert itself, more prepared to accept occasional disjunctures and setbacks as the inevitable price of far-reaching reform. Taking into account the limits of Western influence as well as the volatility of events, a policy of *limited engagement*, encouraging positive evolution without insisting on set outcomes, took on clearer contours. The goal was to avoid "choosing" between Russia and its neighbors and to maintain a commitment to support reform by emphasizing practical assistance, keeping aid tied to reasonable standards of comportment. The situation inside the Soviet successor states was not necessarily conducive to moderation, however, and it was not clear that a policy of limited engagement would be adequate to the task of encouraging change without courting excessive risks.

With due allowance for overgeneralization, the terms "partnership," "limited engagement," and "neocontainment" may be used to characterize three distinct Western policy options in regard to the challenge of post-Soviet transition. Each option refers to a relatively coherent set of policy recommendations, and each implies a certain mode of interpretation concerning the dynamics of Russian reform. Hymns of praise to partnership continue to be sung by responsible figures in Washington and Moscow, but the substance of policy on both sides has become considerably more circumspect, and the possibility of a rapid disintegration of East–West relations, under the press of unexpected events or a sudden change in leadership, cannot be ruled out. The challenge for the West should be to tread carefully among these contrasting options, no one of which can be presumed to be altogether satisfactory taken by itself, while avoiding alarmist conclusions that foreclose positive outcomes prematurely. These are not only conceptual problems but also practical ones. Their resolution depends above all on progress in institutionalizing an alternative security order that engages all the states of Eurasia in the effort to confront the challenges of the post–Cold War world order.

Eurasia's New Security Architecture

The classic Soviet military threat was focused in Europe, and the centerpiece of Western defense policy during the entire Cold War era was the

NATO alliance. NATO always had wide-ranging political functions, but its primary responsibility was to deter aggression by the Soviet Union. With the demise of the Warsaw Pact on 1 July 1991, it could fairly be described as an alliance without a mission. Lacking the Warsaw Pact to deter, the "scenario which constituted the main frame of reference for NATO's military and political planning" had disappeared.[15] Despite the elimination of its traditional raison d'être, however, NATO demonstrated impressive staying power. The decision to rebuild a new Eurasian security order around the core of a transformed North Atlantic alliance might be described as the most fundamental of all Western responses to military developments in the former USSR.

Soon after the disassembling of the Soviet Union, the administration of U.S. President George Bush announced the intention gradually to reduce the American military presence in Europe from 300,000 to approximately 150,000 active duty personnel. In September 1992, the U.S. Senate voted to deepen these cuts, and Washington fixed the goal of a build-down to a force level of about 100,000 (including 75,000 army personnel) by late 1996.[16] Meanwhile, most other NATO members were significantly reducing their military budgets, while Canada opted to withdraw its military forces from Europe altogether. Planned reductions went considerably beyond those demanded by the Conventional Forces in Europe (CFE) Treaty of November 1990 and the CFE 1A follow-up agreement, described by the North Atlantic Council meeting in Copenhagen during June 1991 as "the key-stone for a stable and lasting peace on the continent."[17]

While it accepted the logic of force reductions, Washington made clear that on the institutional level no alternative to NATO as an anchor for European security was deemed acceptable. Survival demanded adaptation, and at its 1991 Copenhagen summit, the North Atlantic Council took a first step toward revitalizing the alliance by issuing a statement on "NATO's Core Security Functions in the New Europe," which listed four fundamental tasks:

1. To provide . . . a stable security environment in Europe . . . in which no country would be able to coerce any European nation or to impose hegemony through the threat or use of force;
2. To serve . . . as a transatlantic forum for Allied consultations on any issue that affect[s] their vital interests;
3. To deter and defend against any threat of aggression against the territory of any NATO member state;
4. To preserve the strategic balance within Europe.[18]

The document placed special emphasis on the role of the alliance as a forum for communication and coordination, and as an arbiter for Europe's changing balance of power. It also noted the complementary security functions of European institutions such as the European Community (EC), the Western European Union (WEU), and the Council on Security and Cooperation in Europe (CSCE), and supported the creation of a European identity in security and defense to "underline the preparedness of the Europeans to take a greater share of responsibility for their security" and "to reinforce transatlantic solidarity." A strong emphasis was placed on NATO's "peculiar position" as the only organ capable of performing all four core security functions, and the final communiqué stressed the alliance's role as the "essential forum" for European security coordination.[19]

The North Atlantic Council summit in Rome of 7–8 November 1991 culminated a first phase of evolution. The council sought to redefine NATO's military role by publishing a "New Strategic Concept" that underlined the continuing importance of collective defense, called for significant nuclear and conventional force reductions but with the maintenance of an "appropriate mix" of same (cuts of up to 50 percent were programmed, though the target date was pushed forward to the year 2000), urged the development of multinational formations under a reinforced integrated command, and placed a new emphasis on mobility, rapid reaction, and conflict management. A centerpiece of the program was the announced creation of a multinational rapid reaction corps of from fifty thousand to seventy thousand men under British command as a potential vehicle for out-of-area interventions. The notion of *interlocking institutions* was coined to characterize a new European security architecture "in which NATO, the CSCE, the European Community, the WEU, and the Council of Europe complement each other." The development of a European security identity and defense function was acknowledged, but strictly as a European pillar of the alliance, whose "enduring value" as the keystone of the European security order was reiterated.[20] Finally, the council sought to address the security vacuum that had appeared in Eastern Europe with the collapse of Soviet power by announcing the creation of a North Atlantic Cooperation Council (NACC) to provide formal linkage between NATO and the countries of the former Warsaw Pact, as well as what would soon become the Soviet successor states.[21]

NATO's new look compared favorably with the extreme caution that characterized the international initiatives of the EC's Maastricht summit one month later. As a foundation for a new European security order it was nonetheless not altogether convincing. The concept of interlocking institutions merely assigned a new name to an existing reality; the latent conflict between NATO, the CSCE, and the EC as forums for security coordination was not convincingly resolved. The tasks of peacekeeping and conflict management, as subsequent events painfully demonstrated, were more easily evoked than accomplished. And the NACC was clearly only a first step toward integrating the new Eurasia into a larger security framework. In its own estimation, NATO had made the turn toward a post–Cold War security order, but there was some room for skepticism. "NATO will endure," wrote Richard Betts, "because popular organizations can survive for a long time from inertia. The longer peace lasts, however, the more NATO will become a shell ... bereft of serious strategic activity."[22] There was more than inertia to NATO's persistence, however. Its capacity for renewal rested on three substantial realities. First, no serious rival to the alliance as a forum for security coordination was in place. Second, the alliance continued to fulfill certain military-technical functions that were relevant to Europe's security needs. Finally, the survival of NATO was perceived in Washington to correspond to the best interests of the United States.

NATO's greatest strength remained the unconvincing nature of possible alternatives. After the fall of the Berlin Wall, the CSCE swelled to encompass no fewer than fifty-six member states. It had become "a small European UN," and by absorbing the Soviet successor states had taken on a burden "that it will not be able to master anytime soon."[23] The November 1990 Charter of Paris gave the CSCE a flexible orientation toward security problems, and it maintains a large network of multilateral negotiating forums. But, required to operate by consensus and without autonomous military forces at its disposal, the CSCE is in no position to confront problems on the ground. The CSCE is certainly more than "an artifact of the Cold War," and it will have a role to play in any European security system built on interlocking institutions.[24] At present, however, it is too weak, dispersed, and divided to offer an attractive forum for real security coordination.

The short-term prospects for a uniquely European defense and security identity are no more promising. These prospects hinge on the further development of the WEU, a process that has only just begun. Though the WEU came into existence in 1954, its revival as a working organ dates only to 1984. Unlike NATO, the WEU's responsibilities are not formally limited to a specific geographic area, but the organization is only partially representative. Its eleven members include most key European powers, but exclude European Union (EU) members Denmark and Ireland and NATO members Norway, Iceland, and Turkey, as well as all of Eastern Europe. It lacks an integrated command structure, has limited operational experience, and is inadequately equipped with the essential tools of communication, intelligence, and command and control. Not least, its leaders assert a self-limiting perception of the organization's responsibilities. According to Secretary

General Willem van Eekelin, the WEU aspires to function as "the defense component in the work of European unification and as an instrument for strengthening the European pillar of the Atlantic Alliance."[25] Josef Joffe's characterization of the organization as "a sleeping beauty that continues to resist the rousing kisses of innumerable princes" is cruel, but perhaps not entirely inappropriate.[26]

To point out the limitations of the CSCE and the WEU is not to exclude all possibility of their future growth. The CSCE is potentially as capable of serving as a forum for transatlantic security cooperation as is NATO. The clumsiness produced by consensual decision making could be addressed with the creation of a Security Council–type forum granting key members special prerogatives, or an EC-style troika as a directing organ. In February 1991 Roland Dumas of France and Hans-Dietrich Genscher of Germany urged the "progressive development of an organic relationship" between the EC and the WEU that could shift the latter organization from its present status as a wing of the European Council into something resembling an armed branch of the EU. The plans announced in May 1992 for the creation of a joint Franco-German Eurocorps of thirty-five thousand men (on the basis of the Franco-German joint brigade in existence since 1990), to operate outside the NATO command and with other European nations encouraged to join, lends a certain substance to Europe's aspiration for an autonomous defense capacity. The Eurocorps' tasks are said to include the defense of Western Europe, humanitarian assistance, and peacekeeping operations. They thus overlap with NATO's classic mission, as well as with the mission defined for NATO's rapid reaction corps.[27] One possible scenario foresees the WEU gradually assuming greater operational responsibility as it merges with the EU, the creation of a jointly controlled European nuclear force on the basis of the existing French and British arsenals, and a progressive disengagement by the United States as NATO "withers away," with the CSCE left to assure a stable transatlantic linkage.[28] Such a result would represent a real revolution in European security affairs, but it presupposes a lengthy period of adaptation as well as what might prove to be an unrealistically high degree of coordination and common purpose among Europeans. In the meantime, only NATO is in a position to respond to the fundamental challenges of Eurasian security.

These challenges are no less significant now than in the past. The alliance keeps the United States engaged in Europe at a time when America's domestic preoccupations have become more compelling. This is perceived to be important precisely because of general uncertainty about what might eventually emerge from the cauldron of instability in the postcommunist East. Both as a "hedge against disasters" and as "our insurance policy against military threats that might emerge in the former Soviet Union," NATO's role as a mechanism for keeping the American balancer committed to Europe is vital.[29] The transatlantic link institutionalized in NATO is also considered useful to help calm fears of a potential imbalance of power within Europe in the wake of German unification. Although the extent to which it is legitimate to speak of a German "problem" may be disputed, unification in the context of the ebbing of Russian influence from East-Central Europe has reanimated long-standing concerns over the hegemonic ambitions of the heirs of Bismarck. America's role inside NATO, according to Michael Mandelbaum, "is no longer deterrence but reassurance," with the goal of preempting defensive reactions to German "rethinking."[30] The protean notion of "instability" has also been invoked as a new responsibility for the alliance that is directly relevant to the most prominent security challenge of the post–Cold War era. Collective security based on multilateral peace enforcement has been touted by some as a positive alternative to Cold War bipolarism, and NATO is uniquely equipped to impose order in regional conflict scenarios where diplomatic mechanisms fail.[31]

Not least, NATO has striven with some success to engage the former Warsaw Pact member states and newly independent countries of Eurasia in an open-ended process of security cooperation. The implementation of an annual NACC Work Plan beginning in 1992, including consultations on security issues and extensive military-to-military contacts, was a practical but limited step in that direction.[32] At its Brussels summit in January 1994, NATO took the effort further by approving the Framework Document for a Partnership for Peace program (PFP), intended, "within the overall framework of the NACC," to move "from general common activities to individual, tailored programs of cooperation between NATO and each of its partners."[33] Invitations were issued to all states participating in the NACC as well as to other CSCE members. General goals were said to include the facilitation of transparency in defense planning; democratic control of armed forces; preparation for cooperative peacekeeping, search and rescue, and humanitarian missions; and gradual movement toward interoperability with NATO forces. A scarcely disguised goal of the PFP was also to forestall insistent demands from Central European states for full NATO membership.[34] In the words of NATO's Assistant Secretary General for Political Affairs Gebhardt von Moltke, "Partnership for Peace restores this question to its proper place, namely, at the end rather than at the beginning of an evolutionary process."[35] An additional goal was to craft a forum that could encompass Russia without destabilizing existing Western institutions. Russia joined the PFP in June 1994 after a lengthy internal debate, though in his remarks at the ceremonial signing of the Framework Agreement Kozyrev reiterated his preference for a new Eurasian security architecture coordinated not by NATO but rather the CSCE.[36] Moscow's reluctance was disconcerting, but NATO had nonetheless accomplished its basic goal of engaging the East without altering its own internal dynamics and decision-making procedures.

Nagging doubts about the future of NATO nonetheless remain. For most of its existence, NATO's legitimacy rested on the ethos of a crusade. With the infidel's camp dispersed, and in the absence of any credible threat on a comparable scale, the alliance's ability to regenerate itself on new foundations can only be problematic.

Skeptics begin by noting that despite the close links of past decades, the dominant U.S. role in Europe remains something of a historical anomaly. Without the cement of an external threat to bind them, it is difficult to see how European and American interests can be prevented from drifting apart. Efforts to define a new military rationale for the alliance also fail entirely to convince. Even in the worst case, defined by some version of the Weimar analogy, the Russian Federation is in no position to re-create the kind of military threat to Europe once posed by the Warsaw Pact. NATO's still considerable nuclear strike capacity, it is argued, is particularly anachronistic. The NACC and PFP programs open the door to the East, but ambiguity concerning where they are intended to lead is considerable, and the Kremlin remains hostile to any formal extension of the alliance to the nations of Central Europe if Russia itself is excluded. Peacekeeping operations in Central Europe and the Balkans might seem to offer a convenient set of responsibilities for an alliance in search of new roles to play—"out of area or out of business" as it is put—but there is very little consensus about how such operations should be organized, and the experience of engagement in the Yugoslav crisis has not been encouraging. Given its history and general orientation, NATO is not ideally suited for the role of security manager in postcommunist Eastern Europe. Charles Glaser speaks of the need for an "extended transition strategy" for preserving the alliance over "a couple of decades in the face of the uncertainties surrounding both Russia and Western Europe."[37] His conclusion is pragmatic, but it may prove to be overoptimistic concerning the capacity of NATO to meet new security challenges effectively, the prospects for a positive alliance role in the East, and the kind of relationship with Europe that the Russian Federation will eventually manage to achieve.

Despite these cautions, on an institutional level Western responses to the Soviet collapse have been both prudent and effective. The huge arsenals accumulated during the Cold War have been reduced, but in the context of programs for modernization and streamlining that allowed for a variety of military contingencies. NATO has weathered the storm as the centerpiece of Western defense policy despite the disappearance of its traditional mission. In the context of the NACC and the PFP, the former Warsaw Pact member states have been engaged in a positive dialogue over military policy and security issues. The dangerous alternative of broadening NATO in such a way as to draw a new line of demarcation between East and West, whether at the former Soviet or present Russian border, has been for the time being avoided. These are halfway solutions, but they do not foreclose more positive alternatives. What such alternatives might be remains to be determined. Moscow's proposal for "upgrading the Conference on Security and Cooperation in Europe into a broader and more universal organization" to which NATO could eventually be subordinated is not particularly convincing.[38] The dilemma of a "security vacuum" in Central Europe has been left unresolved, but given the lack of compelling solutions the current ambiguous status quo may well last for some time.

New Nuclear Dilemmas

During the 1960s, the Soviet Union strained to overcome the United States' considerable strategic advantage and spurned invitations to an arms control dialogue. It was only when something like a rough strategic parity had been created that the era of Strategic Arms Limitations Talks (SALT) could open in November 1969 with the first SALT I sessions. During the next decade, both SALT I and SALT II sought to formalize parity on the basis of a stable deterrence regime. The larger competitive framework within which the negotiations unfolded, however, was not conducive to arms reductions. When the Soviet delegation walked out of the Geneva negotiations on Intermediate-Range Nuclear Forces (INF) and the accompanying START (Strategic Arms Reductions Talks) forum (which had originally been planned as SALT III) in November 1983 in protest against NATO deployments of cruise and Pershing II missiles in Europe, a generation of arms control efforts seemed to have come to a sudden end. Despite some modest accomplishments, the momentum of the nuclear arms race had scarcely been affected.

The process was reanimated from 1985 onward by Soviet General Secretary and President Mikhail Gorbachev's arms control offensive. The INF Treaty of 19 September 1987, the 19 November 1991 CFE Treaty, and the 31 July 1991 START I Treaty, which culminated Gorbachev's arms control agenda, moved well beyond the cautiously defined ceilings of the SALT era toward deep cuts in conventional forces and strategic deployments. The subsequent START II accord and the 1993 Chemical Weapons Convention went further in the same direction, without substantially recasting the conceptual foundations and practical goals of the arms control process itself.[39] These goals may be defined as the reinforcement of the premises of deterrence at the lowest force levels commensurate with stability by raising the costs of counterforce strategies and encouraging a new emphasis on survivability and retaliation. Gorbachev's more ambitious project for a break with the logic of deterrence and total nuclear disarmament by the year 2000, first outlined in a statement of 15 January 1986, was soon tempered by opposition from within the Soviet policy establishment and had no practical effect on the unfolding of policy.[40]

The key to the arms control achievements of the late 1980s and 1990s was the political impetus provided by Soviet perestroika. Gorbachev used arms control to spearhead a concerted effort to normalize relations with the West as a foundation for domestic reform. In search of that end, and probably personally convinced of the ultimate lack of utility of nuclear arms beyond the core function of deterrence, he was ready to accept disproportionate Soviet reductions in order to press the West toward accords. In the course of 1992 the new Russian leadership of Yeltsin and Kozyrev publicly embraced many of the tenets of Gorbachev-era new thinking, and with the signing of the Lisbon Protocol, the START II accord, and the Chemical Weapons Convention, the momentum of the arms control process seemed to be maintained.

Not all issues had been resolved, however. The United States continued to request a modification of the ABM Treaty to permit the testing and deployment of theater ballistic missile defenses in the face of Russian skepticism. The implementation of the START I agreements remained contingent on Ukrainian accession to the NPT. And the START II accord, in addition to requiring the entry into force of START I, faced the difficult challenge of ratification by the Russian parliament. Once again, however, it was the larger political context that became the real complicating factor. Soviet-American arms control efforts took the form of a dialogue between equals. Each side represented a stable polity with a clear sense of long-term goals and a firm grip, within the limits of technological capacity, on its strategic arsenal.[41] The breakdown of order that accompanied the Soviet collapse called into question the basic assumptions of continuity, reliability, and rationality that had been a basis for arms control negotiations in the past. It also created a new geopolitical situation for the Russian Federation that made many of the assumptions underpinning its inherited strategic posture irrelevant to current challenges.

Given Russia's poor economic circumstances and new strategic situation, the radical solution of denuclearization might have been considered a perfectly rational option. The old Soviet arsenal was always somewhat less dependable a shield than it was made out to be. It was imbalanced in favor of the potentially vulnerable fixed intercontinental ballistic missile leg of the strategic triad, and the basing and deployment of its strategic submarine fleet was severely restricted by geographical constraints. A myriad of technical deficiencies also called into question the Soviet Union's capacity actually to carry out its own strategic doctrine of retaliatory strikes if called upon to do so. And the very existence of the arsenal evoked fear and aggressive reaction on the part of potential adversaries. The breakup of the USSR added considerably to these problems. The Soviet Ballistic Missile Early Warning System (BMEWS) was overnight rendered highly unreliable. Loss of strategic facilities located on the territory of non-Russian republics shattered the integrity of the infrastructure that had maintained the integrity of the Soviet strategic nuclear forces in the past, and the new Russia lacked the resources to make good on the losses anytime soon. Demoralization and poor discipline created an acute threat to nuclear safety, both as concerned the reliability of command and control procedures and the physical securing of weapons and nuclear raw materials. Given the ultimate improbability of the risk of premeditated nuclear attack, one might have posed the question whether the nuclear game was worth the candle.[42]

Regardless of the cogency of such arguments, the political dynamic of post-Soviet transition makes it highly improbable that they will be taken seriously. The perception that the nuclear strategic arsenal is now the last remaining assurance that a badly weakened Russia will continue to be respected as a great power is widespread. The sense that Russian state interests have been undermined by a flawed transition pursued according to Western guidelines has made it difficult for any leader in the Kremlin to contemplate further asymmetrical arms control arrangements and has made the ratification of START II highly problematic. Financial constraints also make it difficult for Russia to dismantle existing weapons systems rapidly without significant Western assistance. Not least, Russia's new geopolitical situation has dramatically changed its perception of strategic threats. The new Russia cannot afford the luxury of pursuing a global rivalry with the United States and no longer needs to respond blow for blow to American strategic innovations. It must, however, be concerned about the arch of instability to its south and east that includes China as well as threshold nuclear powers such as India, Pakistan, Iran, and North Korea. Russia borders on a seismic zone where the role of nuclear weapons as a tool of political leverage appears to be growing rather than declining. Its new geostrategic situation, particularly in view of the psychological legacy of the Soviet breakdown, is not conducive to unilateral disarmament.

Despite these cautions, there is a great potential for demilitarization built into the nature of the post-Soviet transition. Russia's lowered horizons should encourage further substantial reductions in the old strategic arsenal configured for global nuclear war with the United States. A strong nonproliferation regime works in Russia's best interests as well as in the interests of the international community, particularly to the extent that it helps reduce the salience of nuclear weapons in the new geopolitics of Eurasia. It is clearly to Russia's advantage to maintain stable relations with the United States and other Western powers if at all possible, and cooperation in nuclear arms reductions can make an important contribution toward that end.

The Western response to these new opportunities has been extremely cautious. Programs to assist with the securing, disabling, and dismantling of weapons systems, such as the Safe and Secure Dismantlement Program, and to sustain or relocate members of the Russian scientific community made redundant by the breakup of the USSR are laudable and should be continued and extended. They do not, however, address the real heart of the problem. In Europe, the United Kingdom and France have proceeded with the modernization of their nuclear arsenals almost as if the Cold War had never ended, and the United States has sought to maintain the broad lines of the arms control agenda inherited from the administration of President George Bush without significant innovation. A classified Pentagon study outlining nuclear policy through the year 2003, and publicly endorsed by President Bill Clinton in September 1994, placed a strong emphasis on continuity. Further strategic arms talks with Moscow beyond those required to assure implementation of START I and START II were put off indefinitely. The modernization of the U.S. arsenal and its adaptation to new tasks, such as theater missile defense, was scheduled to continue. Over four hundred nuclear weapons were to remain in Europe, with the old flexible response option of first use in the event of conventional attack left intact. The report approved reductions in U.S. warhead requirements, called for cutbacks in the strategic bomber fleet, and recommended the removal of nuclear arms from U.S. surface ships, but these were modest gestures in the larger context. According to the Pentagon guidelines, even with START II in effect, the United States would retain between three thousand and thirty-five hundred strategic weapons, and war plans would maintain the goal of destroying up to twenty-five hundred targets in Russia with nuclear strikes in the event of war. U.S. Secretary of Defense William Perry justified the commitments by referring to "the small but real danger that reform in Russia might fail and a new government arise hostile to the United States."[43]

Those who felt that in view of that danger the Yeltsin government should be given as much encouragement as possible to reduce the size of its nuclear arsenal were clearly not in the ascendancy. Addressing the United Nations in New York on 26 September 1994, less than a week after the new U.S. strategic guidelines had been revealed, Yeltsin proposed a new treaty between the five declared nuclear powers that would reduce the number of nuclear vectors considerably below START II levels, provide for a permanent nuclear test ban, and create a regime to block the production of enriched uranium for nuclear reactors. These kinds of steps closely corresponded to Moscow's new strategic imperatives, but they did not receive an enthusiastic response. The time for such measures might eventually arrive, opined one U.S. Defense Department official, "but not now."[44]

The caution with which the United States approached the challenge of arms control threatened to complicate its simultaneous commitment to nonproliferation. Two distinct but related issues were at stake, both with far-reaching policy implications. Most pressing, and a fundamental goal of Western policy, was the renewal of the Nuclear Nonproliferation Treaty (NPT), scheduled to be decided at the April 1995 NPT Review and Extension Conference. Simultaneously, a new variant on the issue of nonproliferation was posed by the dispersion of the former Soviet nuclear arsenal on the territories of the four newly independent states of Belarus, Kazakhstan, Russia, and Ukraine. If Belarus and Kazakhstan proved relatively forthcoming in accepting programs for denuclearization, the same could not be said of Ukraine, which made compliance contingent on financial compensation and international guarantees for Ukrainian sovereignty and repeatedly reneged on commitments to adhere to the NPT.

All four of the NPT review conferences conducted at five-year intervals since the original treaty went into effect in 1970 have devoted considerable attention to the lack of progress in implementing Article 6, which commits the five recognized nuclear weapon states to "good faith" negotiations toward the goal of nuclear disarmament. Whether the current arms control agendas of the nuclear powers may be considered to be in accordance with the spirit of that commitment is an open question. At the present moment, implementation of the START treaties is blocked, and even should the START II provisions be observed to the letter, there will still be more deployed weapons in the arsenals of the nuclear superpowers than when the NPT was signed in 1968. France, the United Kingdom, and the People's Republic of China define their arsenals as weapons of last resort but also maintain commitments to testing and to strategic innovation.

Among the over 160 parties to the NPT who will be called upon to decide, by majority vote, whether and for how long to renew the treaty, there is considerable skepticism about the nuclear weapon states' good faith compliance with Article 6 and about the intentions of those states to exploit their capacity in search of new kinds of political leverage. Even if the NPT is comfortably renewed, which remains the most likely outcome, the effectiveness of the nonproliferation regime will ultimately rest not on enforced constraints (although verification will certainly be important), but on voluntary compliance by national leaders who perceive their best interests to be served by self-restraint. The best way to reinforce such perceptions will be for the nuclear weapon states to set the example by limiting their doctrines and deployments to the core function of minimal deterrence against nuclear first use. "The time between the end of the Cold War and the 1995 NPT review conference," write Wolfgang Panofsky and George Bunn, "constitutes a unique window of opportunity for the nuclear-weapon states to review and restate their nuclear weapons employment doctrines, with the goal of minimizing the perceived military and political role of such weapons in international affairs. Accomplishing this goal would greatly strengthen the non-proliferation regime."[45] A considerably more ambitious approach to Russian-American arms control would be entirely consonant with such a goal.

The issue of denuclearization in independent Ukraine has been equally challenging. Although there are significant barriers that stand in the way of Ukraine's achieving operational control over the nuclear weapons it has inherited from the USSR and to its developing and maintaining a credible nuclear strike force over time, there has also been a current of opinion in Kiev that a nuclear arsenal, no matter what its deficiencies, will serve as an ultimate guarantor of sovereignty and an intimidating deterrent to external aggression. While striving to consolidate Ukrainian sovereignty in almost every way possible, the West has drawn the line at Kiev's aspirations to accede to the status of a nuclear weapon state. Washington has placed strong pressure on Kiev to comply with the Lisbon Protocol of May 1992 and the Trilateral Agreement of January 1994 and has offered substantial financial compensation in exchange for Ukrainian compliance.

These pressures have to some extent been counterproductive. Ukraine is a young state with a fragile sense of national identity in the midst of an extraordinarily painful economic and social transition. The impression that its importance to the West has been virtually limited to the inconvenience factor posed by a residual nuclear arsenal has not encouraged cooperative behavior. Moreover, the Russian Federation is objectively capable of posing a military threat to Ukrainian territorial integrity, for which some kind of provisions must be made. Some partisans of a neocontainment orientation have implied that a Ukrainian nuclear option should indeed be tolerated as a challenge to Russian imperial pressure. A variant on the argument calls attention to the process of reassociation under way between Russia and its neighbors and laments the emergence of a new "strategic threat" in the form of a Russian-sponsored security zone in the CIS area drawn together within the shadow of the Russian nuclear shield.[46] "The [U.S.] administration has largely looked at Ukraine as a non-proliferation problem," writes F. Stephen Larrabee, "which has tended to obscure the larger crisis—the strategic issue that is at stake."[47] The essence of that issue is Ukraine's viability as a sovereign state. An implicit conclusion is that the United States should be more tolerant in discussing proliferation issues with Ukraine and gear its policies more strongly toward support for Ukrainian autonomy and statehood.

Arguments that openly or by implication support or tolerate the emergence of a nuclear Ukraine have obvious flaws. First of all, they surrender the game on the key issue of nuclear nonproliferation: the political efficacy of access to nuclear weapons. If Ukraine's sovereignty and territorial integrity are decisively reinforced by its status as a nuclear weapon state, this will also hold true for any number of other aspiring regional powers. Second, Ukraine itself is an inherently unstable polity that could well confront civil unrest and political instability in the near future, placing control over its nuclear weapons systems at risk. Third, it is quite doubtful that the kind of nuclear capacity that Ukraine would be able to muster could be a credible deterrent in the threat scenarios it is most likely to confront. Such scenarios include Russian encouragement for destabilizing internal unrest or limited military action against exposed border areas, inherently ambiguous gestures that would not merit the ultimate recourse of nuclear attack. These kinds of threats can be more effectively deterred by other, less dramatic kinds of security guarantees. For these reasons and more, the nuclear option for an independent Ukraine is almost certainly a dead end. The West's interests will be well served by policies seeking to strengthen Ukrainian sovereignty through political support and economic assistance, but barring some kind of egregious Russian provocation, that support should be made contingent on Ukrainian affiliation with the NPT and compliance with denuclearization as defined by the Trilateral Agreement. Nor is a process of limited reassociation between Russia and Ukraine, to the extent that it is undertaken voluntarily and in a spirit of mutually beneficial cooperation, necessarily harmful, particularly if it reduces the potential for coercive conflict behavior in the region.

Western responses to the strategic implications of the Soviet collapse have sought to maintain continuity in the arms control process and made a priority of nonproliferation by acknowledging Russia's status as the legitimate heir of the Soviet superpower and pressuring Belarus, Kazakhstan, and Ukraine to surrender their arsenals and adhere to the NPT. Caution has prevailed, and the possibility of making use of Russia's new geostrategic circumstances to press for deep cuts beyond those defined by START II has not been exploited. The overarching policy goal appears to be what has been defined as a "low salience" nuclear strategic environment in which U.S. dominance would remain intact, strategic doctrine would gradually move away from preparation for global war against a peer competitor toward deterrence or compellence strategies aimed at non–status quo regional powers or rogue states, and a renewed nonproliferation regime would be put to work to block the emergence of new nuclear weapon states.[48]

Such a perspective risks undervaluing what might be considered the most important lesson of the Soviet breakdown, which is that the comfortable assumptions of deterrence strategies may ultimately prove to be disastrously wrong. The most fundamental of these assumptions is that nuclear weapons are under control. What the consequences of the Soviet breakdown would seem to demonstrate conclusively is how flawed such an assumption can be. A nuclear weapon state may become caught up in a sudden crisis of political order with completely unforeseen consequences. Proliferation may occur overnight as national disintegration gives rise to newly independent states in possession of pieces of what was once an integrated arsenal. Political confrontations, such as the failed coup of August 1991 or the bloodletting in Moscow in September–October 1993, may call into question the integrity of command authority and ultimate control over the decision for nuclear use. National disintegration may turn highly skilled nuclear scientists into international mercenaries, ready to sell their expertise to the highest bidder. Nuclear safety procedures may break down against a background of social demoralization and impoverishment, leading to the abusive transfer and uncontrolled dissemination of nuclear weapons or raw materials.[49] These problems have to some extent been contained in the case of the Soviet Union, but there is no reason that they cannot recur: "If the Soviet Union can disintegrate," asks Michael MccGwire, "why not China, or India, or the new Russian state?"[50]

The Soviet collapse calls attention to the dangers inherent in all deterrence strategies that make security dependent on a credible nuclear response. It also calls attention to the risks of reliance on nuclear weapons as an ultimate guarantor of security. "The security of the Soviet state," writes William Walker, "in its deepest sense, was mortally wounded by its obsession with nuclear and other military hardware, and with the styles of production and illusions of grandeur associated with them."[51] Western responses to the Soviet apocalypse should take these warnings to heart. In addition to "managing" the post-Soviet transition, the West should commit itself to the search for more ambitious alternatives that might ultimately make denuclearization, in Eurasia and beyond, a practical goal as well as a visionary aspiration.

* * *

The substance of Western responses to military developments in the former Soviet Union must be based on an assessment of both threats and opportunities. The old nightmares of a standing-start offensive by the joint forces of the Warsaw Pact or a preemptive nuclear first strike have been rendered obsolete. The new threats that emerge from the instabilities associated with transition are perhaps less imposing, but no less demanding of attention. They include the challenge of maintaining an arms control process with a Russian partner that finds itself confronted by radically changed geostrategic circumstances, the dilemma of "overnight" proliferation posed above all by Ukraine, and the problem of nuclear safety within nuclear weapon states in crisis. The Soviet collapse has given rise to a proliferation of new national armies and paramilitary forces throughout Eurasia, ongoing regional conflicts along the Russian periphery, a reanimation of the arms trade under much less controlled circumstances than those that prevailed in the past, and the possibility of a major war between nuclear-armed adversaries such as Russia and Ukraine. "The post-Soviet military threat," argues Sergei Medvedev with some force, "is no less substantial than the Soviet threat."[52]

Perhaps the single greatest risk inherent in post-Soviet disorder remains the "loss" of Russia, its exclusion from the dynamic of European cooperation and consignment to the status of a vanquished outsider. The problem would be less severe were Russia's transition proceeding more smoothly than is actually the case, but the road will probably continue to be difficult. At present, it appears that the West has abandoned the optimistic premises of partnership and embraced a variant of limited engagement, though perhaps with the essentially negative goal of preventing an uncontrollable nationalist reaction. The shift toward a systematic policy of neocontainment would represent an extreme provocation, likely to conjure up the very ills it seeks to prevent, and has for the time being been set aside.

What are the limits of Western engagement? One limit is almost certainly the integrity of Western institutions. Selective broadening according to relatively demanding criteria may eventually become an option for the EU and NATO, but Russia is too large and distinctive to be incorporated in these institutions without changing their essential nature. Another limit is the centrality of NATO in Western security planning. The Russian option of an expanded role for the CSCE has inherent appeal, but it confronts major practical barriers and directly contradicts the clearly expressed priorities of the United States and its European allies. Some analysts predict the gradual emergence of another "two bloc" system as the basis for a new Eurasian security order, with a NATO zone on one side incorporating the former Warsaw Pact member states of Central Europe, and a CIS zone supervised by Moscow, corresponding to the territory of the former Soviet Union minus the Baltic states, on the other. The scenario is intriguing, but for the moment it is only hypothetical. A final limit is the credibility of the core function of the Western nuclear arsenal to provide deterrence against a nuclear attack launched from Russia or any other potential nuclear-armed adversary. The fulfillment of that function, however, allows the West a considerable amount of leeway in the pursuit of arms control agreements that would cut into existing arsenals and lend positive impetus to the ongoing effort to build a stable nonproliferation regime, as well as keep alive the long-term goal of a more substantial denuclearization.

Notes

1. "An analysis of the main components of the military power of the armed forces," concludes a contemporary Russian evaluation, "leads to the sad conclusion that not only do they not reach the necessary level, but that there is a tendency toward further disintegration." N.P. Klokotov and M.M. Kasenkov, "Voennaia bezopasnost' Rossii: Deklaratsii i realii," *Voennaia mysl'*, vol. 8 (August 1993), p. 28. A thorough analysis of these problems from a European perspective is offered by Andreas Heinemann-Grüder, *Das russische Militär zwischen Staatszerfall und Nationbildung* (Cologne: Berichte des Bundesinstituts für ostwissenschaftliche Studien, no. 27, 1993); and Hans-Henning Schröder, *Eine Armee in der Krise: Die russischen Streitkräfte 1992–93: Risikofaktor oder Garant politischer Stabilität?* (Cologne: Berichte des Bundesinstituts für ostwissenschaftliche und internationale Studien, no. 45, 1993).

2. Paul Goble, "Forget the Soviet Union," *Foreign Policy*, no. 86 (spring 1992), pp. 56–65.

3. Rodric Braithwaite, "Russian Realities and Western Policy," *Survival*, vol. 36, no. 3 (autumn 1994), pp. 11–12.

4. Andrei V. Kozyrev, "Russia and Human Rights," *Slavic Review*, vol. 51, no. 2 (summer 1992), pp. 289–90. This *plaidoyer* for partnership demonstrates the influence of Gorbachev-era "new thinking" on the original foreign policy discourse of the Boris Yeltsin team.

5. Bruce D. Porter and Carol R. Saivetz, "The Once and Future Empire: Russia and the Near Abroad," *Washington Quarterly*, vol. 17, no. 3 (summer 1994), p. 82.

6. See especially Andrei Kozyrev, "The Lagging Partnership," *Foreign Affairs*, vol. 73, no. 3 (May/June 1994), pp. 59–71. Here, Kozyrev asserts that "Russia is predestined to be a great power" and decries "traditional American Sovietologists" who "cannot accept the idea of a strong Russia, whether it be imperial or democratic" (pp. 60, 62).

7. Zbigniew Brzezinski, "The Premature Partnership," *Foreign Affairs*, vol. 73, no. 2 (March/April 1994), pp. 67–82. In an analysis in the same vein, Paul Goble speaks of

the need to display "tough love" toward Russia, including a "balance of power approach in the region backing weaker powers against stronger ones to discourage aggression." Paul Goble, "Russia and Its Neighbors," *Foreign Policy*, no. 90 (spring 1993), pp. 87–88.

8. The analysis in William C. Bodie, "The Threat to America from the Former USSR," *Orbis*, vol. 37, no. 4 (fall 1993), pp. 509–25, tends in this direction.

9. Vladimir Zhirinovskii, *Poslednii brosok na iug* (Moscow: Too Pisatel', 1993), pp. 103–4.

10. For the acme of fatalistic pessimism, see Yuri N. Afanasyev, "Russian Reform Is Dead," *Foreign Affairs*, vol. 73, no. 2 (March/April 1994), pp. 21–26.

11. The nature of the debate and the moderate-liberal consensus outlined here, are described in Alexei G. Arbatov, "Russia's Foreign Policy Alternatives," *International Security*, vol. 18, no. 2 (fall 1993), pp. 5–43.

12. Konstantin E. Sorokin, "The Nuclear Strategy Debate," *Orbis*, vol. 38, no. 1 (winter 1994), pp. 19–40.

13. Maxim Shashenkov, "Russian Peacekeeping in the 'Near Abroad,' " *Survival*, vol. 36, no. 3 (autumn 1994), p. 48. The threats in question include the status of the Russian diaspora in the near abroad, drug trafficking, and uncontrolled immigration into the Russian Federation, as well as more traditional concerns. Russia's new military doctrine emphasizes the importance of stability in regions adjoining Russia's borders. Text in Charles Dick, "The Military Doctrine of the Russian Federation," special section, *Jane's Intelligence Review* (January 1994), pp. 6–12.

14. Brian D. Taylor, "Russian Civil–Military Relations After the October Uprising," *Survival*, vol. 36, no. 1 (spring 1994), pp. 3–29. A discussion of the problem of civil–military relations appearing before the October crisis in the Russian military journal *Voennaia mysl'* leaves open the possibility of military intervention in political affairs in the event of a deep social crisis, but concludes that it is the responsibility of "state and society" to prevent events from arriving at such a pass. V.M. Rodachin, "Armiia i politicheskaia vlast'," *Voennaia mysl'*, vol. 5 (May 1993), pp. 12–19.

15. Gianni Bonvicini and Stefano Silvestri, "The New 'Arc of Crisis' and the European Community," *International Spectator* (April–June 1992), p. 32.

16. David Gow, "U.S. to Keep 100,000 Troops in Europe," *Guardian Weekly*, 14 February 1993, p. 9.

17. "Final Communiqué, 6–7 June 1991, North Atlantic Council, Copenhagen," in *NATO Communiqués 1991* (Brussels: NATO Office of Information and Press, 1992), p. 49.

18. "NATO's Core Security Functions in the New Europe: Statement Issued by the North Atlantic Council Meeting in Ministerial Session in Copenhagen on 6 and 7 June 1991," in *NATO Communiqués 1991*, p. 22.

19. Ibid., pp. 22, 49.

20. "Rome Declaration on Peace and Cooperation," in *NATO Communiqués 1991*, pp. 26–27. On the notion of interlocking institutions, see Hans Binnendijk, "The Emerging European Security Order," *Washington Quarterly*, vol. 14, no. 4 (autumn 1991), pp. 71–81.

21. The NACC concept originated in a joint statement by U.S. Secretary of Defense James Baker and German Foreign Minister Hans-Dietrich Genscher on 10 May 1991. "Partnership with the Countries of Central and Eastern Europe," *NATO Review* (June 1991).

22. Richard K. Betts, "Systems for Peace or Causes of War? Collective Security, Arms Control, and the New Europe," *International Security*, vol. 17, no. 1 (summer 1992), p. 15. An approving summary of the alliance's new look is offered by David M. Abshire, Richard R. Burt, and R. James Woolsey, *The Atlantic Alliance Transformed* (Washington, DC: Center for Strategic and International Studies, 1992).

23. Franz Mendel, "Wo sind die Grenzens Europas?" *Europäische Sicherheit*, 1992, vol. 3, p. 129.

24. Quotation from Gregory F. Treverton, "America's Stakes and Choices in Europe," *Survival*, vol. 34, no. 3 (autumn 1992), p. 123.

25. Willem Frederik van Eekelin, "Die Westeuropäische Union nach Maastricht," *Europäische Sicherheit*, 1992, vol. 3, p. 131.

26. Josef Joffe, "The New Europe: Yesterday's Ghosts," *Foreign Affairs: America and the World 1993*, vol. 72, no. 1 (winter 1993) p. 43.

27. The Eurocorps has been characterized by one team of analysts as "a direct challenge to the NATO Rapid Reaction Corps." Anand Menon, Anthony Fraser, and William Wallace, "A Common European Defense?" *Survival*, vol. 34, no. 3 (autumn 1992), p. 110.

28. A scenario of this kind is developed in Werner Feld, *The Future of European Security and Defense Policy* (Boulder, CO: Lynne Rienner, 1993), pp. 135–49.

29. Treverton, "America's Stakes and Choice in Europe," p. 128; and Richard N. Gardner, "Practical Internationalism: The United States and Collective Security," *SAIS Review*, vol. 12, no. 2 (summer–fall 1992), p. 36.

30. Michael Mandelbaum, "Americans Need to Learn Why America Must Lead," *International Herald Tribune*, 10 June 1993, p. 4. Fred Chernoff elaborates: "The need might someday arise to counterbalance Germany and to keep it working with the West; this could be accomplished much more effectively through NATO by the United States than through the European Community by France, even in combination with the United Kingdom." Fred Chernoff, "Can NATO Outlive the USSR?" *International Relations*, no. 1 (April 1992), p. 5.

31. For statements supportive of and opposed to the concept of collective security as a foundation for a new European security order, see Heinz Gärtner, "Fünf Sicherheitskonzepte für Europa," *Europäische Rundschau*, 1993, vol. 1, pp. 49–51; and Josef Joffe, "Collective Security and the Future of Europe: Failed Dreams and Dead Ends," *Survival*, vol. 34, no. 1 (spring 1992), pp. 36–50.

32. Military-to-military contacts follow in the tradition of a well-established Soviet-American military-to-military relationship, including Incidents at Sea and Dangerous Military Activities agreements, which has been carried over into the post-Soviet period to both sides' satisfaction. John H. McNeill, "Military-to-Military Arrangements for the Prevention of U.S.-Russian Conflict," *Naval War College Review* (spring 1994), pp. 23–29.

33. Gebhardt von Moltke, "Building a Partnership for Peace," *NATO Review*, vol. 3 (June 1994), p. 4. The text of the Framework Document appears in *NATO Review*, vol. 1 (February 1994), pp. 29–30.

34. See, for example, Paul Latawski, "The Polish Road to NATO: Problems and Prospects," *Polish Quarterly of International Affairs*, vol. 3 (summer 1993), pp. 69–75.

35. von Moltke, "Building a Partnership for Peace," p. 7.

36. Andrei V. Kozyrev, "Russia and NATO: A Partnership for a United and Peaceful Europe," *NATO Review*, vol. 4 (August 1994), pp. 3–6. See also Michael Mihalka, "European-Russian Security and NATO's Partnership for Peace," *RFE/RL Research Report*, 26 August 1994, pp. 34–45.

37. Charles L. Glaser, "Why NATO Is Still Best: Future Security Arrangements for Europe," *International Security*, vol. 18, no. 1 (summer 1993), p. 7.

38. Cited from Kozyrev, "The Lagging Partnership," p. 65.

39. That conclusion might be challenged in the case of the Chemical Weapons Convention, which defines the goal of a total ban on such weapons.

40. For Gorbachev's disarmament project, see M.S. Gorbachev, *Izbrannie rechi i stat'i*, 7 vols. (Moscow: Politizdat, 1987–90), vol. 3, pp. 133–44, and vol. 4, pp. 383–

85. Soviet specialized literature tempered these ambitious aspirations considerably, and in his address before the Council of Europe in Strasbourg on 6 July 1989 Gorbachev moved toward "minimal deterrence" as an interim goal. See E. Agaev, "K novoi modeli strategicheskoi stabil'nosti," *Mezhdunarodnaia zhizn'*, 1989, vol. 2, pp. 103–11; and "Obshcheevropeiskii protsess idet vpered," *Pravda*, 7 July 1989, p. 2.

41. The possibility of nuclear attack as a result of accident or inadvertence was never completely eliminated. See Bruce G. Blair, *The Logic of Accidental Nuclear War* (Washington, DC: Brookings Institution, 1993).

42. Sorokin, "The Nuclear Strategy Debate," pp. 20–24.

43. Cited in R. Jeffrey Smith, "U.S. Keeps Nuclear Guard Against Russia," *International Herald Tribune*, 23 September 1994, p. 2.

44. Cited from "At UN, Yeltsin Calls for New Reductions in Nuclear Arsenals," *International Herald Tribune*, 27 September 1994, p. 1.

45. Wolfgang K.H. Panofsky and George Bunn, "The Doctrine of the Nuclear-Weapon States and the Future of Non-Proliferation," *Arms Control Today*, vol. 24, no. 6 (July/August 1994), p. 3.

46. Adrian Karatnycky, "Russia's Nuclear Grasp," *New York Times*, 30 August 1994, p. A21.

47. Quoted in Raymond Garthoff, "Prospects for Ukrainian Denuclearization After the Moscow Trilateral Statement," *Arms Control Today*, vol. 24, no. 2 (March 1994), p. 24.

48. Michael Quinlan, "The Future of Nuclear Weapons: Policy for Western Possessors," *International Affairs*, vol. 69, no. 3 (July 1993), pp. 485–96.

49. The issue was highlighted during the summer of 1994 by a plutonium smuggling scandal. See Matthew L. Wald and Michael R. Gordon, "Russia Treasures Plutonium, But U.S. Wants to Destroy It," *New York Times*, 19 August 1994, pp. A1, A10.

50. Michael MccGwire, "Is There a Future for Nuclear Weapons?" *International Affairs*, vol. 70, no. 2 (April 1994), p. 221.

51. William Walker, "Nuclear Weapons and the Former Soviet Republics," *International Affairs*, vol. 68, no. 2 (April 1992), p. 77.

52. See Sergei Medvedev, "Security Risks in Russia and the CIS," *International Spectator* (January–March 1994), p. 74.

11

U.S. Nuclear Arms Control Policies Toward Russia and the Former Soviet Union

Michael Nacht

With the collapse of the Soviet Union and the end of the Cold War at the end of 1991, there developed a widespread feeling in the United States and elsewhere that matters of nuclear arms control with Russia, and indeed military matters more generally, would be far less important in the future than in the past. Instead, it was argued, domestic economic strength and cooperation and competition among the major economic powers would become the central feature of post–Cold War international relations. This judgment was reflected in the minimal attention that military and arms control matters were given during the 1992 U.S. presidential campaign and in the increased popularity of "international political economy" and the concomitant decline in interest in "security studies" in American graduate programs in political science, international relations, and public policy.

The experience of the first eighteen months of the Clinton administration has proven contrary to these expectations. The role of force in intra- and interstate conflict has remained a central preoccupation of decision makers not only in Washington but also in Western Europe and Moscow, and at the United Nations in New York. Ethnic conflict in the former Yugoslavia, civil war in Rwanda, the assertion of tribalism in Somalia, and the brutal authoritarianism in Haiti all have forced their way on to the top of the foreign policy agenda. The dedicated North Korean nuclear weapons program has received the highest level of attention in Washington because of its threat to South Korean security, the prospect of Pyongyang selling weapons to other rogue states, and the potential that the North Korean program, if unchecked, could destroy the nuclear nonproliferation regime.

With respect to "strategic nuclear weapons"—defined for decades as the nuclear weapons deployed by the Soviet Union and the United States on land- and sea-based ballistic missiles (ICBMs and SLBMs, respectively), long-range bombers, and, more recently, intercontinental-range cruise missiles that could reach the homeland of each superpower when launched from the other—the agenda has become much more complex. The issue is no longer merely control or even reduction of the delivery vehicles, which was addressed in the Strategic Arms Limitation Treaties (SALT) of 1972 and 1979 and the Strategic Arms Reduction Treaties (START) of 1991 and 1993. Instead the Clinton administration has had to grapple with the multilateralization of the former Soviet arsenal, the control of warheads and fissile material as well as delivery vehicles, the rationalization of the deployment of theater missile defenses within the constraints of the Antiballistic Missile Treaty, and the conversion of Russian defense industries to civilian uses.

The Clinton administration's nuclear arms control policies with regard to Russia and the other states of the former Soviet Union appear to reflect three basic objectives. First, rather than an end in itself, they are an integral part of the American national security policy to draw Russia into both Western and global political, economic, and eventually security institutions. Since the political future of Russia and its commitment to democratization are far from certain—especially in light of the attempted coup d'état against Russian President Boris Yeltsin in August 1993 and the strong showing by ultranationalist Vladimir Zhirinovsky in the December 1993 elections—it is in the American national interest to reduce the Russian nuclear arsenal as rapidly as possible. Enhancing U.S.-Russian military ties and promoting reciprocal unilateral nuclear reductions are therefore also part of Washington's national security strategy.

Second, the nuclear arms control policies toward Russia are supportive of the American priority to thwart the global spread of weapons of mass destruction. Significant progress in U.S.-Russian arms control and reductions would demonstrate a commitment to de-emphasizing the role of nuclear weapons in world politics and would, in turn, reinforce the legitimacy of the Nuclear Nonproliferation Treaty (NPT), whose permanent extension was agreed to in May 1995. Admittedly, there are many experts who are skeptical of the linkages between progress in U.S.-Russian nuclear arms control and the incentives of other states to acquire their own nuclear arsenals. These skeptics believe that the impetus behind nuclear proliferation is based in part on individual governments' calculations about their own regional security needs and also in part on the domestic political prestige associated with nuclear weapon acquisition. Nonetheless, the nuclear superpowers are committed under the terms of the NPT to move toward the complete elimination of their nuclear arsenals, and concrete steps in this direction provide a necessary political basis to convince elites in threshold countries that nuclear weapon acquisition is not in their own national interest.

Third, nuclear arms control, although technologically and politically difficult, presents an opportunity for policy *initiatives* by the administration. This is in contrast to the inevitable *reactive* posture that has driven administration policies with respect to regional "hot spots"—Bosnia, Somalia, Haiti, Cuba, and North Korea. Managing the new relationship with Russia, in part through important steps in reducing nuclear arms and strengthening their operational control, represents a major potential foreign policy success for an administration that is facing a highly complex and uncertain international political environment.

The Policy-Making Process

One of the critical features of the administration's approach to nuclear arms control with Russia and the other states of the former Soviet Union is the widespread support for these objectives among senior political appointees across the bureaucratic spectrum. This in itself is highly unusual. The détente initiatives spurred by President Nixon and his chief foreign policy lieutenant, Henry Kissinger, were greeted skeptically, if not with ardent opposition, by Secretary of Defense Schlesinger, his successor, Donald Rumsfeld, and Arms Control and Disarmament Agency Director Fred Iklé. In the Carter administration, there were deep divisions over strategy and tactics toward the Soviet Union between Secretary of State Cyrus Vance and National Security Advisor Zbigniew Brzezinski. In the Reagan years there were intense differences between Secretary of State George Shultz and his top aides, Paul Nitze and Richard Burt, on the one hand, and Secretary of Defense Caspar Weinberger and Assistant Secretary of Defense Richard Perle, on the other. Even on the reasonably harmonious Bush foreign policy decision-making team, there were substantial tensions between Secretary of State James Baker and Secretary of Defense Dick Cheney. On the Clinton team, there is a virtual unanimity of view between Secretary of State Warren Christopher, Secretary of Defense William Perry, National Security Advisor Anthony Lake, and their principal aides about the wisdom of pursuing far-reaching arms reduction agreements, even if there are certain differences over tactics and some natural differences over bureaucratic turf.

The organizational structure for national security decision making in the

Clinton administration was spelled out in Presidential Decision Directive (PDD)–2, issued by President Clinton on 20 January 1993, the first day of his presidency.[1] PDD–2 established the National Security Council (NSC) as "the principal forum for consideration of national security policy issues requiring Presidential determination."[2] The composition of the NSC was stipulated to include the president, the vice president, the secretary of state, and the secretary of defense, as prescribed by statute; the director of central intelligence (DCI) and the chairman of the Joint Chiefs of Staff (JCS), as statutory advisors to the NSC; plus the secretary of the treasury, the U.S. representative to the United Nations, the assistant to the president for national security affairs, the assistant to the president for economic policy, and the chief of staff to the president.

The decision-making processes for national security issues, including arms control, were stipulated by PDD–2 to include the NSC Principals Committee (NSC/PC), the NSC Deputies Committee (NSC/DC), and NSC Interagency Working Groups (NSC/IWGs).[3] The NSC/PC is chaired by the assistant to the president for national security affairs and includes the secretaries of state and defense, the DCI, the chairman of the JCS, and others as appropriate. It is a "forum available for Cabinet-level officials to meet to discuss and resolve issues not requiring the President's participation"[4] and in practice is the body that most shapes significant national security policies for the president's approval. The NSC/DC is chaired by the deputy assistant to the president for national security affairs and includes the undersecretary of defense for policy, the undersecretary of state for political affairs, the deputy DCI, and the vice chairman of the JCS. The NSC/DC in practice screens policy options developed by the IWGs, offers recommendations to the PC, is attentive to policy implementation, and is also responsible for day-to-day crisis management, in which capacity it is designated the Deputies Committee/CM.[5] The NSC/IWGs are established by the Deputies Committee and, in the foreign policy and defense areas, are chaired at the assistant secretary level by the Departments of State and Defense.[6] However, IWGs concerned with intelligence, nonproliferation, arms control, and crisis management are chaired by NSC senior staff directors.[7]

This process was modified somewhat in the summer of 1993, when it was determined that the Arms Control and Disarmament Agency (ACDA) would in fact retain its independence, later buttressed by "revitalization" legislation that was passed in May 1994. As a result, the ACDA director attends PC meetings dealing with arms control or nonproliferation, and he or his designated representative attends DC meetings concerned with these subjects. The assistant directors of ACDA for strategic and Eurasian affairs and for nonproliferation and regional security and their designated associates represent the agency at the IWGs.

An important set of Congressional committees and their staffs are inti-
mately involved in U.S. arms control policy making. The Senate Foreign
Relations, Armed Services, Budget, and Appropriations Committees and
the House International Relations, Armed Services, Budget, and Appropriations Committees all influence U.S. arms control policy, as do the budget
constraints set down by the Office of Management and Budget that are
submitted to the Congress for review and approval. Senators Sam Nunn and
Richard Lugar of Senate Armed Services, Senators Claiborne Pell, Joseph
Biden, and Jesse Helms of Senate Foreign Relations, Congressman Lee
Hamilton of House International Relations, and their staffs are especially
engaged on Russian nuclear arms control issues.

It is important to realize that there are differences *within* as well as
between agencies of government that increase the fragmentation of authority that characterizes the policy-making process. Within the Department of
Defense, for example, both the assistant secretary of defense for international security policy, who reports to the undersecretary of defense for
policy, and the assistant to the secretary for atomic energy, who reports to
the undersecretary of defense for acquisition, are concerned with initiatives
to ensure the safety and security of Russian nuclear weapons. Key personnel in the Senate Foreign Relations and Armed Services Committees hold
very different views about the most appropriate means of pursuing nuclear
arms control. No wonder then that, despite reasonable ideological agreement, there are intense debates before policies are established and a continuing tug-of-war for influence and control even after they are established.
Moreover, the policy-making process is sensitive to the views articulated by
nongovernmental organizations, scholars, journalists, and prominent experts
who are in turn linked to particular positions and individuals within the
administration. This cacophony of policy voices, reflected in all aspects of
policy making—and in stark contrast to the early détente period when
Henry Kissinger, with the blessing of President Nixon, exerted extraordinary influence over all aspects of national security policy—makes it difficult at times for external observers to appreciate accurately how specific
policy positions are arrived at.

Major Issues

There are four main issues at the center of current U.S. nuclear arms control
policy toward Russia and the other states of the former Soviet Union: START,
ABM Treaty clarification, Nunn–Lugar funding, and defense conversion. The
sections that follow summarize and assess the state of play in each of these
areas and then point to some possible new initiatives on the horizon.[8]

START

When President Ronald Reagan took office in 1981, he was critical of the SALT agreements that had been completed by Presidents Nixon and Carter on the grounds that these accords did not *reduce* the nuclear arsenals of the superpowers and, in some categories, such as multiple independently target-able re-entry vehicles (MIRVs), permitted their rapid expansion. Instead he proposed Strategic Arms *Reduction* Talks that would remove tangible threats to the forces and populations of each society. After many years of negotiation and profound shifts in Soviet politics initiated by General Secre-tary Mikhail Gorbachev, the START I agreement was signed on 31 July 1991 by President George Bush and Secretary Gorbachev; the agreement called for significantly reduced limits for ICBMs and their associated launchers and warheads, SLBM launchers and warheads, and heavy bomb-ers and their armaments, including long-range, nuclear air-launched cruise missiles (ALCMs). Overall, this agreement, if implemented, would reduce the number of deployed strategic warheads on each side from roughly ten thousand to six thousand over a seven-year period. The U.S. Senate con-sented to ratification on 1 October 1992.[9]

In contemporary analyses of the Soviet politics of the time, it is widely held that this agreement helped stimulate the eventual effort to overthrow Gorbachev in mid-August 1991. Although the attempted coup d'état failed, of course, it enormously strengthened the political clout of Boris Yeltsin and accelerated the demise of the Soviet Union, which ceased to exist at the end of 1991. Consequently, a vital nuclear arms control treaty had been completed between two parties, one of which no longer existed! This bi-zarre situation led to extensive negotiations between Moscow and Washing-ton, producing the so-called Lisbon START Protocol. The protocol is considered an amendment to the START I Treaty and provides for Belarus, Ukraine, and Kazakhstan (all of which have nuclear weapons deployed on their territory) to succeed to the Soviet Union's obligation under the treaty. All three states also pledged to adhere to the NPT in the shortest possible time and committed themselves to eliminate all nuclear weapons from their territory within seven years. The U.S. Senate consented to ratification on 1 October 1992, and Belarus, Kazakhstan, and Russia all ratified the protocol, with Belarus and Kazakhstan acceding to the NPT. Ukraine acceded to the NPT in December 1994, and the START Treaty then entered into force.

After extensive additional negotiations, Presidents Bush and Yeltsin met in Moscow at the very end of the Bush administration and signed the Strategic Arms Reduction Treaty (START II). This treaty was a major step forward, calling for the elimination of all MIRVed ICBMs and reductions in strategic warhead limits on each side to between three thousand and thirty-five hundred by the year 2003 (or by the year 2000, if the United States could assist Russia to meet that date).

Therefore the Clinton "inheritance" was a START I agreement that required Ukrainian accession to the NPT in order to enter into force and a START II accord leading to deep reductions that was dependent on the implementation of START I but not yet ratified by either the U.S. Senate or the Russian Duma. Ukrainian NPT accession has turned out to be far more difficult than originally anticipated, becoming a subject of intense debate in Ukrainian domestic politics. Many Ukrainians, reflecting opinions in the Ukrainian legislature (the Rada), did not wish to give up their nuclear weapons and accede to the NPT either because they thought the weapons were an essential deterrent against Russian aggression or because they wanted substantial compensation for their return.[10]

Much of 1993 then focused on Clinton administration efforts to find the key to Ukrainian NPT accession. Ukrainian President Leonid Kravchuk and the Rada, seeking to extract compensation for these weapons, played complex political and diplomatic games with both the United States and Russia. The result was the Trilateral Statement signed by the United States, Russia, and Ukraine in Moscow on 14 January 1994, which provided for "fair and timely compensation to Ukraine, Kazakhstan and Belarus as the nuclear warheads on their territory are transferred to Russia for dismantling."[11] The three presidents agreed on "simultaneous actions on transfer of nuclear warheads from Ukraine and delivery of compensation to Ukraine in the form of fuel assemblies for nuclear power stations."[12] The Trilateral Statement also builds on a bilateral U.S.-Russian Agreement on Highly Enriched Uranium in August 1992. This latter agreement commits both parties to cooperate in the conversion of highly enriched uranium (HEU) resulting from nuclear weapon dismantlement into low-enriched uranium (LEU) for use as commercial reactor fuel. The agreement called for the U.S. Department of Energy to purchase the LEU converted from the HEU at Russian facilities. The Trilateral Statement similarly called for U.S. technical and financial assistance for the safe and secure dismantling of nuclear forces and storage of fissile materials, including a minimum of $175 million to Ukraine (this figure has since more than doubled). Moreover, both Russia and the United States provided security assurances to Ukraine consistent with the principles of the Conference on Security and Cooperation in Europe (CSCE) Final Act once Ukraine becomes a non-nuclear weapon state party to the NPT and START I enters into force.

In July 1994, President Leonid Kravchuk was defeated in his reelection bid, primarily because of the disastrous state of the Ukrainian economy, and was replaced by President Leonid Kuchma, a former factory manager with close Russian ties. President Kuchma then delivered on the Ukrainian commitment by adhering to the NPT at the Budapest Summit in December 1994.

Even if all Ukrainian nuclear weapons are eventually returned to Russia, the START regime is still not fully clarified. This is because the Russian Duma never ratified START II, which was completed during the very pro-American phase of Russian foreign policy in early 1993. Since a pro-nationalist sentiment was reflected in the December 1993 elections, Yeltsin and his colleagues have adopted a more independent foreign policy, and there is substantial criticism in the Duma and among Russian military officers that START II is not in the Russian national interest because it negotiates away the chief weapon of its nuclear arsenal—MIRVed heavy ICBMs. There is some prospect, therefore, that START II will face further serious delays even after START I is implemented, and that it might even have to be renegotiated.

The uncertain political status of START II has raised questions about appropriate U.S. policy beyond START II. Some American officials believe that START II goes far enough to cut central strategic systems, whereas others would like to see both Presidents Clinton and Yeltsin commit to a new structure of reductions after START II that would move both forces well below the three thousand level that is the "floor" of the START II agreement. Because of severe budgetary pressures facing both governments, it is also possible that reciprocal unilateral measures could be enacted that would bring both forces below three thousand. In the fall of 1994, the United States is scheduled to release the results of its Nuclear Posture Review (NPR). If complex arms control agreements are seen as too laborious to negotiate or too difficult to obtain legislative approval, both sides might use NPR-like unilateral force sizing exercises to produce the same result. The difference between the two paths, of course, is that the arms control agreements would be legally binding, whereas the reciprocal unilateral measures do not carry any such status and, in theory, are easily reversible.

Through the end of this century, assuming that the basic moderate tone of Russian politics holds, both sides will draw down their central strategic systems considerably. Indeed, they have already reached agreements on "detargeting"—that is, not to target each other with these weapons—and the United States has taken its long-range bombers off alert. With these operational measures and the removal of major counterforce systems from both arsenals, substantial stabilization through arms control is in progress. How far it progresses is dependent in large part on the vicissitudes of Russian and Ukrainian politics, both of which are difficult to discern.

ABM/TMD Demarcation

The bedrock of modern strategic arms control is the Antiballistic Missile (ABM) Treaty signed in 1972 as part of the SALT I agreements. The treaty limited the United States and the Soviet Union to minimal deployments of defenses against offensive strategic weapons. The rationale for the agreement was that, with each side largely defenseless, neither side had an incentive to strike first, since leaders of each society realized they would be destroyed by the retaliatory attack. Then, when the political climate changed drastically in the Soviet Union, with the ABM Treaty in force, it was possible to reach agreement on deep cuts in offensive forces.

Therefore, for many students of this arcane subject, retention of the ABM Treaty is a sine qua non for a stable U.S.-Russian strategic relationship. For other specialists, the logic of the treaty was never persuasive, and they have consistently sought to undermine it. Indeed, the Reagan administration's Strategic Defense Initiative (SDI) was really aimed at weakening, if not dissolving, the treaty. SDI, however, proved to be technologically unfeasible at reasonable cost.

The Clinton administration faces a different problem. As evidenced by the use of Iraqi Scud missiles in the 1991 Persian Gulf War, countries are developing ballistic missiles that could threaten U.S. forces abroad as well as American friends and allies. The People's Republic of China has developed a ballistic missile, the CSS–2, with a range of several hundred kilometers, and has sold it to Saudi Arabia. The North Koreans and the Chinese are working on longer-range missiles with higher accuracy and greater payloads. With strong support in the Congress, the Clinton administration has supported the development, testing, and deployment of theater missile defenses (TMD) that could defend against such systems but that would *not* provide a defense against strategic ballistic missiles.

The two issues of the ABM Treaty and TMD are joined because the treaty is not clear on what constitutes a "strategic" launcher, missile interceptor, or radar. At the time—twenty-two years ago—TMD systems were not envisaged. The Clinton administration seeks to achieve the dual goals of preserving the ABM Treaty, and therefore strategic stability with Russia, while permitting deployment of TMD systems against regional threats. Therefore it has initiated negotiations with Russia through the diplomatic mechanism established to review the ABM Treaty (the Standing Consultative Commission—SCC—which meets when required in Geneva) to seek "clarification" of the treaty.

One of the issues raised in the negotiations concerns the peak velocity of the interceptor missile. When the ABM Treaty was being negotiated in

1972, a senior Defense Department official, Johnny Foster, offered the view that a peak interceptor missile velocity of five kilometers per second could be used to intercept an attacking missile with a range of thirty-five hundred kilometers (far below the range of intercontinental strategic systems, which are nominally pegged at more than five thousand kilometers). Foster evidently argued that missile defense systems with peak velocities greater than five kilometers per second could intercept missiles with ranges well in excess of thirty-five hundred kilometers and therefore defined this peak velocity as the demarcation between theater and strategic ballistic missiles. This analysis, known as the "Foster Box," has been a subject of contention in the open debate about whether it makes sense to seek this clarification through diplomatic negotiations with Russia. [13]

Several reservations have been offered about this Clinton policy. Some are concerned that this negotiation exaggerates the threat and will lead to the demise of the ABM Treaty. Others believe that the TMD systems can be deployed without consulting the Russians and that negotiations will lead to constraints that will unduly hamper U.S. deployments. The administration argues that the first two arguments are erroneous: one has to examine the threat down the road, not today's threat, given the long lead time to develop and deploy TMD systems, and the projected threat requires such TMD deployments; moreover, the negotiation is designed to clarify the ABM Treaty precisely in order to preserve its effectiveness. No TMD would be deployed that has a significant strategic missile defense capability. The administration also contends that the second set of arguments is flawed: negotiation is required both to preserve the treaty with the Russians and to satisfy Congressional concerns; in addition, the negotiation posture is designed to protect the possible deployment of any TMD system that has technological merit and is under serious consideration for deployment. [14]

It is uncertain when and how this issue will be resolved. The changing international environment suggests that ballistic missile proliferation will increase as an international problem, thereby strengthening the demand for effective TMD systems. The United States and Russia have a great deal riding on their ability to reach an agreement that permits TMD deployments while preserving the ABM Treaty.

Nunn–Lugar Safety, Security, and Dismantlement Initiatives

The collapse of the Soviet Union instantaneously "multilateralized" the nuclear arms control problem into a set of issues involving Russia, Belarus, Kazakhstan, and Ukraine. In 1992 Senators Sam Nunn and Richard Lugar sponsored a bill that authorized the Department of Defense to spend $400 million to assist activities related to weapon dismantlement in the newly independent states of the former Soviet Union. Subsequently, the National Defense Appropriations Act for FY 1993 raised this amount to $800 million, and it was raised the following year to $1.2 billion.[15] This "Nunn–Lugar" fund is to promote the safety, security, and dismantlement (SSD) of nuclear weapons from the arsenals of the NIS. Umbrella agreements have been signed with each of the four states, and more than thirty agreements were completed by mid-1994. SSD assistance is aimed at accelerating reductions required under START I and is also sometimes characterized under the term "cooperative threat reduction" (CTR).

Four types of assistance are provided.[16] The first is to provide critical support for the *physical dismantlement of former strategic offensive arms* in Kazakhstan, Russia, and Ukraine. The second is to *enhance the safety* of these weapons in all four of the NIS. The third is to *help prevent further proliferation of weapons of mass destruction.* And the fourth is to *help improve the implementation of arms control agreements* in the four NIS. Provision of emergency response equipment and armored blankets is an example of SSD assistance.

There is some controversy over the effectiveness of the SSD program, and some members of the House Appropriations Committee are especially critical that the pace is too slow and the effectiveness too weak.

A new phase is planned for 1995 to increase the "transparency" of these weapons by developing cooperative warhead accountability schemes, whereby numbers and locations of warheads are shared by all parties. It remains to be seen how far these transparency measures will proceed. If successfully implemented, "transparency" could be a central element of the future of U.S.-Russian nuclear arms control.

Defense Conversion

A fourth element of nuclear arms control includes a set of measures that have followed from agreements reached between Vice President Gore and Prime Minister Chernomyrdin. Through these agreements a U.S.-Russian Commission on Conversion of Defense Industry has been established.[17] The Gore–Chernomyrdin agreements call for work in several areas. An important step is the effort to convert nuclear research and development complexes to industrial research and development enterprises. A second is to conduct a series of entrepreneurial workshops—three had in fact been conducted through the first half of 1994—for defense technology conversion in Russia. And third, workshops have been jointly sponsored by the ACDA, the U.S. Department of Energy Laboratories (Los Alamos National

Laboratory, Lawrence Livermore National Laboratory, Sandia National Laboratory), and MINATOM, which controls the Russian nuclear laboratories, including Arzamas–16 and Cheliabinsk–70. Efforts at cooperative defense conversion are in the earliest stages of development. They had been strongly pushed—not only for Russia but for China—by William Perry when he was deputy secretary of defense. It remains to be seen how far these activities will proceed, since they are very intrusive into areas that have been highly classified in both societies.

The Future Agenda

This review of nuclear arms control initiatives involving the United States, Russia, and the other NIS suggests a far more active and complex agenda than was either anticipated at the start of the Clinton administration or is generally known to the policy community. The trends are apparent: multilateralization of the efforts; concentration on warheads and fissile material as well as launch vehicles; and movement toward more intrusive measures of cooperative threat reduction. Obviously the necessary conditions for these activities to proceed are the continuation of a government in Moscow that supports democratic processes and an approach to nuclear security that emphasizes cooperation more than competition. If these trends continue, a substantial amount of nuclear disarmament will in fact take effect even if a START III framework is not established for some time. Successful implementation of START I and START II, plus the SSD program, plus defense conversion initiatives would have a massive effect on the nuclear arsenals of both Russia and the United States and would reduce these arsenals to levels not seen since the mid-1960s, greatly enhancing their safety and security.

Consideration is also being given in both Moscow and Washington to bringing the Chinese and possibly the French and British into the strategic arms control dialogue. These countries have all claimed that the two nuclear superpowers would have to reduce their arsenals to much smaller numbers before they in turn would be willing to participate in such discussions. But it is at least plausible that some form of multilateral nuclear arms control dialogue could be initiated in which information is shared that could lead to greater "transparency" of all five sets of nuclear forces.

To the general public and even to many policy elites, nuclear arms control may be forgotten—but it is far from gone. The agenda is increasingly complex, but the stakes are no less important today than they were thirty years ago when the first serious U.S.-Soviet nuclear arms dialogue was initiated. Reaching and implementing agreements that ensure the irreversibility of nuclear reductions would strengthen the likelihood that what strategist

Tom Schelling called "the tradition of non-use" of nuclear weapons will continue far into the future. Maintaining this tradition is in the interests of us all.

Notes

This analysis reflects the personal views of the author and is not representative of the position of the U.S. government or the Arms Control and Disarmament Agency.

1. See "Organization of the National Security Council" (White House, Washington, DC, 20 January 1993, mimeo).

2. Ibid., p. 1.

3. Ibid., pp. 2–4.

4. Ibid., p. 2.

5. Ibid., p. 3.

6. Ibid.

7. Ibid., p. 4.

8. A useful source for factual information on these subjects is *New Independent States Issues Reader* (Washington, DC: U.S. Arms Control and Disarmament Agency, 1994).

9. Ibid., p. 135.

10. Russian-Ukrainian relations are complicated by both a major dispute over the disposition of the Black Sea fleet and the issue of Crimean sovereignty. The Crimean Peninsula was ceded to Ukraine by Soviet Premier Nikita Khrushchev in the mid-1950s but is predominantly populated by members of the Russian nationality group, who tend to have strong pro-Russian and anti-Ukrainian sentiments.

11. *New Independent States Issues Reader*, pp. 21–22.

12. Ibid.

13. For a description of the U.S. TMD systems under development, see *Ballistic Missile Defense: 1994 Report to the Congress* (Washington, DC: Ballistic Missile Defense Organization, 1994). Also see "Ballistic Missile Defense: Information on Theater High Altitude Area Defense (THAAD) and Other Theater Missile Defense Systems" (statement of Brad Hathaway, associate director for systems development and production issues, National Security and International Affairs Division, General Accounting Office, testimony before the Committee on Foreign Relations, U.S. Senate, 3 May 1994). A useful evaluation of the TMD Treaty-related issues is contained in Steven A. Hildreth, "The ABM Treaty and Theater Missile Defense: Proposed Changes and Potential Implications," *Congressional Research Service Report for Congress* 94–374 F, 2 May 1994.

14. Senate testimony in support of the administration's position can be found in Sidney N. Graybeal, "Testimony Before the Senate Foreign Relations Committee on Effective Theater Missile Defenses and the ABM Treaty," 3 May 1994. Testimony critical of the administration's position include Spurgeon M. Keeny Jr., "Statement Before the Senate Foreign Relations Committee," 3 May 1994; and "Statement of John B. Rhinelander on the ABM Treaty and Anti-Tactical Ballistic Missiles Before Senate Committee on Foreign Relations," 3 May 1994. Press accounts of the negotiating positions on interceptor velocities include Bill Gertz, "U.S. Accepts Russian Speed Limits on Missile Defenses," *Washington Times*, 1 July 1994, p. A3; and Thomas W. Lippman, "U.S. Accepts Russian Demand for Missile Limits," *Washington Post*, 2 July 1994. See also John Holum, "Don't Put Allies at Risk," *New York Times*, 25 October 1994.

15. See *New Independent States Issues Reader*, p. 1.

16. Ibid., pp. 2–3.

17. Ibid., pp. 25–27. Also see "Vice President's Statement to the Press at the Signing Ceremony with Russian Prime Minister Viktor Chernomyrdin" (23 June 1994, mimeo).

12

CONCLUSION
The Importance of Nuclear Weapons

George Quester

This chapter will attempt a retrospective overview of the nuclear problems that have been addressed in detail throughout the previous chapters of this volume, specifically, the problems facing the former Soviet Union, that is, the Russian littoral.

It might have been possible to anticipate some of these generic problems in advance as the inevitable price of the breakup of a nuclear power. Regardless of this, it is of course not possible to go back to the unified Soviet Union and the single nuclear force it possessed.

And given the ideological combativeness of the Cold War, and the hypothetical threats of a nuclear holocaust that went with it, it is hardly even arguable that Americans or Russians or others would want to go back. As such, the nuclear issue may be remarkably parallel to the ethnic and economic issues detailed in other volumes in this series, a tale of problems and setbacks spoiling any total joy at the changes after 1989, but one hardly changing the net satisfaction that the Cold War is over.

The nuclear problems are problems nonetheless, and possibly serious problems. Most of the world assumes that the end of the Cold War produced a marked decrease in the net likelihood of thermonuclear war. This may well be so, even if we can never agree on what the real risk of such a war was during the years from 1949 to 1989. Yet given that we cannot be sure of what the real risk was, and given that we have to deal with all the problems outlined in this book, it is also depressingly possible that the net result of the new development here is actually negative, that the total risk of a nuclear calamity or a nuclear holocaust has somehow gone up rather than down.

The Inherent "Use Them or Lose Them" Problem

The first of the problems to be noted here is, as stipulated at the outset, central to the very notion of mutual assured destruction and mutual deterrence—the political and military leaders of each side must be left with something as the price of withholding the nuclear destruction they can unleash.[1]

If some or all leaders on the former Soviet side were dedicated communists, what are they to make of the total defeat and total renunciation of communism? How do we assure that no one feels strongly enough about this lost cause to want to drag the whole world down to destruction in a last-gasp retaliation? Consider this: Marshal Akhromeev was regarded as one of the more reasonable of the senior Soviet military officers in the last years of the Cold War, someone with whom one could talk about shifting away from threatening weapons on each side. Yet Akhromeev, seeing the failure of the 1991 coup attempt against Gorbachev, elected to take his own life.

For the management of nuclear missile forces in a superpower, it is hard to imagine something more threatening than a political change that pushes such a leader to suicide, to a feeling that he has nothing more to lose. As the Cold War has retreated further and further into the past, it might be reasonable to conclude that this bitterness of the "defeat" of Marxism–Leninism must be behind us, that the worst is over. Yet it is dangerous to underestimate the trauma that the end of the Cold War has inflicted on the more committed communists, so that the end of our concerns here may still be out of reach. And there are other inherent problems in this area of command and control that may get worse with time rather than better.

As outlined in the chapters by Bruce G. Blair, William C. Potter, and Oleg Bukharin, some aspects of the command and control issue seem to have been better handled in the Cold War Soviet Union than in the United States or any of the other nuclear weapon states. The closed and tightly centralized nature of the Soviet Union generated a secrecy and a system of management that presumably would keep nuclear weapons from slipping out of control.

Yet what was a rigid system may also then have been a brittle system, one not well suited to the more open and pluralistic Russia that has followed. Just as the police state of the gulags has given way to mafias and crime and threats to domestic law and order, so there is continual concern about whether experienced Soviet bomb designers will now be kept from selling their services to Iran or North Korea, and whether every last nuclear warhead is accounted for, and about whether all Russian fissionable material is safely controlled.

In the old Soviet Union the public did not know nearly as much about their country's nuclear arsenal as the American public knew about that of the United States. If this meant tighter control then, it could mean looser control now.

Secession and Nuclear Deterrence

The defeat of communism was unforeseen by analysts of nuclear strategy, and so was the breakup of a nuclear power. The Nuclear Nonproliferation Treaty and the other treaties dealing with nuclear issues really do not make any provision for such a case. What if Scotland were to secede from Great Britain? How would the nuclear weapons be handled? What if South Carolina or North Dakota were to secede from the United States? Empty questions indeed. What if Ukraine and Kazakhstan and Belarus were to secede from the Soviet Union? Not such empty questions as it turns out, as discussed in great detail in the chapters by Sherman W. Garnett, Vyachaslau Paznyak, and Murat Laumulin.

There are many Americans who welcome the secessions that occurred as reflecting the real wishes of the peoples involved; equally welcome is the breakup of the geopolitical colossus that threatened the rest of Eurasia in the days of the tsars, and then again since the defeat of Hitler. Depending on their own ethnicity, and on the extent of their interest in the news, Americans thus would agree with the official stance of their government that Latvia, Lithuania, and Estonia were entitled to independence. Going beyond the official U.S. stance, many might think it equally valid that Kazakhs, or Uzbekhs, or Armenians, or Ukrainians should also gain independence if they want it.

It would be an unusual American, however, who would desire such self-determination enough for its own sake (or enough for its contribution to the balance of power and the security of Western Europe) to welcome nuclear proliferation as its underpinning. John Mearsheimer[2] and others who make the argument indeed speak for many of their countrymen in welcoming Ukrainian independence; but they are much more on their own in endorsing Ukraine's retention of Soviet nuclear weapons as a reinforcement for this independence (and not only because the missiles the Ukrainians retained were, bizarrely, the strategic rather than the tactical nuclear weapons—strategic missiles difficult for Ukraine to employ against Moscow, but less difficult against New York).

How might the United States and the rest of the world then most surely persuade Ukraine and Kazakhstan to give up the nuclear weapons on their soil, weapons configured for targets in the United States, weapons that nuclear strategists in Kiev argued should be retained as a deterrent to future Russian military interventions?

At this point we are reminded of some of the same trade-offs between basic deterrence and extended nuclear deterrence that used to be so central to American relations with NATO, when West Germany and all of Western Europe faced such a powerful and plausible threat of attack from the Warsaw Pact.

Gallois defended the French nuclear program by arguing that it was self-evident that French bombs would be used against Moscow if Paris were ever about to be occupied by Russian forces, while it was not believable that American nuclear weapons would be used in such a punishment of the Soviet Union, if America had not yet been attacked itself.[3] Yet Gallois's argument for French nuclear forces could just as logically have been used to justify an independent German nuclear force: who would escalate to nuclear war if West Germany were attacked conventionally if the Germans were not able to do so themselves?

By one means or another, the United States succeeded for all the years of the Cold War in negating and overcoming the arguments of Gallois, and in making *extended* nuclear deterrence credible to the Soviets, or at least to the West Germans. The alternative to extended nuclear deterrence for West Germany and South Korea might well have been nuclear proliferation, as the nonavailability of an American nuclear umbrella might have driven Bonn and Seoul to seek their own *basic* nuclear deterrence.

This is all very abstract, of course, and has to be set against political and other realities. As discussed carefully in the chapters by Garnett, Michael Nacht, John W.R. Lepingwell, and Steven E. Miller, as well as in the companion volume on conventional military issues edited by Bruce Parrott, much will depend on the evolution of cultural, political, and economic relationships between Russia and its neighbors. Some Ukrainian nuclear strategists have insisted that Kiev needs nuclear weapons to deter Moscow from restoring the old Russian Empire or the old Soviet Union, but how much has this reflected the realities of what Ukrainians and Russians were thinking about? How credibly could any kind of American conventional deterrent be extended to shield Ukraine against Russian attack (or, perhaps more important, to shield Ukraine against the intimidating shadow of the mere possibility of such an attack, as faced by Finland during the Cold War).

And if the Kazakhs made a similar case vis-à-vis possible Chinese pressures on their border, how easy or difficult would it be to maintain a Russian extended nuclear deterrence on behalf of this newly independent state?

Russian Strategy Versus Soviet Strategy

Even if the Soviet nuclear arsenal can be transferred entirely to Russian control, which would indeed be the fondest wish of most American analysts, many such analysts are nonetheless disturbed by yet another twist of nuclear policy in this region.

The Soviets had long proposed to the United States a policy of "no first use" of nuclear weapons, linked perhaps to nuclear-free zones across Europe and other areas. The American response to such proposals throughout the Cold War was to reject them as an attempt to "make Europe safe for conventional war," and to pave the way for an exploitation of the Soviet superiority in conventional armaments.

Late in the Cold War, Moscow escalated the pressure somewhat, perhaps to encourage the European antinuclear movements, by announcing unilaterally that it would never use nuclear weapons first, no longer making this in any way dependent on a similar advance pledge by the West. (If one indeed contemplates the logic of no first use, there is no reason to make one's own commitment to such a policy contingent on a similar pledge by an adversary; whether one uses weapons of mass destruction or not is—by the very definition of the no-first-use pledge—contingent simply on what the adversary *does*.)

Moscow did not make this pledge as repeatedly, or as loudly and clearly, as Beijing; the Chinese have indeed been unique in how resolutely they have proclaimed that they will never use their nuclear weapons unless someone else has done so. But the pledge was indeed on the record, even if Soviet analysts and military officers often had difficulty in remembering whether this was in fact now their declared national policy. And it certainly made political and military sense, as it had back in the days of the Stockholm Peace Petition and the Rapacki Plan, as long as Moscow and the Warsaw Pact were calculated to have conventional forces superior to NATO.

It has thus come as somewhat of a shock to those American analysts who favored such a pledge for the United States to see the Russian military and the democratic Russian government now backing away from no first use, and moving instead to a duplicate of NATO's old "flexible response."[4]

A hardheaded "realistic" strategist might chime in that this makes all-too-perfect sense: whichever side is ahead in conventional weapons should try to phase out the shadow of nuclear escalation; and whichever side is behind in conventional military power needs to bring this shadow to bear. The sides in the conventional confrontation have simply been reversed.

The United States surely does not want to reify Russian fears of some grand alliance of all of Russia's neighbors girding for some new conventional invasion of Russia itself, thus driving Moscow to introduce nuclear deterrence. Yet one consequence of the breakup of the Soviet Union and the magnitude of what has happened since 1989 is that such scenarios become usable by some of the strategic planners and military briefers in Moscow, with worrisome prospects for the entire system.

Here we have an issue that very much interlocks this volume with the volume edited by Bruce Parrott. Some obvious problems have to be noted here, as demonstrated in the chapters by Nacht, Craig Nation, and Lepingwell. One cannot switch so very easily back and forth between no first use and first use without bruising the moral sensitivities of the publics involved and casting the credibility of threats or pledges into even more doubt.

Cynics about no first use have questioned whether any nation, including China, can be trusted to endorse no first use of weapons of mass destruction when its national interest might seem to demand it. Cynics of a different stripe (we have already mentioned Pierre Gallois as a most-quoted example, but there have been many others) have questioned whether a nation like the United States would ever actually initiate the use of nuclear weapons when an ally was being attacked only conventionally or otherwise, and when American cities were still intact as hostages.

Morality, Ideology, and Nuclear Deterrence

One of the more central philosophical problems of American nuclear deterrence reasoning since World War II has related to presumptions about the real feelings of the Russians and others governed from the Kremlin. Could one try to deter conventional war, and nuclear war, by threatening all these people with nuclear retaliation and mass destruction if these people were assumed to be governed against their will?

The United States ended World War II by bombing Japanese cities, first with mass conventional bombing and then with the only use of nuclear weapons in history. It had similarly striven, with less clear success, to win the war against Nazi Germany by bombing German cities, often quite literally bombing them to the ground; and the atomic bomb would definitely have been used against the Germans if they had not been lucky enough to lose the war by conventional means before the first such bombs were ready.

The bombings of World War II were rationalized in part by a pretense that military targets were being struck in Dresden and Hamburg and in Tokyo, Hiroshima, and Nagasaki. They were rationalized also by a conclusion that most Germans had supported Hitler and his aggressions, and that most of the Japanese had supported Japan's militarism and aggression, so that the masses of people being bombed were collectively guilty and appropriate targets of retaliation.

Hitler had made it easier by characterizing World War II as a war between Germans and other inferior ethnicities. Stalin had made it much more difficult in the Cold War, however, by characterizing the struggle as simply pitting the poorer people of the world against all their richer capitalist exploiters. And the United States similarly was loathe to paint the enemy as "Russian" here, regarding the adversary rather as the arrogant and doctrinaire Communist Party, which governed the Russians and the other ethnic groups of the USSR against their will, just as they governed the Poles and Czechs and East Germans against their will, just as they would have liked to govern Danes and West Germans as well.[5]

To threaten the innocent, to punish the guilty, or to deter the potentially guilty, is what nuclear deterrence and mutual assured destruction were all about, causing a substantial disquiet whenever anyone thought about these linkages at all carefully. The Roman Catholic Bishops' Letter of 1983[6] was only one manifestation of this basic moral problem with the nuclear deterrence of the Cold War: that it flew in the face of all of Western moral tradition; the role of military force had always been not to attack opposing civilians (especially if they were "innocent" civilians), but rather to attack the opposing military, and thus to protect one's own civilians.

By Western moral traditions, the strategic jargon labeled "counterforce" attacks was acceptable, while that labeled "countervalue" was reprehensible. Yet by the basic logic of mutual deterrence and crisis stability, the prevention of World War III depended on avoiding counterforce capabilities and on maintaining countervalue threats.

The introduction of democracy into Russia thus intersects with this basic moral paradox of mutual deterrence in two very opposite ways. First, as noted, we have seen announcements that nuclear forces are no longer aimed at cities. But a second, very opposite, logical inference could have been drawn from developments in Russia. Perhaps it was immoral before 1989 to aim at Russian civilians as the way to deter Soviet leaders, since the Russians had no more real voice in electing these leaders than the Ukrainians or the Estonians. But now that Yeltsin and his government were the product of a real election process, it would be more moral to punish the entire people, since they bore some responsibility for whatever required retaliation.

This logic might be quite tight, amounting to a proposition that nuclear deterrence is morally acceptable only between democracies and not between a democracy and a dictatorship or between two dictatorships. Yet it goes against our popular intuitions, against the widespread feeling that wars are impossible between two such democracies, that nuclear deterrence between the United States and Britain, or the United States and France, and now between the United States and Russia is unnecessary and unthinkable.

For proof that it is at least still "thinkable," consider the following developments. France's official doctrine on nuclear targeting in the 1960s, in a culture that excels in Cartesian rationality, had adopted a policy of *tous azimuts*, aiming in "all directions," aiming at every other nuclear power, and not just at the Soviet Union, on the elementary logic that the mere existence of any missiles in the world that could destroy Paris required preparation to retaliate for such destruction, and thus definitively to deter such destruction. The French "all-azimuth" policy was dropped in the 1970s, as France reverted to targeting the USSR as the principal enemy. But in France one consequence of the end of the Cold War has been a return of the "all-azimuth" theory. If Russia is a democracy, French missiles are not to be aimed exclusively at Russia, but neither are they to be "aimed" nowhere. Rather, as in the 1960s, they are to be aimed "everywhere."[7]

External Nuclear Proliferation

The breakup of the Soviet Union produced a substantially unanticipated round of nuclear proliferation in Ukraine, Belarus, and Kazakhstan, as discussed in the chapters by Laumulin, Paznyak, and Garnett.

As also noted, it has produced concerns that unaccounted-for Soviet nuclear weapons might slip into the hands of North Koreans, Serbs, Libyans, or Iranians, or that unemployed nuclear weapon designers might go abroad to make a fortune showing such countries how to utilize plutonium or enriched uranium for the production of atomic bombs.

There were instances even before the breakup of the USSR in which Soviet assistance was provided to foreign countries that might later prove troublesome. Such assistance to communist China, before the Sino-Soviet rift became pronounced, certainly accelerated the Chinese acquisition of nuclear weapons; Soviet commentators on the Nuclear Nonproliferation Treaty and on the general question of nuclear proliferation after the 1960s have commented that this experience had taught Moscow a bitter lesson.

Yet nuclear assistance was also offered in the construction of power reactors across Eastern Europe, and in Cuba and North Korea. In the case of Cuba, Soviet work on the reactors was halted when Castro declined to sign the NPT or the Latin American Nuclear Free Zone Treaty (the Treaty of Tlatelolco), and the residue of what was delivered and installed in Cuba does not raise concerns about possible nuclear weapons. In the East Euro-pean cases, the concerns at home and abroad are mostly about nuclear safety and the possibility of a major nuclear accident comparable to Cher-nobyl. As noted in the chapter by Paznyak, safety is also a major source of concern inside the former Soviet Union, particularly in Belarus and Ukraine.

It is in North Korea, of course, where the most serious post–Cold War proliferation concerns have arisen, as the Pyongyang regime, hoping to head off what happened to Communist Party rule in Romania, East Ger-many, and Russia, has refused to comply with its commitments under the NPT. North Korea had ratified the NPT, almost surely under Soviet pres-sure, in 1985, for Soviet nuclear assistance would otherwise have been withheld or delayed, as it was in Cuba. Yet the assistance that was delivered became the groundwork for the now menacing possibility that North Korea might have enough plutonium for one or two, or perhaps even five, atomic bombs; and the Pyongyang regime has kept such rumors alive by denying the International Atomic Energy Agency (IAEA) demand for the "special inspections" required to rule out this possibility.[8]

One could devote an entire book to a fuller discussion of the strategic game Pyongyang, deliberately or inadvertently, is playing here in maintain-ing the rumors and possibilities of nuclear proliferation. It fits with the most elementary theories of nuclear deterrence that a regime that is so threatened by the forces of history, economically, politically, and socially, and that is perhaps outmatched by the conventional forces of hostile neighbors, should reach for nuclear weapons as a deterrent to all such forces as the reassur-ance of its continued existence. North Korea, in the wake of events in Eastern Europe and the Soviet Union, had become a "pariah state," a candi-date for the "dustbin of history"; and the mere rumors of nuclear prolifera-tion had been used before as an antidote to such "pariahtude" by Israel and South Africa, and by Taiwan and South Korea.[9]

North Korea is indeed a "littoral state" for Russia, lying just west of Vladivostok. One most directly relevant question for this project thus per-tains to what the outside world can expect from Russian cooperation in inducing North Korea to give up this fling with nuclear proliferation.10 How reliable are the Russian arrangements designed to keep warhead de-signers and missile designers from going to work in Pyongyang? How many old networks and personal contacts are there, dating back to the time when Stalin put Kim Il Sung in power, that might be exploitable now in leading Kim Jong Il and his regime into a more reasonable relationship with the outside world?

Since 1992, most speculation about any outside influence on Pyongyang's nuclear policies has involved the United States and China. The relative lack of reference to Russia is indeed somewhat surprising here.

The "Overall Importance" of Nuclear Weapons

One of the issues more broadly debated among American strategic analysts after the Cold War has been whether military weapons, and in particular nuclear weapons, have now lost most of their importance, as compared with economic power and the basic political and cultural vitalities of various societies.

Liberals and others in America now often present themselves as being unimpressed by nuclear arsenals, ridiculing anyone who suggests that the United States not now quickly disarm.

Simply by the way it is defined, this volume might suggest an opposite view. If nuclear weapons are not important, why would we have an entire book on the nuclear aspects of Russia's relations with its neighbors? But there is more than this sorting of issues into an array of chapters to suggest that nuclear weapons remain very important.

As noted above in the simple comparison of Cuba and North Korea (the two regimes in the world that most openly lament and disapprove of what happened in Moscow after 1989), the world has to worry much more about Pyongyang than about Havana, simply because Pyongyang has a nuclear weapon card to play and Havana does not.

If nuclear weapons did not exist, as noted throughout this discussion, the West would have had to be much *more* worried before 1989 about how to defend itself (most probably burning away much more economic power in preparing for a conventional defense), and *since* 1989 *less* worried. But much more important, if nuclear weapons did not exist, there would be far less need to direct so much attention to Russia or to the rest of the former Soviet Union; indeed, there might not be the kind of interest that drives this entire research venture and all its published volumes.

In a world without nuclear weapons, Japan and Germany might be saliently more important than France and Britain. If someone claims that these two defeated Axis partners are already more important because of their economic power, the structure of the United Nations Security Council still does not reflect this. In any event, Bonn and Tokyo would be even more important in a world without nuclear weapons, while Paris and London would be less so.

In a world without nuclear weapons, Moscow would, moreover, be less important than any of the four capitals noted above, behind Paris and London and Bonn and Tokyo, in terms of how much anyone on the outside had to care or worry about the functioning of the Russian economy and Russian democracy. And this is of course even more true for Kiev, and for every one of the other capitals discussed so knowledgeably in all these volumes.

Without nuclear weapons, the outside world's concerns would have been satisfied by the simple news that the old Russian Empire, which had become the USSR, had ceased to exist and that ethnic Russia was now confronted by a littoral of politically independent states.

The real world analyzed in this book is, of course, a nuclear world, a world where Russia remains a nuclear superpower, and where even Ukraine outranks France and Britain and China in the destructive potential of its still separate nuclear arsenal. And the reality is also that even as small a "nuclear arsenal" as is suspected in Pyongyang (another sort of inheritance from the old Soviet system) has been big enough to make Pyongyang important.

Nuclear weapons remain very significant. The ongoing relations between Russia and its littoral demonstrate this all too well.

Notes

1. On the basic logic of the nuclear confrontation here, see Bernard Brodie, *The Absolute Weapon* (New York: Harcourt Brace, 1946).

2. John J. Mearsheimer, "The Case for a Ukrainian Deterrent," *Foreign Affairs*, vol. 72, no. 3 (summer 1993), pp. 50–66.

3. Pierre Gallois, *The Balance of Terror* (Boston: Houghton-Mifflin, 1961).

4. See James F. Holcomb and Michael M. Boll, *Russia's New Doctrine: Two Views* (Carlisle, PA: U.S. Army War College, 1994).

5. For an elaboration around these points, see Colin Gray, "Nuclear Strategy: The Case for a Theory of Victory," *International Security*, vol. 4, no. 1 (summer 1979), pp. 54–87.

6. *The Challenge of Peace: God's Promise and Our Response* (Washington, DC: National Conference of Catholic Bishops, 1983).

7. For details on post-1989 developments in French nuclear strategy, see David S. Yost, "Nuclear Weapons Issues in France," in *Strategic Views from the Second Tier*, eds. John C. Hopkins and Weixing Hu (San Diego: University of California Institute on Global Conflict and Cooperation, 1993).

8. On developments in North Korea, see Selig Harrison, "The North Korean Nuclear Crisis," *Arms Control Today*, vol. 24, no. 9 (November 1994), pp. 18–20.

9. The notion of a "pariah state" was defined by Robert E. Harkavy, "The Pariah State Syndrome," *Orbis*, vol. 2, no. 3 (fall 1977), pp. 623–49.

10. See Steven J. Blank, *Russian Policy and the Korean Crisis* (Carlisle, PA: U.S. Army War College, 1994).

Appendix: Project Participants

List of Workshop Participants, 11–15 July 1994
The Nuclear Challenge in Russia and
the New States of Eurasia

Olga Alexandrova, Federal Institute for Russian, East European and International Studies
Roy Allison, Royal Institute of International Affairs
Jonathan Aves, Centre for Defence Studies, King's College
Bess Brown, Radio Free Europe/Radio Liberty Research Institute
Oleg Bukharin, Moscow Institute of Physics and Technology
Julian Cooper, University of Birmingham
Roland Dannreuther, International Institute for Strategic Studies
Christopher Davis, Oxford University
Karen Dawisha, University of Maryland
Renee de Nevers, International Institute for Strategic Studies and Hoover Institution
Lawrence Freedman, Department of War Studies, King's College
Sherman Garnett, Carnegie Endowment for International Peace
Raymond Garthoff, The Brookings Institution
Elaine Holoboff, Department of War Studies, King's College
Major General Nicholas Krawciw, U.S. Army, Ret.
Taras Kuzio, School of Slavonic and East European Studies, University of London
Murat Laumulin, Ministry of Foreign Affairs, Kazakhstan
John Lepingwell, Radio Free Europe/Radio Liberty Research Institute
Janine Ludlam, Russian Littoral Project

Michael M cGwire, Cambridge University
Steven Miller, Harvard University
David Mussington, International Institute for Strategic Studies
Michael Nacht, University of Maryland
Craig Nation, Johns Hopkins University Bologna Center
Piotr Ogrodzinski, Department of Strategic Research, Ministry of Foreign Affairs, Poland
Bruce Parrott, Johns Hopkins University, School of Advanced International Studies
Fiona Paton, Department of War Studies, King's College
Vyachaslau Paznyak, Centre for Strategic Initiatives, Minsk
Wolfgang Pfeiler, Ernst Moritz Arndt University
William Potter, Monterey Institute of International Studies
Alex Pravda, Oxford University
Aline Quester, Center for Naval Analyses
George Quester, University of Maryland
Kjetil Ribe, Department of War Studies, King's College
Anatolii Rozanov, Belarusian State University
Anna Scherbakova, Monterey Institute of International Studies
Tatiana Shakleina, Institute of USA and Canada Studies, Moscow
Maxim Shashenkov, Oxford University
Mikhail Tsypkin, Naval Postgraduate School, Monterey

Index

ABM Treaty. *See* Antiballistic Missile (ABM) Treaty
Accidental launch, 94–95
Accident response equipment, 49
ACDA. *See* Arms Control and Disarmament Agency
ADMs. *See* Atomic demolitions munitions
Akhromeev, Marshall, 253
Aktau (Kazakhstan), 21, 182
Algeria, 18
All-azimuth theory, 259
Allison, Roy, 157
All-Union Research Institute for Nonorganic Substances, 24
Almaty (Kazakhstan), 206
Almaty agreement, 157–58
Americium–241, 52
Antiballistic Missile (ABM) Treaty, 116, 227, 247–48
Arbatov, Alexei, 73, 91–92, 107
Arkin, William, 25
Armenia, 15
Armored blankets, 48
Arms Control and Disarmament Agency (ACDA), 242
Arzamas–16 (Russia), 16
Aspin, Les, 141, 143
Assured destruction. *See* Mutual assured destruction
Atomic demolitions munitions (ADMs), 45–46
Atomic Energy Agency (Kazakhstan), 184, 187, 208

Authoritarianism, 215

Balance of power system, 4
Ballistic missile early-warning systems (BMEWS), 108, 228
BASCAN. *See* Basic Automated Command System
Basic Automated Command System (BASCAN), 86*n.43*
Belarus, 13, 15, 29, 47, 95, 101, 130–31, 192, 230, 244
  compensation for weapons repatriation, 161–62
  denuclearization in, 163–70, 171, 173
  disincentives to nuclear option, 166–68
  emergency response, 49
  export controls in, 19, 162–63, 177*n.60*
  HEU in, 37, 39
  intelligence agency cooperation in, 170–71
  military doctrine of, 156–57
  military infrastructure, 166
  nuclear policy of, 155–63
  nuclear power plants in, 173–74*n.8*
  psychological backlash in, 167
  public opinion in, 167–68
  and Russia, 157, 159, 160–62, 169–70
  Soviet legacy to, 153–55
  U.S. assistance to, 162, 163, 177*n.60*
Belarusian Popular Front (BPF), 171
Belarus Nuclear and Radiation Safety Agency. *See* Gospromatomnadzor

Belous, Vladimir, 111
Belov, Petr, 110–11
Beryllium, 21
Black market, 36, 42
Black Sea fleet, 129, 134, 145,
    251*n.10*
Blocking devices, 60–61, 65–66,
    79*n.2*
BMEWS. *See* Ballistic missile
    early-warning systems
BPF. *See* Belarusian Popular Front
Braithwaite, Rodric, 214
Brzezinski, Zbigniew, 216
Bunn, George, 231
Bureau for Coordination of Activities
    Against Organized Crime (CIS),
    50
Burrows, William, 25
Bush, George, 61, 244
Buteiko, Anton, 140

Canada, 220
Carter, Ashton, 58*n.28*
Central European Initiative, 135
CFE Treaty. *See* Conventional Forces
    in Europe (CFE) Treaty
Charter of Paris (1990), 222
Chaus, Piotr, 158, 159
Cheliabinsk–65 (Russia), 37, 43, 45,
    48
Chemical Weapons Convention,
    226–27
Chernobyl, 166–67, 260
Chernomyrdin, Viktor, 218, 249
China, 92, 93, 230, 247, 250, 259
    Central Asian claims of, 202–04
    and Kazakhstan, 192, 198, 202–08
    military ambitions of, 204–05
    no first use policy, 256
    Russian nuclear assistance to, 18
Chornovil, Viacheslav, 130–31
CIS. *See* Commonwealth of
    Independent States
Clinton, Bill, 50, 94, 143, 145, 192,
    229, 242
Cochran, T., 45–46
Cocked gun posture, 94
Cold War, 3, 90

Commission for Military and
    Technological Cooperation
    (Russia), 18
Committee for State Security
    (Belarus), 170, 178*n.76*
Commonwealth of Independent States
    (CIS), 96, 100, 214, 235
    and Belarus, 158, 169
    command and control systems, 101,
    103–04
    and Kazakhstan, 181, 182, 186, 199,
    209
    and Ukraine, 129, 130, 133, 142
Comprehensive Test Ban (CTB), 10,
    27
Conference on Interaction and
    Confidence-Building Measures in
    Asia, 208
Conventional Forces in Europe (CFE)
    Treaty, 81*n.16*, 220, 226
Convention on the Physical Protection
    of Nuclear Material, 13, 15, 154
Cooperative Threat Reduction (CTR)
    program, 42–43, 44, 48, 114, 162,
    248–49
Council on Security and Cooperation
    in Europe (CSCE), 221, 222, 223,
    234–35
Counterforce attacks, 258
Countervalue attacks, 258
Crimea, 251*n.10*
Cruise missiles, 66–67
CSCE. *See* Council on Security and
    Cooperation in Europe
CTB. *See* Comprehensive Test Ban
CTR program. *See* Cooperative Threat
    Reduction (CTR) program
Cuba, 259–60, 261

Dead hand concept, 75–77, 86*n.51*
Dealerting, 94–95, 98, 99*n.24*
Declassification, 54
Decree on Measures to Implement the
    Treaty on the Nonproliferation of
    Nuclear Weapons (Belarus), 160
Defense conversion, 249–50
Democratization, 215
Desert Storm, 8

Detargeting, 9, 78, 94–95, 246
Deterrence, 3, 6, 89, 91–94, 227, 231, 253
  and Belarusian nuclear policy, 156–57, 174–75n.23
  and Kazakhstan, 199
  and morality, 9, 257–59
  and no first use policy, 105–07
  and secession, 254–55
  See also Extended deterrence
Direct command, 62
Directorate of Economic Security (Belarus), 170
DRCS. *See* Duplicating radio command system
Dual citizenship, 199, 207
Dual-use items, 21
Dumas, Roland, 223
Duplicating radio command system (DRCS), 86n.43

Early-warning satellites, 85n.39
Early-warning systems, 101, 103–04, 108, 120n.19, 228
EC. *See* European Community
England. *See* Great Britain
Environmental sampling, 55
Estonia, 15, 21
Ethnicity, 127
Euratom, 43
European Community (EC), 221, 223, 234
European security architecture, 219–26
Export Control Commission (Russia), 18
Export controls, 15–20, 21
Extended deterrence, 5, 106–07, 255

First use policy. *See* No first use policy
Flexible response, 5, 256
Foster, Johnny, 248
Foster Box, 248
France, 92, 250, 255, 261
  all-azimuth theory, 259
  dismantlement assistance, 49
  nuclear arsenal, 229, 230
  security assurances to Ukraine, 82n.17

Franco-German Eurocorps, 223
Freeh, Louis, 15
Fuel storage sites, 23–24

Gaidar, Egor, 214
Gas centrifuge, 36
Gaseous diffusion, 36
Gates, Robert, 185
"General Safety Criteria for the Russian Fissile Material Storage Facility", 44
Genscher, Hans-Dietrich, 223
Geopolitics, 4
Germany, 27, 28, 224, 261
Glaser, Charles, 225
Gorbachev, Mikhail, 12, 47, 61, 63, 226–27, 244
Gore, Al, 249
Gosatomnadzor, 24, 41, 42, 56, 57n.4
Gospromatomnadzor, 160
Grachev, Pavel, 81n.12, 105, 106, 141, 198
Gravity bombs, 61, 67
Great Britain, 4, 92, 250, 261
  and Belarus, 160
  materials control assistance, 43
  nuclear arsenal, 229, 230
  security assurances to Ukraine, 82n.17
Greenpeace, 23
Gun-type fission bomb, 36

Hafnium, 21
Hard-target kill (HTK) capability, 108–09
Hersh, Seymour, 16
HEU. *See* Highly enriched uranium
Highly enriched uranium (HEU), 15–16, 20–21, 23, 24, 35–36, 245
  detection of, 40
  disposal options for, 44
  production ban, 51
  from warhead dismantlement, 43
Hitler, Adolph, 258
HTK capability. *See* Hard-target kill capability

IAEA. *See* International Atomic
  Energy Agency
Ianaev, Vice President, 63
Implosion-type fission bomb, 36
INF. *See* Intermediate Range Nuclear
  Forces
INFCIRC–66 type safeguards, 22
Institute of Power Engineering
  Problems, 20, 24
Interlocking institutions, 221–22
Intermediate Range Nuclear Forces
  (INF), 226
International Atomic Energy Agency
  (IAEA), 10, 13, 15
  and Belarus, 153–54, 157
  and Kazakhstan, 184, 185–86, 187,
    208
  and materials control assistance, 43
  and North Korea, 29, 260
  safeguard agreements, 21–22
International CHETEK Corporation,
  17
International Nuclear Fuel Cycle
  Evaluation, 11
International Science and Technology
  Center, 43
Inventory shrinkage, 40–41
Iran, 18, 186, 198
Iraq, 8
Islam, 186, 198
Islamic Republic of Eastern
  Turkestan, 203
Israel, 27, 28
Izvestiia (newspaper), 207

Japan, 261
Jean, M., 204
Joffe, Josef, 223

Kalahari Desert, 12
Kamp, Karl-Heinz, 166
Karaganov, Sergei, 91
KATEP. *See* Kazakh State Atomic
  Energy Industrial Corporation
Kazakhstan, 13, 15, 21, 29, 95, 230,
  244, 254–55
  arms industry, 201–02
  and China, 202–08

Kazakhstan *(continued)*
  emergency response, 49
  HEU in, 37, 39
  materials control in, 43
  national army of, 208–09
  and nonproliferation regime,
    185–87, 191–92
  and NPT, 193–95
  nuclear policy in, 181–209
    and antinuclear movement,
      187–89, 205–06
    contradictory nature of, 195–97
    development of, 185
    political parties and internal
      struggle, 189–91
  reactors in, 21, 182
  and Russia, 181–82, 186, 191–92,
    194, 195–96, 197–202
  and China, 206–08
  possible military alliance, 200–202,
    207
  Russian military doctrine, 198–200
  security guarantees, 209
  Soviet nuclear legacy to, 182–83
  and START I, 192
  uranium deposits in, 182
  uranium trade, 183–84
  warhead removal from, 101
  Western assistance to, 193
Kazakh State Atomic Energy
  Industrial Corporation (KATEP),
  184
KAZBEK network, 85*n.40*, 86*n.43*
Kazlouski, Pavel, 158
KGB (Belarus). *See* Committee for
  State Security (Belarus)
Kharkiv Technical Institute (Ukraine),
  21
Khasbulatov, Ruslan, 112
Khizha, Georgii, 18
Kokoshin, Andrei, 62
Kola Peninsula, 23
Korea. *See* North Korea; South Korea
Kostenko, Iurii, 131–32
Kozyrev, Andrei, 214–15, 216, 224–25
  and North Korea, 29
  and START II, 112
Krasnoiarsk–26 (Russia), 37, 51–53

Kravchenko, Piotr, 155, 157–58, 162
Kravchuk, Leonid, 65, 126–27,
    132–33, 136–37, 142–43, 245
Kuchma, Leonid, 117, 128–29, 146,
    219, 246
Kurchatov Institute, 23, 57n.2

Laboratory for Observation of
    Radioactive Contamination, 188
Larrabee, F. Stephen, 232
Latvia, 15, 21
Launch-on-warning, 59, 72–78, 94
    and "dead hand" concept, 75–77
    hair-trigger timeline of, 73–75
LEU. *See* Low enriched uranium
Limited engagement policy, 219, 234
Lisbon Protocol, 169, 195, 196, 214,
    227, 244
    and Belarus, 159–60
    and Kazakhstan, 181, 185–86, 208
    and Ukraine, 138–39
Lithuania, 15, 21
Lobnor test site (China), 205–06
London Suppliers Group, 11
Low enriched uranium (LEU), 37, 245
Low salience nuclear strategy, 233
Lukashenka, Aliaksandr, 161

Mackinder, Halford J., 4
Managed access inspections, 54
Mandelbaum, Michael, 224
MAPI. *See* Ministry of Atomic Power
    and Industry
Markey Amendment, 58n.21
Maslin, Colonel General, 90
Massandra protocols, 103, 129, 134,
    148n.10
Material control and accounting, 24,
    40–41
McGuire, Michael, 233
Mearsheimer, John, 254
Medvedev, Sergei, 234
Mikhailov, Viktor, 17
MINATOM. *See* Ministry of Atomic
    Energy
Ministry of Atomic Energy
    (MINATOM), 37, 42, 52–53, 56
    creation of, 57n.4

Ministry of Atomic Energy *(continued)*
    and export controls, 17
    and national safeguards, 25–26
    stockpile management, 70
    and warhead dismantlement, 43
Ministry of Atomic Power and
    Industry (MAPI), 13, 17, 57n.4
Ministry of Defense (Russia), 37, 56
Ministry of Foreign Affairs (Soviet
    Union), 13
Ministry of Medium Machine
    Building (Soviet Union), 57n.4
Ministry of Shipbuilding (Russia), 23,
    57n.2
Minsk accord, 19
Minuteman III missiles, 78
MIRVs. *See* Multiple independently
    targetable reentry vehicles
Missiles, 60, 64–67, 78, 103, 109–11,
    117
Mixed oxide (MOX) fuel, 44, 45
Moldova, 13, 32n.9
MOX fuel. *See* Mixed oxide (MIX)
    fuel
Multiple independently targetable
    reentry vehicles (MIRVs), 109,
    117
Mutual assured destruction, 6, 109, 253
MX Peacekeeper missiles, 78

NACC. *See* North Atlantic
    Cooperation Council
Nationalism, 171, 173, 215
National Nuclear Center
    (Kazakhstan), 184, 187
National Security Council (NSC), 242
NATO. *See* North Atlantic Treaty
    Organization
"NATO's Core Security Functions in
    the New Europe", 220–21
Nazarbaev, Nursultan, 182, 186, 188,
    202
Neo-containment, 216, 234
Neutrality, 131
Nevada-Semipalatinsk movement,
    188, 205–06
"New Strategic Concept" (NATO),
    221

Nitze, Paul, 108
Nixon, Richard, 80–81*n.11*
No first use policy, 5, 9, 97–98,
    105–07, 256–57
Nonproliferation. *See* Nuclear
    nonproliferation regime
North Atlantic Cooperation Council
    (NACC), 221–22, 225, 226
North Atlantic Council, 220–21
North Atlantic Treaty Organization
    (NATO), 92, 93, 212, 234
  changing role of, 220–24
  future of, 225–26
  and no first use policy, 98, 105
North Korea, 28–29, 239–40, 260–61
NPT. *See* Nuclear Nonproliferation
    Treaty
NSC. *See* National Security Council
NSG. *See* Nuclear Suppliers Group
Nuclear Exporters Committee. *See*
    Zangger Committee
Nuclear free zones, 5, 9, 156, 256
Nuclear inheritance, 20
Nuclear nonproliferation regime,
    10–31
  export controls, 15–20
  international controls, 20–22
  and Kazakhstan, 185–87
  national safeguards, 22–26
  1994 status report, 14
  policy recommendations, 29–31
  post Soviet period, 13–26
  problem countries for, 27–29
  and Soviet Union, 11–13
  technical aspects of, 35–56
Nuclear Nonproliferation Treaty
    (NPT), 10, 13, 89, 214, 230–31,
    240–41
  and Belarus, 154, 157, 159–60, 169
  Extension Conference (1995),
    26–27, 30
  good faith negotiations requirement,
    230–31
  and Kazakhstan, 181, 185, 193–95,
    209
  and Russian first-use policy, 106
  and safeguard agreements, 21
  South African compliance with, 12

Nuclear Nonproliferation Treaty
    (continued)
  Soviet support for, 11
  and Ukraine, 67–68, 95, 132, 137,
    140, 144, 245–46
Nuclear Posture Review, 246
Nuclear Suppliers Group (NSG), 10,
    21, 30
Nuclear Threat Reduction Act, 53
Nuclear weapons
  command and control issues, 253
  elimination of, 47–56
    and materials production halt, 50–53
    safeguard system, 55–56
    and security agencies, 49–50
    threat assessment, 49–50
    verification agreements, 54–55
    Western assistance for, 48–49
    Western response to, 229
  importance of, 252–62
  materials control from
      dismantlement of, 43–45
  near theft of, 25
  Russian control of, 59–79
  security of, 45–47
  "use them or lose them" problem,
      253–54
  See also specific weapons and
    delivery systems
Nunn-Lugar legislation. *See*
    Cooperative Threat Reduction
    (CTR) program

Oak Ridge plant (U.S.), 54
Organized crime, 50, 72

Pakistan, 18
Panofsky, Wolfgang, 231
Pan-Slavism, 168
Partial Test Ban Treaty (1963), 11
Partnership for Peace (PFP), 224–25,
    226
PCK. *See* People's Congress of
    Kazakhstan
Peaceful nuclear explosives (PNEs),
    17, 19
People's Congress of Kazakhstan
    (PCK), 190

People's Unity of Kazakhstan Union (PUKU), 190
Perkhushkovo (Russia), 79*n.2*
Permission command, 62
Perry, William, 229, 250
PFP. *See* Partnership for Peace
PGMs. *See* Precision-guided munitions
Pikayev, Alexander, 91
Pliushch, Ivan, 137
Plutonium, 35–36, 52
    disposal options for, 44–45
    production, 36
    production ban, 51
    storage facilities, 25–26
    vitrification of, 45
    from warhead dismantlement, 43
Plutonium–239, 36
PNEs. *See* Peaceful nuclear explosives
Poland, 135
Precision-guided munitions (PGMs), 105, 108
Preemption, 73, 83–85*n.35*
Presidential Decision Directive (PDD–2), 242
Primary, 36
Privalov, Leonid, 158
Production Association Maiak (Russia), 48
PUKU. *See* People's Unity of Kazakhstan Union

Radets'kiy, Vladimir, 145, 219
Radiation leakage, 64
Radioactive waste, 189
Rail car security, 49
Rapacki Plan, 5
Reagan, Ronald, 244
Remote sensing, 55
Research and training facilities, 20
Research reactors, 20
Retaliation, 73, 83–85*n.35*, 107–08
Rocky Flats (U.S.), 44
Rogov, Sergei, 91, 95, 107
Russia, 4, 7–8, 10, 22, 212–13, 224, 234, 261–62
    alert levels in, 85*n.41*
    and Belarus, 157, 159, 160–62, 165, 169–70

Russia *(continued)*
    command posts, 73
    defense conversion in, 249–50
    denuclearization in, 95–97, 227–28
    disillusionment in, 215
    enrichment plants in, 37, 38–39
    export controls in, 17–20
    and fissile material control, 35, 36
        national safeguards for, 41–42, 55–56
        Western assistance for, 42–43
    and Kazakhstan, 181–82, 186, 191–92, 194–202, 206–08
    materials production cutoff, 51
    military, 218
        defense budget, 62
        equipment deterioration, 103
        strategic rocket forces, 102–04
        subordination to civilian authority, 62–63
        troop strength, 213
    neoimperialism in, 216
    1991 coup attempt, 63
    and North Korea, 28–29
    nuclear policy of, 89–98, 256–57
        agenda, 94–98
        and conventional attacks, 92–93
        doctrine and force restructuring, 104–09
        estimation of war, 90
        force structure debates, 109–11
        and international status, 90–93
        in 1993 military doctrine, 93–98, 105–09
        no first use, 97–98, 105–07
        and proliferation, 92
    nuclear stockpile, 69–70, 90
    nuclear weapons control, 59–79
        demoralization in, 228
        launch-on-warning strategy, 72–78
        and political incoherence, 62–64
        and rogue commanders, 60–61
        and smuggling, 69–72
        threat of anarchy, 59–61
        and Ukraine's bid for nuclear status, 64–69
    nuclear workforce, 19–20
    peacemaking role of, 215

Russia *(continued)*
  plutonium and HEU inventories, 37
  political violence in, 216
  production reactors in, 51–53
  security interests, 218
  strategic legacy of, 101–04
  and Ukraine, 127, 128–32, 146, 232
  warhead dismantlement, 43–45, 47–56
  Western views of instability in,
    213–19
  See also Soviet Union; Trilateral
    Agreement
Russian Air Defense Forces (VPVO),
  104
Russian Special Operations
  (*Spetsnaz*), 25, 45

SALT. *See* Strategic Arms Limitation
  Talks
Sandia National Laboratory, 49
Satarov, Georgii, 112
Schlesinger, James, 80–81*n.11*
SDI. *See* Strategic Defense Initiative
Seabed Treaty, 15
Secondary, 36
Security, 22–26
  of fissile materials, 35–43
    control and accountancy system,
      40–41
    and facilities, 37–39
    and human reliability, 41
    materials detection, 40
    safeguards for, 40–42
    Western assistance for, 42–43
  at military facilities, 25
  of nuclear weapons, 45–47
  rail car, 49
  and warhead dismantlement, 43–45
  See also Smuggling
Semipalatinsk (Kazakhstan), 21, 181,
  183, 185, 187, 188, 193
Sergeev, Igor, 102, 114
Shaposhnikov, Marshal, 65
Shirkovski, Eduard, 178*n.76*
Shmarov, Valerii, 140
Shumeiko, Vladimir, 114
Shushkevich, Stanislau, 158, 161, 163
Siberian Chemical Combine (Russia), 48

Silo-based missiles, 60
Smuggling, 15–16, 50, 69–72
Socialist Party of Kazakhstan (SPK),
  190
Solzhenitsyn, Aleksandr, 198
Soskovets, Oleg, 18
Sosny (Russia), 24
South Africa, 12, 27, 28
South Korea, 4, 5, 12
Soviet Union, 3, 226–27, 228, 256–57,
  259
  alert levels in, 80*n.6*, 85*n.41*
  and Kazakhstan, 181
  launch-on-warning strategy, 94
  materials control and accountancy
    system, 41
  materials production cutoff, 51
  nonproliferation regime, 10–13, 26,
    27–28
  nuclear export policy, 11, 12–13, 17
  nuclear fuel cycle, 22–23
  strategic exercises by, 84–85*n.35*
  and Western security policy, 212
  See also Russia
Spetsnaz. See Russian Special
  Operations
SPK. *See* Socialist Party of Kazakhstan
SS–18 missiles, 64, 103
SS–19 missiles, 65, 66, 117
SS–24 missiles, 64, 65, 66, 103, 117
SS–25 missiles, 64, 103, 109, 110–11,
  117
SSD program, 249, 250
Stalin, Joseph, 258
START I, 97, 112, 115–16, 169, 214,
  227, 240
  implementation, 250
  and Kazakhstan, 181, 191, 192, 193,
    195, 196, 199, 208
  and Russian arsenal, 90
  and Ukraine, 112, 137, 138, 141, 191
START II, 97, 103, 104, 214, 227
  critics of, 92
  and force structure debates, 109–11
  implementation, 250
    costs, 113–14
  prospects, 100–101
  and Kazakhstan, 191, 193

START II *(continued)*
opposition to, 114
ratification possibility, 111–15, 228
ratification without implementation, 113–18
and Russian arsenal, 90
and U.S. arms control policy, 244–46
and Western aid, 114
See also Lisbon Protocol
State Committee for the Defense Industry (Russia), 23
State Committee for the Supervision of Nuclear and Radiation Safety. *See* Gosatomnadzor
Storage facilities, 23–24, 43, 48, 49
Strategic Arms Limitation Talks (SALT), 108, 226, 240
Strategic Arms Reduction Talks. *See* START I; START II
Strategic bombers, 61, 66–67, 103
Strategic Defense Initiative (SDI), 247
Strategic weapons, 46–47
Submarines, 60–61, 73, 79*n.3*, 103
Sweden, 43
Swedish Nuclear Physics Inspectorate, 184

Tactical weapons, 46, 47–48
Tajikistan, 202
Talbott, Strobe, 140, 143
Tarasiuk, Borys, 140
Tecksnabeksport, 17
Theater missile defense (TMD), 247–48
TMD. *See* Theater missile defense
Tolubko, Vladimir, 149*n.21*
Tomsk–7 (Russia), 37, 43, 44, 48, 51–53
Trans-Siberian Railway, 4
Treaty for the Prohibition of Nuclear Weapons in Latin America (1967), 11
Treaty on Collective Security, 199
Trilateral Agreement (1994), 28, 65, 68, 101, 126, 129, 132, 140, 141, 143–45, 146, 219, 231, 245
Tu–95 Bear bombers, 103
Tu–160 Blackjack bombers, 103

Turkestan. *See* Xinjiang Province (China)
Turkey, 198

Ukraine, 15, 29, 98, 196, 215, 230, 244, 254–55
armed forces of, 134, 141–43
and CIS, 101, 129, 130, 133, 142
conventional balance with Russia, 81–82*n.16*
denuclearization in, 95–97, 231–32
assistance and compensation for, 145, 151*n.42*
conditions for, 137–40
diplomatic response to, 140–41
diplomatic recognition of, 135
emergency response, 49
export controls in, 19
HEU in, 37, 39, 44
materials control in, 43
nationalism in, 173
and NPT, 13
nuclear policy of, 125–46, 171, 172
accommodationist stance, 128–30
compromise in, 132–36
domestic factors, 126–28
external factors, 128–32
and military, 141–43
nationalist position on, 130–32, 148*n.20*
and nuclear diplomacy, 136–45
sources and orientation of, 126–36
nuclear status bid, 64–69
as problem country, 28
reactors in, 21
and Russia, 127, 128–32
safeguards in, 21–22
security assurances for, 82*n.17*
and START I, 112, 137, 138, 141, 191
and START II, 117–18
and U.S., 101, 125, 134, 136, 138–41, 146, 232
warhead repatriation from, 47
warheads and delivery systems, 103
See also Trilateral Agreement
Ulba Metallurgy Plant (Kazakhstan), 21, 182–83

United Kingdom. *See* Great Britain
United States, 4, 5, 7–8, 12, 212, 215,
 233, 255–57
 arms control policy, 229–30,
  239–51
 agenda for, 250–51
 bias of, 61
 major issues in, 243–50
 process, 241–43
 and Belarus, 159, 160, 161–62, 165,
  192
 conventional superiority of, 93
 and CTR program, 42–43, 44
 and deterrence, 91–92, 257–59
 European military presence, 220,
  223–24, 225
 foreign policy agenda of, 91
 HEU purchases from Russia, 44
 and Kazakhstan, 185, 194, 195–96,
  208
 and materials production ban, 49–50
 nonproliferation policy, 29–31,
  230–31
 and Russia, 53, 96
 Soviet cooperation with, 12, 26
 and Ukraine, 82*n.17*, 96, 101, 125,
  134, 136, 138–41, 146, 232
 warhead dismantlement assistance,
  48–49, 162
 warhead reduction in, 115, 116
 See also Trilateral Agreement
Ural Electrochemistry Plant (Russia),
 48
Uranium
 in Kazakhstan, 182, 183–84
 mining, 20
 See also Highly enriched uranium;
  Low enriched uranium
Uranium–235, 36, 72

Ust'-Kamenogorsk (Kazakhstan), 21,
 37, 182–83
Uzbekistan, 15, 21

Van Eekelin, Willem, 223
Verification agreements, 54–55, 231
Vietnam, 4
Vitrification, 45, 57*n.8*
Voennaia mysl' (journal), 107
Volkov, Lev, 109, 111
Von Moltke, Gebhardt, 224
VPVO. *See* Russian Air Defense
 Forces

Walker, William, 233
Warsaw Pact, 212, 220
Western European Union (WEU), 21,
 222–23
WEU. *See* Western European Union
Windrem, Robert, 25
World War II, 257–58

Xinjiang Province (China), 203, 205

Yazov, General, 63
Yeltsin, Boris, 18, 57*n.4*, 62, 63, 65,
 216, 227, 230
 and detargeting, 9, 94
 foreign policy, 214
 and Kazakhstan, 186
 parliamentary opposition to, 216–17
 and START I, 116
 and START II, 112, 115
 and Trilateral Agreement, 143

Zangger Committee, 11
Zero alert posture, 79, 95, 99*n.24*
Zhirinovsky, Vladimir, 198, 217, 240
Zirconium, 21